DISCIPLESHIP from
JESUS'S PERSPECTIVE

To Hadassah, my unborn daughter, who along with this book was once just an idea continuously formulating within my mind. Now they are fully conceived. Day by day they are taking shape, becoming more fully developed and refined. By God's grace both of these babies will see the light of day for the first time this year.

DISCIPLESHIP from JESUS'S PERSPECTIVE

Rediscovering and Reinstituting the Master Plan

GEORGE GRAY

iUniverse, Inc.
Bloomington

Discipleship from Jesus's Perspective
Rediscovering and Reinstituting the Master Plan

iUniverse books may be ordered through booksellers or by contacting:

iUniverse
1663 Liberty Drive
Bloomington, IN 47403
www.iuniverse.com
1-800-Authors (1-800-288-4677)

ISBN: 978-1-4759-5959-8 (sc)
ISBN: 978-1-4759-5958-1 (hc)
ISBN: 978-1-4759-5957-4 (ebk)

Library of Congress Control Number: 2012921231

Printed in the United States of America

iUniverse rev. date: 11/12/2012

Contents

Preface

Something should perhaps be said as to the nature of this undertaking with regard to how exactly I ended up here formulating and publishing this material. In terms of human acknowledgements I will first need to mention my father Bobby Cooksey, who more than anyone else was responsible for sending me on the theological journey culminating in this book. I was just out of high school when we worked together in the plumbing construction trade and business he ran for some time. All throughout the day as we were performing our daily tasks we exchanged volumes of theological discussion, debate and intrigue. My father had served as a pastor in the past with the Foursquare Church and had been to Bible College. I had not yet entered into formal study. One of the matters of foremost concern for both of us was the centrality of the earthly Jesus to every other concern of the Church. Adherence to His expressed will as recorded in the gospels dominated my philosophy of life, and I found ready support for this concept throughout scripture. We wondered together where the church that was once identified by this same perspective had gone and what new directions they were headed in.

In that same vein of thinking, but more specifically, I came across what seemed to me to be without question the primary objective of the Church according to her Lord in Matthew 28:19-20. I concluded that a Christian just couldn't go wrong as long as he or she was some way involved in the objectives stated in the Great Commission. It is called "great" due to the scope and supremacy of the undertaking. It is a "commission" in the sense that it is not to be undertaken on an individual basis. Only by walking side by side with Christ and hand in hand with one another can anything of this magnitude be accomplished. At that time I was not aware of all of the finer points that arise once one's ability to translate from the original Greek is secured. I only knew what the King James Bible was telling me about going into the entire world and "teaching" all nations. The transition from *teaching* to *making disciples* would come later as I began to realize there was something more behind those words.

Armed with this indisputable evidence I ventured out at the age of 22 to the mission field in Ghana, West Africa to do my part of that grand objective: teach all nations. Even though I was an Art major at the time, opportunities to teach and write came to me and I saw it as God's leading. I preached on the Great Commission and the Life of Christ. At the Assemblies of God Literature Center in Accra, I helped develop gospel literature for new converts in a comic book format for the low literacy rate context we were in. One of the main emphases of the tracts was the teachings of Christ. I understood Jesus's statement of "teaching them to observe everything I have commanded you," to mean "put my teachings first."

Once I returned from the mission field I determined to pursue a formal education so that one day I could teach in Bible College overseas. This was the best way in my mind to obey Jesus's command to "teach" all nations. Whatever position I found myself in along the way, I pushed the theme of Christo centrism to the forefront. I taught in Christian School at first and pursued correspondence courses, but eventually felt that wouldn't be enough to secure a professorship. I then turned to Houston Baptist University and loved every minute of those seven years of formal education. During this time one thing remained crystal clear and drove me onward: that is to, as Paul said, apprehend the reason I had been apprehended by this calling to make disciples. I was uncommonly gripped by the Great Commission to the point of necessity. It was my guiding light in an uncertain sea of theological relativism. I even made it the theme of my Master's Thesis: The Primary Objective of the Church: Selected Speeches of Jesus Christ. But in the back of my mind, a handbook-for-discipleship idea was constantly brewing and bubbling up within me.

To a degree, my college years were also a time of exploration. I was and still am Assemblies of God by preference, but by conviction I am non-denominational. I learned some very helpful principles along the way. I owe the Vineyard denomination for teaching me the value of the small and intimate home group method. You will find that this particular approach best fits the teaching context for the application of this book's lessons. Also there is the holiness emphasis of John Wesley. As I studied Christian History I found like-mindedness in this great leader who didn't stop short of sinless perfection as a possibility for this life (even if it may be only a temporary achievement). I recall so many times during my college years being so fond of his writings that I would purposely situate myself by his volumes in the library when I would go there to study. And this is how I ended up with a brief stint in the United Methodist Church. I served as the Chair of Evangelism and did the children's sermons and sometimes the regular sermons while there. I eventually found myself in the Christian Church. I connected with them in the area of devotion to the Word of God as the only word that matters. We also shared a desire for world missions. I served in that local congregation as the Missions Ministry Leader, which in a way lead to the writing of this book.

In the year 2000 I completed my graduate degree, having secured special recognition in the area of New Testament Greek. I was also licensed and ordained by the Baptist Church, which I hope they don't come to regret. In that same year I believe the Lord lead me to my current profession (Case Manager/ Chaplain for Star of Hope Mission). I was blessed to introduce those same principles into the Spiritual Recovery Program for the homeless men I have worked with for the past twelve years. I started out looking for material that would be perfect for making disciples. I discovered Bill Gothard's Commands of Christ series online through the Institute of Basic Life Principles. We actually began to teach this material for a few years and in the process, I gained some new insights from his book. This was the fact that Jesus explicitly stated it was his "commands" that were to be adhered to. This was more precise than just the general idea of learning from his teachings. Zeroing in on the commands helped me narrow my search and therefore make it easier to write a manual on the subject. Plus they don't eliminate the teachings but give you a way to practice them. It is the practice that qualifies the disciple just as it qualifies the medical doctor.

At first the recovery program was not part of the plan. I had actually been working on a series of PowerPoint slides for the mission field (continuing with the burden to make disciples of all nations). I had finally decided to put it all down on paper (or computer) and have a discipleship course ready for when the opportunity to travel overseas presented itself. In the process the leadership at the Star of Hope Mission got wind of it and invited me to incorporate it into the Spiritual Recovery Program. It was a ton of material and it took four teachers twice a week to pull it off. So now I was faced with the fact that I was the only instructor who really knew the context of each slide and would have to make that available to the others in a form of commentary attached to each one. It comes out to be a great teaching tool as well as something else. I could now see the initial framework materializing for a book on the subject. I had already attempted to publish the teaching tool, but it seemed only a book could serve that purpose initially. But now I had it. Through the worldwide publication of this book, I finally had a way to literally make disciples of all nations!

In addition to the series by Bill Gothard I am indebted to many other authors that I have considered in the writing of this book because they have addressed the commands of Christ in their own way. Those who stand out the most are as follows. Paul S. Minear comes to mind as a heavyweight scholar, who opened up to me untold richness in the commands he did address even though there were but a handful he could accept as authentic.[1] I also appreciated Dan Esterline's approach of introducing fifty-two of Jesus's commands in a journaling format.[2] He was highly adept and bringing out the Greek infrastructure behind every command as well as turning the exercise into a weekly devotional rather than merely an academic effort. Finally there is Hugh P. Jeter, who I found to be a kindred spirit in my search for enlightenment.[3] I thoroughly enjoyed his uplifting spirit and approach to such a worthy subject.

I also want to thank those who have entered into the struggle that has made this book possible. Thanks to my wife Eleanor for tolerating the untold hours that such an undertaking of this magnitude this requires. Thanks to the editorial team who helped me improve and polish the presentation of this material. Thanks to my former Greek professor, Dr. David Capes, for working through this manuscript and the kind words of support. To my old friend and great missionary statesman Dr. Doug Jeter (Hugh's son) who put his everything into not only reading but editing this manuscript. Finally, to the father who was kind enough to adopt me; Robert Gray who having spent a lifetime in education, was well

[1] Minear, Paul, S., *Commands of Christ: Authority and Implications* (Nashville-New York: Abingdon Press, 1972).
[2] Esterline, Dan, A., Sr. *A Weekly Discipleship Journal: 52 Commands of Christ* (Enumclaw, Washington: Winepress, 2003).
[3] Jeter, Hugh, P., *Commands of Christ* (Houston, Texas: 1stBooks, 2003).

equipped to provide the final proof read for this text and made the book even better.

My hope is that the Church as a whole will rally together to take responsibility for what Christ has called not just one man to do, but all of us to do. This way we can achieve something that Jesus would really be proud of! He promises to be with us in a special way as we turn our attention to the accomplishment of His will.

George Gray
2012
Humble, Texas

Introduction

Calling the Church to a Christ-centered discipleship method is a lot like calling eyes to see, ears to hear, or birds to fly. What a strange apparition it would be, for example, to see birds walking through the streets and crosswalks, riding in the backs of cabs, and checking in and out of airports. What an odd business it would be to explain to them that they have no need of public transportation but should rely instead on their own wings. If this impossible dream became a reality I could just imagine one of them protesting that "transportation is transportation; we don't need to add personal flight to it."

I feel just as bewildered when I have to go around to different churches and try to explain the very purpose for which they were created. One would think that some things would be, as the Declaration of Independence suggests, "self-evident." However, the current state of affairs in discipleship seems to suggest something very different. Just like the multiple methods of transportation fictitiously made available to nonflying fowls, the Christian Church today seems to believe discipleship is equally open to multiple avenues of expression. The operation is altogether subjective, and they have forgotten what their own "wings" are for. Somewhere along the line, Christians have disconnected from their purpose. The design has detached from the Designer; so we foolishly muddle along with far inferior solutions.

Discipleship has come to mean any sort of spiritual growth, which is just like saying flying means any sort of transportation. Discipleship is not just spiritual formation but a certain *type* of spiritual formation. The Church has forgotten that more important than becoming a disciple is *whose* disciple you are becoming. It is not about teaching someone to pray and read his or her Bible; it is about learning how Jesus wants us to pray and read our Bible. It is not about the doctrine of the Church but the doctrine of Jesus Christ, the head of the Church. It is not about attending a church service but attending to the Lord Jesus's view of what it means to be the church. You simply cannot make a Christian disciple without a Master/servant relationship between Jesus of Nazareth and a true believer. The key is to remember that in Christ's system of making disciples there can never be any other substitute for the Master Himself.

This is where many so-called discipleship programs miss the target and the point. Christian leaders erroneously assume that just as Jesus had his disciples, they are to have theirs. But we were never commanded to make disciples of ourselves. That is why the Lord limited the curriculum for this enterprise to the commands He gave His first disciples. Discipleship is nothing more than adhering to Jesus's expressed will. It is treating every command He gave His disciples as if He were giving it personally to us. We become Jesus's disciples by practicing Jesus's commands and, in the process, gaining His point of view, philosophy, and image.

The title of the book suggests that there is a particular standpoint to be gained from a thorough investigation of the facts. This perspective is none other than that of the Son of God. Oftentimes we will seek out the professional opinions of those considered experts in any field—or perhaps even the author of a particular successful methodology—in order to maximize our own success in an area. However, once God Himself directly brings to bear His own wisdom in such a matter, it can never be presented as if He were just another expert opinion to be compared and contrasted with the rest.

This is precisely the point of this manuscript; for if indeed Jesus's perspective on any matter can be conclusively established, the need for any further debate is rendered null and void. At that point, all further reflection will first have to consider what the Master has already set in motion. My contention is that this particular perspective of perspectives and viewpoint of viewpoints has yet to be fully recognized within the Christian faith. Making disciples of Jesus today is not the primary objective, nor has it been prone to much in the way of objectivity at all. It has not been developed to the point of specificity at all but is lost in a sea of relativism and overgeneralization. There is no standard operating procedure for this, the most important of all objectives relating to the Church. The purpose of this book is to provide just such a procedure along with its prospective rationale. It is as the subtitle suggests to develop a method to "rediscover and reinstitute" the master plan (that of Jesus himself).

As such, the book is easily divided into theory and practice. The first and shorter section is devoted to theory, and that is the area where caution is recommended. Providing a theory of impenetrable logic requires that one investigate a great deal beyond the surface of a matter. So while the beginning chapters (which address the exegesis of pivotal passages) might be the most intellectually stimulating for some, it could present the greatest of challenges for others. Therefore, one is encouraged to use that section as a reference point and perhaps move on to the implications section should they be overwhelmed with the technical aspects of the investigation.

Regardless of those realities, there is no doubt in my mind that the practical section will prove to be so incredibly useful it will make the whole effort entirely worthwhile. It is my sincere desire that you will thoroughly enjoy this presentation and that it will become an extremely beneficial tool in the serious attempt we all are required to make toward this greatest of causes known to man: making disciples the way Jesus intended.

As you begin to work through the second half of the book, where you are to apply the imperatives to your life, there are a few items that may need clarification. First is to notice the particular levels of growth attributed to each section of development. It spans infanthood to adulthood (patterned after Erik Erikson's Stages of Psychosocial Development[4]) in an effort to emphasize the progression of growth that will necessarily occur as you work through the material in the same succession the first disciples did. I believe Jesus purposely offered easier and softer concepts in the beginning and left the more challenging material for those who were prepared to receive it due to having achieved a more advanced level of maturity. Therefore, it is recommended to address the material in the proper sequence. Additionally, it is suggested that some sort of recognition be offered once a particular level of advancement has been achieved.

Secondly, the question naturally arises as to the best teaching method to cover these lessons. Even though it is theoretically possible to engage this material on both an individual and corporate (large classroom) level, it is recommended that a small-group format be used with the additional option of an accountability partner. We must replicate as much as possible the original circumstances the first group of twelve disciples experienced.

---

4   Erikson, Erik H., *The Life Cycle Completed* (New York: W.W. Norton & Company, 1982), 56.

There is also the issue of which translation of the Bible is preferred. I have found in my own interaction with the original language that the New American Standard Bible is one of the best due to the fact that they attempt to adhere to the original wording as much as possible. I will use this version along with the New King James throughout this document unless I am translating the passage myself. At that point my own translation will be utilized as an attempt to dig even further into the hidden value that tends to resurface any time you examine the originals yourself. A personal translation will also serve to demonstrate to the reader that the exegesis of the passage has come from a thorough investigation of the facts. It is in the *Exegesis of Pivotal Passages* section that you will encounter my own translation.

PART ONE:
Jesus's Perspective:
Rediscovery
Knowing the Master's Objective

I

Exegesis of Pivotal Passages

In order to arrive at the perspective of Jesus Christ on any matter it is imperative that those passages in the gospels that record his particular viewpoint are fully considered. Modern scholarship has tended to shy away from such an exercise in suspicion that the text is somehow not trustworthy.[5] The assumption is that the original words of Jesus must have been tampered with in order to control the direction of the Church in a way that best suited those who remained.

Placing new words in the mouth of the original leader does not necessarily guarantee any results; for as it is today, those words are either forgotten or manipulated on the interpretive and applicative levels. We can basically make the Master say whatever we want regardless of what is actually written. Therefore, it is not necessary to change the original.

Nor can I imagine it a remote possibility that any such fabrication would have been tolerated by the early Church whose heart and soul breathed the oral gospel tradition. To alter the original message of the gospels would defeat the primary reason for their existence. They were written for the very purpose of making disciples of Jesus, not to further personal political agendas.

Inherent in these doubts about the reliability of the documents is also a lack of faith toward any possibility that God's hand was uniquely involved in their preservation or that anyone had a serious enough relationship with Christ that it would render such a miserable deed unimaginable. Scholarship that is agnostic at its core should not become the gathering

---

5   Johnson, Luke Timothy, *The Real Jesus: The Misguided Quest for the Historical Jesus and the Truth of the Traditional Gospels* (HarperSanFranciso: 1996), 23.

point for all future discussion on such critical matters of faith. To demythologize scripture is to remove the supernatural, for the Bible is not a book of myths. To remove the supernatural is to remove deity. To remove deity is to remove any reason for further discussion about spiritual matters: hence we have uncovered the plot of Satan.

The author of this manuscript does not share the presupposition that the "historical Jesus" is someone very different from the person presented to us in the gospels. On the contrary, scripture is valued as the most trustworthy source available and therefore indispensable to arriving at a reasonable conclusion on any matter. I accept those gospel records that were canonized and reject those that were not. I consider this issue of determining what is and what is not accepted as a gospel to have long since been resolved. It is not about changing the original writings as much as it is having the courage to accept them at face value. The point at which they are being tampered with today is not so much on the written level as it is on the level of their interpretation and application.

On the issue of how disciples are to be made, there is only one passage that actually addresses it directly. Yet it is addressed and with great detail and significance. For it is in what is known as the Great Commission that we find the process spelled out in a manner that leaves no doubt whatsoever as to the Lord's original intentions. It is especially noteworthy that these instructions are among the final words to the Church prior to Jesus's ascension. Knowing that this would be His last chance for direct communication, Christ is presented as laying out the ground rules for how His church is to function henceforth.

If there is a desire to know what discipleship is all about the place to begin is Matthew 28:18b-20: "I was given all authority in heaven and upon earth. Therefore, having gone, make disciples of all the nations, baptizing them into the name of the Father, Son and Holy Spirit, teaching them to keep all things that I commanded to you. And behold, I myself am with you every day until the end of the world" (author's translation).

MATTHEW 28:18-20

At first glance there appears to be a smattering of ideas with little to gather it in a singular direction. It is only by looking beneath the surface and discovering the actual Greek infrastructure that everything begins to fall into place. A clear pattern emerges that cannot be denied. As will become apparent in the unfolding commentary, the central issue revolves around one single expression in the original Greek. This one word that translates into two in English is the mandate that pumps the life-giving blood to the rest of the body. It is the verb μαθητεύσατε (*mathēteusate*), which represents the primary activity that is to define Christianity, namely to "make disciples."

After a careful study of the syntax and grammatical structure, it can be said with full confidence that this one term is the center of the universe for the Christian Church. The sun does not revolve around the earth but the earth revolves around the radiant splendor of this fiery orb called discipleship. Furthermore, it is just such an accurate understanding the nature and order of things that means life or death for the kingdom of God. There is a rare atmosphere that one experiences when approaching this portion of scripture. It is as if Jesus has appeared on the scene once again as the eternal Logos to set in place the principles by which this spiritual universe will continue to function in an orderly sequence from henceforth. Let us examine this passage line by line so as not to overlook any important detail.

In 18, it says, "I was given all authority in heaven and upon earth." The context is the risen Messiah in Galilee meeting with the nucleus of the church in order to provide them with final instructions for the continued advancement of his kingdom in his absence. He approaches them as the King of Kings and Lord of Lords as the victor over hell and the grave. As such He is appropriately "worshipped," in verse 17, yet some still doubted. Perhaps it is that very doubt that causes Him to reemphasize at this point His supreme authority. However, it is also necessary when laying down the policy and procedure for all future engagement that one's right to do so is firmly established. Furthermore, as a message to all future generations it will serve them well as a reminder of just who is supposed to ultimately be in charge. This is not for Christ's sake, as if He is desperate to hold on to power, but for the sake of those who will tend to drift toward their own priorities in His absence as well as the absence of their own faith walk. For we now approach a critical juncture of change from "seeing is believing" to "We walk by faith, not by sight" (1 Corinthians 5:7). All that will remain are these final words of direction and our resolve to either repeat or replace them. It is for this very reason that believers must "die daily" (1 Corinthians 15:31) to further the kingdom. The self-denial, taking up the cross, and following must continue (Luke 9:23). No longer is there an earthly personality to cling to but only His message, and the Holy Spirit's reminder to oblige.

The term used in this sentence that will most readily determine its meaning is ἐξουσία (*exousia*). The Greek Lexicon offers five possible meanings that all seem to rotate around this idea of authorization: 1. the right to act; 2. ability or power; 3. authority or absolute power; 4. ruling power or official power; and 5. means of exercising power. Number three is offered as the closest to the intended meaning in Matthew 28:18 by Gingrich's lexicon.[6] The fact that this authority Jesus speaks of is described as "all authority in heaven and on earth" leans heavily in favor of Gingrich's conclusions by supporting this idea of *absolute* power and authority. One gets the idea that there is no further appeal process by which any higher authority could be summoned. This is as high up the ladder as a man can possibly go. Yet it is also interesting to note that this supreme authority and final say was handed over to Christ. The implication can only be that this was the decision of the Father (Luke 10:22). It causes the recollection of that well-known passage of scripture in Philippians 2:9-11 that states, "Therefore God also has highly exalted Him and given Him the name which is above every name, that at the name of Jesus every knee should bow, of those in heaven, and of those on earth, and of those under the earth, and that every tongue should confess that Jesus Christ is Lord, to the glory of God the Father." Ultimately the point is substantiated that this absolute power that was handed over to Christ could have come from none other than the Father. Who else would be capable of possessing authority on a universal dimension?

19-20a: "Therefore, having gone, make disciples of all nations, baptizing them in the name of the Father, Son and Holy Spirit, teaching them to keep all things I commanded you." Notice first that my translation does not start with "go" as do many other translations. Even the New American Standard Bible translates πορευθέντες as "go" but at least has the decency to offer an explanation in the notes: "Or *having gone*; Gr. aorist part." They correctly surmise that due to the fact that πορευθέντες is an aorist participle, it cannot be properly translated as if it were an

---

6   Gingrich, Wilbur F., *Shorter Lexicon of the Greek New Testament* (Chicago and London: The University of Chicago Press, 1965), 75.

imperative (e.g., order or mandate).[7] Aorist means it is to be translated as if took place before the actual activity that is being insisted upon. This is why *having gone* is preferred over *as you go*. "As you go" means it is occurring at the same time as the *making of disciples*. *As you go* is not aorist participle but *present* participle and is therefore an incorrect translation. Translating it *go* is also wrong because it is suggesting that it is an *imperative* and not a *participle*. Examples of imperatives are go, tell, preach, teach, baptize, make disciples, sing, submit, love, etc. Notice how they all can express a direct order from a superior. However, when you place those same terms in a participle form, you will notice how they all become verbal adjectives: going, telling, preaching, teaching, baptizing, discipling, singing, submitting, loving, etc. As such, they all will naturally end in "ing." You cannot translate a participle without that. Therefore it is totally incorrect to start Matthew 28:19 with the word *go*. This is an error in the translation process.

When the translation begins with *go* as the directive, it increases the possibility that the understanding of the passage will immediately begin heading in the wrong direction. This has unfortunately been the case for many generations. The actual imperative of the sentence is not *go* but *make disciples*. The going, baptizing, and teaching tell us *how* to make disciples of all nations.[8] In Greek grammar, any time you have an imperative statement followed by a string of participles it constitutes the development of a main and subordinate clause. Notice the pattern below:

I. Main clause
   A. Subordinate clause
   B. Subordinate clause
   C. Subordinate cause

When it is read in the original Greek, the above structure naturally falls into place and the actual order of things is clearly understood. However, when one tries to transfer that into another language, it can come out a bit jumbled. Great care must be taken to rearrange each term in its proper sequence for the English way of communicating and thinking. Since

[7]   Black, David A., *Learn to Read New Testament Greek* (Nashville, TN: B&H Publishing Group, 1994), 138.
[8]   Ibid., 187.

this has not yet been attempted, what we currently have in our English translations looks like this:

    A. Having gone
I. Make disciples of all nations
    B. Baptizing them in the name of the Father, Son, and Holy Spirit
    C. Teaching them to keep all things I commanded you.

It is easy to see that the typical translation is a bit disoriented. The arrangement above reflects the actual sequence of the original language. However, this sequence must be reordered to make sense in our language. A translation that better communicates what is meant in the original language might be like so: "Therefore, make disciples by going into the entire world, baptizing them in the name of the Father, Son, and Holy Spirit and teaching them to practice everything I commanded you."

I. Make disciples by
    A. Going into the entire world.
    B. Baptizing them in the name of the Father, Son, and Holy Spirit
    C. Teaching them to practice everything I commanded you.

This way the main clause is in the correct position and is properly followed by all of the subordinate clauses that tell you how to perform the task at hand. It is not unusual in Greek to see participles out of place. Routinely they will be positioned both before and after the main clause, expecting the reader to realign them in his or her thinking.[9] If you fail to do so the message comes out a bit jumbled.

The point of all this internal investigation in terms of Greek grammar and syntax is to help us arrive at just exactly what the principle aim of the Great Commission is. The bottom line is that Jesus is communicating in no uncertain terms what is the primary objective: making disciples. Even that fact was hidden for some time as these very words (make disciples) were originally translated as *teach* in the King James Version. But the term

---

[9] Ibid.

for *teach* in Greek is διδάσκω (*didaskō*), which is not even close to the actual word we have in verse 19, namely μαθητεύσατε (*mathēteusate*).

For centuries this Great Commission has remained under a cloud of uncertainty just because greater care was not taken in the translation process. It is hard, therefore, to doubt that Satan was and is working behind the scenes to keep this message from getting out to the public in a completely understandable format. This is one of those improvements in modern translations that was long overdue. Today, *make disciples* is the common terminology used in most translations. Once you isolate the mandate and its subsidiaries, confusion about the Great Commission is greatly diminished. Instead of many ideas that are disconnected you are left with a singular objective and the steps to achieve it.

So now that we have everything accurately restructured for maximum clarity we can move on to the particular message the author likely wants to communicate. The first thing that stands out with a great deal of particularity is not what is said but what is not said. There is no mention here of "preaching the gospel" or "that repentance for forgiveness of sins would be proclaimed" (Mark 16:15; Luke 24:47). It is repentance and faith rather than works that allows one to enter into the kingdom of God (Mark 1:14; John 3:16). So it is rather curious that Matthew never mentions faith. He only focuses on making disciples through baptism and teaching.

However, as is so often the case, if you speak only of grace there is a good chance that self-serving individuals will gladly take you up on it and never consider the hard work that is to follow. Such an empty faith would no doubt be reprehensible to the Jewish perspective. We know the Gospel of Matthew was written to a Jewish audience. Perhaps this is the very reason "faith in the gospel" is not presented as the only thing required. Rather, it is at best implied by the fact that it is not possible to introduce a lengthy and severe training process to an unmotivated doubter. Unrelenting dedication is always preceded by burning desire.

In Judaism, it is that desire that is first tested before one is baptized in water, which is understood as a sort of initiation or rite of passage into the religion. The individual Gentile approaches Judaism expressing his wish to unite with the children of God. At that point, the person is examined according to the nature of his or her faith. If the questioners are convinced as to their belief, they are prepared for water baptism by further teaching.[10] This is perhaps why it is possible not to mention what Matthew and his audience considered the obvious prerequisite. Common heritage allows for common knowledge. It seems that this is likely the scenario we see in the Matthew account. Thankfully we have the other commissioning accounts to provide the less discerning with the rest of the story.

There is one marked departure, however, from typical Jewish protocol. That is the act of offering this message and training process to the heathen. To go into all the world and approach sinners with the good news and invite them to become part of the family of God would have been quite beyond the norm in Judaism. It was the Gentile who was to approach the Jew, not vice versa. This proactive method is no doubt part of the new wine that Jesus is offering that will not be contained in the old wine skins of Jewish tradition. Yet at the same time we see that the making of disciples is that aspect of Judaism that remains intact and is to continue to be part and parcel of the Christian experience today. Yet even this exercise is reshaped by Jesus and ends up with His unique signature.

We know that typically, application is made to rabbis who chose from those applicants whom they considered to have the best potential. More than likely they would have chosen the ones who thought, acted, and looked most like them. However, Jesus was proactive in His selection process. There was no application procedure. It was simply Him acting in his Father's best interest and tapping that person on the shoulder that God led Him to. Also personal ambition was frowned upon. The objective for every student in Judaism was eventually to rise to the status of master. Not so with Jesus's disciples. There would always remain throughout all time the one and only Master: Jesus. We are not dealing here with a mere man but the Son of the living God.

Very few in the Jewish faith could rise to the level of rabbi or even be a student of a rabbi. In Christianity everyone is called to become a student of the one and only rabbi, Jesus. He is permanently our Master and we are permanently His and one another's servants.

---

[10] Daube, David, *The New Testament and Rabbinic Judaism* (Peabody, Massachusetts: Hendrickson 1998), 113-14.

Discipleship was about apprenticeship. The dictionary definition for μαθητής (*disciple*) means just that: "pupil" or "apprentice."[11] It was learning how things are to be done and then trying your hand at it under supervision. You see that principle clearly demonstrated in Jesus's discipleship process (Matthew 10; Mark 6; Luke 9-10). But it is mostly about learning. It involves a lot of heart-to-heart discussion over open campfires. There is both small-group interaction and the further exchange of a trusted few. We see the dynamic of a group of twelve and the more intimate gatherings of only three on special occasions. There is the day-to-day trial-and-error of making assertions and seeing those either accepted or rejected by the Person in charge. There is the exchange of ideas and either the exaltation or humiliation that follows.

An excellent book that further examines these principles in the context of the experience of the first disciples as they follow Christ is *The Training of the Twelve* by A. B. Bruce.[12] No modern-day disciple should be without it. It does much to help us bridge the gap between what we understand discipleship to be and what it was in the beginning.

The mandate of our Lord is to repeat the process that He first initiated. We are to replicate as much as possible the original exchange by placing ourselves under His direction as did the first disciples. We are to take what the first disciples left us of His commands and do everything we can to put those into practice. We are to examine our philosophy of life, attitude, and lifestyle and reorient it toward that which we are discovering about what our Lord expects of us. This is not a movement with a natural leader, but a supernatural one. His command is our ultimate leader, and our appointed leaders are those who have best mastered the Master.

Thus far we have unfolded two out of three aspects of making disciples as enumerated by our Lord in Matthew 28:18-19. We see that the task at hand is heavy on the side of works with the grace aspect merely implied. It is all stated as a call to action.

There are certain objectives that must be accomplished in order to further the kingdom of God in an exponential fashion. Making disciples ensures that. For making a disciple will definitely produce multiplied

---

[11] Gingrich, F. Wilbur, *Shorter Lexicon of the Greek New Testament* (Chicago and London: The University of Chicago Press, 1965), 129.

[12] Bruce, A. B., *The Training of the Twelve* (Grand Rapids, Michigan: Kregel Publications, 1971), 1-545.

returns when compared to just making a new convert.[13] The first two objectives are to go global and to baptize them in the Trinitarian formula. Then the real work begins (as if covering the whole face of the earth is not enough). One is to painstakingly teach the new convert how to carry out each and every one of the some 254 of Jesus's commands as recorded in the Gospels. The final stage of this process is stated in Matthew 28:20a: "teaching them to keep everything I commanded you."

So a teacher is required as well as a specific type of curriculum. The instructor is to focus on something precise. He is not to focus on Jesus's philosophy, ideas, or principles per se, although all of those things provide the context necessary for a clear understanding. He is to focus on the commands (ἐνετειλάμην) that normally follow those things. Typically, Jesus will follow a general teaching with a homework list, or "to-do" list if you will.[14] That is to be the area with the greatest emphasis. In other words, Jesus is not interested in filling our head with facts but in us putting those facts to work. It is in the fulfillment of the objective that we are changed in a way that is not possible by information alone. This is why the teacher's stated goal is not to help the student acquire knowledge as much as it is to acquire the knowledge necessary to perform a particular task. It is the means to an end and not the end in itself. We are to teach them to *keep* (τηρεῖν) the commands, not just to *know* the commands. For Jesus, it can safely be said that "actions speak louder than words." He is never recorded as saying, "I love you" at all. But no one can ever doubt His love because of what He did. Love is not saying something to someone, it is doing something for someone. Talk is cheap and love must be proven in service (Mark 10:45; Luke 6:46).

Likewise, when you consider the fact that Jesus chose the word *keep* rather than *practice* or *obey*, it proves there is additional insight that must not be dismissed. When the translator goes into this passage, everything within him wants to ignore the word keep and replace it with something more sensible and agreeable to the Western psyche and style of communication. But if that is done the deeper meaning is lost forever. It is not by accident that the dictionary definition of this term not only deals

---

[13] Hull, Bill, *The Disciple Making Pastor* (Grand Rapids, Michigan: Baker Books, 2007), 78.

[14] Stassen, Glen H. and David P. Gushee, *Kingdom Ethics* (Downers Grove, Illinois: InterVarsity Press, 2003), 135.

with the *observance* of a particular law or rule but with the *treasuring* of that particular rule. It contains the idea of *watching over, guarding, or preserving* something.[15] This is so important and tends to separate the truly devout soul from the pretender. In other words we are not to approach Jesus's commands as a long list of dos and don'ts that are impossible, irrelevant, and burdensome. Far from it. They are a treasure trove of wisdom from the Person we admire most in life. We should rather preserve them in a book, chisel them on tablets, and adorn our homes' façades with them. All the days of our lives we should consider them our greatest discovery. Having come to this conclusion, all efforts would be made then to safeguard this valuable resource from infiltration both without and within. And as our most precious resource it would then receive the place of highest honor in our institutions. It would remain on the tip of every tongue and make up our collective conscience. It would demonstrate the core values of how we are recognized as a people, namely our strict adherence to and love for the imperatives of our Lord Jesus Christ.

It is significant that the word *all* ($\pi \acute{\alpha} \nu \tau \alpha$) is used repeatedly in this passage. First Jesus has *all* authority in heaven and on Earth. Next we are told to go into *all* the world. And finally we are to teach them to practice *all things* he commanded the first disciples. It is a very thorough and comprehensive program. In fact it can seem a bit overwhelming when considered from the perspective of personal responsibility. Yet there is reassurance that we are not in this enterprise alone. We are promised all the infinite resources of eternity as our Lord pledges to go with us every (*all*) day until the end of time. Thankfully it is not just a mission but a commission.

The central figure of our faith has in effect drawn out a target for us to hit together. To miss the mark is to commit sin. In the center of that target is the bull's eye of obedience. If He is truly our Lord we have no other option. If we truly love Him we have no other privilege. By grace His every wish is our command and His every command is our wish.

MARK 7:1-23

Seeing discipleship from Jesus's perspective means understanding what his underlying values are. The magnitude of this passage lies in its ability

---

[15]   Gingrich, Wilber F., *Shorter Lexicon of the Greek New Testament* (Chicago and London: The University of Chicago Press, 1965), 217.

to clearly distinguish Jesus's philosophy of ministry from the religious leadership of his day. Christ came to Earth not only to become a human sacrifice but, in the process, to set the religious world back on proper course with God. It is apparent from His teaching that He also came to set the record straight theologically. More than any other prophet God had sent in the past, it is the Son of God who can most clearly communicate both who God is and what He expects from His people. Only the Son can *exegete*, or *explain* the Father (John 1:18). For only the Son has had face-to-face contact with Him throughout eternity (John 1:1ff). Carefully consider each word of this majestic treatise so as to come away with a common rationale by which true discipleship can begin. In this indictment the Lord effectively sets the current religious framework on its head. He introduces a paradigm shift that effectively rearranges all former predispositions from an outside—in to an inside—out point of reference. Each of the following verses of Mark 7: 1-23 are the authors' translation.

7:1-2: "The Pharisees and some of the scribes from Jerusalem huddled toward him noticing some of his disciples eating bread with common hands (that is unwashed hands)." The first term that is addressed in the Greek word order is συνάγονται (*sunagontai*). The word signifies a *gathering together* or an *assembly*.[16] This term has a passive or middle voice. Since it would not make sense for them to have been gathered by an outside force, the proper way of seeing this event is in the middle voice. That means they gathered themselves together—thus the use of the term *huddled*. It is clear that the assembly preceded the movement toward Jesus because there are two separate terms to indicate each event (συνάγονται means "assembled" and πρὸς means "toward"). It appears that this faultfinding brigade was launched from headquarters in Jerusalem. Jerusalem would naturally serve as the ultimate base of operations for the ritually clean because it highly surpassed Galilee and the Gentile contaminated Samaria.

Right away the author is able to communicate the Pharisaic tendency to major on the minors (Matthew 23:24). One is struck by the insignificance of the ordeal. Surely there must have been something much, much worse that could have been addressed instead. It appears as a small matter to people today, but this was not a matter of sanitation or "moral rectitude"

---

[16] Rienecker, Fritz and Cleon Rogers, *Linguistic Key to the Greek New Testament* (Grand Rapids, Michigan: Zondervan Publishing House, 1976), 106.

but "fitness for the cult."[17] Ceremonial cleanliness was part of their faith. The Pharisees believed that impurity could be passed from the hands to the mouth and from there into the heart.[18] They were obsessed about anything that might defile them externally, hence avoiding dirty items as well as people. Washing hands before meals would have been extremely important to them, and they typically would utilize large stone water-pots in the process.[19]

The scribes are also mentioned but with the same distinction as the disciples. There were "certain ones" or "some" (τινες) of the scribes present. Perhaps it was a more virulent stream of the sect who was engaged in the everyday affairs of society. It should also be noted in general that the scribes were "not copyists but scholars and therefore experts in the interpretation of the law."[20] As such they may have felt a responsibility to clarify scriptural matters.

What did the inspectors notice? That "some" of Jesus's disciples were eating with "common" (κοιναῖς) hands. The reverse realities of the initial charge are just as interesting as the accusation. That would mean that some of them did ritually wash their hands before eating the bread—including Jesus.

Something must be said about the condition of the hands. Typically, translations (e.g., KJV, TEV, New International Version, RSV, JB, and NEV) render κοιναῖς (koinais) as either "unclean" or "defiled (KJV, TEV, NIV, RSV, JB and NEV)." However this goes beyond the scope of that term. It means nothing more than "common."[21] This fact necessitates further explanation by Mark ("that is, unwashed"). It is to be understood in the sense of being accessible to the general public,[22] like a currency that

---

[17]   Booth, Roger P., Jesus *and the Laws of Purity: Tradition History and Legal History in Mark 7* (Sheffield, England: JSOT Press, 1986), 118.

[18]   Melton, Loyd D., PhD, Lecture tapes for New Testament History. Cassette 8, Trinity College and Seminary, 1999.

[19]   Ibid.

[20]   Brooks, James A., *The New American Commentary: Mark* (Nashville, Tennessee: Broadman Press, 1991), 50.

[21]   Bauer, Walter, *A Greek-English Lexicon of the New Testament and Other Early Christian Literature,* transl. and eds. William F. Arndt and F. Wilbur Gingrich (Chicago: The University of Chicago Press, 1957), 458.

[22]   Booth, 120.

would pass through many hands unrestrained. One has to conclude for oneself what is meant, but it is clear that those things that are "uncommon" (or a "low-traffic" item) would be considered to possess a higher measure of cleanliness.

When we consider the mention of *bread* in the text a number of issues arise. One is the fact that the preceding chapter of Mark relates the story of the multiplication of bread and fish. It is a remote possibility that the very *bread* of this debate was heaven sent.[23] Even if that is not the case, there is a stark contrast that strikes the reader as they fall from the pinnacle of euphoric celebration and inclusion in chapter 6 to the miry pit of miserly religious analysis and exclusion in chapter 7.

7:3-4: (For the Pharisees and all Jews will not eat without first washing their hands vigorously; holding on firmly to the traditions of the elders. Nor will they eat when returning from the marketplace unless they baptize themselves. They received and held firmly to all sorts of stipulations such as baptisms of cups, pitchers, brass kettles and even dining cots.)

Once again it seemed more logical to connect verses three and four into one thought. This thought is really a digression from the first two verses and thus can best be expressed within the perimeters of a parenthesis.[24] It is notable that not only the religious elite but all Jewry seem to be held in contempt in this passage. Some have suggested that this is simply an addition of the early church and should be edited out.[25] Others call it hyperbole.[26] The second conclusion is more reasonable. "The Jews" became synonymous with the religious authorities who wished to dispose of Jesus, and later, Christianity. The author of the book of John is especially fond of this term. But it clearly can't mean all Jews because Jesus himself was Jewish. Perhaps it became simply a figure of speech by the time the New Testament books were written. No doubt it was fitting for the context since it was at this time that Christianity was forming a separate identity from the Judaism that had become a militant opposition. Was it simply another

---

[23] Geddert, Timothy J., *Believers Church Bible Commentary: Mark* (Scottsdale, Pennsylvania: Herald Press, 2001), 163.

[24] Nicoll, W. R., ed., *The Expositor's Greek Testament* (Grand Rapids, Michigan: Wm. B. Eerdmans Publishing Company, 1961), 386.

[25] Booth, 198.

[26] Brooks, 114.

way of saying, "The scribes and the Pharisees as well as their devotees," as is done throughout this text? This is a possibility.

Nevertheless, the main point here is to demonstrate the lengths the elite are willing to go to in obtaining ritual purity. It was not simply an issue of one's dirtiness but of one's doxology. As a matter of fact, it had become so serious to them at this time that a violation of ceremonial cleanliness was considered worse than bloodshed.[27] They would apparently rather starve than eat with unwashed hands.

There is a peculiar term used in this passage to describe the way they wash. The translation above renders it *vigorously*. However, the literal translation is "with fist." This particular expression cannot be found in any literary sources so scholars are left to speculate as to its intended meaning.[28] Faced with this uncertainty, one is forced to uncover what may be behind the surface of these terms.

There are only two legitimate avenues to traverse in this area. It is either a Greek or an Aramaic puzzle that must be pieced together. If the Aramaic did precede the Greek it could account for the unusual terminology at some points. Often a word can be translated more than one way. In this case, the original Aramaic term can mean either "a jug" or "a span from the fingers to the elbow."[29] Some translations (LB and JB, for example) have opted for this solution, translating the passage as washing "up to the elbows." "With water jugs" would also be possible in this approach. A first-century burned house (AD 70) has been discovered with a stone water pot (and a stone table and bowls, etc. because stone was held to be ritually clean) so "with water jars" would not be completely out of the question.[30] But we cannot be absolutely certain about this conclusion since there is no existing Aramaic text.

In an effort to work with the empirical data that is available, one is obligated to consider the Greek language. The term πυγμῇ (*pugmē*) is

---

[27] Charlesworth, James H., *Jesus within Judaism* (New York: Doubleday, 1988), 73.

[28] Schmidt, K. L., *Theological Dictionary of the New Testament*, Gerhard Friedrich etd. Vol. VI (Πε–Ρ) (Grand Rapids, Michigan: Wm. B. Eerdmans Publishing Co., 1968.), 916.

[29] Schmidt, 916.

[30] Charlesworth, 106.

chosen. This term is typically used in the context of a "fight with fists."[31] "Pugilism" is an expression that denotes a resistance, struggle, or conflict. Therefore, in seeking terminology that will fit both its typical usage and the scriptural context, one is compelled to render the passage as "thoroughly or vigorously." This follows more closely the train of thought in the chapter where there is an expression of intensity in terms of "seizing or holding firmly to" a particular tradition. The fervor with which the authorities are attached to this obsession is striking. Perhaps that determination found physical outlet within the washing exercise itself.

Something more must be said about these prized traditions. Who were the elders? Where did the tradition originate? There was no body of literature in Jesus's day that could be referred to in support of the Pharisees. They were following an oral tradition that had been handed down by the generations of rabbis that had preceded them.[32] In that day writing materials were scarce and costly. Instead, the students were trained to lock the very statements and mannerisms of the rabbi into their memory banks.[33] All of society was geared toward this sort of activity, so that indeed oral tradition became a legitimate source of information. This data amounted to a great volume of material once it was put into writing in the second-century AD.

The author goes on in a seemingly endless tirade of all the outlandish practices of the scribes and Pharisees. They can't even eat until everything is perfect. If they were to go out to the market, for example, that too would defile them and warrant a complete submersion of their bodies in water before eating (literally: *and from marketplace unless they baptize themselves not they eat*). It is significant here that the washing terminology changes. In verse 3 the word νίψωνται (*nipsōntai*) is used. But in verse 4 it changes to βαπτίσωνται (*baptisōntai*). It appears that most translations (KJV, LB, PME, RSV, TEV, NIV, JB, and NEB) are reluctant to translate the second term as it is given, perhaps because of its theological baggage. Three of the above-mentioned versions render the term "sprinkling." But this holds some validity since oldest Greek manuscripts use this instead of

---

[31] Schmidt, 915.
[32] Donahue, John R., SJ Harrington and Daniel J. Harrington, eds., *Sacra Pagina Series. Vol. 2, The Gospel of Mark* (Collegeville, Minnesota: The Liturgical Press, 2002), 219.
[33] Melton, cassette 11.

"baptizing." Yet in early Christianity there is little difference theologically between pouring and submerging since both methods are used in water baptism ceremonies, according to the Didache.[34] So we are forced to come full circle and consider the fact that the author of this passage chose to select a different and more controversial term at this point. The choice of "baptism" or "sprinkling" instead of just "washing" heightens the religious significance of the practice.

Their overzealous behavior is exposed in its extreme. It shows their scrutiny of even one's pots and pans and various other kitchen utensils. "All sorts of stipulations," above, is literally "many other things"—ἄλλα πολλά in the original. Again we are confronted with the term κρατεῖν (kratein), which means "seize" or "hold onto firmly." We sense their blind and uncompromising devotion to tradition as they find themselves *straining* at the gnat and swallowing the camel (Matthew 23:24). Cups, pitchers, kettles, and cots are more important to them than their fellow man. Such regulations were normally relegated to the priesthood alone but these religious leaders had imposed them on everyone.[35]

7:5: "The scribes and the Pharisees asked him, 'Why don't your disciples walk according to the tradition of the elders, instead of eating the bread with common hands?'" No doubt the adversaries were looking for something Jesus Himself would be guilty of but had to settle for easier prey among his band of ruffians. From their point of view the disciples were entirely unorthodox in their behavior. Nevertheless, Christ was indirectly made the target by addressing a matter that He was ultimately responsible for as their leader. They must have felt that if they could demonstrate how Jesus had failed to instruct his disciples in the most basic rules of piety, then they would be able to "undermine His authority as a teacher."[36] Surely the scribes and Pharisees must have been mortified by the scathing reply of the Lord.

7:6-7: "but He said to them, 'Isaiah was right when he prophesied about you hypocrites. It is written: These people honor me with the lips, but their heart is far away—distant from me. But in vain they worship

---

34   Niederwimmer, Kurt, *The Didache: A Commentary*, trans. Linda M. Maloney, ed. Harold W. Attridge (Minneapolis: Fortress Press, 1998), 125.

35   Geddert, 164.

36   Keck, Leander E., ed. *The New Interpreter's Bible*. Vol. VIII (Nashville: Abingdon Press, 1994), 606.

me; Teaching commandments of men as doctrine." 7:8: "While letting go of God's commandments you latch on to man's tradition." 7:9: "He was saying to them, 'You set aside the commandment of God beautifully, so that your own tradition might be established.'"

As is typical of Jesus throughout the gospels, He is able to really get down to business in a hurry. He is portrayed as knowing the true motives of individuals who approach Him, and rather than addressing their external speech, He exposes their hidden agenda (John 4; Matthew 19:21; 22:18; John 2:24-25). They support their accusations with tradition, and Jesus supports His with scripture. He quotes Isaiah 29:13. Jesus's quotation is reported as following the septuagint ("LXX") but exchanging "commandments of men *and* doctrine" with "commandments of men *as* doctrine."[37] This counterproposal exposes them as hypocrites and idolaters. That massive body of oral tradition that had been passed down for generations was just what Jesus called it—lip service. Rabbis could count on their pupils to put their words to memory, and no doubt those same disciples looked forward to the day when their own teachings would be immortalized. Herein lies the problem. Jesus put his finger on a corrupt system that bordered on idolatry if not addressed. Their predisposition to covet recognition blinded them to the question of whether they should be seeking it to begin with. It was in the scribes' and Pharisees' personal interest to continue the legacy of honoring the elders so that they themselves could enjoy the same honor. So Jesus uncovered the political reality of what had been passed off as devotion to God. They were not devoted to God and His word but to their own word. History records the Pharisees' tendency to require more of the people than what scripture indicates.[38]

Notice the double emphasis in the original Greek on the distance of their hearts. Most translations just have "far" or "far away" in verse 6. But the sentence in the Greek language has two terms back to back (πόρρω; ἀπέχει). *Porrō* means "far away"[39] and *apachei* means "distant."[40]

---

[37] Donahue, 221.

[38] Whiston, William, transl., *Josephus: Complete Works* (Grand Rapids, Michigan: Kregel Publications, 1963), vol. 13; *Antiquities of the Jews*, by Flavius Josephus, 10, 6, p. 281.

[39] Gingrich, F. Wilbur, *Shorter Lexicon of the Greek New Testament* (Chicago and London: The University of Chicago Press, 1965), 180.

[40] Bauer, 85.

The fact is the author could have chosen just one word to communicate the meaning. Instead he used repetition to emphasize the depths that the religious leaders had sunken to. They had become oh so distant in their relationship with God.

The Pharisees don't realize what they have lost in the process. The very word of God has been abandoned as well as their relationship with the One who has preserved it. They have issued a direct insult to God by replacing His word with their own. Jesus makes this clear in the antithetical parallelism of Jewish communication. This comparison of opposites was characteristic of Semitic speech.[41] He contrasts the treatment with the things of God to the treatment of the things of man. They "release" (ἀφέντες) one and "embrace" (κρατεῖτε—this is the third time this word is used) the other (vs. 8). Then in verse 9 he increases the intensity of the language.[42] The first indication that further elaboration is to follow is the imperfect term ἔλεγεν, which means he "kept saying" instead of "he said." On this occasion they "strike out"[43] (ἀθετεῖτε) one and "establish" (στήσητε) the other. But this time it is not the tradition of the elders that is being promoted—it is "their own" (ὑμῶν) tradition. It has been suggested that verse 9 is simply a repeat of verse 8.[44] However, it rather seems to hold the very key to understanding the judgment against the Pharisees. Without the realization that a shift took place from upholding the tradition of elders to upholding their own tradition, there is no justification in accusing them of hypocrisy (vs. 6). So Jesus uncovers their ulterior motive, which is ultimately to glorify themselves. All of this apparent devotion to the tradition of the elders was simply pretence to get their own agenda established.

7:10-14: "For Moses said: 'Honor your father and mother,' and "Whoever curses father or mother is to die—put him to death!' But you . . . you say, 'If a man should say to the father or the mother "Korban" (it is a gift), then however they might have benefited from him is no longer possible.' You tie the hands of the man so that he is no longer able to do anything for his father or mother. Therefore you have nullified the word of God with your tradition, which you passed on. You do all sorts of things like this."

---

41 Brooks, 117.

42 Geddert, 165.

43 Rienecker, 107.

44 Nicoll, 388.

Not only does Jesus make an accusation, He backs it up with a specific example. Surely the Pharisees and scribes must have been wishing this diatribe would soon come to an end so they could slither away in retreat. Instead, however, the evidence mounts against them. Every word is like a nail that fastens the lid of the coffin over them ever more securely with each penetrating blow. They must have come to the realization with each failure to match up to Him intellectually that Jesus of Nazareth had indeed become a serious threat to their way of life. One can almost imagine the widening eyes gripped with fear as the Savior verbally tore them limb from limb. Like a prosecuting attorney, Jesus produces damaging evidence that clearly finds them guilty of abandoning the very Word of God. Somehow He is able to show how those who claim to love the law the most are actually the ones who are out to replace it. He is proving beyond reasonable doubt that these men are indeed hypocrites.

He does so by showing proof of their allegiance to tradition over scripture. In blatant disregard for their parents they would offer their property as a gift to the temple. Therefore they are guilty of breaking one of the Ten Commandments in order to keep their own traditions. Notice the double negative at the end of verse 10. *To die* (infinitive) is followed by *put him to death* (imperative) in the Greek (θανάτῳ; τελευτάτω). Perhaps this is why the King James Version translates the passage "let him *die the death*." Death is mentioned twice as it is in the Greek. Perhaps this is to emphasize the gravity of the situation. Other translations (NEB; JB; LB; NIV; and TEV) thus render it *must die*. The bottom line is that it is a horrible thing to badmouth one's parents. That is a violation of the Fifth Commandment and is worthy of death according to Moses. But the Pharisees and scribes seemed to have no such conscience. Even their parents had to go if they got in the way. Their allegiance to the traditions betrays their desire for personal advancement over keeping the law. They would never have expected to see themselves as opponents of Moses, but Jesus demonstrated that this was indeed the case. He devastates them by showing just how deep and wide the chasm is between them and Moses. In other words, Moses says one thing but *you* say something completely different. In the original language this stark contrast is done through the repetition of terms once more.[45] In the translation of verse 11 above it

---

[45] Black, David Alan, *Learn to Read New Testament Greek* (Nashville, Tennessee: Broadman & Holman Publishers, 1994), 63.

shows that *you* is repeated (ὑμεῖς δὲ λέγετε—you, but you say). *Korban* is an oath that means one is dedicating property to God or the Temple. As such it was unavailable for regular use until such time as the donor chose to release it.[46] The matter is explained in Leviticus 27. It has also been verified archeologically. A first-century ossuary lid was discovered with the term *Korban* inscribed on it.[47] Through the *Korban* tradition the Pharisees and scribes "tie the hands" of the family so they are not able to honor their parents. The actual word order in verse 12 is "No longer do you allow him anything to do for the father or mother."

The intensity of the crime seems to escalate with each statement.[48] In verse 8 they released the Word. In verse 9 they set it aside. Now in verse 13 he further accuses them of canceling it out altogether by replacing it. He ends the matter with noting that they are continually doing things like this. The term πολλὰ (*polla*) here shows contempt[49] for the fact that these types of restrictions are "endless." It is as if they are always coming up with something new to threaten God's word.

7:14-16: "Having called the crowd to himself again he kept saying to them: 'Everyone listen to me and understand. There is absolutely nothing that can defile a man that comes into him from the outside. On the contrary, the things that come out of a man are what defile the man'"

At this point it is as though Jesus sees a window of opportunity. Having sealed their (religious leaders) fate, it is now time to chart a new course. It is time to be released from the bondage of Pharisaic dogma. There is a valuable principle that, if applied, could cause a paradigm shift that would revolutionize Jewish culture. But having heard the opposing view for so long, the crowd must essentially be deprogrammed (if that were possible). So the Christ goes over the matter again and again (imperfect tense—"kept saying") to make sure the message is driven home. Saying a man cannot be defiled (made common) externally was to turn the Jewish world upside down. As the above translation indicates he was emphatically stating that "absolutely nothing" coming into a man can defile him. This particular expression was chosen to communicate the emphasis displayed in the original Greek word order. The noun "nothing" is placed out of order so

---

46   Geddert, 165.

47   Keck, 606.

48   Geddert, 165.

49   Nicoll, 388.

that it may be stressed in the sentence. Normally the verb precedes the noun.[50] This is such a radical statement that some scholars have suggested it could not have come from Jesus.[51] But it is more likely that since the Pharisees had been openly debated and defeated on this matter of ritual purity a teachable moment was born.

The emphasis of the teaching centers on the terms "coming into" and "coming out from." This fact is crystallized by the actuality that those words are reduplicated in the Greek for emphasis. The phrase contains these repeated prepositions: εἰσπορευόμενον εἰς and ἐκ, ἐκπορευόμενά (coming into, into and out of, coming out). He could have raised the tone in his voice when he came to these terms, saying, "It's not about what *comes in*, but what *comes out!*" "On the contrary" was chosen in the above translation to take place of the "but" due to the fact that "ἀλλά" conveys a little more than that.

Once again we can also see the antithetical parallelism mentioned earlier. Contrasting repetition of thought or just simply repetition of thought is more important than rhyme in Hebrew poetry. So the speech of Jesus in response to the religious leaders is not only a masterful and watertight piece of litigation, also it is a rhetorical work of art. Understandably such a reply can only come from someone who had an eternity to fashion His rebuttal. Verse 16 is omitted in most modern translations.[52] The best manuscripts do not contain this verse.[53] It reads ει τις εχει ωτα ακουειν ακουετω ("If anyone has ears to hear let him hear"). Although it seems redundant, perhaps it should be reconsidered. After all, it is fitting that a monumental statement should be followed with such a remark.

7:17-23: "When he managed to pull himself away from the crowd he entered into a house where his disciples began to question him about the parable. He said to them, 'Are you without understanding as well; You? Haven't you considered that everything coming into, inside the man from the outside is not able to corrupt him? That it is not going into his heart but his belly? It passes through the digestive system and out the drain. 'Now,' he said, 'it's the things that come out of a man, those are the things that corrupt a man. For a man's heart is where the evil plans are devised.

---

50   Black, 183.
51   Donahue and Harrington, 224.
52   Ibid.
53   Cole, 185.

From there come such things as fornication, thefts, murders, adulteries, greed, evil intentions, deceit, sensuality, an evil eye, blasphemy, arrogance and foolishness. All of these evil things come from within and they are what corrupt a person.'"

From the outset there are some notable variants from the typical translation. First, the picture of the reluctance of the crowd to release him is normally omitted. This is not stated in the text per se but is suggested by the fact that the preposition "into" is repeated and "from" follows. The expression "entered into" or "into" (εἰσῆλθεν εἰς) shows that perhaps there was some effort expended in the process. The closest thing to the above rendering is the Living Bible, which states, "Then he went into a house *to get away* from the crowds." Of course there is nothing unusual about seeing him navigate around and sometimes avoid the throngs. That seems to be a common occurrence in his ministry (Mark 1:45, 2:1, 7:24; Matthew 14:13; John 6:1, 3, and 15).

The house did not provide the restful seclusion Jesus must have desired. Instead, the disciples wanted to probe Him further about the mysterious statement or parable. Some have suggested the term should be rendered "riddle" instead of "parable," but *riddle* is a totally different Greek word (αἴνιγμα).[54] The term is this passage is παραβολήν (*parabolēn*), which can practically be transliterated as "parable".

It is as though Jesus is saying, "Oh no, not you too! You mean to tell me that even *you* don't get it?" The second-person plural pronoun (*you*) is emphasized through repetition (ὑμεῖς, ἐστε). Yet He then proceeds to clarify the direction and origin of the things that are able to corrupt a person. It is not what comes into the body but what comes out of the heart that matters. The digestive system functions one way and the conscience another. Contrary to the popular teaching of the day, one's hands can't really corrupt the food, which will in turn corrupt (used instead of "defile" for κοινῶσαι) the person (used for ἄνθρωπον, or "man," in order to make the final statement in verse 23 as inclusive as it was meant to be) partaking of it. It is an input/output argument. It's not what you take in that matters but what you give out. Food enters the stomach, is digested, and then exits the body. It has no affect whatsoever on the heart. The Pharisees would say, "You are what you eat." Jesus says you are what you believe.

---

54 Pring, J. T., ed., *The Oxford Dictionary of Modern Greek* (Oxford: Clarendon Press, 1982), 167.

Even though Jesus appears put off by His companions, the extended explanation does much to clarify the matter. After all, the initial statement was not specific enough. This method of "public retort and private explanation" was a common rabbinical method of training students in the first century.[55] With the disciples He goes a little further and identifies what exactly is going into the body, its destination, what exactly comes out, and where it originates. The detail of the offenses that corrupt a person is extensive. This typical list of vices can also be found in Paul's writings. However, the evil devising ($\delta\iota\alpha\lambda o\gamma\iota\sigma\mu o\grave{\iota}$ $o\acute{\iota}$ $\kappa\alpha\kappa o\grave{\iota}$) and evil eye ($\acute{o}\phi\theta\alpha\lambda\mu\grave{o}\varsigma$ $\pi o\nu\eta\rho\acute{o}\varsigma$) are not found in Paul's lists.[56] Evil devising is self-explanatory but the *evil eye* warrants some illumination. The *Linguistic Key to the Greek New Testament* uses the term "envy" to define the expression.[57] This is helpful because on the surface the term has no modern correlation. It is a figure of speech common to the first century that expresses the jealous gaze that withholds appreciation for another's success.[58]

Nevertheless, the purpose for this long list of crimes is not to condemn the sinner but to prevent harm from ever occurring in the first place. Jesus's approach as expressed in the Sermon on the Mount is briefly touched on here. It is the thought-life that precedes every diabolical act known to mankind. Therefore it is the heart and mind that must be addressed as the source of the problem rather than the aftereffects. The regulations of the scribes and the Pharisees were intended to be a hedge of protection around the law. They were devised to keep the law from being violated. Instead they began to replace the law. Jesus replaced the hedge.

To sum it all up there is one key difference between Jesus and the Pharisees/scribes. Jesus really does want to protect God's law from being violated, whereas the religious leaders only want to protect their own philosophies from being violated. They use the supposed desire to protect the law as a cover-up for furthering their own agenda. This agenda expands more and more with each passing generation to the point that it begins to eclipse the actual word of God. They claim that the tradition of

---

[55] Daube, David, *The New Testament and Rabbinic Judaism* (Peabody, Massachusetts: Hendrickson Publishers, 1956), 141.

[56] Donahue and Harrington, 224-29.

[57] Rienecker, 108.

[58] Bivin, David and Roy Blizzard Jr., *Understanding the Difficult Words of Jesus* (Austin, Texas: Center for Judaic-Christian Studies, 1983), 144.

the elders (which they will soon become part of) is there as a hedge or a fence protecting the law (word of God) from being trampled. Therefore it is to be wholeheartedly embraced and cherished. Jesus was skeptical of manmade tradition and proved how it was not a protection to the law but a threat to it. In the end these traditions and formulas by which the average person could remain ritually uncontaminated proved to be nothing more than a distraction from the true matters of the heart. It is man's heart more than his hands that must be purified.

The kingdom of God is in a completely reversed order from every other kingdom ever known to man. It starts not from without on the battlefield of flesh and bones but from within on the battlefield of ideas, thoughts, and motives. Jesus knew that this was the place to start if you want to protect God's commandments from being violated. Behavior always follows what is going on in the heart and mind of the individual. To change the person you don't start with behavior but with the attitude. Once a person is born again, he or she has a natural hunger for righteousness (keeping the law). A change in the heart provides a new perspective toward all of life. It is that motivation from within that ends up providing a hedge of protection for the Holy Word of God.

Both parties were concerned about prevention. Jesus proves in this passage that his method of preventing the Word from being violated far surpasses that of His opponents. For example, all the traditions in the world will not be able to prevent murder because they don't address the causes of murder (the sixth of the Ten Commandments). Jesus's approach to preventing murder is to force us to look at our anger. We are to notice how it functions in different circumstances and take preventive measures to ensure that it doesn't escalate into violence. He does the same thing with adultery and the lust that leads to it, as well as breaking vows and the causes of that. In one issue after another He consistently addresses the matter in terms of cause and effect (Matthew 5:21-48). Trying to stop something bad from happening at the effect stage is too late. You must go to the root of every problem. This is the key to understanding the teaching of our Lord. Learning and practicing the imperatives of our Lord is what it means to be a disciple. To change our behavior we must first address our attitudes. Our thought life is the place to begin. All bad behavior begins in the heart and the mind, and that is the only place to properly address it.

MATTHEW 23:8-10

This is the last of the pivotal passages considered to lay the groundwork for a discipleship that can beyond all reasonable doubt be identified as Christ centered. A Christ-centered discipleship is one that first takes into consideration the way Christ insisted this practice be carried out. We saw Him clearly spelling it out in Matthew 28:19-20. Second, centering discipleship on the Master teacher requires possession the philosophical key that will unlock the mysteries of His discourse. That golden key is provided for us in Mark 7:1-23, should we possess the willingness and determination to uncover it. Finally, in order to ensure that our discipleship is of Christ, by Christ, and for Christ, certain ground rules must be set in place from the outset that will ensure man never reaches beyond that holy perimeter. Everything that can considered outside the Master is not more but less than the sum of Him. It is to settle for less.

The passage that demonstrates the necessity of this resolve to loyalty is Matthew 23:8-10: "But don't you ever be called rabbi; for one is your teacher, and you are all brothers. Don't ever call (anyone) on earth your father; for one is your Father in heaven. Neither may you be called leaders, for one is your leader, the Messiah (author's translation)."

This little snippet is couched between a scathing rebuke of the scribes and Pharisees who loved the notoriety their offices provided. Religious pride and position was the item that most infuriated the Lord, for such an approach to discipleship was godless. He wanted his disciples to be different. He never wanted them to desire recognition or power to exercise control over others. The whole idea that one can work one's way up the corporate spiritual ladder through various levels of personal achievement is flawed from the beginning. For any advances that are made spiritually are initiated from heaven. The lesson of the Beatitudes proves this fact. For each level of spiritual achievement mentioned is not the result of personal accomplishment but personal blessing from God. Blessed are the poor in spirit, they who mourn, the meek, those who hunger and thirst for righteousness, etc. The individual is not blessed as a result of the personal achievement but to be poor in spirit. To be poor in spirit in the first place is the result of a divine blessing. So to parade around as if one's achievements are the results of individual effort alone is an insult to God. It is taking credit for what God has wrought in an individual's life. It is taking away the glory of God and claiming it as one's own. It sounds awfully close to the mentality of Satan himself. No one is good but the Father.

The first sentence above contains the words *μὴ κληθῆτε* in the original Greek. This translates to "don't ever be called" because it is an aorist subjunctive preceded by the adverb "*μή*." When this combination is found it is known as a subjunctive of prohibition.[59] It is used to forbid the matter from ever getting started. It is as if Jesus said to them, "I don't ever want to hear of any one of you being called a rabbi, do you hear me? Don't even consider it!" The first half of the sentence in verse 8 says what not to do, but the second half explains instead what to do, which is to give up on gaining the control that will never be available to anyone but the Lord. Jesus's system of discipleship is diametrically opposed to the Pharisees' in one crucial aspect and that is that the student will always remain so. The student will never work his way up to master level in Jesus's program. There is one permanent instructor and the rest are brothers. This is so critical because everything to follow rises or falls on it. He is laying the groundwork for just exactly what is to be the nature of the Church from here on out. What is the focal point? What is the direction from which, once having drifted, every effort is made to find the way back? What is that internal compass that lets the Church know it is on track with the will of God? This core value and principle is found right here, in verse 8. It is the centrality of the Messiah and His teachings alone.

Being called "rabbi" is to be called "my great one" in the Hebrew language. It is addressed to the great teachers of the day. It is understandable that one would desire to work his way up to that honorable position in Jewish society. Plus it is already evident that this is really what was driving the disciples in following Jesus in the first place. They longed for places of honor and were frequently discussing among themselves who would be the greatest (Luke 9:46; Mark 9:34). The problem with this attitude is just what Jesus was trying to explain in the seventh chapter of Mark. The wisdom of man can and often does end up competing with the wisdom of God. Unless everything is kept in its proper perspective, all is lost.

As great and as gifted as so many people are, they can never rise to a supernatural level in their discourse as did the Messiah. He was the greatest teacher ever known to man. Just as a pipeline can never rise from the level

---

59   Brooks, James A. and Carlton L. Winbery, *Syntax of New Testament Greek* (Lanham, MD; University of America Inc., 1979), 118.

of a channel to a source of living water, so can mankind never rise to the level of a source of eternal wisdom. Humanity is at best a bearer of good news—a vessel, if you will. All of man's paltry attempts to educate and be educated are useless compared to the wisdom and knowledge that is hidden in Christ (Colossians 2:3). There was only one Man who ever walked the earth who truly deserved the title "My great One," and that is the Messiah. A disciple of Christ is always a disciple because it is simply not humanly possible to be anything more. He rejects the idea that any other teacher of the Lord's caliber can ever exist. Success is mastering the Master, not becoming one. He is above all instructors and all knowledge of man.

All scripture either leads up to Him or branches out of Him. As the cornerstone, it is His philosophy and teachings that provide the starting point by which all further discussion is measured (Mark 12:10). We are not to measure Christ's message by the messages of His disciples but vice versa. All scripture, whether Old or New is only properly interpreted and explained by Christ (John 1:18). The believer is not to be of Paul, Apollos, Cephas, or even Moses but of Christ (1 Corinthians 3:4). Once Christ enters the equation there is only one teacher who really matters. All others stand silent before him. His message is the hinge by which everything else in the New Testament pivots. He identified Himself to be the vine from which His followers would branch out (John 15:1). This means more than would seem at first. Not only is it a statement about a devoted spiritual life, but it explains just how the dedicated individual is to approach scripture. If understood as a tree, the Old Testament should be seen as the roots, the gospels as the trunk, and the rest of the New Testament as the branches.

It is important to remember the sequence that the first disciples went through before an attempt is made to imitate them. The first item that was indelibly imprinted in their heart of hearts and soul of souls was the life and teachings of the Messiah and not the further explanations and undershepherding of the epistles. By the time the epistles were written, the teachings of Christ were already firmly embedded in the psyche of the Church by means of oral transmission.[60] Practically everything He said and did was put to memory and recited verbatim. It was the common knowledge and currency of the early church. The fact that writing material was hard to come by ended up being a blessing. This blessing was not by

---

[60] Gerhardsson, Birger, *The Origins of the Gospel Traditions* (Philadelphia: Fortress Press, 1977), 19-49.

accident, for it is the plan of God that His followers hide these teachings in their hearts first before any further discussion is allowed to take place. This ensures that all following considerations would be bathed in and informed by the ultimate wisdom of the Son. The church today would do well to repeat this practice if it also intends to offer a discipleship program that is loyal to Christ. A certain order should be maintained in the presentation and teaching of scripture as well as the memorization of all those messages that come straight from the head of the Church. Memorization is one way to keep the teaching of Christ in the forefront, which is the whole point of Matthew 23:8. To say we have one teacher is to say that primary consideration should always be given to the canon of Christ. The wise man will build his house on the rock (Matthew 7:24). The teaching of Christ serves as the essential and foundational element by which all further considerations are either rejected or upheld. Everything rises or falls on His initial intellectual investment.

Verse 9 makes the middle section of the sandwiched statements about the Messiah by introducing the honor due to the heavenly Father. Why the sudden shift from Christ to Father and then back to Christ again? It could very well tie in to the first statement about having one Teacher. For the one teaching of the one Master instructor that should stand out the most is his message about God the Father. It was a message that bubbled up within the unique Father—Son connection He experienced as a member of the Trinity. No man ever has understood the personal level of intimacy and oneness that was Jesus's daily bread. This is the center of His reality as a human being and what He in all likelihood wanted to share with the rest of mankind. He no doubt wanted all people to comprehend just exactly what they were missing out on by having only superficial relationships with God. One of the ways He may have proposed to change the hearts and minds of individuals was the introduction of the Lord's Prayer. In that prayer, which is obviously meant to center the family of God, the title by which the Church is to address God on a regular basis is none other than "Father." As it is reconsidered day after day and meditated upon moment by moment, it is likely expected that this will become, for God's people, the common perspective by which their lives are ordered and reordered.

What is interesting about this second statement in a list of names not available for a disciple's usage is that the term "anyone" is missing. One could conclude, however, that by the pattern seen in all three verses it is certainly implied. Nevertheless, it cannot be included in the translation

31

other than in parenthesis. I have translated it as follows: "Don't ever call (anyone) on earth your father; for one is your Father in heaven." A shift is made in this second sentence from passive to active as they are instructed now not to call someone else "father," instead of not allowing themselves to be called "father." The emphasis here is again loyalty to divinity over humanity. They are not to pursue such status for themselves or to look to others for qualifications they are not capable of possessing as human beings. Although such a statement seems hardly necessary to even mention to reasonable people, it is easy to see even in the current supposedly enlightened state of modern affairs that this is likely the command of Christ that is most often violated. Reverence is given to the founders of a nation by referring to them as our forefathers, or the fathers of our nation. Christian history considers godly leaders of the past as the fathers of the early church. It is common knowledge that priests are regularly addressed by that very term. And should Protestants be eager to accuse, it can easily be pointed out how their ministers prefer to be addressed as "reverend." Does humanity really deserve reverence? And be that as it may, has the Church considered why its advanced degrees dare to assume the heavenly knowledge and title of "master" or "doctor" of divinity? It is clear from the tenor of Jesus's message in this portion of scripture that sweeping reforms are called for at the highest levels—that is if those individuals see themselves as under the Messiah's authority.

But what about one's biological father? Technically even he cannot be omitted from the comprehensive nature of the expression "anyone on earth." Again, going back to the previous statement about Jesus's primary teaching objective, it is clear that even one's own father can become a hindrance to the proper divine perspective. Is it not possible to rely solely on one's father (the sole provider during this period of history) for sustenance and thereby forget that it is actually one's Father in heaven who is responsible for one's daily bread? From the perspective of the parent, it takes a great measure of faith to actually live by total reliance on a heavenly Father as opposed to self-reliance. The tendency is to take personal responsibility for one's own affairs without considering that anything more is required.

In the end it is concluded that this second statement about fatherhood is no easier to understand and live out than the other two. For we know that it is impossible to go through life without teachers, fathers, and leaders. Yet we are presented with the command to limit the plural to the singular.

There is one teacher. There is one father. There is one leader. Basically He is once again asking us to do the impossible. Therefore one must conclude this to be another way of saying to keep Him first. Although we may know of teachers, fathers, and leaders, as far as believers are concerned there is only one. To keep the Church from repeating Peter's near drowning, Christ is insisting that all eyes remain fixed on Him.

Is that not the central issue of this entire passage? That is, what will it take for the followers of Christ to remain in their places with hands raised to their brow in salute to the King of kings and Lord of lords rather than look in the mirror and imagine that they are somehow taking His place in His absence? This vacancy was never intended for man and was clearly assigned to the Holy Spirit alone (John 14:16-17). The Greek Orthodox Church does well to leave an empty throne toward the right side in the front of the church to remind parishioners that His place can never be filled by mortal man. Similar and even more strident efforts should be made throughout all Christendom in an effort to give heed to the wishes of the Lord so stated in these verses.

The evidence presented above demonstrates just how easy it is to fall prey to the same error of the scribes and Pharisees. The desire to advance in status and be acknowledged as the spiritual elite plagues us all, and the only remedy is what the Great Physician orders in verse 11: "The greatest among you shall be your servant." The answer is this: both to see ourselves as the permanent student and Him as the permanent Master (vs. 8). Only then will the Church begin to value His perspective more than its own. The evidence of this epidemic of preoccupation with individual perspective over the Master's is the paltry adherence to His plans, or even the awareness that such a detailed agenda exists. The extent of the "attention deficit disorder" is clearly demonstrated by the fact that Christianity for the most part has only incorporated a few of His some 254 commands into their standard operating procedure. About the only two things they do pay attention to are water baptism and communion, and there is little agreement over how those matters are to be understood and implemented. Like the Pharisees, Christianity as a whole is also guilty of allowing denominational policy, bylaws, and other traditions to usurp the leadership of its true rabbi and his Father. A great overhaul is long overdue where the Church is allowed to decrease and Christ is allowed to increase. Jesus's teaching must be allowed to regain a place of prominence and preeminence among his supposed followers. Once this is achieved, the world will have the opportunity to be transformed in a greater degree than ever before, for it will no longer see individuals but the Christ who is in them. Currently the wisdom of the Messiah is the Church's best-kept secret.

Finally there is verse 10: "Neither be called leaders, for one is your leader; the Messiah." The basic formula of this triad of thought is maintained in this last statement. The third line shifts back from the idea of not calling someone else father to not being called leader. It is a shift from active to passive (or middle) voice. Each time, we are reminded that there is only one person in charge. There is one teacher, one father and one leader. What is being communicated is that the servant of God is not to ever imagine that such an honorable title in any one of these three categories is possible. The admiration the scribes and Pharisees are seeking is beyond the reach of humanity, so they should be soundly rebuked for it. Just like their tradition began to override the very word of God, the respect they hungered for extended beyond the reasonable boundaries of what is appropriate for mankind.

The word here for "leaders" is "καθηγηταί." This is a very interesting word and has been translated a number of ways. It has been understood as "master," "master teacher, and guide."[61] *Kathēgētai* is the combination of *kata* and *hēgēomai*, which will narrow down the options for a clearer understanding. *Kata* is simply to say "according to." *Hēgēomai* is where we get the word hegemony, which basically means "power, dominion, or authority." Placed together, the combination of the two communicates the idea that this person is "according to authority." It is to say that this individual is the authoritative figure of the movement. So it is translated "leader" in terms of the top official who represents the organization. Some phrases that are commonly used that might apply to this term include "The *leader* of the free world," or "Take me to your *leader*." But the reason for not translating it as "master" is due to the fact that the usual term for "master" (*kurios*—Lord, Master) is not used here.

The followers of Christ are not to be addressed as leaders for there is one Leader, the Christ. Instead of leaders, the followers are to be addressed

---

61 Strong, James: *The Exhaustive Concordance of the Bible: Showing Every Word of the Text of the Common English Version of the Canonical Books, and Every Occurrence of Each Word in Regular Order*. Electronic ed. (Ontario, Canada: Woodside Bible Fellowship, 1996), S. G2519.

as either "brothers" (vs. 8) or "servants" (verse 10). The shoes of Christ cannot be filled by mortal man. The central figure of the Christian faith must always be its founder. The greatest threat to that is the coveting of greater positions of authority or any tendency to imagine that a substitute messiah must be found. The power hungry will never do as a disciple (Matthew 5:3). The biggest challenge for the disciples then and now is to keep Christ in the forefront and themselves in the background. This is what it means to say there is only "one leader" when there are actually great multitudes of leaders in the Church—that the under management so downplays its own significance and elevates His that it is no longer noticeable. It so emphasizes His teaching over theirs so their teaching is hardly perceptible. The objective is to keep Jesus as the "main text" and his followers as a "footnote" at best. It is easier to decrease when the Messiah stands before the Church in person. It is much harder to decrease when He stands before the Church by faith alone. Nevertheless, "He must increase, but I must decrease" (John 3:30). The greatest responsibility of a disciple of Jesus Christ is to keep everyone's eyes fixed on the Master.

This statement by Jesus is in preparation of the time when the disciples would no longer see him. The twenty-third chapter of Matthew represents the time frame just prior to His final departure. But herein lies the dilemma. It is expected and inevitable that the movement He leaves behind would begin to function in some sort of an organized fashion. That being the case, how is it possible to say everyone is a servant and no one is a leader of servants?

There are two things wrong with that question. The first is to imply that Christ is not present in both a personal and a written word dimension. Remember, He did say that as efforts are made to carry out the Great Commission, "Behold: I Myself am with you always, even to the end of time" (Matthew 28:20). This passage of scripture is known by that title (Commission) for this very reason. Nevertheless, although He is still with us, it is not in a tangible form; consequently there is the challenge of keeping His will ever before us as if He was.

The second problem with that question is the assumption that servant and leader are two mutually exclusive words. In Jesus's system it is clear that whatever position a person finds himself in the hierarchy of the church's organizational structure, he will redefine that position in terms of service. All leadership in the Church of Christ is servant leadership. The only way servant leadership can remain singular—namely, having only one leader—is if the rest of the leaders disappear. This is exactly what is required. Being a leader in the Church means the individual so loses sight of himself that it is as if he is no longer present. The more invisible the servant leader, the more visible is the Christ. Being a leader in the Church is more about being led. Christ is calling all Church leaders to renounce headship and take on the title of servant. Disciples are not leaders first and servants second. They are servants first, who just happen to minister in a structured environment. Christ decides where the individual can best serve within that organizational structure. Individual politics are the evil of all evils in this system. Institutionalization is a given; humble service is not.

He stated that we have "one leader, the Christ." It is interesting that he didn't say, "You have one leader, the Father." It is that earthly figure, "the Messiah," the historical Jesus (canonical), who provides everything the disciples need to complete the mission. He did not tell them that the rest of the instructions would be provided through heavenly messages from His throne. No, he said the Holy Spirit would come to them and remind them of *what he had already said* to them during his sojourn here on Earth (John 14:26). This is not to downplay the place of prayer or to say that communication with the heavenly Christ is irrelevant. It is to say that the earthly experience is the only human example provided and it is not to be overlooked or downplayed in terms of its immense significance.

The term "Christ" means "Messiah." Messiah has never been understood in heavenly terms. Throughout Jewish history it meant an earthly king who would restore the nation of Israel to independence and secure for them a permanent place of world dominance. In order to carry out discipleship in a meaningful fashion the Church must get its head out of the clouds, so to speak. A heavenly Being cannot serve as a practical example for an earthly disciple. This is one of the reasons he came to Earth—namely to show us what a true relationship with God looks like. Without that practical example firmly in place, the Church tends to overspiritualize its progress while its lifestyle tends to go by the wayside. The Incarnation is not just an interesting theological consideration. It is the only resource that has been provided for Christian discipleship.

Perhaps this is the very reason for the existence of the gospels themselves. They alone provide the material that opens up the rest of the world to the life and teachings of the one and only "teacher" and "leader" of the Christian faith. Without this information, discipleship is not possible. The boundaries have been drawn for discipleship by the original founder. In this passage (28:19-20) Jesus as well as Matthew set forth the parameters of the target. At the center of that objective He places His own commands to the first disciples. According to Jesus, discipleship must be Christ centered. This means it revolves around the historical record of the earthly Messiah and His interaction with the first disciples.

II

Implications of Exegesis

Matthew 28:19-20

The Authoritarian Approach

If there is one phrase that makes us cringe, it is "chain of command." We live in an egalitarian-driven society that is essentially in denial of hierarchy. As a matter of fact, that very idea is frowned upon and censored. However, we are reluctantly forced to admit to the ugly truth of subjection every time we pay our taxes, report for jury duty, run a business, or manage a military unit. Yet we turn right around and demand our rights across the board, whether at the job, home, school, or even church. But if we ever hope to understand Jesus's perspective on discipleship we will have to come to terms with the fact that Jesus refuses to come to us in any other way than what can best be described as an authoritarian.

He can only be correctly understood as Lord and Master. As such, He has the right to address us as a king addresses his subjects and does so when appropriate. He doesn't call for a steering committee or a council meeting. He doesn't poll the general population first to determine the will of the majority. No. He unapologetically reigns by edict. He expects that His command is the final word. He sees His role as the giver of the command and our role as the one responsible for carrying it out. Nobody returns to Him at a later date and suggests a better way of doing things, nor do they become involved at any level unless invited to do so. The Great Commission is not only a place to find the primary objective of the church. Because of its distant Eastern context it tends to present us with a highly countercultural dilemma as well.

So it is when Jesus defines the parameters for any matter. He does so in a highly authoritative manner. For instance, He says He is the way, truth, and life. That is the nonnegotiable and unchangeable revelation of God, and any attempt to change it is dangerous and heretical. It is a threat to the kingdom of God. Discipleship is another area He has finalized. Therefore, every other approach to discipleship becomes not just an option but an opposition. He never left the matter of discipleship open for debate. He stated the way he wanted it handled and that was final. Such an approach is so foreign to our postmodern predisposition that we find ourselves not only confused but resistant to and therefore inadvertently outside of the will of God. Perhaps this is why there are so many books and pamphlets available presenting one method after another, as if the matter had never been settled. However, it was decided and narrowly defined by Jesus as consisting of one thing and one thing only: teaching others to keep His commands. By making disciples some other way the Church has demonstrated that it is either ignorant of or is disregarding of God's will. The square peg of hierarchy misfits the rounded ear holes of postmodernism. Only the transforming power of the Holy Spirit will reshape our receptivity and open us up to divine revelation. We must overcome the prejudices of our upbringing to succeed.

Just look at how the Great Commission is worded from the very beginning. It all starts out with what can only be correctly perceived as his declaration of supreme command. He states, "All authority in heaven and earth is given to me." One of the definitions of this term is the "right" to do something. He alone is authorized to set forth the agenda. As the head of the Church, He has all the rights and privileges pertaining thereto. Rather than skimming past this statement we should pause, reflect, and fall down on our knees to worship Him. This essentially means that as our superior, He is not to be questioned. To question Him would be to say that you have the right to do so. Not only does He have all the rights on Earth but all the rights in heaven. This is an incredible statement that the Western psyche has great difficulty absorbing. We believe we are "endowed by our Creator with inalienable rights." We are the one in the driver's seat. But we forget about the part of the Creator providing that for us. So immediately we see that tension between what Jesus is proclaiming in Matthew 28 and what we believe about our own liberties. We do have a choice, this is definitely true. Unfortunately, however, the only choice we really have is to either stay in control or release that control back over to the Creator.

To participate in the advancement of the kingdom we must refrain from imposing democratic ideals upon the Word of God and renounce our idolatrous attachment to equal rights. We must repent and exchange our demands for His. We must continually remind ourselves that the context of the gospels is first-century Judaism. The Bible is essentially an Eastern document and the sooner we realize it the sooner we will be prepared to arrive at the correct interpretation.

On that broad road that leads to destruction lies the great multitudes of mankind who have failed to take the scriptures seriously. They have done so not by failing to read it but by failing to let it read them. We must stop reshaping the text in a way that makes us feel more comfortable in our supposedly advanced society. We must once and for all abandon this idea that there is a single ounce of Western philosophy ever mentioned in any of its pages. Such modern textual interpretations are anachronistic at best. We must go back to the historical basics and remind ourselves again and again that we are reading a two thousand-year-old Middle Eastern document! It will never be properly understood any other way. Not only is a true understanding of the Word of God at stake but even the very salvation of our souls. For unless we believe (trust in) the Lord (Master) Jesus (Savior) Christ (Messiah), we cannot be saved (Acts 16:31). In other words, salvation requires that we submit to God. It requires surrendering to our Superior. It necessitates trusting in someone other and greater than you. All of these things are repulsive to the self-reliant, independent, and rebellious. Is Christ saying, "It's my way or the highway"? I believe the answer to that question is a resounding *yes!* Not only does everything have to be His way, the alternative is the road that leads to perdition (Matthew 7:13).

Lordship is simply one topic that modern minds find difficult to even comprehend, much less embrace. Like a newly transplanted organ, our body tends to reject it in favor of the old. But unless we discover a way to do so, we will find ourselves on the wrong side of eternity. We must not fail, under any circumstances, to accept Him for who He is, lest happily we discover too late that we have called him "Lord" in vain. If there was ever a generation that overuses the term "Lord," it is ours. For Sunday after Sunday we sing Lord this and Lord that. We talk about how the Lord has blessed us and what the Lord is accomplishing in our lives yet we have no idea what that word means. For when it is all said and done we find that we alone were the lords and masters of our own destinies. If we were honest we could not help but look over our lives with remorse and regret. If we really wanted to tell the truth, we would add one more song to the Praise and Worship service. We would sing with Frank Sinatra, "I did it my way." Jesus says to those who only give Him lip service on judgment day, "I never knew you; depart from me" (Matthew 7:23). This is just how crucial it is to have a total reversal from our will to His in our relationship with the Messiah.

Dictatorship is a bad word in our day and age, but it is safe to say that it was not so in Jesus's day, and is still not so in the Middle East. For not all monarchs were tyrants. For them a godly individual leader is to be preferred over an unruly mob. For narrow is the way that leads to life and few will there be who find it. Have you ever stopped to consider that it is the broad road that leads to destruction, which also happens to be the choice of the majority? So why have we made a god out of the majority vote? There were good kings and bad kings. We serve the good and wonderful King of kings and Lord of lords. One day every knee shall bow and every tongue confess this fact. We should get used to the idea of kingdom rule, for sooner or later it will be the permanent reality. The greatest honor remains for those who refuse to wait for the final kingdom to commence but are even now humbly bowing before the King in their hearts and lifestyles.

Lordship and the surrender it implies is essential to the Christian faith, for Jesus said from the very beginning what is required: "the kingdom of God is at hand: repent and believe the gospel" (Mark 1:15). Since salvation means entering into a kingdom, then the reverse is also true. Refusal to enter a kingdom means damnation. It doesn't mean entering into a personal agenda, democracy, or any other individual preference. Since He knows us better than we know ourselves, a government of, for, and by the Christ is superior to that of, for, and by the people. Democracy may be the best that sinful humanity can come up with for now, but we should never forget that all history is inexorably moving toward the institution of a final monarchy. It is literally God's kingdom. To enter His kingdom now, you must change because God should not and will not change. You must relinquish the right to be heard and to be counted and even to cast a vote. That is why Jesus states in no uncertain terms that the individual has to have a change of mind (repent) and a change of allegiance (believe). In other words we must fall down on our knees before the King in total surrender before we are allowed access.

What is required to enter the kingdom is also required to continue functioning within its borders. To be a productive citizen, one thing is essential: a continued attitude of bonding or abiding in Him. He is the vine and we are the branches, and disconnecting from Him results in uselessness (John 15). Without Him we can do absolutely nothing. The branch cannot bear fruit independently; it relies on the sustenance of the vine. Just like the electrical switch in the breaker box in our houses, there is no other option than to stay locked into one's place in the hierarchy of the kingdom. It is a place of complete and total dependence. The more we rely on ourselves, the less productive we become and thus a pruning is in order. It is that interconnectedness, even to the point of losing our own identity, that makes us one. This is the only way that there can continue to be one leader (Matthew 23:10) in the Church. He sends us into the world in the same way the Father sent Him (John 20:21). He was so one with the Father that to see Him was to see the Father (John 14:9). The words and works he did were not His own (John 5:19). He always did those things that pleased the Father (John 8:29). So, just as He lost His identity in the Father, so are we to lose our identity in Him. What is required is yielding to the point being indistinguishable from the Christ.

So open up to the idea of taking orders as a servant and renounce the idea that you have control over anything. For our love relationship with the Lord is not based on what He can do for us but what we can do for Him. Did the Messiah not state in John 15:10: "If you keep my commandments you will abide in my love just as I have kept my Father's commandments and abide in His love"? He's already done everything He can do.

Conversion Prerequisite Included

One of the most interesting things about the Great Commission is the great omission within that grand objective. It is as if it is already widely understood that discipleship cannot proceed without the individual first being converted over to the Christian faith. The Commissioning accounts in Mark and Luke are helpful in confirming that apparent foreknowledge. Mark on the other hand seems to leave out discipleship in favor of world evangelism. He records Jesus as saying, "Go into the entire world and preach the gospel to every creature" (Mark 16:15). Luke states something similar, namely "that repentance and remission of sins should be preached in his name among all nations, beginning at Jerusalem" (Luke 24:47). So the question is, has each of them left out something?

Rather than purposely omitting vital information, I would rather say that some are just hitting the high points and others are expanding on those ideas. I don't believe Matthew was purposely excluding conversion. However, he was purposely including additional vital information that would help provide a fuller picture of everything Jesus intended to transpire in His worldwide program of kingdom expansion. The most probable reason for multiple gospels is not multiple opinions but the desire to provide a fuller picture than was first presented in the original abbreviated version of Mark. Mark provided a launching pad for further discussion.

Another item that clarifies Matthew's approach was his audience. It is a well-known fact that Matthew was written in a way so as to persuade Jews to believe. That doesn't mean he felt free to use any means to advance his objective, it only means the Jewish flavor of the Messiah was evident and therefore utilized. It also means that the emphasis will not be placed on the faith that is a foregone conclusion but the exact nature of the training program that is not yet known. In Judaism, conversion is to be tested prior to discipleship. The rite of passage once conversion has been confirmed is water baptism. So once baptism is mentioned, it is already understood that the conversion issue was thoroughly addressed.

This is why we can say that the conversion prerequisite is included in the Great Commission (Matthew 28:19-20). Even if Matthew does not directly use the word "gospel," he indirectly implies it by using the word "baptize." It is present, just not to the eye of the beholding Gentile. Does it also show a leaning toward law over grace? Perhaps it is at least stated in such a way as to have a greater appeal to those who believe they are to earn their salvation, so they will not be too quick to reject the whole enterprise before it has a chance to be fully considered. No doubt there is some statement here about the dangers of easy believism. Disciples would do well to better understand their salvation in terms of commitment over mere mental ascent.

Overall, we can only be indebted to Matthew for allowing the culture of his day to bring out even more pertinent information about Jesus that was previously unknown to us. For had this not been the case, we would have never known what Jesus had to say about the way discipleship is best carried out. Discipleship would not have been addressed at all in a specific manner.

A Specific Objective

The current state of affairs in the discipline of spiritual formation demonstrates one of two possibilities. Either the Church as a whole has overlooked Jesus's statement on discipleship or it is not taking it seriously. The reason for this conclusion is the vast number of approaches to discipleship that flood the market today as if the matter had never been resolved. The term "discipleship" has now become synonymous with the idea of "spiritual growth." But if you pay closer attention to exactly what Jesus said about it, you are forced to a different conclusion. According to Jesus, discipleship is not equivalent to spiritual growth. Discipleship is a certain *type* of spiritual growth. From the information provided in Matthew 28:19-20 we see first of all that it is to be the training that immediately follows conversion. Secondly we see that this training process is comprised of two actions that are to take place in a very specific way. They are to be baptized in a certain way and then taught in a certain way. Water baptism is to be undertaken in the name of the Father, Son, and Holy Spirit. The teaching component is to be undertaken in a way that will ensure the students are called to action. They are to activate a narrowly defined agenda; namely, all of Jesus's commands to the original disciples.

One can only hope that the reason for this grave oversight on the part of the Church is the difficulty of the translation in Matthew 28:19ff. After all, for centuries many did not even know that the imperative to "make disciples" was stated here in this passage. The King James Version had mistranslated *mathēteusate* (*make disciples*) as "teach" instead. Another problem that arises with this Great Commission passage is the failure to connect the dots. Once the term "make disciples" was rediscovered that should not have been the end of the correction process. For the rest of the translation also appears somewhat disconnected. It is not easy to tell from the English translation for example that the passage not only tells you to make disciples, but *how* to make disciples. Efforts need to be made to clarify in the English grammar what is clear in the Greek grammar. This could easily be done simply by adding the word "by" at the appropriate juncture. For example, notice how such a simple correction can bring the whole enterprise together as a seamless unit: "Therefore, make disciples *by* going into the entire world, baptizing them in the name of the Father, Son and Holy Spirit and teaching them to practice everything I commanded you." Once it has been firmly established as to both the mandate to make disciples as well as the exact procedure required to do so, there should be no need for further discussion. It should all now be about following through with what was specified.

But can these excuses hold water? Has the Church really been totally in the dark on discipleship? Even if you don't connect the dots you are still left with a great deal of material in the form of mandates from Christ that are being unattended to. Even if you don't know what it takes to make a disciple, you know what Jesus wanted. You are well aware of the fact that he said to "teach them to keep everything I commanded you," even if you don't naturally connect that to the disciple-making process. If we were just to heed to that one statement, discipleship would already be covered without us even realizing it. For it all boils down to keeping all of Jesus's commands. As it is now, the state of affairs in the Church is far removed from that possibility. It seems that the only two of the some two hundred and fifty four of Jesus's commands that are being seriously addressed are that of water baptism and communion. On the one hand we have a long way to go, but on the other hand it is a relatively easy matter to correct.

This error in judgment just reinforces what was stated earlier about the careless way so many of us approach scripture; missing vital information. It also illustrates what happens when you don't allow the Master Teacher his due place of primacy in the New Testament. All revelation must hinge off His teaching rather than being seen as separate, competing, or equal to His. It is all equally God's Word, but it is not equally placed when building an overall perspective. There is a sequence. Christ's wisdom is the cornerstone that every subsequent statement is measured by. As the foundation upon which all else is built it must be mastered first. This is not a philosophical argument alone but a statement of faith. We must confess with the writer of Hebrews, "God, after He spoke long ago to the fathers in the prophets in many portions and in many ways, in these last days has spoken to us in His Son, whom He appointed heir of all things, though whom also He made the world" (1:1-2). The message of the New Testament is by and large about the Son as the clearest of all the revelations of God. We must also confess with John, "No one has seen God at any time; the only begotten of God who is in the bosom of the Father, He has explained Him." Every other author of scripture came from Earth. Jesus is the only voice that comes directly from heaven. He alone has the inside story. The centrality of Christ's word is something that must not be underestimated, for the cost for that oversight is astronomical. It causes an erosion of focus and purpose that ends up with a Church that operates more like a headless horseman than a fully functioning human body. Today we have a body of believers that speak for themselves. Rather than being responsive to the impulses of the brain, they all function independently because they have a mind of their own. It is an orchestra without a conductor providing cacophony rather than harmony. Let's return to Jesus Christ, our one true head. Let's put our head back on our shoulders.

Command Driven

When you view the Great Commission with all of its variables it can seem a little overwhelming in scope and complexity. So how can we simplify this process? You have before you a number of challenges that must be met in order to produce a disciple, but what do all of these things have in common? What is another way of stating the three principles of making disciples? Can it all be summed up in one action?

For instance, Jesus said we could receive credit for completing the entire Bible if we only did one thing: "Treat others the way you want to be treated." It is said that there are some 614 regulations in the Old Testament and these can all be fulfilled with this one rule. Likewise the Commission speaks of worldwide gospel proclamation. Every creature is to be reached. All nations are to be covered. All converts are to be discipled. They are to be baptized in the name of the Father, Son, and Holy Spirit. They are then to be taught to keep everything Jesus commanded. So what is the solution? How can all of these objectives be streamlined into one principle that, having stayed locked into and focused upon, will result in complete success? Well, if you want to narrow down the Commission into a singular objective, it is this: pinpoint Jesus's commands. The Commission itself is a command. It is a command to keep the commands. We are commanded to make disciples that way. We are commanded to go into the entire world. We are commanded to baptize in the name of the Father, Son, and Holy Spirit. We are commanded to teach obedience to the Messiah. They are all commands. As you follow through with each one of His specific orders you will also find that you have fulfilled the Great Commission in the process.

The command to "make disciples" is one of some two hundred and fifty-four imperatives found in the gospel records. To be a true disciple you must address each of those imperatives one at a time until you can say you completed them all. This is not just one way of making disciples, it is the only way because it is the only technique Jesus has authorized. He has decided that the bull's eye on this discipleship target is one thing and one thing only: His orders. Our decision is this: Are we going to accept this target or replace it with our own? There are two ways to hit the center of a target. One is to fasten the target down, step back a good distance, and aim for the red dot in the middle. The second way is to fire at will and then paint the target around the exact spot the arrow just happened to land. From a general observation of the way discipleship is done today, I would say we are using the second option. Each person has his own view, yet he is actually calling it God's view. He is saying, "Look, I have completed God's will because I have hit the center of the target."

It seems to stem from this idea that discipleship is a topic strictly reserved for the seasoned veteran. The way it works is that you find someone who is well advanced in years and ministry experience. Then you interview him on his particular practice for spiritual growth. If he is a successful minister, then the value of his opinion is even more paramount. In this approach, discipleship is viewed like any other skill. But in this case it is a spiritual skill that is being mastered. Therefore, you choose the preeminent sage in the field of spiritual formation and follow that master so you can achieve the levels he has acquired. It is much like the field of martial arts where you are challenged to work your way up the multiple levels of skill development. This is fine for spiritual growth in general, but again, discipleship is not general; it is specific. It is inexorably linked to the Messiah and His first adherents. In this method the master ends up with his own disciples rather than disciples of Christ. Trying to make a disciple without Christ's Commands is like trying to make chocolate chip cookies without chocolate chips. Those are not cookies in general but a specific *type* of cookie with specific ingredients. No matter how advanced the chef is or how successful his reputation, there are essential items that must be included in this particular product no matter how you approach it.

What if Christ had told us to go into the world and make disciples of Thanksgiving by roasting turkeys, setting the traditional table, and "teaching them to keep everything I commanded you about gratitude"? Could we claim success by going out and opening up burger restaurants?

How about fried chicken? We can only claim success when we correctly follow His instructions. Just like today's spiritual leaders, we say, "Well, the bottom line is that people are being fed and we are making a profit, right?" Wrong. What is true about spiritual growth in general is not true about discipleship. He is the manna who came down from heaven that if we eat of we will never die. The Christians must feast on Christ and Christ alone in their initial development. They have to eat, drink, and sleep Christ—his philosophy, his teaching, his commands to the point that they become totally identified with Him, body and soul. Herein lies the problem with Christianity today: the student does not look, think, or act anything like the Master. There is an identity crisis that would simply not be there if we had ever paid attention to Christ in the first place.

It is interesting when observing that bull's eye Jesus pointed us toward that it consists strictly of obedience to His directives. Why is that so? Why isn't it focused on His great teachings, parables, power, or wisdom? One reason is that a teaching can be the most inspiring event of human history, but if it has no adherence, neither it nor its author is valued. For Jesus, one can safely say that obedience proved both friendship and love. He said, "You are my friends if you do whatsoever I command you" (John 15:14). And again, "If you keep my commandments you will abide in my love, just as I have kept my father's commandments and abide in His love" (John 15:10). For Jesus, it can truly be said that "action speaks louder than words." "Greater love has no man than this: that a man lay down his life for his friends" (John 15:13). He is never recorded as saying "I love you" as is so prevalent in our culture today. He said little about His passion for us but did much to show it. It is hypocritical to say and not do. This is the very thing that so opposed him to the Pharisees. They claimed all sorts of things and spoke openly of their devotion to God but did nothing. To understand this is to understand the heart of Christ. Lip service is offensive to Christ, but love in action is near and dear to His heart.

Secondly, He saw His life as an investment; a seed if you will that would provide a significant return over the long haul. In John 12:24 He states: "Most assuredly, I say to you, unless a grain of wheat falls into the ground and dies, it remains alone; but if it dies, it produces much grain." He saw His life and the lives of his followers as seeds or plants that were expected to produce. He was the vine and we the branches. Every branch that bears fruit is pruned to bear more fruit. And every branch that fails to bear fruit is eliminated (John 15:2). This communicates His expectations for results from His followers. They too were expected to invest their lives in the kingdom. Like Him they were to turn themselves over to the will of God to be used in whatever way seemed best to the Father. He was totally yielded to the point of taking no action or saying any word that was not given to Him from above (John 5:19; 14:10). He was so completely surrendered to the Father that to see Him was to see the Father (John 14:9). Only as we walk in obedience can we make an investment in the kingdom and only as we make an investment can we expect results. By placing our attention toward His commands, Christ is saying He is highly concerned about both sowing and reaping; both investing and multiplying that investment. The results He expects are guaranteed so long as the participant follows through with His strategies. This is why there is no tolerance in his kingdom for a lack of results.

Finally, when considering why the emphasis is on "command" over philosophy, it is interesting to notice the following. If you focus on principles alone and not the execution of those principles, all you are left with is a good idea. However, if you concentrate on the carrying out of those principles, the theory and the practice of the objective are preserved. The proposal is dignified only when ratified and activated. Otherwise it is rejected by the failure to recognize and implement its intrinsic value.

It is a well-known fact in medical history that it was not always common practice to sterilize one's hands before and after surgery. In the nineteenth century, Dr. Ignaz Semmelweis discovered that disinfecting his hands before childbirth dramatically reduced puerperal fever (deadly for mothers) in obstetrical clinics where the mortality rate at that time was 10 to 35 percent. [62]Although his idea was brilliant, it may have led to his ending up in an insane asylum and was widely rejected until after his death. Ironically, he died in 1856 of septicemia, the very thing he was trying to prevent. Who knows how many deaths could have been prevented during that period had his discovery been taken seriously? Today, asepsis (the state of being free from disease-causing contaminants) is common practice among all physicians.

Jesus chose "command obedience" because in this way His wonderful theories and proposals remain both cherished and fulfilled. Once they are fulfilled, many lives will be saved. Command means valuing the teaching

---

[62] Shlager, Neil, ed. *Science and Its Times*. Vol. 5. (Detroit: Gale Group, 2000), 371.

enough to insist it is practiced. Command incorporates everything, for to keep the command you first need to understand what it means. In order to keep the command effectively we must consider everything that leads up to it: the historical context, the immediate context (in interacting with the disciples), the principle, the theory, the audience, the size of the audience, the lifestyle of the instructor, and the general philosophy of the instructor, to name a few. Command is not less, it is infinitely more.

A Comprehensive Plan

Notice how many "alls" are mentioned in the Great Commission: "I was given *all* authority in heaven and upon earth. Therefore, having gone, make disciples of *all* the nations, baptizing them into the name of the Father, Son and Holy Spirit, teaching them to keep *all* things that I commanded to you. And behold, I myself am with you *every* day until the end of the world."

First we see that we have all the resources we need. Other than communicating the fact that He is assuming full command, Jesus is also opening up to our disposing all the power of eternity necessary to accomplish this grand objective. The bottom line is that He is partnering with us in a God-sized undertaking. When you consider the sheer magnitude of this proposal it is breathtaking. Some things are easier said than done, and this is surely the greatest example of that. He is not saying to include any other nation that is interested. He is saying to proactively cover the entire globe, nation by nation until everyone has heard. Some have tried to specify even further that the word for nations here is where we get the phrase "ethnic groups." But this word is also regularly translated "gentiles" as well. Yet it is immaterial whether you choose all ethnic groups or all nations, for what is really meant here is all "creatures" (Mark 16:15)! Once you encounter this term there is no longer any doubt as to what is intended by saying all nations, ethnic groups, or gentiles. Basically it means everybody! Everybody ought to know who Jesus is. Not only ought they know, they *are* to know, according to Jesus.

The point of contention for the original recipients of this message was more about race relations than anything else. When Jesus made this statement it was not a popular concept to include anyone other than Jews in the salvation process. So you can just imagine what kind of jolt this must have been to their predispositions. They must have thought, *Not only do we have to allow some Gentiles, but everybody in the whole world?* From the recorded church history in Acts we see that this command was not well received or implemented by those who originally heard it. For us the point of contention is more about logistics. How can we possibly cover every person on Earth? How on earth is this possible? That is exactly, I believe, the question Christ intends for us to come to. That way we will be forced to enlist all the powers of the universe to accomplish this impossible mission. The scope of it necessitates divine intervention. He also wants us to conclude that we were never meant to take on such a challenge alone. He insists that we stay intimately connected with Him throughout the entire process. Notice the last verse as He promises to be with us to the end.

Next we see the complete Godhead is mentioned in the baptismal process. We are not just baptized into one person but all three members of the Trinity. There is not just one name that is appealed to but three. Father, Son, and Holy Spirit comprise the full extent of the eternal community. When you read this statement or think about the writing of it, you wonder why the sentence seems to drag on and on. Why was it necessary to extend it to the limits rather than just mentioning one name as do the baptisms in Acts? One possible answer has to do with the audience that is actually being addressed from the context of first-century Judaism. In transferring to a fuller revelation about not only the Father but His Son, it is necessary to include this fact in the initiation rite of passage. In the process you find it necessary to complete the full circle of persons by mentioning the Holy Spirit. This is the sequence of enlightenment one becomes privy to once they have accepted the gospel message. Again it seems to have something to do with the comprehensive nature of this plan of God. He wants everything done thoroughly and completely. This is not a venture where you shoot from the hip and hope you make some sort of impression. No, it is a serious matter that deserves the utmost attention to detail. It is the most important thing the Church accomplishes in this world.

The fourth matter that is to be addressed in an all-inclusive manner is the training material by which disciples are said to be made. Instead of just a handful of commands or a "to-do" list comprised of those core values that will make up the believer's identity in the world, we are required to ensure that every single command Jesus ever uttered be considered and implemented. What they were required therefore to do (and did accomplish in the writing of the gospels) was to recall (with the aid of the

Holy Spirit) as much as possible everything the Master said and did so as not to miss any of His directives. Not only was each command essential, but the context, which would help provide a better understanding of it. One can't help but wonder if this is the pattern exercised when writing the gospels. Since they are clearly not biographical in nature, what are they? Are they command centered? If they were paying attention to Jesus, it is at least a possibility. This may provide the key to understanding these documents better. The gospel testimonials are filled with commands from beginning to end. However, that may just reflect the fact that when one takes charge, the expectation is that orders will be both handed down and executed.

Overall the point again is that these matters are of the utmost significance and therefore should not be approached haphazardly. It requires a systematic line-by-line, precept-by-precept approach that takes Jesus and His leadership very seriously. It is time then to call in the scholars and parse every Greek verb and untangle every grammar knot; to measure and remeasure the sentence structure and historical context. For this is our heart and soul. This is what defines us as true followers of Jesus Christ. It is not about what we say but what we do in response to Jesus's initiatives. Let no stone be unturned in the process of seriously considering every desire of the Master. His every wish is our command and His command is our every wish. This is what true devotion looks like.

Finally we are reassured with the promise of Jesus's personal presence with us throughout the process. Thank God the statement by Thomas Kelly is true: "He asks all, but He gives all."[63] The most wonderful characteristic of the commission is the "co" aspect. He does not just promise to help get us started. No. He promises in no uncertain terms that He will personally be there with us, side by side, until the job is complete. In the original Greek the phrase is "all the days," or "each and every day." Whew! What a relief! Thank God that the living Christ is in our midst as the impetus that drives us forward in the expansion of His eternal kingdom. Christ in us is the hope of glory (Colossians 1:27)! Again this demonstrates the urgency and significance of this undertaking. It has to succeed; it cannot fail. The only way to ensure that is that He remains personally involved in every aspect of its execution.

---

[63] Foster, Richard J. and James Bryan Smith, eds., *Devotional Classics* (San Francisco, CA: HarperSanFrancisco, 1993), 208.

Success Is Taking Action

From the Great Commission we learn that discipleship is more an apprenticeship than scholarship. An academic approach may end once class is dismissed. Apprenticeship on the other hand is an on-the-job-training process whereby the participant gains the skills necessary to carry out a specific objective on his or her own. The relationship expressed in Matthew 28:20 is closer to an employer/employee model than an instructor/student model. Jesus explicitly states that disciples are not made by teaching them His commands but by teaching them to *keep* His commands. Therefore, success has not been achieved until these principles become a practical part of one's daily experience. In athletics, it is the difference between an intimate knowledge of the play and executing that play flawlessly (Hebrews 12:1). In terms of military success it is the difference between a strategy and its implementation (Ephesians 6:10).

I believe these analogies are closer to the perspective of the Lord than any other due to the fact that we find ourselves in a contest between good and evil. The kingdom of darkness is at war with the kingdom of God. Jesus said, "I will build my church; and the gates of hell will not overpower it." It is about reclaiming the territory that has been captured by the enemy. That territory is the hearts and minds of mankind. Jesus's strategy is to send lights out into the darkness that they may see our good works and glorify our heavenly Father (Matthew 5:16). As they see the way our lifestyles outshine everyone else they will be attracted to join in. However, if we too are "darkness," there is nothing to be visibly attracted to. We are darkness when we disengage.

Currently it appears that the church is more darkness than light. Recent Gallup polls indicate that there is little difference in the behaviors between churchgoers and nonchurchgoers. They have basically the same rates of divorce and unwed pregnancies, for example. Yet Jesus taught that wrong divorce (divorce for any other reason than infidelity) is adultery. Generally speaking we are not so much the disciples of Christ as we are the disciples of our own culture. Our mouths say we are Christ centered but our actions say we are culture centered. We paint a portrait of Christ that best fits our comfort zone rather than accepting the hard-hitting revolutionary figure we find in the gospels. People are not even students of the text much less practitioners. Rather than accepting Jesus as our Lord and adhering to His demands, we either bypass Him or stampede right over the top of Him on the way to the latest discipleship fad.

But we need to remember that faith without works is dead (James 2:17). God help us resurrect our innate good intentions toward the Lord and transition ourselves from lip service to active duty. Everyone wants to know Christ but nobody wants to obey Him. Jesus stated the truth about His generation and ours when he said, "This people draws nigh unto me with their mouth, and honors me with their lips; but their heart is far from me. But in vain they do worship me, teaching for doctrines the commandments of men" (Matthew 15:8). But to be a disciple we must obey him. Jesus quoted Hosea 6:6 when he said, "I will have mercy and not sacrifice" (Matthew 9:13). The complete statement in Hosea is, "For I desired mercy, and not sacrifice; and the knowledge of God more than burnt offerings." If all you do is attend services, stop! It's time to attend to the agenda of the Lord. Grab a mitt and get in the game! Followers of Christ are not those who admire Him from a distance but who prove their love by taking action on His proposals.

This is why the program I have produced leans heavily on application. I have taken 254 of Jesus's commands and divided those up into 92 categories. Each category has a PowerPoint slide teaching what the Lord is telling us to do along with discussion questions about how we can put the commands to work. The testing that goes along with the classroom instruction is strictly based on application and not simply a restatement of principles.

The bottom line regarding the testing is this: 1. Do you have a working knowledge of the requirement? 2. How many of the objectives have you accomplished? 3. How do you plan to accomplish those objectives that you have yet to complete? As we continue to develop the training process we will steer more toward the direction of achievement rather than attendance. As each of the ninety-two objectives is accomplished, it may be somewhat helpful to provide acknowledgement of some sort, such as merit badges, stars, stripes, or colored belts. Anything that can be done to focus our attention on following through with Christ's objectives is paramount if we are serious about making disciples in the specific manner we were instructed in Matthew 28:19-20.

For now perhaps the best way to approach this material is to divide up in to small groups and present one command per week with the challenge to complete that specific objective before the group reconvenes the following week. At that point each person will state how he or she attempted to follow through with the command and determine whether or not this attempt was a valid application. A record will be kept as to how many of Jesus's commands have been completed until each person can say he or she has finished them all. Another possibility is to teach the objective and then take action on it that very day. This way the leader can demonstrate the correct method and verify that the mission was completed accurately. Not all commands will lend themselves to an "on-the-job-training" approach, but many should. Suggested exercises should be provided for every command so the disciple will know how best to proceed in each instance.

The Primary Objective

Have you ever asked yourself, What is the main objective of the church? Why do we exist? What is our purpose? What is our mission? These are questions that are not really open to debate. These issues have already been decided by God. It is just a matter of locating in scripture where exactly each particular issue is addressed. I don't know of a single Christian denomination that doesn't proclaim the Bible to be the supreme authority on every matter. All agree that this is the final word. It is there to resolve all disputes once the answer is located in the Word of God. On the other hand, I don't know of a single denomination that really abides by that policy. It is kind of like saying we are Christ centered, or that Jesus is our Lord. Everyone agrees to that theoretically, but in practice very little of Christ or his teachings are anywhere to be seen. If you were to ask that same person to tell you anything Christ said in the gospels or actually test them on Jesus's teaching, they would be woefully lacking in either theory or practice. But Lordship is about practice. The same thing occurs when a church is approached for something unbiblical they are practicing. A scripture is presented and then usually reasoned away in favor of tradition, saying, "This is the way we have always done so and so." Just like the Pharisees, we have a written code, tradition, bylaws, etc. that finalize standard operating procedure. The time for deliberation has expired.

Such is the unfortunate reality of the condition of the Church today. Everything has already been decided, and there is no more room for questions. There may have been a small window of opportunity at the very beginning of the movement whereby the newly discovered scriptural principle was unapologetically embraced against the establishment of the denomination it had seceded from. But now that this issue has been settled, that window of opportunity has passed. The free and vibrant winds of the Holy Spirit have been hushed and subdued by the relentless march toward institutionalization.

If you are a regular attendee of church services, what do you see? What really is the primary objective of this organization you are a member of? On the surface I see it is operating much like any other business. It offers a product and expects a certain profit that will sustain the salaries of the elite. This product is a spiritual atmosphere whereby a person can drive through and have their spiritual needs attended to; much like our clothing, banking, and sustenance are provided for at other institutions. We don't attend church to serve but to be served. We come in and take our seats, much as we do at any movie theater, and wait for the "show" to begin. As the customer we have the right to criticize the level of service we received. We never stop and ask ourselves if this is what Christ expects because we are the king, not Him. Everyone knows the customer is king. As king we demand a certain level of comfort and performance or we will take our business elsewhere. If there is one thing we have done well it is our building projects. Multimillion-dollar facilities go up all around us to appeal to the refined consumer. How far we have drifted from the wishes of the one we call the "head" of the Church.

The shift has yet to take place from "the customer is always right" to "the Christ is always right." He is really the only person we are obligated to. How well have we done with that so far? Well, it is interesting to note that there is nowhere in scripture where the Christ (a former carpenter) commands us to erect church buildings. Why is that then a primary objective? There is nowhere in scripture that Christ commands us to hold worship services. Why is that a primary objective? The word "sermon" is not to be found in the New Testament. Why is that a primary objective? The answer is that, just like the Pharisees and their synagogues, we have built everything around ourselves and what we want rather than stopping to consider what Jesus wants.

What does He want? What direction did He intend his church to take? Where in scripture can you find this clearly delineated? Once again we turn to Matthew 28:19-20, where we find the primary objective, the mission or purpose, if you will, of the church: "Therefore, having gone, make disciples of all nations, baptizing them in the name of the Father,

Son, and Holy Spirit, teaching them to keep all things I commanded you."

The purpose of the church is to make disciples. Anything else is beside the point. All our time, resources, and manpower is to be used moving in one direction and one direction only: to convert the lost and train them to obey Jesus. This Christian consumer industry that has developed is simply a disgrace. Christ is calling everyone back to the drawing board. He's calling on all churches to make His priority theirs. Bring discipleship back to the center of all you do.

Advancing Side by Side

One of the most encouraging things about making disciples is the way it is sandwiched by the very presence and power of Jesus Christ. We are not sent away to conquer the world in our own power and out of our own resources. This entire enterprise is accomplished within His caress. Notice how He emphasizes that He has all authority in heaven and Earth. Then He immediately follows that up with our part in the overall scheme of things. Because we are the body of Christ, His authority is our authority. His mission is our mission. His resources are our resources. This is not simply an edict coming from a distant dictator. It is a rejoicing of the fact that this divine wave of enthusiasm is the one we will ride all the way into eternity. The severity of the undertaking is sandwiched at the beginning by an enthusiastic, "Are you with me?" and at the end by the promise that He will always be with us.

The greatest challenge for the first disciples as well as today's disciples is the fact that we are woefully inadequate for such an achievement on our own. It's like starting a five-year-old quarterback in the Super Bowl. When we consider the immensity of the objective and that every person on Earth is to be notified, it is quite beyond our ability to comprehend, much less seriously consider. This all-inclusive objective must certainly qualify as one of those areas Jesus usually keeps from us due to the fact that we simply do not possess the capacity to grasp it. However, his near departure may have placed him under a greater constraint to divulge it. Like he said to Nicodemus, "If I have told you earthly things and you do not believe, how will you believe if I tell you heavenly things?" (John 3:14) And it is as he later told the disciples, "I still have many things to say to you, but you cannot bear them now" (John 16:12). Perhaps this provides some of the reason as well, as to why this portion of scripture has been so neglected by the Church. We simply can't get our finite minds around it.

This is why the statement at the end of Matthew is so important. "Behold, I myself am with you always, even to the end of time" (Matthew 28:20). This is the only other imperative in the Great Commission besides the command to "make disciples." He in effect supports our faces with his two nail-scarred hands, looks us in the eye, and says, "Look at me, I will never abandon you. I will be right there by your side from now on." Whew! What a relief! And I thought I had to do this all by myself! That's the good news about making disciples. When we go we never go alone. Not only has He sent us the Holy Spirit as a personal guide and source of encouragement, He has promised that He will also minister side by side with us in this grand undertaking. He will personally ensure that this matter of utmost importance is administered with the highest care and concern.

Therefore the key to the highest levels of success and achievement in this enterprise is just how yielded to Him we can remain. It is through abiding in Him that greatest productivity is guaranteed (John 15:5). His success came from such a complete surrender to the Father that He practically lost his identity. To see Him was to see the Father. We are called to that same oneness with Christ, so that to see us is to see the Lord. That is when all of the resources of heaven will finally be unleashed and the exponential dimension of the harvest will come.

Mark 7:1-23

The Inside-Out Kingdom

What does it take to become a great champion? To become a gold medalist in the Olympics? Something had to spark their interest; perhaps as a child they were inspired by some great athlete. It was that inspiration that eventually drove them to achieve their dream. They didn't just wake up one day and decide to become a perfectionist. They didn't become a purist because they were ordered to by their coach or parents. But make no mistake about it, they did become every bit an uncompromising worker to be able to compete and prevail at the highest levels. It all started inside their own hearts and souls, and they began a quest to see just how much they could achieve if they really put their minds to it. But what was it exactly that caused that spark within them to become a lifelong passion and flame? The passion was not only to compete on a higher level but to surpass over every other competitor on Earth. At some point in their lives they were convinced that this is the greatest thing ever. They became a true believer in themselves and their mission.

The overall purpose of Jesus's lengthy indictment against the Pharisees was to demonstrate their fundamental difference of perspective. A paradigm shift of epic proportions was necessary to get the religious leaders (and the country they had led astray) back on track with the Father. They basically had the right idea but the wrong method to achieve it. It was kind of like waking up in a backward or upside-down world. It is a world where people walk on their hands and travel backward everywhere they commute. That is the world Jesus stepped into.

The objective of the religious leadership was to keep Israel holy so as to remain within the favor of God. It was their constant disobedience that led them to the state they found themselves in, under the bondage of one foreign dictator after another. Their approach was external, in terms of behavioral modification. They intended to keep the people from committing sin or from missing the mark. It was an attempt to change things from the outside in. But in the end they found themselves only dealing with the symptoms and not the actual disease of sin itself. At least we can say this was the conclusion of the Master. Yet it does not appear that the Pharisees or the nation ever fully accepted that evaluation. Nevertheless, the case was convincingly made by Jesus that external matters have no influence over the heart. Quite the contrary, it is the thoughts that serve as the root cause of the bad behavior. The bottom line for Christ was the contention that it is the heart and mind of individuals that must undergo a radical transformation. Good behavior starts with a change of heart.

This is the point Jesus is trying to make in Mark chapter seven. Both parties were for eliminating sin. One party said to attack the problem at the symptom level, the other party said to attack at the root level. The Pharisees were much like an overbearing parent who slavishly forced his children to achieve greatness rather than inspiring them toward self-discovery and self-determination. A desire to please God must come from within; it cannot be forced. Sin is not pleasing to God. The original Greek word for sin is ἁμαρτία (*hamartia*). It simply means to "miss the mark." So the analogy of training for the Olympics is highly applicable. What inspires the archery contestant to aim toward the center of the target? Is it not the passion to succeed? Where does that passion come from? It comes from within. Will the contestant drive the arrow into the center of the red dot every time? Will he split one arrow after another? No. He will miss the mark from time to time. But will he miss the mark fewer times than anyone else on Earth? Yes, and as such will be crowned the champion. This is the attitude toward sin that the Master was attempting to inspire mankind to achieve. He was trying to spark something inside us that would one day become a burning passion for excellence. It is a love for the sport that drives one toward perfection. It is a love of God that drives one to maturity in discipleship.

The implications for today's believers are as follows. None of those things such as inspiration, passion, enthusiasm, love, repentance, and faith can be seen. They are lodged deep within the human spirit. Therefore, we have to find a way to stop inspecting the behavior of the individual and start inspecting his or her intimacy level with Christ. And where that is deficient, we must do everything we can to inspire them toward that divine connection. Repentance and faith is the place to start. Each individual must come to his or her own conclusion that the direction they are headed is not the best option. They must have a change of mind (repentance) concerning their typical pattern of living out their lives. Just like anything, once we have that "eureka" moment, we immediately shift gears. For instance, let's say I do my taxes and it shows that I will be refunded fewer than a hundred dollars. But when I take it to a professional, he finds one thousand dollars. What will transpire in my mind is an immediate shift that will probably change the way I do things from now on. That's what we are looking for in individuals who are coming to Christ. We must ask the disciples we are training where that eureka moment was in their life, where they had a change of heart, and were motivated then to place their faith in something better. If we find in the process that there was no reversal of heart and mind, they need to be brought to a saving knowledge of Jesus Christ through repentance.

Hence from the very beginning he is calling for both repentance and belief. Notice how he shapes the debate in Mark 1:15: "the kingdom of God is at hand: repent and believe in the gospel." He could have said, "The kingdom of God is near, change your ways!" To repent is not an outward but an inward change. It literally means to "change your mind." Belief is similar. It is not an outward activity but an internal resolve. It is a shift from a doubting and rejecting predisposition to a trusting and accepting disposition. Scripture emphasizes this fact that salvation cannot come through works but by faith (Ephesians 2:8). Favorable activities on behalf of others are excellent but are not to be confused with faith. It is a genuine faith that leads to good actions, not the good actions that lead to faith. Contrary to popular opinion the kingdom of God was not to come by force, and might is not necessarily right. This will be the first kingdom ever to begin in the heart and end up in the hierarchy. Jesus spoke of the kingdom as a seed. It is the smallest of seeds that ends up as the largest of plants (Matthew 13:31). It is hidden in the soil of the earth and unnoticed for the longest until it grows to the point of tremendous impact all over the world. This is accomplished without a single shot being fired. It is upside down from every other kingdom ever known to man because he typically refuses to see things God's way. Christ came into a backward and upside-down world and did everything He could to turn things around. He wanted to get the people of God headed in the right direction with the Father.

Today is no different. He still wants us to focus on winning over the hearts and minds of individuals so they will enter into His kingdom by faith. We don't have to wait for a literal kingdom to come, for we already possess the capability to live according to eternal kingdom principles. We pray every day, "Your kingdom come; Your will be done." The truth of the matter is that once His will is done, the kingdom has already fully arrived! To want His kingdom to come is also to want His will to be done. This is the very message Jesus is endeavoring to communicate in His (the Lord's) prayer. He uses parallelism to restate the matter in a different way. He says the same thing twice on purpose. We know that one day "every knee shall bow and every tongue shall confess that Jesus Christ is Lord" (Philippians 2:11). But the question is, Who is willing to bow now, when it may not be in our best interest? Who is willing to confess now under every cloud of suspicion and doubt that Jesus Christ is Lord? Who is willing to attempt to carry out God's will now that their hearts have changed? When you are born again, you can see the kingdom of God or the will of God. By God's grace you can then begin to carry out that will. Sin will no longer reign in your mortal body, and therefore you will be free to perform every command of Christ, thereby becoming more like Him. It is becoming like Him that changes the world from the inside out. They see our good works and then glorify our Father in heaven (Matthew 5:16). He invested his life and we will invest ours in the expansion of God's will. This kingdom is advanced one heart at a time. Remember, Jesus said, "Nor will they say, 'Look, here it is!' or, 'There it is!' For behold, the kingdom of God is within you" (Luke 17:21).

Another important factor that we derive from this passage of scripture is the key to unlocking the mystery of Christ's teachings. If you don't understand the inside-out dynamic of His perspective, you will easily miss the point of much of His instruction. Many people erroneously teach that Jesus said things He did not because of this very reason. I've heard them say, "I've never committed adultery, but Jesus said I am still guilty of it since I have secretly desired another person," or "I've never committed murder but Jesus said I'm guilty of it since I have secretly desired another person's demise." This faulty conclusion is the result of a total misunderstanding of Jesus's objective in the Sermon on the Mount. What he was saying was that if you simply focus on not committing adultery or murder rather than everything that leads up to it, you will fail. It is also the result of not paying close attention to the exact wording He uses. He didn't say thinking about doing something is the same as doing it. He said thinking about it is doing it in your "heart." Therefore, if you can control your heart and mind you can more easily control your actions. This is the whole point of Mark 7:1-23: to correct your behavior by focusing inwardly rather than outwardly. To make a change on the outside, a change on the inside is necessary. As I stated before, Jesus and the Pharisees had the same goal: not to violate the Ten Commandments. They just had different methods for achieving the same goal. Jesus's methods always work in contrast to his opponents'. What you see in the Sermon on the Mount and other teachings of Jesus is the practicing of that theory he divulged in Mark chapter 7. We must master the perspective of Jesus in Mark so that we will be fully equipped to accurately apply His lessons to our lives.

Setting the Record Straight

Perhaps Jesus's greatest contribution to mankind outside his self-sacrifice was in the realm of theology. Theology is a term that simply means, in the Greek, "a word about God." *Theo* means "God" and *logos* means "a word." The fact that heaven and Earth are separated means that it is inevitable that mankind will from time to time drift away in their understanding of God. We are left to speculate about our relationship with Him since it is strictly a matter of faith and not sight. We have only the documents He left us to keep us grounded. But once those documents are neglected (as is often the case), error naturally overtakes us.

Such an error was spreading like poison among the people of God when Jesus arrived on the scene, and He alone held the heavenly antidote. I think it is safe to say that the religious leadership had begun to see God strictly as a judge. Because of this faulty perspective God was becoming in the minds of the people a cosmic "killjoy," just waiting for the opportunity to strike down any person who stepped out of line. It was a relationship based on fear alone. Jesus made every attempt to turn that sort of thinking around and appealed to mankind to see God as a loving heavenly Father. The Lord's Prayer is essential in this regard. Our daily communication with God and understanding of Him is transformed once this pattern of thinking is allowed to saturate our inner man. This loving and forgiving father figure he spoke of was full of grace and therefore became a threat to the God of justice in the mind of some. It made Jesus appear anti-law in some circles.

There is always that tension between the two extremes of law and grace, and the generation Jesus came into was squarely locked into the law side of the debate. Our current generation, on the other hand, seems locked into the other extreme where it is all grace and no law. My contention is that by introducing the Fatherhood of God concept, Jesus hoped to bring all generations back toward the center a bit. The idea of fatherhood contains the perfect balance of law and grace in one authoritative figure. Upon the fathers fell the responsibility of both tolerance and intolerance; loving embrace and chastening. Therefore, the false accusation of Jesus coming to "destroy the law" was simply that. It was a fabrication that did not seriously take into consideration all that Jesus was communicating. He was, on the contrary, a great deal more concerned about the law than were the religious leaders who had in effect replaced it with their own traditions. As is often the case it is the accuser who is actually guilty of the very thing he or she is trying to pin on his or her counterpart. If there were no concern over the violation of God's law, would there be any need for God's Son to be sacrificed? Not at all. He simply would have forgiven us. The crucifixion of Christ contains just as much a passion for justice as it does for grace. The two are not mutually exclusive in the mind of Christ, but both are essential: "but grace and truth came through Jesus Christ" (John 1:17). The Father is both just and the justifier (Romans 3:26). It was the Pharisees and not Jesus who saw God in the wrong light.

Without a love relationship with the Father there is no obedience to the law, for forced compliance is not true obedience. Conversely, with a love relationship both the law as well as everything that is considered above and beyond the law can be accomplished.

As the official ambassador from heaven for the reestablishment of pure religion, He left us with these theological principles whereby the mismanagement of the faith could be rectified in full. He taught us to aim for fatherhood in our understanding of God and to direct our attention to our relationships with both God and man. This was not just an appeal to the masses; it was a direct attempt to reorder the theological framework that the current administration had misaligned. Much like a chiropractor, he came to "straighten out the spine" where the "vertebra had twisted out of their proper positions, resulting in a tremendous amount of pain, discomfort, and unproductiveness." He arrived on the scene not just as the practicing physician but as the original creator and designer of the spinal column itself. If we are not careful we will miss that fact about Jesus and thereby overlook one of the key purposes of His sojourn here. When God is with us, we should make every effort to find out exactly what it is He wants from us. His message was not just for the current generation but all generations to follow. Ignoring Him could result in mankind's ultimate demise, whereas carefully attending to His every need and concern can only improve things on every level of human existence.

We all look forward to the day when the Lord will return to the earth to rule and reign throughout eternity. We believe at that time that all religious debate and confusion will cease. We believe that our partial knowledge about heavenly things will become complete knowledge, thereby paving the way for worldwide unity. Well, it's easy to forget that this has already happened. That person was already here and has faithfully provided all the solutions we need. He didn't come as anyone less than who he is: the Son of God. His role as Messiah is to set the record straight between God and man and thereby lay the groundwork for the final restoration of an imperfect world. He left us with the blueprint of the kingdom to come. If we will carefully reconsider his message we will find the very principles whereby this new and permanent reality will be upheld.

Take another look at the words of Christ, for they are the infrastructure of eternity. This is why He can say with complete confidence: "Heaven and earth will pass away, but my words will not pass away" (Matthew 24:35). And "He that rejects me, and receives not my words, has one that judges him: the word that I have spoken, the same shall judge him in the last day" (John 12:48).

He came with all the answers for both the Church and the world. It is up to us to recognize them and respond appropriately. He is greater than Solomon and Jonah (Matthew 12:41). No sage or prophet can ever compare to Him for no man has ever descended directly from heaven. It can never be said of a man what was said of Him by God on the mount of the transfiguration: "This is my beloved Son, in whom I am well pleased; listen to him!" (Matthew 17:5)

With Jesus you have the firsthand account of the living God, not a secondhand word from a earthbound messenger. We have before us a written account of the greatest insight ever offered to mankind. We can treasure His wisdom and allow it to revolutionize the way we do church or we can neglect His written guidance at our own peril as we are faced with those same words and principles on judgment day. I believe He is calling the churches back to Himself. He is calling them to renounce worldly wisdom and everything that has no direct connection to the "red letters." May Christianity experience a revival of all those who want to return to the Lordship of Christ by a renewed effort to place ourselves back under the authority of his words as recorded in the gospel records. To obey is better than sacrifice. Today we see a ton of sacrifice and an ounce of obedience. That ghastly statistic must be reversed before it is too late.

The following indictment from Luke 11:32 and Matthew 12:41 applies not only to that generation of the first century but this generation of the twenty-first century if we fail to incorporate the teachings of Jesus the Messiah into the fabric of our everyday life in the Church: "The men of Nineveh will stand up with this generation at the judgment, and will condemn it because they repented at the preaching of Jonah; and behold something greater than Jonah is here. The Queen of the South will rise up with this generation at the judgment and will condemn it, because she came from the ends of the earth to hear the wisdom of Solomon; and behold, something greater than Solomon is here."

As it is now those teachings are accepted and alluded to from time to time, but they are not paramount. They are not referred to when making daily decisions about the business affairs of the Church. They are not the core of our teaching or message. They are not second nature, having been put to memory or hidden in our hearts. They are not even required reading! They are not elevated to the point that we are so familiar with them that they identify us with Jesus as a people. We are not so fond of them that they have become part of our subconscious and as such rule and reign over our lives and the life of the Church. We do not so honor them that we can truly say the Master's teachings have in effect served as the head of our organization in the physical absence of the Master. They never sink down to the daily behavior level. There is no testing given that will ensure that an individual church member is well acquainted with this material. We don't promote those who are most familiar with Christ's perspective and demote those who are least familiar with it. We don't have any recognition for those who complete Christ's commands as opposed to those who don't. And the list goes on . . .

To say Jesus came to set the record straight is to say that he laid the groundwork for a proper relationship with God. His perspective is in effect the compass that keeps us headed in a heavenly direction. Much work has to be done to ground ourselves in the fresh revelation he offered to mankind so as to ensure that we are not building in vain. He presented himself as the Chief Cornerstone. Therefore Christ and his teaching must serve as the canon within the canon: the nonnegotiable principles by which every forethought and afterthought is measured.

An Ounce of Prevention

The scribes and Pharisees began with a noble objective. That objective was to find a way to prevent the law (for example, the Ten Commandments) from being violated. Therefore, an elaborate system of regulations for the carrying out of everyday tasks was developed that if followed to the letter would prevent the masses from veering off course and trampling over the face of God's Holy Word. They served much like cattle prodders keeping the teeming throng in line and on course toward the day of their eventual slaughter. However, I don't believe that was the original intention. The idea was to save rather than lose lives. They felt that if the nation could be held in check from violating the commands, then the wrath of God would be averted. The greater the compliance the less likely a foreign empire would be called upon to dominate their very existence. So to accomplish this, the religious hierarchy built a hedge of tradition around the law to protect it in the same way you build a barrier around a garden to prevent it from being trampled upon.

It is at this very point, namely prevention, where Jesus and the religious leaders actually agreed. Jesus held the highest regard for scripture and was one with the principle that the will of God is to be fully treasured, protected, and complied with. Only He was even more a stickler than His opponents, for what may have begun as a good intention for them ended up no more than a pathetic attempt at self-preservation. In His holiness, Jesus was able to detect this backslidden condition and was in effect calling them back to perfection. However, when you believe you are perfect already it is hard to do anything but give rather than receive advice. Had they the ears to hear it they would have immediately replaced their overgrown hedge of tradition with his perfected hedge of preventive care and maintenance.

The information in Mark 7:1-23 explains how this new hedge works and is indispensable to the disciple of Christ. Without it you will not come to the proper conclusions about any further instruction from the Master. When you delve into the historical background of this text and see the prevailing wisdom of the time as compared to the wisdom of Christ, a clear pattern emerges that aids the reader in making a great deal more sense of previously unintelligible material. It contains the basic philosophical predisposition of Christ that henceforth determines the direction and aim of all future instruction. Trying to make sense of His teaching objectives without this information is like trying to understand a movie without having been present for the introduction. It sets the stage for all that is to follow. It is the intellectual context that underpins and informs every subsequent deduction and conclusion. But what does that context consist of exactly?

First there is, in Jesus's philosophy, this idea about addressing the problem at the preseed level. For example, rather than teaching people to keep their oaths, you teach them to never make oaths in the first place. That is 100 percent effective. But the percentages go way down once you start trying to keep the oath you no longer desire to keep. Again, rather than teaching individuals to only retaliate in kind, teach them to never retaliate. It is a lot easier to stay innocent by not attempting a payback than to control your payback once it has begun. The objective is to thwart the evil kernel from ever taking root in the first place.

On the seed level there is the prevention of the negative and promotion of the positive. Fostering positive attitudes and beliefs also prevents the negative seedling attitudes that lead to wrongdoing. By contrasting the

Beatitudes with Mark 7:21-22 we see how the threat of the negative counterpart can be eliminated by the appropriate positive predisposition. Being poor in spirit and mournful prevents pride and foolishness. Meekness prevents deeds of coveting. A hunger and thirst for righteousness prevents evil thoughts. Being merciful prevents envy and slander. Purity of heart prevents wickedness. I believe the Beatitudes unveil the heart and mind of Christ. It is in acquiring His spiritual DNA that we find ourselves shielded from as well as triumphant over the negative influence. It is making a change in a far deeper dimension than the typical superficial religious approach. Stopping incorrect activity without doesn't necessarily result in the change of heart necessary to end the transgression on a consistent or genuine basis. We are told, for example, if you want to avoid open heart surgery, you should exercise, eat right, and take your medicine. However, until something or someone makes a "believer" out of us, we will continue along our self-destructive routines. Our hearts and minds have to be convinced before our bodies kick in. All the work to be done, whether it be the acquisition of positive or the elimination of the negative, is done on the inside first.

Second, there is this aspect of dealing with the matter at the root cause level. Once the evil thought has penetrated into the "soil level" of our hearts and minds it begins to develop into a root, stem, and flowery weed. The best way to handle that wildflower is not to mow over the top of it but to dislodge it from the soil (soul) of the individual at the root level. For example, if you want to avoid adultery, address your questionable secret desires and thought life; for those are the root causes of adultery. If you want to avoid murder, deal with your inordinate and uncontrolled anger issues; for those are the root causes of murder. If you want to stop the necessity to swear, strengthen your noes and yeses; for that weak commitment to your word is the root cause of the need to constantly appeal to the oath-making process.

Overall we see that Jesus focuses on the heart and the Pharisee focuses on the hands. It was just as Jesus concluded in Matthew 24:25-26: "you clean the outside of the cup and of the dish, but inside they are full of robbery and self-indulgence. You blind Pharisee, first clean the inside of the cup and of the dish, so that the outside of it may become clean also." Outward conformity just wasn't thorough enough. So once you do finally see the solution to the problem and begin to do "spiritual heart surgery," you will then see how much more difficult it is and the need therefore for a higher power. Kingdom attitudes can never be mastered outside of conversion. Except a man be born again, he cannot see the kingdom of God (John 3:3). Salvation provides the electric charge necessary to get the dead battery functioning again so that our vehicle can start heading in the right direction. One does not hunger and thirst for righteousness until they are "blessed" to do so (Matthew 5:6). We are not to marvel that He says to us we must be born again.

So what are the major implications for believers today? First, it is this internal transformational grid and framework that we must take with us as we attempt to make sense of the rest of the story. We must apply that framework to everything Jesus said thereafter. It is an indispensable ingredient in forming proper conclusions about what Jesus taught. When this predisposition is allowed to pervade the context of the discussion a clearer understanding is automatically achieved. Whereas when we attempt to make sense of Jesus's teaching without it our conclusions will come out twisted; for Jesus does say a lot of hard things that sometimes seem impossible to accept. Often, however, it is because He is appealing to the necessary transformation of the inner man through illustrations that involve external realities.

For example, the appeal to eat his flesh and drink his blood is really an appeal to accept him as Lord and Savior. But many people walked away with cannibalism lodged in their brain. Again the appeal to rip out your eyeball and cast it away from you is an appeal to deal with the secret desires that will lead to adultery if they continue to go unchecked. People misunderstand Jesus because unlike Him, they are superficial in their understanding of spiritual things. Many people have also mistakenly said that Jesus taught that being angry with someone is the same as killing them and lusting after a woman is the same as committing adultery with her. This is because they are not aware of this principle introduced in Mark chapter seven of addressing your thoughts before they get out of control. Nobody really believes a bad thought is the same as doing it. If the choice, for example, was presented to you of a bad thought, bad injury, or death being perpetrated against you, how many of us would say it doesn't matter, that it is all the same? Nor did Jesus ever suggest that. He did not say once you have thought about it you have already committed adultery. Pay closer attention. He said, "has already committed adultery with her *in his heart*" (Matthew 5:28). He sees that as priming the pump, so to speak, for the actual despicable act, which is far worse! He is agreeing with and carrying forth that statement by David to "Keep me from my secret sin, so that I may be innocent of the great transgression" (Psalm 19:13). Again it is the thought life where all the work is to be done in Jesus's program for diminishing sin and its negative consequences.

Many a botched interpretation of Jesus's teachings is because they simply are not familiar with this fact that Christ wants to prevent major sin from occurring by dealing with the lesser sins that lead up to it. He didn't come to the earth just to pay the bill for sin but to equip mankind to get the upper hand over it. If he had come to pay the bill only, why all the teaching? Why all the training? Why the making of disciples? To pay the price, all that was required was the shedding of his blood. It wasn't required for him to live the life of a first-century Jewish carpenter turned itinerate preacher. He lived a full life to show us how to do it!

He came to provide the game plan for a victorious and abundant life as opposed to living life as a failure: "The thief comes only to steal and kill and destroy; I came that they may have life, and have it abundantly" (John 10:10). If ever there was a passage taken out of context, this has to be the supreme example. First, notice that He is telling us why He came! Does it sound like He is saying, "I came to settle a legal matter between you and the Father"? Certainly we agree that justification is part of the equation, but here in this passage it is sanctification that is emphasized so heavily. Yet so many have missed both of those objectives and turned this into a passage for earthly rewards in terms of prosperity. Again, it is by approaching Christ on a superficial level that you come out with such results. You must apply the grid of *internal transformation* to everything He says to come to an accurate conclusion.

"Life abundant" means not being bound by sin. Notice another of his sayings that confirms this: "Jesus answered them, 'Truly, truly, I say to you, everyone who commits sin is the slave of sin. The slave does not remain in the house forever; the Son does remain forever. So if the Son makes you free, you will be free indeed.'" The stealing, killing, and destroying of the thief is done through the bondage of sin, but the Son wants to deliver us from that bondage to the freedom that makes up the abundant life. For in that abundant life there is fruitfulness for the kingdom of God. A sinful life will not produce so will need to be pruned (*catharsis* in Greek), so that more fruit can be produced (John 15:2). The abundant life is a spiritually productive life!

The second implication that is intertwined with the first is that we must get more serious about eliminating sin in our lives. Perhaps due to the influence of Martin Luther, the Church as a whole has buried its head in the sand when it comes to self-examination and dealing with the complexities of the sinful nature. Luther encouraged others to "sin boldly," as if it really didn't matter anymore since the issue was legally resolved in heaven. This seems to be the typical perspective today. It is as if we are saying since sin is inevitable, why wrestle with it anymore? There is no way you are going to be able to eliminate it in your life as long as you are in this physical body; as if only human beings sin. To err is human, to forgive divine, as the expression goes. Just accept the fact that you are a sinner and will always be a sinner. Great! What a wonderful plan to change the world!

No, on the contrary—such a plan ends up allowing the world to change the Church. "He that loves the world, the love of the Father is not in him" (1 John 2:15). "Go and sin no more" (John 8:11). "Shall we continue in sin that grace might abound? God forbid!" (Romans 6:1-2) "Sin shall therefore no longer reign in your mortal body" (Romans 6:12). "I write unto you that you sin not" (1 John 2:1). "He cannot keep sinning because he is born of God" (1 John 3:9). "Be perfect as your heavenly Father is perfect" (Matthew 5:48).

These messages only scratch the surface of the unending assault against sin on just about every page of the New Testament. Yet we are faced with the fact that we so often fall short of it, which is probably the reason for that oft-repeated theme. For although the New Testament author writes to the church so that they will not sin, he follows that statement with, "but if anyone sins, we have an advocate with the Father, Jesus Christ the righteous." The overall teaching of Christ and his followers is not to eliminate sin altogether but to keep the upper hand on it at the very least. Perfection in the sense of a perfect score on every test in life is not possible. But perfection in the sense of maturing to the point of keeping one's mistakes down to a bare minimum is. This second view of perfection is closer to the original Greek word Jesus used in Matthew 5:48 when He appealed to us to be like the Father. Just like we use preventive medicine to avert serious illness and even death, it is even more important that we use Jesus's preventive methods to avoid serious spiritual illness and death. To do so our understanding of sin has to move from an elementary to adult level.

The statement "sin is sin," for example, must be eliminated from our vocabulary, for it is an adolescent conclusion. It is this oversimplification of the sin problem that leads to a total disconnect with Jesus and His message. It is basically saying that no sin is any worse than any other. Such a statement is so unreasonable as to defy all logic. Such logic exercised out in the real world would mean that driving five miles over the speed limit and being a mass murderer deserves the same punishment under the law, for after all, wrongdoing is wrongdoing. People say such things because they don't want to struggle with the difficult questions. They want a philosophy of sin that is easier on them; one that says, "Oh well, nobody can stop sinning any way so why try at all?" They forget that Jesus said these things: "Enter through the narrow gate; for the gate is wide and the way is broad that leads to destruction, and there are many who enter through it. For the gate is small and the way is narrow that leads to life and there are few who find it," and "And then I will declare to them, 'I never knew you; depart from me you who practice lawlessness'" (Matthew 7:13-14; 23). To believe all sin is the same is basically to disagree with Jesus, who teaches us the best way to overcome the worst sin is by taking every sinful thought captive to His obedience. The apostle's statement in 2 Corinthians 10:5 about "bringing into captivity every thought to the obedience of Christ" does not stand alone; it is a restatement of the principles of the Christ who preceded him.

There are greater and lesser sins that lead to greater and lesser consequences both in this life and the next. To get anywhere with Jesus, we have to get past this roadblock of denial. Did Christ not say to Pilate, "He who delivered me to you has the *greater* sin?" How can that be if there is no such thing as greater and lesser sins? Did Christ not teach that greater sins deserve greater punishment by saying, "Whoever says to his brother, 'You good for nothing' shall be guilty before the supreme court; and whoever says, 'You fool,' shall be guilty enough to go into the fiery hell?" If all sin is the same, there is no purpose for this teaching since it is communicating how anger escalates into violence and murder thereby providing a scale to prevent it from reaching dangerous levels.

Why prevent greater sins if there are none? It doesn't matter, you say, because they all lead to hell. Is that what Jesus said? He taught that some sin is worse than others and each sin deserves its appropriate level of punishment. He also taught that each positive action deserves its appropriate level of reward: "He who receives a prophet in the name of a prophet shall receive a prophet's reward; and he who receives a righteous man in the name of a righteous man shall receive a righteous man's reward. And whoever in the name of a disciple gives to one of these little ones even a cup of cold water to drink; truly I say to you, he shall not lose his reward." He also taught that "every careless word that people speak, they shall give an accounting for in the day of judgment. For by your words you will be justified, and by your words you will be condemned."

Why is God going to so much trouble about recording every word that comes out of our mouths positive or negative if it serves no purpose? If one negative word will send you to hell for eternity, why all the fuss? Could it be that the afterlife is a little more complex than what we had originally thought? Could it be that eternity will possess infinite levels of achievement and failures and the appropriate level of punishment and reward for both? Could it be that one's status will reflect a lifetime of choices?

I believe so. This is why Jesus spent so much time teaching us how to overcome sin. The more successful we are in that effort the more productive we can be in furthering His kingdom. It is a contest that each of us wants to win. The contest isn't who can be the most perfect and sinless person. The contest is who can stay in the best spiritual shape to be as productive a champion spiritual athlete as possible. He gives each of us gifts that are expected to produce certain results, which will receive great reward, or if there are no results, great damnation (Matthew 25:14-30). The competition is about who can make the most disciples in this world because the kingdom of God is advanced one heart at a time. Remember, sin is not doing wrong as much as it is "not doing right." The word *sin* means *missing the mark*.

We must understand the true nature of sin to go about life with the proper focus and direction. You can tell that the writer of Hebrews really understood Jesus's system well when he gave this example of what looks to be an Olympic athlete in 12:1-2: "Therefore, since we have so great a cloud of witnesses surrounding us, let us also lay aside every encumbrance and the sin which so easily entangles us, and let us run with endurance the race that is set before us, fixing our eyes on Jesus, the author and perfecter of faith, who for the joy set before Him endured the cross, despising the shame, and was sat down at the right hand of the throne of God."

The bottom line is to be winners! We can win over sin and win this battle against good and evil if we approach it for what it is. It is a life and death struggle between two opposing teams. Everyone who has gone on before us is watching us. We are in the game and they are watching the game. Who will be the most valuable player? Who will leave memories about their victories in Christ that will last beyond a lifetime? Let's be like Paul, who also seemed to fully grasp what the Christ who preceded him had taught about sin: "I press on toward the goal for the prize of the upward call of God in Christ Jesus. Let us therefore, as many as are perfect, have this attitude." The simple fact of the matter is this: we can actually achieve infinitely more for the Lord by maintaining the upper hand over sin. That is the message of Christ that every New Testament author understood and that it is about time that the twenty-first-century Church understood it as well.

Thirdly and finally, in terms of the implications of Jesus's teaching on sin, we will have to do away with this oft repeated and relied upon idea that "we are all sinners." Ironically, reformation theology may have overstepped the boundaries of God's word in insisting "*simul justus et peccator,*" which is the idea that we are simultaneously a saint and a sinner. Unfortunately that is found nowhere in the Old or New Testaments. All throughout the New Testament the people of God are not addressed as "sinners." On the contrary, they are always referred to as "saints" or "holy ones" in the Greek. Instead it is those individuals who are outside of the Christian faith that are referred to as sinners and seen as the believer's complete opposite. Martin Luther was correct in concluding that the sinful nature is forever with us. But the idea of throwing in the towel because of that is total heresy. The scripture always contrasts the "righteous" on one hand with the "sinner" on the other. One of many examples in the New Testament is this: "And if it is with difficulty that the righteous is saved, what will become of the godless man and the sinner?" (1 Peter 4:18) It is easy to see that the two types of individuals are in complete contrast to one another, just as light and darkness. We cannot be light and darkness simultaneously but are either one or the other.

Notice 1 John and how it is contrasted again: "This is the message that we have heard from Him and announce to you, that God is light, and in Him there is no darkness at all. If we say that we have fellowship with Him and yet walk in the darkness, we lie and do not practice the truth; but if we walk in the light as He Himself is the light, we have fellowship with one another and the blood of Jesus His Son cleanses us from all sin" (1:5-7). Here the "walking in darkness" is contrasted to "walking in the light." What that means is lifestyle—your daily routine or procedure. Our lifestyle should be noticeably different from that of the sinner. Do we make mistakes? Yes! Do we need forgiveness? Yes! Do we make that an excuse to sin on a regular basis? Not at all!

Once our lifestyle ceases to go in a positive direction and throws caution to the wind, we now find ourselves in the category of "sinner." A sinner is one who continually sins with no intentions of ever changing. To say we are a sinner in the biblical sense is to say we are pure 100 percent darkness. It is not to say we only have a tendency to be selfish or to struggle with a sinful nature. It is to say we are totally against God. Therefore, we should not carry around that banner as if we discovered a great liberating truth. If you believe long enough you are a sinner, that is exactly what you will become and then you will cease to be a saint. Darkness is the absence of light. The two cannot coexist. Your humanity has either been ignited by Christ or it remains unlit and is therefore void. This hits the proverbial nail on the head in terms of exactly what is wrong with the Church today. We think we can be both full and empty. We think we can have our cake and eat it too. We take great pride in calling ourselves sinners to take all of the pressure off as if there is no price whatsoever to pay for such folly. This is the very reason the Church has failed to make an impact on the world; for with this split personality of saint/sinner—*we are the world.*

Notice how at the very beginning of the passage above in 1 John there is an extremely interesting statement. He declares that what they are passing on to us is Jesus's perspective about sin. With Jesus it is black and white. If you walk with Him, you will walk in the light and as a saint. If you walk in darkness you have no fellowship with Christ. If you are standing in the shadows with only your face glowing, you are still in the darkness. You have to move forward and step inside the brightness of His orb so that you are fully visible. We are either in or out, not half in and half out. Those individuals are not worthy of Christ. With Jesus we always aim for refinement. The higher we climb toward that goal the more we achieve for Him and His kingdom. The lower we descend the less we accomplish. He as our heavenly coach is constantly pushing us upward. There is no room for a lazy and self-indulgent Christianity in Jesus. It is the narrow way to life or the highway to hell. We are to cut out by the roots all the sins He mentioned in Mark chapter 7 and add all the virtues in Matthew chapter 5. But you say, "It is impossible!" No one is righteous or can be. But Jesus answers, "Blessed are they that hunger and thirst for righteousness for they shall be filled." Jesus is saying that with His help you can be more than you ever thought possible.

Matthew 23:8-10

A Central Earthly Figure

There is a Son of God and a Son of Man dimension to unravel in the process of understanding this message of the centrality of Christ. Calling Jesus the Son of God is a statement of faith about His being a deity. Discipleship from Jesus's perspective includes this idea of never reaching beyond the anointed one for additional insight because there is no further insight outside of God's Son. How is it possible to replace the mind of God with the mind of man and expect to go forward? He possesses the only firsthand account of the Father (John 1:18). One does not graduate from the gospels to the epistles, for example, because there is nothing more complex and sophisticated than the wisdom of Christ. Rather than a further development of elementary principles, the rest of the New Testament only restates in descending significance what is already fully refined in the earthly ministry of Christ. Nothing exists beyond the Christ, but rather everything else is merely an extension of Him. We are all simply reacting to God's personal impact on the world.

He said He was the vine and his disciples where the branches. He did not say, "I am the vine and someday you will also be the vine." The men who took over the Church upon Jesus's departure were not the new leaders of the Church. They did not take the movement in a new direction. Instead they protected and promoted what they had already received from his Majesty on High. They did this because they had learned directly from God the Son that this movement is not about them, it is to all revolve around the King of Glory. They were called to put a seal on it by both treasuring what they had received and rejecting the idea that any further development of either His teaching or leadership was possible.

There is not thesis, antithesis, and synthesis developing after Jesus ascends to the Father. Instead, Jesus provides perfect knowledge that will bring everything together into a perfect union. All the final editing was done by the Messiah. He is the hinge that binds the Old and New Testaments or Covenants together. This Son of God and His teachings provide the greatest resource for a better understanding of both. That is why hermeneutics falls short if it only considers Old and New Testament history without a heavy emphasis on the gospel records in deriving at an accurate interpretation of an epistle; for no epistle can be fully understood without first providing the context presented by the life and teachings of God's Son.

Secondly, the centrality of Christ for discipleship cannot be fully grasped without entirely comprehending the significance of Jesus as the Son of Man. This is a very important distinction that may seem unnecessary at first but once understood will streamline discipleship in such a way as to make it more manageable, achievable, and successful. Notice what Jesus says in Matthew 23:10: "Do not be called leaders; for One is your Leader, that is, Christ." By saying "Christ," Jesus is referring to his ministry to them as the earthly Messiah. The Messiah (*anointed one*) is never understood to be a heavenly figure in Jewish theology. He is the earthly monarch and military conqueror who overpowers the world and places it at the feet of the nation of Israel. The disciples understood Jesus to be that person. Jesus was to be the anointed King, and as such they expected they would soon rule and reign with him in a literal kingdom in Jerusalem. There is no pie in the sky in Jewish theology; everything is tied to earthly reality. Heaven is not the final destination for them; the final objective is heaven on earth. They saw themselves as being discipled by the very person who was going to make all of this happen. It is their training by this great man that you could see, touch and exchange ideas with that was to shape their very destinies. So what Jesus is telling them here is that it is their *earthly sojourn with him in the flesh* that will guide them in the future. He said you have one leader—that flesh and blood man you have known as the Messiah.

It is impossible to be discipled in the spirit. Discipleship is a person-to-person activity. It requires a relationship with another human being who is considered your superior. It has to be someone you can watch and observe and interact with on a daily basis. Our theology today has become too heavenly minded to be any earthly good. The Christ we prefer is the one in heaven who we can keep at a safe distance. We prefer mental ascent both with our salvation and our supposed spiritual growth. We can't face Him in his human form as He commands allegiance in every facet of our daily thoughts and experience. To become a disciple of Jesus of Nazareth the first thing to do is pull your head out of the clouds and take a good hard look at yourself in terms of your motives and the direction your life is headed. It requires diving into the scripture and placing yourself in the disciples' shoes.

A Limited Frame of Reference

To say there is one teacher and one leader in this enterprise is to say that certain restrictions are being imposed on the discipleship process that, once breached, will result in failure. Even though such conclusions are obvious when you read what Christ said, one feels obligated to state this fact overtly so as to ensure that one is not laboring in vain. Discipleship is singular and not plural in the following sense. Although we value the entire word of God from cover to cover as such, discipleship is not comprehensive scripturally. According to Jesus, making disciples has more to do with *who you are a disciple of* than the fact that you are being discipled. The focus, aim, goal, purpose, objective, and prize all have to do with keeping the central earthly figure central.

The first way to accomplish this is to use the gospels exclusively in your disciple-making process. Although we are aware of the fact that the gospels do not occur in a vacuum and that the Old Testament scriptures are a prerequisite to a full understanding of the gospels, we also remember that it is this central character called Jesus of Nazareth who will provide the only pattern upon which this entire enterprise will either rise or fall. As much as we admire the great men and prophets of God, we are not called to be disciples of Moses or Elijah. If we drift off and begin to focus exclusively on the teachings and example of Moses, Solomon, or even Paul, we will find ourselves heading in the wrong direction when it comes to discipleship. We are called to be disciples of Jesus only. There has to be a singular foundation that is sure enough to build your entire life upon. There must be a standard measuring point by which all further reflection is examined. We need a nonnegotiable framework that to tamper with is to violate the very core elements of our identity; our DNA so to speak. It is far deeper than our fingerprints; it is the heart and soul of every true believer: the image of Christ.

The second way to accomplish this is to keep the Lord's teaching and leadership as the "gold standard," so to speak. We are so to honor the earthly Jesus's teachings that we consider our own unworthy of consideration by comparison. Our teaching is so inferior that we can't even call ourselves a teacher at all. Our leadership is so inferior when compared to Christ's that we can't even call it leadership. The teaching of the Son of God is the gold standard in terms of being a canon within the canon. It is through Jesus's teaching that we make better sense of all scripture that both preceded and follows Him since He is actually the author of it all.

The third way to do that is to put an end to all politics in the Church. The striving after power, position, and status is not Christ-centered behavior. Rather it is in the role of a servant that we will find our calling, whatever the assignment consists of. We are never to lead but always to be led and be led by a certain someone in particular: Jesus of Nazareth. The Lord said that we are not to be like the religious leaders of the day who kept jockeying for position until they reached the highest point. That top position is forever filled. It will never be available to any disciple. So the key to success is to decide how we will decrease and He will increase. The overall challenge is to keep the absent teacher and leader forever the present teacher and leader in our hearts, minds, and daily activities.

This teaching by Christ about not having any other leader and teacher was in preparation for the day He would soon depart. The disciples were to face the challenging reality that we face every day: how to function without a visible head and still keep what has passed away from passing away. This is why His recorded Word becomes so important, for it is the only objective element He has left us with. Without this material we have no tangible resource to keep Christ ever before us as the only teacher and only head. The best leaders know how to keep Him in the forefront and themselves in the background. They do so by putting His every word to memory so that every decision on current affairs is deeply informed by the mind of Christ. They also do so by keeping discipleship exclusively about Jesus and His commands.

He has given us the challenge of keeping Him first. It is up to us how we will achieve that. The major thing to realize for this endeavor to succeed is that the Messiah's headship is not automatic. If we don't take decisive action the original Master of the disciple-making process will eventually be replaced by the traditions of men (just as the law was replaced by the tradition of the Pharisees). I believe wholeheartedly that this is the current state of affairs in the Church today. Christ is the head of the church *only if we honor his documented will.*

Notice also how Jesus places this further limit or specification on discipleship just prior to his final departure in Matthew 28:19-20. He says we are to make disciples by teaching them to keep everything he "commanded" them. He did not say everything I will continue to command you in the future, but everything I have already commanded you during the past three years of My ministry with you.

Why did Jesus place this limitation on discipleship? Why was it to end with his departure? Jesus knew that once he returned to the Father, the relationship between Him and his disciples would change. They would no longer have that personal contact with Him on a flesh and blood level. Jesus stepped into a world where making disciples was a common occurrence; just like becoming a carpenter was a common occurrence. He wrapped himself in the earthly garb of current affairs and turned it into something spectacular. He put his own signature on the discipleship process while he ministered down here on earth.

Once he completed his mission he returned to the Father, leaving behind the pattern to be followed henceforth. He limited the disciple-making process to the procedure He went through in making His first set of disciples. He did that because that would be his only chance to enter into the current situation and provide a tangible pattern that could be recognized and repeated.

Permanent Tenure

The overall objective of this passage of scripture was to contrast Jesus's version of discipleship to the current perspective of first century Judaism; especially the Pharisees. In every other instance of discipleship known to man there is this expectation that the student will one day advance to the status of "master." This leads to pride and loss of focus on the things of God. This is precisely where Jesus steps in and forbids such a foregone conclusion. In Jesus's system He is always the Master and we are always the servant. Therefore, the greatest among the constituency is the one showing himself to be the best servant. That is the highest position available in the type of discipleship that truly identifies itself as Christian. Christ's disciples are a brotherhood of servants.

How can we ever equal, much less surpass, the greatest Teacher who ever lived? If it is so, we would be foolish to imagine ourselves ever matching Him to the point of fulfilling His role as the top instructor in Christianity, just as there are top rabbis in Judaism. Jesus is trying to communicate to us that we are in a different ballgame now. God's very

Son has visited us and instituted a special sort of discipleship that will never again be matched. Therefore it is imperative that we keep it all intact by carrying it out in exactly the manner in which He started.

It is a test of our humility as well as our ultimate loyalty. In Matthew 23:8-10 Jesus suddenly applies the breaks, if you will. Figuratively speaking, the disciples then peeled themselves off the vehicle's front window and began to wonder why. At that point He attempted to drive home this understanding that you will never be the master because your Master is more than a mere man. It is not within the human range of possibility to replace divinity. They were constantly jockeying for position. Jesus had to stop them time and time again from their desire to at least be the head disciple. But Jesus wouldn't even give them that. Humility is without a doubt the most essential of all ingredients to be the type of disciple Jesus wants and needs. It is simply not natural to us to function in the manner Jesus demands. We can only pray that He will give us the eyes to see this concept that the greatest is the servant.

While the Lord was with them they never once thought about anything but worshiping Him in his power, wisdom, and majesty. However, in his perceived absence, now there is the temptation to imagine possibilities that are beyond the scope of mere humanity. There is the tendency to conclude that here in Christ's absence is a seat that needs to be filled and that we are doing so quite innocently in terms of practical management. Yet our heart of hearts tells us different, that to imagine such a thing is almost as hideous as the perspective of Satan himself, who apparently concluded something very similar.

No, on the contrary, we can never even think such a thing is possible for the sake of our own eternal wellbeing. Instead, what Jesus has done in effect is to provide the same opportunity with Him as he had known with the Father. It is the opportunity to be so one with God that you disappear. It is to so identify yourself with Christ that when you speak it is also Christ speaking. When you think it is also Christ thinking because you are actually so yielded to His philosophy. Keeping the Christ of the gospels as your permanent headmaster is an act of worship; and it is the only way Christian discipleship will ever work.

"Christ My All"
Christ for sickness, Christ for health,

Christ for poverty, Christ for wealth,
Christ for joy, Christ for sorrow,
Christ today and Christ tomorrow;
Christ my Life, and Christ my Light,
Christ for morning, noon and night,
Christ when all around gives way
Christ my everlasting Stay;
Christ my Rest and Christ my Food
Christ above my highest good,
Christ my Well-beloved Friend
Christ my Pleasure without end;
Christ my Savior, Christ my Lord;
Christ my Portion, Christ my God,
Christ my Shepherd, I His sheep;
Christ Himself my soul to keep;
Christ my Leader, Christ my Peace
Christ hath wrought my soul's release,
Christ my Righteousness divine
Christ for me, for He is mine;
Christ my Wisdom, Christ my Meat,
Christ restores my wandering feet,
Christ my Advocate and Priest
Christ who ne'er forgets the least;
Christ my Teacher, Christ my Guide,
Christ my Rock, in Christ I hide,
Christ the Ever-living Bread,
Christ His precious Blood hath shed;
Christ hath brought me nigh to God,
Christ the everlasting Word,
Christ my Master, Christ my Head,
Christ, who for my sins hath bled;
Christ my Glory, Christ my Crown,
Christ the Plant of great renown,
Christ my Comforter on High,
Christ my Hope draws ever nigh.

—Author unknown

III

Other Statements That Reveal Perspective

MATTHEW 10:24

"A disciple is not above his teacher, nor a slave above his master." Although we know this statement is priming the pump of preparation for a disciple to accept persecution and hardship, there is problem at the outset with the initial premise. In the above quote from Jesus the disciple/teacher relationship is found to be comparable to the slave/master relationship of first-century Jewish society. What was common knowledge at the time is now uncommon. This statement demonstrates the first-century predisposition toward hierarchy that is expected in the master/apprentice association. Therefore, for discipleship to occur in any context, there has to be a principal figure that is viewed by all as the superior intellect and example. Once that authority is questioned the relationship is compromised.

In our day the idea of a master/slave relationship is appalling. We recoil in disgust at the very thought of it in our modern age where everyone demands access to the same level playing field; and if not there will be a lawsuit to ensure it will be in short order. Submission to authority is not accepted *prima facie*; it only occurs when there is no other option. The only time it really plays out well is in the corporate world, where failure to comply will result in termination of employment. It seems it is only either the corporate ladder or a military command structure that is still somewhat receptive to the chain-of-command perspective. Yet in our society, even those institutions are undermined once it is perceived that advancement is discriminatory. Percentages are always expected to show equal representation of each group, especially those who are perceived as the minority.

So we have no real reference point in our cultural experience that will connect us with Jesus's statement on a gut level. Jesus's society couldn't have been further from the principle of equal rights, which the West idolizes. There were the "haves" and the "have nots." Although we know that Jesus likely most identified himself with the poor *am haaretz* ("people of the land," in Hebrew), slavery was a regular part of their everyday economy. As it is in many third-world countries today, high poverty rates and the lack of employment opportunities ended up forcing many people into a life of servitude. It was not protested but accepted as an unfortunate fact of life. As long as the masters were fair with their slaves they were not considered evil or wrong. Slaves were not to resist their fate but serve dutifully and fulfill their obligations. So although slavery was indeed the very thing Israel was saved from and brought out of, the harsh reality was that the current situation they lived in demanded it. The bottom line about it was that since it was inevitable, they were to make sure they did not forget how they were once slaves. Of all countries, they should be known for treating them the best. Many slaves refused to leave their masters even when the opportunity was offered. This possibility was provided for in Old Testament law, where, if the slave so chose, he could permanently attach himself to the master's household. It was just such a context that Paul had in mind when constantly referring to himself as the "bond slave" (δοῦλος, or *doulos*) of Christ throughout the New Testament.

The hard fact of the matter is that Jesus appeals to the master/slave relationship as a legitimate case in point of how a disciple and his teacher should relate. To Him it is a fact of life that contains a universal principle worthy of use in an illustration. It is as if He is saying, "Everybody knows this to be the case." Nobody in Israel, the entire Roman Empire, or even the whole world would have disagreed with this statement at that time. Therefore, we will be forced to accept it as a very good point from the Lord that has only in recent history become countercultural. What was accepted in that day and time means conversely that what is happening in our day would have been rejected. This current rebellious spirit of entitlement and demanding of one's rights has no place in Jesus's system of discipleship. The first rule of the kingdom is poverty of spirit. There is to be no such defiant sort of attitude that says, "You will have to earn your respect before I give it to you." Sometimes it is just the fact of who someone is or their standing and rank that demands respect; for it has already been earned. At some point we will need to find the willingness to come down from our high horses and bow on our knees to the King if we ever even hope to even be considered for Jesus's discipleship program.

In terms of Jesus's perspective toward discipleship in this statement; it is clear that the expectation is one of total surrender to the point of oneness with Christ. Once the union is accomplished, so is the identification of the disciple as a target for hatred and all of the unfortunate dangers that go along with that predisposition.

MATTHEW 10:42

"And whoever in the name of a disciple gives to one of these little ones even a cup of cold water to drink; truly I say to you, he shall not lose his reward." In this passage there are a number of levels of reward based on the status of the individual being received. He first of all states in 10:40 that those who receive them (his disciples) receive Him. He sees his disciples as an extension of himself. This concept is born out in Acts when Jesus accuses Saul of persecuting Him—the risen Lord—even though it was actually the Lord's disciples he was pursuing (9:4). We also see it in Paul's statement that he is "always carrying about in the body the dying of Jesus, so that the life of Jesus also may be manifested in our body" (2 Corinthians 4:10). It is also implied in many other statements such as the fact that the church is seen as the "body" of Christ in this world.

Next he lists different levels of achievement in righteousness that includes the appropriate level of reward in terms of how well certain individuals are received. There is a reward for receiving a prophet in the name of a prophet; a righteous man in the name of a righteous man. Finally there is even a reward for offering a cup of cold water "in the name of a disciple." There is a heavy emphasis on reward for the smallest consideration. I believe this is an encouragement to try even harder. For if there is this much ado over the least of actions, what awaits the one who puts forth even greater effort?

In terms of getting a grasp on Jesus's perspective toward discipleship, it is clear here that although He expects everyone to undergo this cross-carrying discipline, the challenge of discipleship in its entirety will likely not be widely accepted. People will have to be inspired to enter into this contest of contests. Those who do rise to the occasion will likely be few in number, causing it to then default into the category of a notable achievement; although any way you slice it, it is an enormous task. As such it will have its reward in heaven. If there is a reward for simply doing a small deed in the name of a disciple, how much more will the reward be for actually serving as a disciple?

I believe it will be monumental, according to the level of sacrifice; for notice what Jesus said to the first disciples: "Truly I say to you, that you who have followed Me, in the regeneration when the Son of Man will sit on His glorious throne, you also shall sit upon twelve thrones, judging the twelve tribes of Israel. And everyone who has left houses or brothers or sisters or father or mother or children or farms for My name's sake, will receive many times as much and will inherit eternal life" (Matthew 19:28-29). Since a disciple is an adherent to as well as an advocate of Jesus's some 254 commands, it is not hard to see the immensity of the objective for the average believer. The standard supporter observes from a distance and never really gets his or her hands dirty. Yet the call is for everyone to get a mitt (or a sword, spiritually speaking) and get in the game!

We have before us a confrontation between good and evil that is of epic proportions. All the world wars in history pale in comparison. Discipleship is not to be presented as an option; it is a requirement for every soul that names the name of Christ. Nobody is called to sit. Everybody is called to serve. Each person is gifted in a unique way so as to provide the military unit with its optimum potential. Judgment day will consist of what we did or didn't do with the talents he has given us (Matthew 25:14-30). It is the expansion of the kingdom of God, not observing religious traditions, that is of paramount interest to Christ. He says, "I desire mercy and not sacrifice" (Matthew 9:13).

MATTHEW 12:49

"Stretching out his hand toward his disciples, he said, 'Behold my mother and my brothers!'" Jesus was fond of those who were willing to scrap their own daily agenda and even welfare in order to fully comprehend and carry out the will of God. He considered such individuals part of his immediate family. He was even more loyal to them than He was of the natural family He was born into due to their failure to fully believe in Him as more than an earthly brother or son (Mark 3:21-32; 6:4; John 2:4; 7:5). It also demonstrates to us the sacredness of the ties that bind the true family of

God together. That bond of companionship that trumped every other earthly tie found its greatest expression in that small inner circle of men He called His disciples.

Jesus's perspective of discipleship leaned heavily toward this idea of maintaining a core personal community of fellowship that would provide matchless opportunities for conversation, discussion, dialogue, and interaction on every level of practical experience. Imagine the long walks they must have taken, and for hours and hours on end the deep philosophical exchanges between them as compared to the brief and distant interactions with the crowds. They were not just experiencing Him in a classroom environment; they lived with Him day in and day out for three years or so. They knew His every move, expression, pattern, and personality trait. They were dumbfounded and mystified by His towering wisdom and supernatural deeds. Yet they had also become the best of friends; the kind you hang out with and whose company you enjoy even though you are with that person all the time.

The implications of this reality are multifaceted. First is the fact that since their discipleship process included spending massive amounts of time together, how can we hope to accomplish anything similar in our hit-and-miss or happenstance culture? They did not just meet on Sunday mornings for an hour and a half. They were together seven days a week. Add to that fact that they worked together all day and it is simply a twenty-four/seven connection. It was intense and personal. Jesus's approach was "hands on." It makes what we call discipleship today laughable. To improve the situation we simply must find a way to increase our interaction with one another. One of the best ways to do this is the home church model. That is not a modern development; it is what was occurring from the very beginning. Action must be taken to move the community from formal to informal; monologue to dialogue; superficial to interpersonal; and independent and self-sufficient to dependent and interconnected.

One thing I experienced firsthand in terms of that sense of community that is so often second nature elsewhere was when I pursued my wife in the context of her Filipino culture. In order to properly ask for her hand in marriage, I not only had to approach her father but her eldest sibling as well. We had a number of serious discussions first among her immediate community before the green light was given to follow through on the engagement. I actually had to first submit a letter to the entire community to make them aware of my intentions and for them to ponder. There is safety in numbers, and it is all designed to provide for the greatest good to each individual member of the family or community. Moreover, it is a common occurrence that once a serious problem occurs, one is to collect as many different views on the matter as possible. My wife rarely attempts to solve complex issues alone. She always garners as much support from every member of her family and special friends as possible. Also, when I get involved in personal matters of other family members, I am encouraged rather than discouraged to do so. The point is that what is second nature elsewhere is foreign in the West. So in bringing our discipleship process to the next level, we will be forced to question our culture a little bit more and open ourselves up to the different sorts of thinking that provided the context for Jesus's teaching on the matter. If you don't understand or participate in the Eastern mind-set to some extent, you cannot fully understand and participate in the teaching of Jesus.

Another facet of what we are missing in today's discipleship is what I call the *Koinonia* aspect. It is a Greek word meaning "to have all things in common." Whatever is mine is yours; whatever is yours is mine. It is what you see transpiring in the early chapters of the book of Acts as a possible further development of what Jesus and his disciples had previously experienced. Because of the fact that everything we are provided comes from our heavenly Father, it is natural then to expect that it be lovingly shared among His children. The word "us" in the Lord's Prayer says more than it first appears. "Give us this day our daily bread" means that this shared sense of community is to always be with us. They were daily meeting in their homes, breaking bread and exchanging ideas and resources. The supernatural element of Jesus in terms of signs and wonders was still being carried out by the apostles. There is the need in discipleship for both authority structure and interpersonal structure; even more so what would be called a brotherhood that becomes a part of your extended family. Or, as Jesus saw it, the biological family was probably more an extension of His spiritual family. More important than focusing on the family was to focus on the family of God.

LUKE 14:26-27

"If anyone comes to me and does not hate his own father and mother and wife and children and brothers and sisters, yes, and even his own life, he cannot be my disciple. Whoever does not carry his own cross and come after me cannot be my disciple." We move from the good life and close family ties rather abruptly now to a policy of disengagement and nonattachment to worldly comforts and associations. These are the basic institutions and infrastructures that we all expect to fall back on in crisis. He is in effect removing our safety net. Jesus's point of view on this matter is that the disciple will not necessarily be able to rely on such resources due to his ultimate allegiance to the kingdom of God over the kingdoms of the world or the direction that society happens to be headed in at any particular time. Just as Jesus's own allegiance was more toward the disciples than His own family, our ties with those who do the will of God must also supersede all other relationships. The only hope is that both our heavenly and earthly families will consist of those who fit that category. Nevertheless, the absolute core of the issue at stake in this passage is to have no other gods before Him.

We must be careful not to read too much into the term "hate," which I believe was chosen for dramatic impact. Sometimes we have to be shaken from our comfort zone and only the strongest language has the ability to cut through to the heart of an individual. Jesus often uses hyperbole and metaphor. It is unwise to take him literally when the language is so strong that it is obvious to everyone that He is simply driving home a point. What is the point here exactly? He is warning us that discipleship is not for the faint of heart. We will from time to time be tested to the very limits of our sanity. Not even are our very lives guaranteed to us. Discipleship is a calling to a life of self-sacrifice at the highest levels. It is basically a call to step in where Christ left off. Where did He leave off? His mortal sacrifice ended at the cross. He is only saying to us that our sacrifice could also end up as the ultimate sacrifice due to following closely to Him and His commands over the prevailing customs of our age. Before we jump into Jesus's discipleship program we must ask ourselves if we have what it takes. Much like signing up for military service, we must think it over carefully and ask ourselves if we are truly prepared for any and every eventuality. Only when we are fully aware of the dangers involved and yet remain fully resolved are we obliged to serve for the duration of our commitment and not to retreat at the first sign of adversity.

This is not a command for raw recruits; it is a tough steak that is meant for only the strongest and most mature among us to chew on over and over again until it can be digested. This sort of rhetoric was not employed in the beginning. Jesus waited to share this cold hard fact until after the disciples had come to the conclusion deep in their hearts and souls that He was indeed the Christ; the Son of the living God. As He moved closer to His own demise and destiny, Jesus's language about such matters progressed from a tiny flicker to an engulfing flame.

The same care should be taken as modern disciples are made. Advanced principles and directives do not belong in the introductory levels and stages of discipleship. Those objectives are to be withheld until the time the individual is firmly established enough to handle them. For the disciples that was several years into a lengthy, intense, and personal exchange with Christ.

LUKE 14:33

"So then, none of you can be my disciple who does not give up all his own possessions." This statement by the Lord follows two brief parables about making sure you have enough resources to finish the job. First He gives the example of an individual who is building a tower. How ridiculous would it be to start on a project without ever even considering whether you have enough resources to complete it? It is so unusual that this person who began the work but was unable to finish it would never hear the end of it. The second short parable is like the first. This time the context is a battle between two kings. Before they enter into the struggle they must first be adequately assured that they are sufficiently equipped to win the battle and therefore profit from the experience. If they don't have what it takes it would be highly advisable to not enter into the conflict in the first place and make preparations for a peaceful transition.

It is a message about counting the cost of discipleship. Christ-centered discipleship is so demanding that it requires an individual to really just sit down and think it over first before undertaking such a significant commitment. "No one, having put his hand to the plow, and looking back, is fit for the kingdom of God" (Luke 9:62). He is telling us that if you want to be a disciple, make sure you have what it takes to fulfill your obligation. If not you should never enlist in the first place. You have to ask yourself whether you are willing to give up everything you have—everything you hold dear and all your worldly possessions are hanging in the balance.

I've heard it said that until you find a cause worth dying for you have never really lived. So many today are simply satisfied with their material possessions, as if creature comforts were the only things that matter. Paul reminded us that we will leave this Earth the same way we arrived: naked (1 Timothy 6:7)! Yet "keeping up with the Joneses" represents the height of our life's ambition. How tragic is it that we have traded in the fountain of living water for broken cisterns (Jeremiah 2:13)? Why do we prefer idols over the real and living God? Why do we treasure our twenty-seven-thousand-some-odd days (average life span) on Earth over the uncountable number of days spent in eternity? Why have we held on so tightly to what we can't keep and so loosely to what we can't lose? Why have we done the opposite of what Jesus taught by storing up treasure on earth? "When the Son of man comes, will He find faith on the earth?" (Luke 18:8) Nary can a disciple be found in times of affluence.

None of us can be His disciple if we don't give up our possessions. What a strong statement and a hard line to draw in the sand. It makes you wonder whether discipleship is even possible for the majority of believers today. When statements such as the ones noted above are made, it is a lot easier to determine who is and isn't legitimate.

But it also brings up another serious issue. Are there such things as believers who are not disciples? Are there individuals in the Church who espouse certain private beliefs but whose level of commitment to them is very low? On the other hand, are there true disciples in the Church who are willing to take on the yoke and plow through life as those who are totally surrendered to the Master? Well, we know there are definitely all stages of commitment, yet the calling from the Lord is to make disciples of them all (Matthew 28:19). The overall situation matches the parable Jesus gave about the Sower (Mark 4:1-20). There are different stages and types of nonproductive soil and there are different stages and types of productive soil. So from looking at the current situation in the Church, it appears that indeed there are all levels of disciples present as well as those who have yet to take on the challenge of discipleship. I would say it is that last category that faces the greatest peril.

Jesus talked about three types of people in the kingdom of God given various amounts of money to invest (Matthew 25:14-30). Regardless of how much each person was given, the bottom line was: Did they produce? Did they invest their talents in any way so as to provide at least some kind of a return in the end? Was the master able to capitalize on his investments? When all three participants were called forth to give an account of their stewardship, it is the last person who receives the harshest punishment, whereas the others receive additional capital to invest. The most frightening aspect of the parable is this. The person who buried his talent received eternal damnation. It is similar to the teaching in John 15 about the vine and the branches. Here again there is an investor and invested. The Father is pictured as the owner and is looking for a profit to come out of His vineyard. To do that He has to get the most produce possible from each branch. So He prunes them back from time to time to get more out of them. Now comes the scary part. Once He sees a branch that is not producing at all, He cuts it off and casts it into the fire. From the point of view of the owner, it just doesn't make sense to keep a branch around that is useless. The wasted energy going into that branch can be refocused, making a useful branch even more useful. The bottom line for any business owner is results.

I think it is a warning to those individuals who think they can get their salvation and then sit on it. If you think you can just coast by in the Christian life, you may not be serving the same Master we all have come to know and love in the gospels. "Test yourselves to see if you are in the faith; examine yourselves! Or do you not recognize this about yourselves that Jesus Christ is in you—unless indeed you fail the test?" (2 Corinthians 13:5)

Just like it is unacceptable for a branch to be fruitless, it is unacceptable for a true believer not to multiply. Every new born babe in Christ is a seed. Unless that seed is planted in some way it remains alone. Jesus saw His life the same way (John 12:24). He saw His death on the cross as the planting of one seed that ended up producing a mountain of seeds.

So it is fitting that this statement of Jesus about detachment from earthly possessions should be punctuated by the parable of the useless salt. Many of us who are called the "salt of the earth" by Jesus have forthwith lost our potency. By investing all of our time, energy, and resources in maintaining a certain standard of living unparalleled throughout the history of man we have ensured our demise. Like senseless salt, we too have made fools of ourselves. The Greek term for the type of salt that is useless in Luke 14:34 is μωρανθῇ (*moranthe*). This term is where we get the English word *moron*. How foolish we have become to sell our souls to the Devil in exchange for a few meaningless years of overindulgence. In the end we must ask ourselves whose disciples we have truly become.

JOHN 8:31-32

"So Jesus was saying to those Jews who had believed Him, 'If you continue in my word, then you are truly disciples of mine; and you will know the truth, and the truth will make you free.'" From Jesus's perspective there is a certain amount of steadfastness that is essential to discipleship. As illustrated in the parable of the sower, it is the nonproductive soil that first receives the Word with gladness, but then, once trouble arises shrivels up and dies. That is not the type of person who will make a good disciple. He lacks a certain key ingredient known as intestinal fortitude. The old expression, "When the going gets tough, the tough get going" applies here. The individuals Jesus chose to be his disciples were those kind of people. Even though they were attracted to the political power and influence that awaited them, they were also the sort of people who could persevere under trial.

Initially this particular group of Jews was warming up to him. In verse 30 it says "many came to believe in him," due to the words he had spoken. Those actual words had to do with his interconnectedness with the Father. He made the point that he did nothing on his own initiative. For a class of people who valued the Father more than anything else, the message of oneness with that Person must have seemed appealing. They all likely would have been striving for just such a unity yet continually falling short. However, their initial warm reception turned cold and callous once they were invited to take the next step toward a more serious and permanent connection with Him as Savior and Lord.

He was basically encouraging those who had now opened up to Him to continue on that path until they reached its destination: their freedom from the bondage of sin. The movement in Jesus's mind was from the initial curiosity about His wording, to further consideration, to discovering the truth (of the gospel), to salvation. However, self-righteousness immediately kicked in, and what had originally been a sovereign move of the Spirit from spark to flicker was extinguished with the icy fingers of dead religion. In the end they chose their spiritual pedigree and supposed affinity with their forefather over a new and living way to the heavenly Father. That initial hope and thrust toward the Father turned out to lack enough power to get them airborne. They in effect never got off the "launching pad," although in the beginning there was at least the appearance of smoke, fire, and liftoff.

Once the going got tough, however, it became apparent what they really were made of. Their hearts were not the fertile ground that was capable of taking the seed to fruition in terms of supporting a root-bearing system whereby long-term growth and reproduction can occur. Instead, it seems as though they could have been better identified with the hardened soil that the seed is unable to penetrate. It just ends up exposed to the elements and to the birds that swoop down and feed upon it. This is a reasonable deduction due to the fact that their shift from belief to disbelief was so dramatic. It hardly seems possible that anything had time to develop. Everything changed within the brief time span in the exchange of dialogue where it shifts from one subject to another. Once it was suggested that further deliverance and a deeper level of commitment was necessary, a protest was immediately underway. As long as Jesus remained in the spotlight and on the hot seat of contention it was okay, but once the light shifted over to them and their shortcomings it was a different story altogether.

To be a disciple of Jesus you must prepare yourself for self-examination and self-denial. You must have what it takes, internally and externally, to persevere under adversity. You can't just follow Him when it suits you or makes you look good. You must stand strong for Him under every storm of criticism and contempt and prevail when you are right. Likewise, you must humbly accept your faults and declare your unworthiness when you are wrong. It takes the type of person who can withstand a great deal of pressure; who can swim upstream against the prevailing tide of public opinion and private turmoil; and who can hold on until the end.

Disciples are diamonds in the rough. The more pressure builds and presses against them on every side the more illustrious they become. Like a marine's sword, disciples begin only as a raw piece of steel. Next they are given over to the flame and their metal is inserted into the heat until it becomes red hot. At that point they are glowing red and pliable and are hammered into shape. Excess metal is ground away until a razor-sharp edge develops. The final touches of refinement are the sanding, polishing, and decorating to the point that they serve as a fine adornment to the military uniform. Yet in all their shining glory they have not yet fulfilled their purpose, which will be found only on the battlefield. I believe that from Jesus's perspective, this is exactly what it takes to be a true disciple.

A true disciple is one who continues in Jesus's word. Jesus's word is extremely challenging—some might even say outrageous at times! The question is, Do we have the guts to stand up to it, to struggle and wrestle with the implications without giving up? Can we hold on for dear life until a small and glimmering ray of hope and understanding finally shines through? That is the type of tenacity essential for the would-be disciple.

JOHN 13:35

"By this all men will know that you are my disciples, if you have love for one another." Love for your fellow servants is the primary thing that identifies you as Jesus's disciple. Without that the entire enterprise falls on its head. The ties that bind this family of God together are to be even more intense than those that unite us to our earthly families. In the preceding verse the command is to "love one another, even as I have loved you . . ." The way He loved them was so deeply as to even place them before the desires of His own biological family. He said the disciples were His family even more so than the others (Matthew 12:49). That is not to say he did not care for the others and consider them his responsibility; after all, he did wait until age thirty or so to begin his ministry, probably due to taking care of them and needing to wait for the right time to hand the reigns over to the next in line. Plus we see even on the cross how he made arrangements for His mother to be looked after in His absence. So what we are referring to here is a love that is even deeper than that which is already immense.

There is to be a special bond between us that is the envy of all the earth. The challenge for them and for us is not in our relationship with the Master as much as it is with the Master's followers. Jesus told the disciples that they were all "brothers," and that the greatest among them was to be their servant. On the other hand, if we "bite and devour one another" (Galatians 5:15), we cannot expect to be identified as a true disciple of Jesus Christ.

The basis of a great deal of the conflict between disciples has to do with a thirst for power. This is most likely why Jesus laid down the ground rules as He did in order to keep the focus on Christ as the only individual who is to be perceived as the person in charge. The rest of us are always to see ourselves as a team of servants and apprentices. If we can ever master this principle we will eliminate one of the greatest causes for contention at its source.

One of the ways to accomplish this worthy objective is to meditate on Matthew 23:8-10 and Matthew 5:3-10. Those passages should be put to memory, prayer, and meditation on a daily basis. We should use those as a soul catharsis that will place ourselves in the proper disposition for service as opposed to seizure (of control). The beatitudes are not just for admiration, they are for spiritual inventory. We must seek daily the mind of Christ with regard to poverty of spirit, mournfulness, meekness, a thirst for righteousness, mercifulness, purity of heart, peacemaking, and experiencing persecution for doing well.

In addition to this our relationship deficit is reaching epidemic proportions in the modern church. So much of our interaction with fellow believers is superficial. Yet Jesus's example is a personal 24/7 work-and-leisure environment. They lived and worked together for around three years! Additionally, you don't get the feeling that Jesus did this because He had to but because He wanted to. Something has to be done to bring fellowship to a new level—that of true discipleship. It should be a Koinonia-shaped (κοινωνία, or "communion") community where all things are shared and we are day after day eating together in one another's homes and becoming the best of friends; where companionship is known at its highest levels and isolation is the exception to the general rule of extended family relationships. There has to be a shift from impersonal to personal; from multimillion-dollar church campuses to individual households.

It may be that we lack a public relationship with one another because we lack a private relationship with God. We are supposed to gather together to celebrate our common commitment to the cause of Christ throughout the week. Instead it seems that when we gather together, that is the only day of the week we ever think about God. It is no wonder there is a disconnect in our relationship with one another, for we have no legitimate context for it in most instances.

If you have ever led people to the Lord and personally discipled them by teaching them to appropriate Christ's commands into their everyday lives, you know there is nothing like it on earth in terms of the way spirits can unite for eternity. The joy of the moment, when on bended knee they turn everything over to God, is much like the joy and celebration we experience when mothers hold their newborn children for the first time. There is often that travail that precedes new birth, where unbelievers struggle in the valley of decision as to whether they can trust (exercise faith) in the Lord Jesus Christ. The unborn individuals consider, reconsider, struggle, and toss and turn until they can wait no longer, and come and fall on their knees and pour out their heart to the Lord. They let go of everything, giving Christ total control of their life—and then something wonderful happens. Suddenly old things pass away and all things become new and these people are activated, energized, and eager to serve. They are ready for any challenge and can't wait for the next assignment.

When you cover each command of Christ they soak it up like a sponge; they are fully engaged and are able to comprehend the significance of every principle. The new converts are compelled to take action right away and demonstrate their devotion to the Lord through obedience. They grow ever closer and ever stronger. You rejoice with them as you do when your own child accomplishes some great feat.

If you are privileged enough to be not only the one who led them to Christ but also baptized them in water, the bond seems to grow even stronger. It is a fellowship of devotion to Christ. The more they grow in His imperatives and in His word and prayer the nearer and dearer they become to you, who are on the same quest.

One fellow disciple I led to the Lord was committing entire chapters of the Gospel of John to memory out of love for the Lord. I was so proud of his zeal, fervor, and passion for Christ. Later, that same person was able to work with me on the mission field and tears fell from my eyes as he shared his testimony.

Yet this powerful bond of love, friendship, and family is not only there when you are the spiritual elder; it is there when you find a kindred spirit. You see that same passion, desire, and power that has also driven you driving someone else to make the type of sacrifices necessary to produce fruit for the kingdom of God. To those who have left all to follow Christ, there is a heart-to-heart connection that can never be broken. Those people are the most honorable among us. They are the world's greatest treasures. They are the light of the world and the salt of the earth. You feel privileged to know them and to make their acquaintance. If you are honored to work side by side with them in the vineyard of the Lord, then it is even a greater privilege and your joy is complete. There is an intense fellowship that will never be properly understood by the world; but that fraternity of faith will make an indelible impression upon them that they will not be able to deny. Who knows how many could come to the Lord because of that impression—or how many, on the other hand, may never come because of the absence of it in our currently detached version of Christianity?

JOHN 15:8

"My Father is glorified by this, that you bear much fruit, and so prove to be my disciples." From Jesus's perspective the final characteristic that identifies one as a true disciple of Christ is productivity. The best way to be productive in the kingdom of God is to expand it. Kingdom expansion comes only one way: through conversions. Once new converts are discipled the result then is even more conversions. This is the fruitfulness that provides the evidence for genuine Christian discipleship. This implies something about Christian maturity. It is in the bearing of "much" fruit that you "prove to be," or, more accurately "become" (γένησθε) His disciples. The difference between bearing some fruit and bearing much fruit is pruning and cultivation. Over much time and effort the branch matures to the point of full productivity.

Secondly, one "becomes" a disciple of Jesus only after this process is complete. He has not reached full discipleship until he has risen to the highest levels of intimacy and productivity. It is obvious there are mature and immature disciples, as we see from the cause-and-effect relationship with the master and his students. Jesus is stating here that "His" disciples are to be identified by their capacity to develop into full maturity. Their maturity is proven in their productivity. The true vine is greatly treasured because the vinedresser knows it is guaranteed to produce. The true branch is greatly treasured for the same reason. Its firm attachment to the true vine guarantees results as well. It is like saying to them, "One of these days you're going to make me proud, and then the world is going to see why I chose you. Once you reach your peak, I will be delighted to say, 'These belong to me.'"

All the previous verses in this chapter speak of guaranteed results as long as there remains an interconnection with Jesus who is identified as the "true vine" (John 15:1). Thankfully in this scenario an unfruitful branch is an anomaly. The picture painted here is that the natural course of events in any grapevine is grape production. The only maintenance required is an occasional pruning to produce even more fruit. So the command to "abide in me" is a command to do what is likely to happen anyway once you truly surrender your life to Christ. Yet it is also true that what had come so naturally to them over the past three years may now prove to be a much greater challenge in Christ's physical absence.

He is telling them that upon His departure their greatest challenge will be to keep Him as the apple of their eye, the central figure of their faith. Should at any time they drift away from that priority their productivity will suffer. A true disciple is not such a person. He is someone who stays intimately familiar with the Lord no matter what the circumstances. If Christ is visibly present or at the Father's right hand, it makes no difference. True devotion to Him can never be shaken because the disciple finds a way to continue that person-to-person contact with Him by faith. Just as the branch and the vine make up a unit for the delivery of the Holy Spirit, the disciple is to remain locked into Christ so that he or she can channel the nourishment that will produce the fruit the Father is looking for. Just as Jesus remained so lovingly and entirely submitted to the will and purposes of the Father so as to be one with Him, we are called to be one with the Son. As the Father sent Jesus, so is Jesus sending us (John 20:21). All productivity is an outgrowth of our level of intimacy with the Son. When we treasure the Son's commands enough to practice them, that bond of love is intensified along with our productivity (John 15:10).

The disciples are "wired into" Christ and the only thing that can prevent the energy from flowing through them is a disconnect of some sort, such as a short in the line or the circuit breakers in the electric boxes of our houses, for example. Once the line is damaged, fuse is blown, or circuit breaker is tripped, the source of power is prevented from channeling into the outlets. We will find ourselves slipping out of place from time to time and in need of a "reset" from the heavenly Father. The effectiveness of our witness depends upon open lines of communication and communion with the Lord.

What is the difference between a true disciple and a false one? A true disciple is connected or one with the true vine. Jesus identifies Himself as the true vine. The natural result of that union is fruitfulness. That is the visible evidence of the invisible connection at the heart level. If there is no serious relationship with Christ, there can be no positive result. Christ is the source of everything meaningful in the Christian faith whether it is regeneration, sanctification, or glorification. If He ceases to be the central focus and figure of the disciple-making enterprise, true Christian discipleship will cease to exist. "Without Me you can do nothing" (John 15:5).

There are many well-meaning but unsuccessful attempts to spur Christian growth in individuals; or in other words, to get them to grow up and become mature believers. All sorts of efforts toward Christian education are planned and executed to get people into the Word; to educate them on the doctrine of that particular organization; or to acquaint them with the particular philosophy of the spiritual leader of the congregation. Small groups are organized; sermons rehashed; Bible studies engaged in; etc. All of these efforts, no matter what method or direction, are falsely labeled Christian discipleship because they are using too broad a brush stroke when what is asked for is something precise. Discipleship is understood as something general rather than something specific. This happens because we are not connected to the vine. If we were truly connected to Christ, then what He said about discipleship is the only thing we would consider as legitimate.

What did Christ say makes a disciple? He only said one thing: "Teaching them to keep everything I have commanded you" (Matthew 28:20). That is not a broad and complex issue, it is a narrowly defined objective. Christian discipleship is nothing more or less than finding a way to carry out Jesus's orders. We believers are all to be the servants of one Master: the Christ. He is basically saying that in order to be His disciples we must pay attention to what He is saying to us and find a way to put that into our everyday practice and experience. What He said to the first twelve disciples He is saying to those of us who will follow in their footsteps. Each of the first twelve did not go on to form their own schools of discipleship. Instead, they remained devoted adherents to the original Master and were teaching others to do the same. That is the heart and soul of true Christian discipleship: to remain devoted adherents to the imperatives of the original Master, Jesus of Nazareth.

Jesus stated with one voice what He wanted discipleship to be. Today there are legions of voices vying for our allegiance. In the building of the tower of Babel they started out with one language but couldn't complete the task once their languages were multiplied. Discipleship today is suffering the same fate. This is an easy problem to solve if you are connected to the vine. He said, "My sheep hear my voice" (John 10:27). Through all the current cacophony of voices, opinions, and languages we must recognize the voice of the Master so we can find our way back home. The confusion comes from the enemy who wants to muddy the water by making us think the issue of discipleship remains unresolved; for once we see clearly just exactly what is expected of us, the kingdom of God will be exponentially advanced. Therefore, Satan effectively lures us into wasting our time and resources on a matter that was never really open to debate to begin with. We write a library of books on a subject that is really very simple and doesn't require much explanation. Like a dog chasing its own tail we wind up confused and disoriented because we imagine discipleship is something different or other than it has always been! We need to just accept what Jesus said about it at the outset and move on. We need to rediscover Jesus's perspective on discipleship and let that alone be our guiding light.

PART TWO:
Jesus's Perspective:
Reinstitution
Keeping the Master's Imperatives

Introduction

Having fully explained Jesus's perspective on how Christian discipleship is achieved, it is now possible to proceed with the reinstitution of that objective. In Matthew 28:19-20 Jesus spelled out three basic steps that were necessary in order to make sure a disciple is made correctly: first is by going into the entire world; second is the baptism of the new convert to the gospel message; and third is the systematic observance of each and every command that Jesus ever uttered to those initial twelve disciples. All three of those objectives have one thing in common: they are all mandates.

The last step is really the most important because it is within that particular aspect of the overall objective that every other step is fulfilled as well. The proclamation of the gospel worldwide and the baptism of those new converts as an initiation into the disciple-making process are after all just as much commanded as anything else Jesus insisted upon. Therefore, when you teach them the third step, you are teaching them to perform the first two steps as well because the first two steps fall under the category of "everything I commanded you." It is as if Jesus said to them, "Teach them to do everything you were told, including what I just said!" This is why it is possible to make disciples by simply focusing on one thing: Jesus's commands. If you go through and find every time Jesus gave an order to his disciples and then apply that to yourself, you are on the right track.

Everything Jesus wanted the first disciples to do He wants us to do as well. That is why he said "teaching *them* [us] to keep everything I have commanded *you* [them]" (emphasis mine). This leads me to believe this must be the reason for the existence of the gospels in the first place. In order to ensure that those instructions could be passed down to all future generations without error, it must have been decided that a faithful record be established. For those first twelve disciples would soon pass away and there would be no more possibility to verify anything firsthand. So I believe the early Church left us with everything they could remember and garnish from the disciples' original experience with Him, and that is the only resource by which that most important ingredient of disciple making, called "commands," can be reapplied.

So hereby is the task that lies before us made certain. If it is the commands Jesus wants it is the commands Jesus will get. We will now proceed through all four Gospels from beginning to end in a harmony aspect to uncover every imperative He ever uttered to or toward His disciples. We proceed with full knowledge of the fact that a great deal of the material overlaps and will be careful not to repeat commands that have already been stated. By using the original Greek and allowing that knowledge to help us easily identify and pull up for consideration every imperative, we will then proceed to fully comprehend and carry forth that particular objective. We will not consider ourselves to have completed this process of discipleship until all 254 of these jewels have been fully realized. God bless this massive undertaking.

How the Lessons Work

A brief introduction as to the overall structure and design of the following lessons is in order and will aid the reader in the learning and application process. You will notice first a number at the top left corner of the lesson to tell you what lesson you are reading. There are 92 lessons in all, which include all 254 of the commands I have found in the gospel records that Jesus gave to his disciples during his earthly ministry. The number 254 is an approximate measurement and includes some commands that may not have been directly addressed to the disciples but were nonetheless duly noted. They have the force of a command—not just to the outside group being addressed but to everyone involved in the context of the discussion. For example, Jesus's command to the Pharisees decide if the tree is good or bad based on the fruit is a good principle for the disciple's to live by as well (Matthew 12:33). I would consider that an indirect command to the disciples. There are also some commands that were not included because they seemed to address a personal issue between Jesus and an individual rather that a general objective that could be applied to everyone. For example, Jesus's command for Peter to go and find a gold coin in a fish's mouth was a personal issue between the two of them and not a general principle that applied to all twelve (Matthew 17:27). Which is to say there is some "give or take" in arriving at these figures.

As you move across from the number you will encounter a title presented to you in the form of a mandate. What I have attempted to do here is sum up the commands that seem to be in the same category into one thought. In some instances, it is a repeat of the only command available for that category, and in others there are a good number of commands that are being lumped into the singular objective. I felt it would be redundant to offer a lesson on each command when it might produce a repetition of the same theme.

After the title will be a scripture reference or list of references. This will include all the places in the four Gospels where this issue is addressed. In some cases it is found in only one book, but in most instances all three Synoptics (the Gospels of Matthew, Mark, and Luke) and sometimes John will be included. This is really where the lesson begins. All scripture references should be read in their entirety before going further so that you will be able to notice where exactly the commands are coming from.

Below the references you will find a short passage that is an attempt to find that particular section of all of the listed references that best expresses the primary objective, thereby in a sense, narrowing the scope of the investigation. This passage of scripture should go to the heart of the issue at hand. Within that passage in most cases you will find the imperatives that will be addressed in that lesson. So there is a progression from general and contextual to specific as if moving from the exterior of a target gradually to the bull's eye.

The bull's eye consists of the section entitled "Command" or "Commands of Christ". There you will find the actual sentences where the imperatives are located. Each sentence will be revisited in its original language to make sure the fullness of the communication is uncovered. It will be retranslated by the author with the actual imperative noted and italicized. Therefore, the translation in the "Commands" section will not necessarily match the reference above it. Instead, it will present to the reader additional insights and possibilities which will anchor the overall teaching more securely in the original concepts. The reader will thereby begin to notice a pattern and learn to pick up on the way a command is identified in passages. It is easier to identify an imperative in Greek than in English. The word itself is marked to indicate it is indeed an imperative.

Once the introductory titles and imperatives are highlighted, the commentary on the passage will begin so as to be careful not to apply the imperative out of context. The circumstances surrounding the command will often bring to light what is expected in terms of our response. Additionally, remarks about the original language will be utilized to ensure that the student is headed in the right direction with regard to comprehension and application.

At the end of the lesson is a chance to reflect on the material presented. An open dialogue is encouraged whereby the general principles are revisited and either confirmed or denied before moving on to the process by which the would-be disciple will apply these matters to his or her life. It comes to the reader in the form of a "Discussion Questions" format.

Finally there is the "Suggested Exercises" portion of the lesson. This is the most critical of all due to the statement by Jesus that making disciples is about teaching them to "*keep* everything I commanded you" in Matthew 28:20. It is in the carrying out of the objective that the disciple is truly confirmed. It is extremely important that the student find some legitimate avenue in which the command can be expressed or fulfilled in real life. The exercises are good suggestions and I feel confident that adherence to those will put a successful end to the matter.

It is suggested that the would-be disciples choose one of the exercises to complete before the group meets the next time and then share their experience with the group. Some method of confirmation should be agreed upon whereby the completed assignment can be verified. Perhaps the leader of the group can decide if the activity performed met the Lord's objective and then sign off on it. Each disciple should keep up with the commands kept and those that still need completing. There may be times when it has to be returned to at a later date.

Some form of recognition should be agreed upon once each growth level is achieved. For example, in karate a different colored belt is earned at each level. Something similar should be awarded the disciple who is moving forward into a new stage of spiritual development. Those who complete all stages of development should also be recognized and offered leadership roles.

It is my prayer that this upcoming adventure will be the most rewarding of your life. God bless the soul striving toward the worthy goal of becoming a true disciple of Jesus of Nazareth.

SECTION ONE:
Spiritual Infant

1

Check It Out

John 1:35-39a

Again the next day John was standing with two of his disciples and he looked at Jesus as he walked, and said, "Behold the lamb of God!" The two disciples heard him speak, and they followed Jesus. And Jesus turned and saw them following, and said to them, "What do you seek?" They said to him, "Rabbi (which translated means Teacher), where are you staying?" He said to them, "Come and you will see."

Command of Christ: *Come* and you will see.

The authoritative invitation as recorded in the first chapter of John is the first of around 254 imperatives we will encounter in the life of Jesus and His behavior toward his disciples. The context is important for understanding this invitation/order from the Master. John the Baptist had just suggested to the Pharisees that he was only setting the stage for the true hero, a title he was not worthy of himself. Then when Jesus shows up, John announces "here is the man." It is obvious that the disciples were looking for the Messiah, and having surmised that the Baptist was not the one after all, went to find out if Jesus was the Messiah. At the point of their questioning Jesus compellingly invites them to come and find out (where He stays). This is the first of Jesus's commands.

With this interaction we have just passed over into a new dimension of revelation, that being of God's own Son. Both the first chapter of John and Hebrews explain how that at this turning point in history, God offers mankind the fullest revelation of Himself thus far. John points out in verse 18 that this perspective is indeed unique by the fact that we now have a firsthand account. As great as the prophets were they were not passing on a firsthand account of God to the people. But Jesus, who was eternally with and equal to God, became the only man capable of presenting the "inside story." Only the Son can truly *explain* (*exegete,* in Greek) the Father. Therefore, just as the first disciples got wind of the superiority of Christ to everything they had ever known before and then made every effort to latch on to that, we too must pass over into that discovery of discoveries and conclusion of conclusions. This will serve as the basis of our willingness to turn everything over to Him as our Lord and Master and to see ourselves as His humble servants and lifelong disciples.

John the Baptist got their curiosity going in referring to Christ as the "Lamb of God, who takes away the sin of the world." Then Jesus follows through with permission for them to just tag along. It's interesting that it is not told in a passive voice but is an imperative right from the get-go. Yet He does not overwhelm them here with a transfiguration or the like. It is simply a willingness to befriend them and satisfy their curiosity about who He is. They would proceed from there to the unthreatening environment of a wedding ceremony, perhaps to provide a positive atmosphere to get to know one another. One lesson we learn from the Master here is to present the truth in stages. He will not, for example, speak of the cross for some time yet to come. As they discover little by little who He is, only then will they be prepared to make a more substantial commitment.

Discussion Questions:

- What was it that initially drew the disciples to Christ? How about you?
- How did Jesus provide a nonthreatening environment for them?
- What is unique about the perspective of Jesus compared to other messengers from God?
- What is unique about the way Jesus invites but at the same time insists?
- How can you take the initiative to plant seeds of hospitality and curiosity?
- How will you use friendship to reach the lost?

- How can you better allow nonbelievers time and space to decide and commit?
- Do you tend to require too much of them (nonbelievers) initially?
- Do you expect growth in infinitesimal or astronomical stages?

Suggested Exercises:

- This week invite someone who doesn't know the Lord over for dinner or out to a ball game. Develop a friendship that over time will naturally lead them to ask questions about your faith. Don't chase them down and corner them with a fire-and-brimstone message right away. At the same time, always be ready to share the reason you are different; be ready with the good news found in John 3:16. Use the natural as a bridge to the supernatural in your presentation of the gospel (John 4:7-10).
- Are you yet to discover who Jesus is but are curious? "Alpha" is a course designed to provide a friendly and comfortable at home environment where individuals can discuss the meaning of life and find out what Christianity is all about on an introductory level. Visit www.alphausa.org to find a meeting near you!

2

Follow Me

John 1:43; Matthew 4:19, 9:9; Mark 1:16, 2:14; and
Luke 5:10, 27

*The next day he purposed to go into Galilee, and he found Philip.
And Jesus said to him, "Follow me"* (John 1:43).

Command of Christ: *Follow* me.

Here we find Jesus taking the initiative to begin a ministry relationship.
Notice that this calling must originate from the Lord and is therefore not
something we can pursue out of our own ambition or desires. Much is
to be said about this since so many want to decide for themselves about
full-time ministry just as they would any other career path. Yet at the
same time we want to know that God is behind it. Therefore, the acid
test each minister must ask is thus: Is this vocation the result of my own
inventiveness or did the idea indeed originate from the body of Christ?
On the other hand, we are all ordered to be disciples. So in that sense
we are all called to reach the lost. Nevertheless, we are not all necessarily
called to be full-time ministers. Nor are we expected to reach the lost on
our own.

Notice also that the calling is given not only as an invitation but also as
a demand. The fact that the word "follow" is an imperative demonstrates
that surrendering to His authority is always the first item on the agenda
with the Lord. Being Lord means, after all, being in charge. He doesn't
make appeals but rather insists on our undying devotion at all times,
even during His initial contact with us. As you will come to discover in

this study, our disciple/Master relationship consists for the most part in attending to a series of direct orders fired out one after another from the central authority figure. In the end what determines our usefulness as well as our level of devotion is how well we adhere to and cherish these directives (John 15:10).

This command to follow is on two levels. First there is the call to relationship. That's what we initially encounter with Jesus's approach to Phillip (John 1:43). This is the first mention in the gospels of the call to "follow." Notice how the translation from the original Greek brings out the interconnectedness of the Master to the disciple. The "me" of this passage is not accusative. If it were, "follow me" would be the natural translation and thought process here. But since it is dative it is best translated as "follow to me," which includes the idea of adhering to an individual. It reminds us of the "abiding" passage in John 15 where He calls Himself the vine and us the branches. We tend to jump ahead to the call for action, but we know that any work for God can only be accomplished out of fellowship first. We want our relationship to be awarded by our performance, but His kingdom is in the reverse order from ours. The relationship must be first. Then and only then can He do His work through us. He is not looking for someone to do the work for Him but someone who will allow Him to do the work through them. We see this in Jesus's own ministry, where He never claims credit for any word or action (John 5:19; 14:10). It is apparent that he wants us to follow in the same vein, as we are to be sent in the same fashion or pattern (John 20:21).

Secondly, we arrive at the purpose for the fellowship. In Matthew 4:19, Mark 1:16, and Luke 5:10 we see the type of work He is calling us to. He informs Peter, Andrew, James, and John of His intentions to make them fishermen of men. It is the exchange of one profession for another as is also the case in his offer to Matthew the tax collector (Matthew 9:9; Mark 2:14; and Luke 5:27). This goal is overwhelming if we take it upon ourselves alone. But thankfully once again it is the end result of three years of interaction with the Son of God that brings them to this point. Again we are tempted to take the ball and run with it, but then we will once again be guilty of a performance-based relationship and we forget that we can't really save anyone independently. This also is the work of God through man and not man for God. The comfort in these words in the Synoptic Gospels is that "he will make us," not "we will make ourselves" fishers of men. So the challenge to us is not necessarily how many have we brought to the Lord, but how many has the Lord brought to Himself through us. Is He able to reach the lost through us yet? Has our relationship not yet matured to that point of divine usefulness?

Discussion Questions:

- Can you decide for yourself about a career in full-time ministry, or is it decided for you?
- How is the call to follow both an invitation and an order?
- How is it revealed that the call to follow IS also a call to relationship when you look at the original Greek grammar of the passage?
- Have you answered the call to relationship?
- Has your fellowship shaped you into a fisherman?
- Who is actually catching the fish—you or God?
- How does your connection lead to their conversion? Give an example.

Suggested Exercises:

- Establish a daily prayer routine. If you already practice this, add to the length of your prayer time and make sure it is completed privately. Also make sure you are free from any devotional materials so as not to get distracted from the direct line of communication that must be developed between you and the Lord. Ask Jesus to make you a better fisher of men and report the results back to the group. What bait did Jesus suggest? How did a closer walk with Him improve your chances?
- Research the gospels in terms of any methods Jesus used to attract people to His message. Report back to the group the list of techniques you were able to come up with. Where you able to utilize any of those methods in your own evangelistic endeavors?

3

Respect God's House

John 2:14-16; Mark 11:17; Matthew 21:13

And he found in the temple those who were selling oxen and sheep and doves, and the money changers seated at their tables. And he made a scourge of cords, and drove them all out of the temple, with the sheep and the oxen; and he poured out the coins of the money changers and overturned their tables; and to those who were selling the doves he said, "Take these things away; stop making my Father's house a place of business" (John 2:14-16).

Commands of Christ: *Take* these things away; don't *make* my Father's house a house of merchandise.

We know the story of Jesus's zeal for God's house in terms of keeping it free from the corruption of money. He clearly does not want it to become just another profit-making venture. Perhaps that is why He never promoted the idea of building synagogues or church buildings for his movement. Sometimes being biblical in your approach means not only doing what is said but not doing what is not said. There is no statement by our Founder about constructing church buildings. We decided to do that on our own, perhaps for the sake of comfort. If anyone would have been in favor of erecting an edifice, surely that person would be a carpenter; but not this one. Jesus knew that soon the age of temple worship would come to an end. He also knew that it was God's plan to relocate His presence in people, and that the individual soul would now become the Temple of God (1 Corinthians 6:19).

117

Actually, the original word for "church" in the New Testament has nothing to do with building or temple construction at all. *Ekklesia* is the Greek word for "church," and it literally means "assembly" or "called out" (*ek*-out; *klesia*-called). When people come together in Jesus's name, there it is: the church in all its glory and splendor. Nevertheless, since most Christians pay little attention to such details, we find ourselves in a world surrounded by church structures of every shape, form, and fashion.

This imperative to respect God's house was actually not initially a direct commandment to the disciples but now has become so as we busy ourselves with construction of worship centers. We must take heed to the warnings of our Lord with regard to what He calls his Father's house. If there must be a building, then that place has to be holy. It is to be countercultural and opposed to sordid gain. It is also to have an atmosphere of prayer. Christ wants them to remove the merchandise and replace it with prayer (Mark 11:17). The only house Jesus wants is a house of prayer.

I think if Jesus were here today, you might just catch Him donning a hardhat. But it would not be for the purpose of construction but for demolition. I could just see Him out there bulldozing every church building in sight and demanding that we come together in our homes as it was in the beginning. Remember, for the first three hundred years there were no church buildings in the Christian religion. It was only when Constantine made Christianity the official religion of the Roman Empire that this practice began.

Overall then, what is Jesus insisting upon? The order is not to make the temple a house of merchandise but a house of prayer. The two imperatives underlined above are "take" and "don't make." Later on in the gospels Jesus adds "prayer" to the equation in his second recorded cleansing of the temple (Mark 11:17; Matthew 21:13). One way to accomplish this is to eliminate the need for so much money by reducing unnecessary expenses. One huge expense is the construction of worship centers. Maybe we should reconsider such building programs and focus more on one another. Another huge expense is salaries. Ministers should consider working a job on the side as a tent-maker, so to speak. Then we can become better equipped to address more important matters, such as prayer and meeting the needs of the community.

Discussion Questions:

- Why do you think Jesus was never interested in church-building projects?
- What is the Greek word for church and how does that clarify our objective?
- What changes need to be made in order to help your church become a house of prayer and not a house of profit?
- How radical would it be to propose that the church building be sold or demolished?
- What reaction would there be if the pastor was required to work a regular job and receive part-time pay from the church? After the initial fallout, would there be a positive or negative gain for the church?
- Do you ever feel as if everyone is just "playing" church where you attend or do you always have a sense that you are part of something genuine and supernatural?

Suggested Exercises:

- Approach the leadership of your church with these ideas for moving the church away from a money-centered approach to a prayer-centered approach and report back to the group with a written report of the reaction you received.

Write out a plan for how you would organize a church that had no building and no full-time paid minister. Use the first chapter of Acts for your guide. Remember the church did not operate in the beginning the way it operates now. Determine whether it is possible to go back to the basics or if it is too late.

4

Repent and Believe

Mark 1:15; Matthew 4:17; John 3:7

The kingdom of God is at hand; repent and believe in the gospel (Mark 1:15).

Commands of Christ: *Repent* and *believe* in the gospel. You *must* be born again.

Our next alert from Jesus comes out of His conversation with Nicodemus as well as His common refrain to the public to "repent and believe the good news." Nicodemus was curious about Jesus and what was going on with Him. He was trying to understand in the flesh what could only come about in the spirit. He is like so many today who have a keen interest in religion but fail to fully surrender to God. That's where Jesus was leading people, back to repentance and trust. Before one is willing to fully commit to something else, he or she must first be convinced in his or her own mind that the alternative is a better option. You can't go straight to faith and bypass the changing of your own mind. This leads to an empty, false commitment and causes you to fall short of salvation. That is why Jesus places repentance before belief.

The Greek word that is translated above as repentance is *metanoeite*. *Meta* means *change* and *noeō* means *mind*. Each individual must come to that conclusion independently, that the way he or she is headed is actually not the best option available. Only then will each person be open to other possibilities, one of which is total surrender to (faith in) God. As human beings made in the image of God, we possess something more than the animal kingdom that preceded us, which is the ability to reason. Unlike the animals that operate primarily by instinct, we are able to examine two possibilities and choose the most virtuous. God expects us to use that enhanced capacity to examine our situation and determine the wisest course of action. Two possibilities are before us: our way or His way. Once we are convinced that our way makes less sense we will be open to considering turning our lives over to God.

That brings us to the second term Jesus is requiring of mankind. You must *believe.* In the original Greek the term for believe is *pisteuete.* That term is translated throughout the New Testament as faith, belief, or trust. It is a misunderstanding of the potency of this terminology that causes many to fall short of a true conversion experience. It is not consent to a historical fact that saves anyone but their commitment to that fact. I often use the illustration of the young lad on the edge of the swimming pool who hesitates to jump into the pool where his father waits with open arms. His actions will ultimately tell us how much trust he really has in his father. It is just that sort of "leap of faith" that is required for salvation to actually occur. It is a letting go of the control we have over our own lives and handing it over to another. However, when it comes to our relationship with God, we are not handing it over only in this one instance but for the rest of our lives.

This is what it takes for one to enter the kingdom of God. Entering the kingdom is another way of saying I have received my Salvation. The only way to enter any domain is by subjecting yourself to the one who owns it. You cannot enter another's kingdom as king but only as a subject of the king. If you try to enter any other way you will not be allowed to proceed. There are two sides of the coin in conversion. One side is what He did for us. The other side is what we do for Him. He laid down His life for us, and now for salvation we are doing the same. We must lay down our life for Him as a living sacrifice. Once we do that, the transaction is complete. It is very much like withdrawing money from your checking account. Unless you provide evidence that this is your checking account, you will not be able to withdraw from it. The transaction is incomplete unless you respond appropriately.

When Jesus announced that the kingdom of God was at hand, the people were not thinking spiritually. They were thinking politically. They were looking forward to the day when their nation would achieve not only independence but world dominance. But I believe Jesus capitalized on that predisposition and mind-set. He knew the phrase "kingdom of God" would instantly spark a flame in the heart of every Israelite to the point of undivided attention. What better lure could the Master use to fish for men? They wanted the world. But what good is it to gain the whole world and lose your soul? He offered them what they wanted in order to provide for them what they really needed. With Jesus the spiritual is the only true and permanent reality (John 6:63). Therefore he was not at all misleading them by suggesting that a new kingdom was on its way; rather, He was preventing them from being mislead. These were not the final days of history as foretold by the prophets, but the days leading up to that ultimate sacrifice that would open up the kingdom of God to the hearts of all men.

They had jumped to a political conclusion, as did his disciples. But they as all of us had to learn that God's kingdom starts from within. It is not from the outside-in like all other kingdoms that have overpowered the world by brute force. But it starts with a change of heart. Nonetheless, there will in time be a physical kingdom, and the disciples will rule on twelve literal thrones with Jesus. But that is yet to come in God's inside-out kingdom, which is reversed from the way we normally relate. When the outside catches up with the inside we will indeed rule and reign with Jesus Christ forever.

So there we have it. Jesus is insisting that we "must be born again." The Master Teacher requires two things for a genuine conversion: repentance and belief. Therefore it would behoove us all to return to the drawing board and ask ourselves these questions to ensure that our names are indeed recorded in the Book of Life. Are we really saved? Can we remember the time we finally changed our mind (repentance) about the direction our life was headed and then turned it completely over to God (faith)? If not, let's take care of that as soon as possible. Trust in the Lord Jesus Christ and be saved. If we are accepting Him as less than Lord, we have not accepted Him at all.

Discussion Questions:

- Is it possible to trust in Christ and enter into His kingdom without first repenting?
- What does it mean to believe in the gospel?

- Is it possible to accept Jesus as Savior without also accepting Him as your Master?
- What are the two sides of the coin that make the salvation transaction complete?
- How did Jesus use the phrase "kingdom of God" to spark the curiosity of the people?
- Explain the following statement: "When the outside catches up with the inside we will indeed rule and reign with Jesus Christ forever."

Suggested Exercises:

- Examine yourself to determine whether or not you are truly in the faith.
- Identify the moment you truly changed your mind about the direction your life was headed and determined it was wrong. Share that experience with the group.
- Identify the time you subsequently exchanged your belief in your way of doing things for a belief in Christ and His way of doing things. At what point did you know that you had fully surrendered? Share that with the group.
- Share how you felt once you turned everything over to God.
- If you never experienced any of the three steps just mentioned, you may have never been saved. Find out which step you are deficient in and determine whether you are ready to make a change. Repent and believe the gospel so you too can become a child of God.

5

Awaken to the Harvest

John 4:35-39

Do you not say, "There are yet four months, and then comes the harvest"? Behold, I say to you, lift up your eyes and look on the fields, that they are white for harvest. Already he who reaps is receiving wages and is gathering fruit for life eternal; so that he who sows and he who reaps may rejoice together. For in this case the saying is true, "One sows and another reaps." I sent you to reap that for which you have not labored; others have labored and you have entered into their labor. From that city many of the Samaritans believed in Him because of the word of the woman who testified, "He told me all the things that I have done."

Command of Christ: *Lift up* your eyes and *look* on the fields, that they are white for harvest.

The implication of the call to "open your eyes" is that there must have been a metaphorical temporary blindness of some sort. Either their eyes were totally shut or they were seeing but not perceiving. The enemy, Satan, will use either avenue to cause confusion. He will throw us off track just enough to interfere with lost humanity finding its way home. In our hard-hearted affluent society, for instance, the enemy will do everything he can to convince us of the futility of our efforts. It seems all too often that nobody is interested anymore, we think, so what's the use? Instead we should abide by the attitude of Jesus: that anyone can come to the Lord as long as you present the message in an attractive way.

124

The woman at the well would have never even been addressed by any other man of God, especially one who knew her sordid past. But the way He presented the gospel was so appealing and irresistible. He found common ground and then built on that. We too must never give up and must be prepared to offer the gospel under any circumstance (Ephesians 6:15). Even if we fail, we have planted a seed and can be sure there will be results from that effort (Psalm 126:6). We are, bottom line, in a battle for souls.

Here, the context is Jesus passing through Samaria and perceiving an unexpected reality. Many more people than would be anticipated were ready to accept the gospel message. Jesus told them that harvest time was now, and not the usual four months down the road. He starts with one woman whom He encounters at the well and ends up with a crowd from the city ready to hear what He has to offer. I doubt the disciples even understood what was happening or what Jesus meant by his harvesting analogy. They seem to have gotten caught up in the moment, not knowing which way to turn. But for Jesus it was about saving the lost (Luke 19:10).

This unforeseen catch is even more surprising considering the context of Samaria. The people living in this area were considered not only an inferior race but the area of the country that could be counted on to compromise their faith for whatever viewpoint had come to power. They were the first to take on the Greco-Roman philosophy and lifestyle. But those pious Jews who held firm to their convictions abided in Judea. Therefore, what the woman stated was correct, that the Jews had no dealings with the Samaritans. In fact they even refused to dirty their sandals with the sod of that district, having made a passageway that took them around the "contaminated" Samaria to reach Galilee. They refused to pass through that land even though the route was shorter. It is a feud that dates back to the divided kingdom of Rehoboam (1 Kings 12:1).

So what Jesus was demanding from the disciples was to awaken to the reality that had just transpired before them. That a whole town of Samaria would be open to the good news was good news indeed, especially since they were willing to receive that message from a Jew. One might expect that over time Samaria could be included with the other Gentile nations as fertile ground for the gospel. But no, already they show a desire to know Jesus. So in agricultural terms, Jesus calls the disciples to consider the unexpected. They are not even paying any notice to their wheat fields because it's too early for harvest. He's alerting them to an unprecedented turn of events. Suddenly it's harvest time all over again! The command issued from Jesus to his disciples is to "lift up" your eyes and "contemplate" (it is *more than see* in the Greek). Now they must reassess their former way of doing things, for what they thought was set in stone has now been reconfigured.

We too must open our eyes to the fact that it is the people and places we least expect that will show the best response. In our day we have seen the third-world countries as the largest growth area for the kingdom of God. But in our own country evangelism is having little to no effect. But more accessible are the outcasts within our own borders. There are an enumerable amount of reasons to disassociate with others, and we tend to look for any excuse. Whether it is race, creed, socioeconomic status, or education, we are too quick to write others off. And that is exactly what Christ is speaking out against. We must learn to be more accepting of those who are in some way different than we are because the kingdom is for all mankind, regardless. It's that small-mindedness that caused the Pharisees to miss out on the greatest event in all of human history, the incarnation.

Discussion Questions:

- Why would the Samaritans have never been expected to be open to spiritual things, namely the presentation of the gospel?
- How did Jesus's lack of prejudice and His creative illustrations provide a solid foundation for acceptance of the gospel from a Samaritan?
- Name a type of person you may dislike or look down upon for some reason. Why is that?
- What can you do to become more accepting and evangelistic?

Suggested Exercises:

- Plan a short-term mission trip to a third-world country. You will return with a totally different perspective toward those you consider "foreigners" in your country.
- You may also want consider inviting a foreign exchange student into your home.

- Teaching an ESL (English as a Second Language) course is another opportunity that will provide assistance to non-English speakers as well as provide a bridge for forming new relationships.
- Make friends with a person at work, school, or church who would not normally be advantageous to you. Break away from your clique.
- Make a list of all people you consider "beneath" you and pray for repentance for thinking that way.
- Pray for God to open your eyes to the unexpected harvest around you.

6

Celebrate

Matthew 5:10-12; Luke 6:22-23

Blessed are you when people insult you and persecute you, and falsely say all kinds of evil against you because of me. Rejoice and be glad, for your reward in heaven is great; for in the same way they persecuted the prophets who were before you (Matthew 5:11-12).

Command of Christ: *Rejoice* and *be glad*, for your reward in heaven is great.

At first glance this beatitude seems a bit out of place from the others. It's hard to see persecution as a blessing, for example. As is so often the case with Jesus, we find ourselves rejoicing when we should be mourning and mourning when we should be rejoicing. The Lord states that a man is blessed that is persecuted for righteousness's sake. Perhaps it is so because only the holiness of the individual, in embodying all of the previous seven Beatitudes, would offend the unrighteous to the point of them taking notice and feeling threatened. Therefore, your persecution is evidence that you have indeed become that child of God you always hoped you could be, and on the other hand are no longer recognizable as a worldly person. It is proof that you have arrived, so to speak, even though your meekness and poverty of spirit will not allow you to say so. Now from that perspective it is indeed appropriate to celebrate such an enormous accomplishment. Few people will ever know this level of saintliness that Jesus exemplified every day. It is the same spiritual attainment that was found in the prophets of

128

the Old Testament. They also endured great hardships and even death for their honest relationship with God and man.

So the order from our Master is to "rejoice and make merry." But I suspect there will not be a great deal of merriment forthcoming because most of us are too busy striving to blend in and remain anonymous. We keep our beliefs private and even berate those who dare express their religious views outside a formal church setting. This perspective has nothing to do with Jesus Christ and His agenda. Those who want "comfortable" religion will not make it as disciples of Christ. They may in fact be surprised to find out they are disciples of the opposition. For when you really become the type of person the Beatitudes describe, you will not be able to conceal it. It will simply be what you have become and who you are. Walking in the truth is simply that; there is no pretense. You simply are who you say you are whether public or private, when it is beneficial, and when it is not. The ultimate aim of virtue is to be free from all duplicity. It is singleness of speech, action, and purpose. What you see is what you get. Integrity is just that. Therefore, if you embody lightness rather than darkness you should not feel obligated to apologize for it. Instead, you find the most prominent place to provide vision to the greatest number of individuals possible.

Though the world may try to snuff you out, their efforts to extinguish one flame will only result in the rise of many more flames all the more intense and all the more brilliant than ever before. If we save our life we will lose it; if we lose it we will save it. Like our Master, our end can never stop our influence but only ensure that it will go even further and have a greater impact than we ever imagined. "If I be lifted up, I will draw all men unto me" (John 12:32).

But here in the Beatitudes He is not referring to death necessarily as he will at a later date, when the disciple has matured and is ready for the ultimate challenge. He is referring here to the insults and how one is made to experience rejection as an outcast when pursing a discipleship. We must remember there is a reward for every sacrifice we make, and enduring the world's distain means we are worthy of a greater honor than before. It means we've been promoted to the highest rank of Christendom. For that we are to be excited, for the reward is not insignificant. Throughout all eternity we will know the privileges that come with that distinction. It is somewhat like the medals of honor awarded to combat veterans but on a much grander and enduring scale. Though persecution is never sought after and never enjoyable, it is an indication that we really are somebody in the kingdom of God. May the Lord help us think differently about these trials—not as desired but not as something to be avoided, either. May the Holy Spirit encourage us to stand firm and confident in who we have become for Christ. What we are is what the world will become; for one day every knee shall bow, and every tongue will indeed confess that Jesus Christ is Lord, to the glory of God the Father (Philippians 2:10-11). We are not behind the times but way ahead of our time! Let's celebrate that!

Discussion Questions:

- Persecution for righteousness's sake is painful, yet it means you have achieved something great in the kingdom of God. What would you call this achievement?
- Has your relationship with Christ alienated you from others? Provide an example.
- How has this teaching from Jesus enabled you to handle rejection differently?
- Discuss the fact that we can rejoice when attacked for two reasons: one because we have reached a high level of achievement in God's kingdom; and two because for having achieved this we can count on a significant reward in eternity.

Suggested Exercises:

- Meditate on and pray for the acquisition of the Beatitudes until they become second nature, until they describe who you are or have become.
- Keep a log of every instance in which it seems you are being insulted, persecuted, and falsely spoken evil of for Jesus's sake.
- Have a "praise celebration" based on those facts you were able to gather.
- Write out a prayer of thanks to God that you are actually different enough to be noticed.
- Have each person in your small group say a prayer of thanksgiving for the criticism they have received for being noticeably different from the world.

7

Never Hide

Matthew 5:13-16

You are the salt of the earth; but if the salt has become tasteless, how can it be made salty again? It is no longer good for anything, except to be thrown out and trampled underfoot by men. You are the light of the world. A city that is set on a hill cannot be hidden; nor does anyone light a lamp and put it under a basket, but on the lamp stand, and it gives light to all who are in the house. Let your light shine before men in such a way that they may see your good works, and glorify your Father who is in heaven.

Command of Christ: *Let* your light *shine* before men . . .

Jesus begins this teaching with statements about who we are. He says, "You are the salt of the earth" and "You are the light of the world." The question is, How do we see ourselves? Do we really believe what Jesus said about us? You must first believe in yourself before anyone else can. That is the place to begin with this teaching, because until we have arrived at the same conclusion, we cannot respond appropriately to the implications. The world says something very different about us. It labels us as "out of touch," "religious fanatics," even "mentally ill." So then we are faced with two different reports. There is what Jesus says we are versus what the world says we are. With those two options the choice is easy; let's go with what Jesus says. Believe first in who you are! You are the light, you are the salt, and you are a faithful child of God in a dark and unbelieving world.

You are the best thing this world has to offer and don't let anyone tell you differently.

This teaching ties in with the previous message on celebration. Being a person marked by the attitudes of poverty in spirit, mournfulness, meekness, hunger for righteousness, mercy, pureness of heart, and peacemaking sets you apart from the world as a glorious light of holiness showing the way to the kingdom. But again it also makes you a target. You stick out like a sore thumb because your standards are so high. You make the sinner uncomfortable because he thought a person like you wasn't possible. Now sinners have to feel guilty about their lifestyles. This leads to persecution, in an effort to cut you down to size and justify their wicked ways.

Because of this we are tempted to keep our beliefs to ourselves. We hide our light and we neutralize our "saltiness." But if we do so we destroy the very purpose for which we were saved. Discipleship is primarily about reaching the lost. The plan of God is to expand His kingdom in the hearts of men all over the world, and then bring in the tangible realities afterward. So we are His ambassadors and we are to spread His message worldwide (Matthew 28:19; Mark 16:15; Luke 24:47; and John 20:21).

So the command is to be bold and to not be ashamed. Don't let the negativity of the enemy steal your joy. Be proud of who you are in the Lord knowing you are (as we said earlier) ahead of your time. You are on the right side of history, and in time you will be vindicated. In time every knee will bow and every tongue will confess that Jesus Christ is Lord. But (as the song goes) the greatest treasure remains for those who humbly choose Him now! All He is really asking of us is to be who we already are: lights. He has set our hearts ablaze with the love of God. Why not do the natural thing? Why not serve our purpose? Anything less would not make sense. Hidden light is useless just as is tasteless salt. It is actually quite foolish to serve tasteless salt at the dinner table. As a matter of fact the Greek word for "losing its taste" is *moronthe*. It is where we get the word, "moron or fool." And if you think about it, it is pretty foolish to hide all your light bulbs. Having tasteless salt is like having nothing at all. Having hidden light is like having no light at all. The bottom line is, *we were made to have an impact*! That is not an inconvenience but a necessity and an honor. May the Lord quench all our fears and fill us with the confidence to stand up and be counted!

Is it fear that motivates us to hide? If so, what are we afraid of? I think we fear rejection, but that's not all. There is also the fear of contamination.

In other words, we believe "mixing it up with the world could rub off on me." In our zeal to be set apart, we can find ourselves going to the extreme of having no dealings with regular people at all. We see this all the time with religious sects—maybe certain Muslims, for example, who purposely dress differently and stay within a small circle of relationships to maintain purity. While their practice of modesty and careful attention to religious observances is certainly not wrong, it is wrong to avoid others like the plague. This was one of the conflicts that arose between Jesus and the Pharisees, who called Him the friend of sinners. But his reply was that he did not come to call the righteous but the sinners to repentance.

As much as I prefer the contemplative life, another example is monasteries. Totally shut off from the world, they cannot have the impact Jesus desires. The teaching of Jesus is to be "in the world but not of the world" (John 17:15). That is the balancing act we have to perform in this world. It is possible, however, to drift into sin, and thereby lose our saltiness that way. So the teaching is overall to avoid uselessness to the kingdom. That balance on the tightrope of usefulness can be lost on one side or the other. Either one can totally cut oneself off from the world, or on the other extreme become totally indistinguishable from the world. Either way we have lost our positive impact.

So let them see who we are without allowing them to change it. Get out there and show the world you care. Get involved in volunteer work, evangelism, community service. Eliminate the "holy huddle" on Sundays only. Stay engaged. Let them see your good works and glorify your Father in heaven. Faith without works is dead, and it deadens our witness.

Discussion Questions:

- Jesus sees you as the salt of the earth and the light of the world. How do you see yourself?
- How does the world see us?
- How can the loss of our saltiness make fools out of Christians?
- Which fear do you struggle with the most: persecution or contamination?
- What good works are you performing that others will see and glorify your heavenly Father for?
- Does the fact that we are the salt and the light mean that we are the only "Jesus" some people will ever see?

Suggested Exercises:

- Every morning when you get up remind yourself by saying in the form of an affirmation: "I am the salt of the earth; I am the light of the world. Without me the world will remain in darkness."
- Search your local paper for a community project your church could get involved in. Let your light shine in that community.
- Put together an emergency relief team that will be trained and ready to be deployed should a natural disaster strike your community.
- Volunteer for a worthy cause.

8

Honor All Scripture

Matthew 5:17-19

Do not think that I came to abolish the Law or the Prophets;
I did not come to abolish but to fulfill. For truly I say to you,
until heaven and earth pass away, not the smallest letter or stroke
shall pass from the Law until all is accomplished. Whoever then
annuls one of the least of these commandments, and teaches others
to do the same shall be called least in the kingdom of heaven; but
whoever keeps and teaches them, he shall be called great in the
kingdom of heaven.

Command of Christ: *Do not ever think* that I came to destroy the law.

The emphasis here is about the way we think. Jesus is ordering us not to
jump to the wrong conclusion about His ministry. It's true that He did
not come to condemn the world but to save it. Therefore, there is this
heavy grace emphasis to the point of getting the wrong impression about
Jesus's standards. Even the gospel of John (1:17) suggests that in contrast
to Moses and the law, Christ came to establish grace and truth. But that's
just the point. It is to establish a basis for the law to be fulfilled, not a basis
to totally eliminate it. Plus the statement includes the term "truth." Grace
and truth together place you in the center. One extreme is all grace and
then sin all you want. The other extreme is all truth and hating sinners.
We don't need just grace; we need grace and truth. The Pharisees saw Jesus
as a liberal, one who not only reached out to sinners but accepted sin.

They painted a picture of Him as being against the Law of Moses. Jesus speaks out in Matthew 5:17-19 to set the record straight.

Not only is there a need to set the record straight in first-century Israel, there is a serious need to set it straight in the modern world. Many of us are guilty of jumping to the wrong conclusion about Jesus and His message. Martin Luther for example encouraged individuals to "sin boldly," as if keeping the law didn't matter anymore. Many people today use the phrase "but that's just the Old Testament" to justify the canceling out of a doctrine that will threaten their sinful lifestyles. People today just like in Jesus's day have gotten the wrong impression. Jesus did not come to replace the Old Testament with the New Testament. The New Testament is an extension and fulfillment of the Old and does not eliminate it. The bottom line is that it is all the word of God, so we must be very careful in what changes we propose. Jesus expressly states that He did not come to destroy the law. Only that which is fulfilled by Him is no longer operational. So Jesus set the ground rules for what can be understood as a change in the way the law is carried out. So technically the law was not totally eliminated but adjusted through refinement. God's principles never change, but the way they are exercised changes.

It is the word "fulfilled" that determines the continued usefulness of any regulation. Jesus said He didn't come to abolish anything but to fulfill it. That can be understood in two ways. One aspect of fulfillment is to abide by something. Jesus is the only person to abide by or keep the law perfectly. So if it is not important, why go to all the trouble? Jesus proved the validity of the law by adhering to it in every respect. The only thing was, He did not approach tradition the same way. This fact made the religious leaders assume that He had disregard for the law. Not so—it was the tradition of men He had contempt for (Mark 7:8-9).

Another dimension of the word *fulfill* has to do with completing one's purpose. Once a piece of fruit has budded, grown, and ripened it is eaten. It can fulfill its purpose once it comes to an end in its development. That is the sense in which Jesus is picturing the law in terms of those particular aspects of it that will change. Some portions of the law will fulfill their purpose by acting as a schoolmaster for the better solutions to follow. The purpose is to produce edible fruit (salvation by grace), but the sacrificial system was the root system and the trunk that Jesus branched out of that led to that ultimate conclusion. Once it has fulfilled its purpose, then that stage of development is "finished." Now that the apple tree (for example) is grown, we don't have to focus on that aspect of the process anymore, it is over. Now we just enjoy the produce.

Hebrews shows us what Jesus already knew: that the sacrifice of His life would replace the entire sacrificial system, with all its tedious regulations. The sacrificial system held the root idea that the crucifixion completed. Physical circumcision matured into spiritual circumcision of the heart. The external reality of the temple compound was replaced by the internal reality of the human heart because now we are the temple of the Holy Spirit. The old principle lives on in a new way while the methods change. Not the smallest letter or stroke of a letter will be eliminated until all is accomplished.

Many misunderstood Jesus because He challenged their conclusions about the law. Challenging conclusions is not challenging the law. There were many ways the people of God had misconstrued scripture over time, and one of the reasons Jesus came to Earth was to correct those divergences. For example, people had gone to an extreme about seeing God primarily as a judge. Jesus kept drawing them back to the idea of "father" for God. Plus his death on the cross proved God was not "out to get us" but was willing to pay the ultimate sacrifice out of love for us. Another issue that had been blown out of proportion was the Sabbath day. Jesus was constantly healing and doing good works on the Sabbath and teaching people to back down from their harsh stance of total inactivity. He stated that the Sabbath was created for man and not man for the Sabbath. Overall He taught us to get the heart of the matter. External law sets perimeters for the heart. But if your heart is right you don't have to be concerned with boundaries, you naturally stay within the confines of love. But it is a circular argument because love is inexorably linked to action. The Ten Commandments show you what actions you will both attend to and avoid so that your love may be proven legitimate.

When Jesus made reference to the "law and the prophets," it was another way of saying the entire Old Testament. *Law* meant the first five books of the Bible and *prophets* can refer to the rest of the Bible. His statement in Matthew 5:17 is, "Do not think that I have come to abolish the law or the prophets." That is His command to them and to us. He did not come to destroy but to fulfill. He makes a towering statement to ensure we don't miss the point. He says "until heaven and earth pass away, not the smallest letter or extension of a letter shall by any means pass from the Law until everything is accomplished."

In the original Greek the term for "smallest letter" is *iota*. Iota (the lowercase i in English) can be the smallest letter in the Greek alphabet, especially when it takes the form of a *subscript* and is hardly noticeable as reduced and stationed beneath the regular sized letter. The smallest letter in Hebrew is the *yod*. The King James Version translates it *jot*. The next phrase translated "extension of a letter" comes from the Greek word *keria*. It means "little horn." But this term is often translated as "tittle." It means the small lines or projections on a letter that distinguish it from other letters. In Hebrew there are a number of letters where the *tittle* is the only thing that makes a difference between them.

If that wasn't enough Jesus goes on to say that anyone who fails to do and teach the very least of the commandments (law of God) will be the least in the kingdom. The greatest in the kingdom is an honor reserved for those who both do and teach the least of the commands (law/prophets). So the Ten Commandments, for example, are not only valuable for today but are eternally significant in the kingdom of God. It is one of the measures of our success or failure in this life! We should never downplay their significance.

So there you have it. The Old Testament (law/prophets) is permanently restored to the place of honor it deserves by the Son of God. We should not see them as separate Testaments for different times although there are some stipulations that have been eliminated over time. It is all eternal having originated from the lips of God (2 Timothy 3:16). It's best to see the whole Bible as a unit with different sections developing over time: the root; the stem; and then the branches. These are three different aspects of the same tree.

Although Jesus did not come to judge, He is saying not to purely associate him with grace alone. For the age of grace will surely be followed by judgment day. All things must be seen as a whole. Jesus said, "The words that I speak, they shall judge you in the last day." So don't get the wrong impression about me, He says. It is those who break the law who won't make it on judgment day, not the ones who keep the law. May none of us have to hear these chilling words on judgment day from our Lord in Matthew 7:23: "And then I will confess to them, I never knew you. Depart from me you who work *lawlessness*."

Jesus loves us just the way we are but too much to let us stay that way. We are not saved by good works but *for* good works. So don't get salvation and sanctification confused with one another. Jesus died not just to save us from hell but to make us holy heroes. Titus 2:14 says, "Who gave himself for us, that He might redeem us from all iniquity, and purify unto himself a peculiar people, zealous of good works."

Discussion Questions:

- How did the Pharisees characterize Jesus's ministry to the extent that Christ felt it necessary to set the record straight?
- What are the two extremes and how does Jesus represent the balanced approach?
- Explain this statement: "God's principles never change but the way they are exercised changes."
- Jesus stated that only that which was "fulfilled" would come to an end. What is one example of a certain practice that is no longer necessary because Jesus fulfilled it? Also explain how this demonstrates that the completion (fulfillment) of one stage of development leads to the beginning of another.
- What are some examples of the ways Jesus rejected their conclusions about the law without rejecting the law itself?
- What steps can you take that will show a greater respect for Old Testament law?
- The fact that not even part of a letter can be altered says what about the scriptures?
- How do we know that Jesus's statement about the narrow road leading to life means keeping the law leads to life?

Suggested Exercises:

- Reread the Old Testament with Jesus's teaching in mind. What portions of it have been fulfilled and what principles remain valid for today and eternity?
- Do research on the question of fulfilled verses unfulfilled scripture or valid versus invalid applications of Old Testament passages.
- Consider learning Hebrew to gain a greater perspective on Old Testament passages.
- Discuss among your discipleship group the value of the Old Testament as the "context" or "setting" for the New and how it is impossible to understand Jesus without it.

- Have each person in your group memorize and quote the Ten Commandments.
- Discuss current law in comparison with Old Testament law. For example, in what cases was the death penalty used as compared with how the death penalty is used today? If the Old Testament law was reinstituted would it result in more or less crime?

9

Never Overlook Anger

Matthew 5:21-26

You have heard that the ancients were told, "You shall not commit murder" and "Whoever commits murder shall be liable to the court." But I say to you that everyone who is angry with his brother shall be guilty before the court; and whoever says to his brother, "You good-for-nothing," shall be guilty before the supreme court; and whoever says, "You fool," shall be guilty enough to go into the fiery hell (Matthew 5:21-22).

Commands of Christ: *Leave* your gift in front of the altar and *go; first be reconciled* with your brother and then *come* and *offer* your gift . . . *Settle* quickly with your adversary on the way.

To fully understand the way Jesus addressed anger, one must understand the concept of the "hedge." In many instances, individuals will build a hedge around their gardens to keep passersby from trampling down the crops or flowers. In that sense they are fencing in the product they value to keep it from being violated. This was the same concept that the religious leaders of Jesus's day had about the law. They felt that the law needed protection from being trampled on by the common people. In order to accomplish this they constructed a "hedge" in the form of tradition as a deterrent. They expected the rules and regulations to keep man so preoccupied as to have no time left over for disobedience. A person's every move was anticipated. Provisions were made to prevent that move from stepping outside of God's will.

However, what was originally a noble goal in the end became nothing but self-aggrandizement. Generation after generation had piled up volumes of tradition for every conceivable circumstance. The goal became to arrive at that lofty position of rabbi so as to ensure that your proposals were added to that long list of contributors. Being a rabbi meant your disciples were forced to adhere to your doctrine. Not only that, they were expected to memorize your teachings to the letter—even to the point of including the facial expressions! Therefore the tradition itself grew to the point that it was more closely adhered to and respected than even the Word of God. Jesus exposed this extreme in Mark 7:7-23 when his disciples were chided for not washing their hands before eating.

The Pharisees were obsessed with "ritual cleanliness." They felt that the strict washings and baptisms of the priestly office in the temple should be required for the general public. Even going out to the market warranted a bath/baptism when the Pharisee returned home. Jesus accused them of making the commandments of men superior to the commandments of God. An example was the use of the word "Corban." Saying that word dedicated the item to the temple, and it could not be reversed. Even if one's elderly parents could benefit from the item, the statement of dedication to the temple could not be changed. In this way Jesus provided evidence of the way the Pharisees' system ended up violating the fifth of the Ten Commandments (to honor father and mother).

In contrast to the Pharisees' flawed "hedge," I believe Jesus offered a better way to keep people from breaking the law. He also wanted to protect the law from being violated so He offered a true "hedge." His method was to stop focusing on eliminating the external action (such as murder or adultery) and to focus instead on what leads up to that ultimate transgression. The way to stop murder is not focusing on the act of murder itself but on what actually led to that point of no return. What was the motivation and how could that premeditation have been addressed to the point that it never got that far? Jesus taught that to prevent murder (prevent representing the hedge), one must focus on anger. Likewise, to prevent adultery one must focus on lust. If you control your thoughts you will never be guilty of committing the sin that those thoughts lead to. Jesus, I believe, in essence replaced their faulty hedge with a legitimate hedge of protection against violating the law. So again, let's be careful not to look at these passages as a rejection of the law or the prophets but instead as what they are: a tremendous respect for the law so as to make every effort to avoid breaking it. Jesus is not arguing against the law of God, He is arguing about their faulty methods of keeping it.

Another common misconception about this passage is that Jesus is saying anger is the same as murder. Nothing could be further from the truth. He is saying that if you don't take your anger seriously, it will destroy you. Unlike many people today who believe all sin is the same, Jesus would beg to differ. Like David, He wishes to be free from the "secret sin" so as not to be guilty of the "great transgression" (Psalm 19:13).

In Matthew 5:21-26 he demonstrates how a smaller sin becomes a bigger and more costly sin. Nobody in his right mind would say that wishing someone was dead is the same as taking that person's life. But that is where we must begin if we never want it to go that far. Jesus advises us first to beware of "escalating profanity." The first stage of anger allows you to write the person off as an idiot by calling him *raca*, which basically means "bone-head." This contempt can escalate into malice by next referring to the individual as a "fool." Jesus suggests that harsher levels of punishment are suitable for each advanced stage of unchecked anger. The first stage of calling the person "stupid" or an "idiot" is worthy of going before the counsel or Sanhedrin. The second-stage "fool" is worthy of much harsher punishment in the flames of hell (Matthew 5:22). Calling someone a fool in that day was probably like calling them "expendable" in our day. It is when we get to the point of demonizing or dehumanizing our opponent that we thereby eliminate him from the right to exist.

Out of this context, Jesus now presents the solution in the form of five orders. The first command is to "leave [*aphes* in Greek] your gift there in front of the altar." I call that refusing to spiritualize everything. I don't just keep going through the motions in terms of my church routine when my relationships are in peril. The kingdom of God is not about attendance to rituals but relationships. When I carry around an unresolved conflict with a brother or sister I am damaging my relationship with both God and man. Plus I'm offering the anger a chance to escalate into something more dangerous. I should instead take immediate action, even if I find myself at the altar in the Temple! To obey is better than sacrifice. The second command is "go" (*hupage*). Next is "be reconciled" (*diallagethi* in Greek) with your brother. Leave the gift at the altar and be reconciled. Then come back and offer your gift. So many people do their duty on Sundays and then act like cutthroats the rest of the week. Jesus is saying you might as well not come to God's house if that's the way you want to live. He doesn't want religious people but righteous people. Once you have left your gift on the altar, have gone away, and been reconciled, then you can return for the fourth imperative, which is "offer." Now you can *offer* (*prosphere* in Greek) your gift.

The final bit of advice in controlling anger given in command form is to "settle [*isthi* in Greek] matters quickly with your adversary who is taking you to court." We tend to get upset if we are sued and sent to jail. But if it was our fault we have no right to be upset. Perhaps we owed a debt and ignored the person and our obligation. We are adding fuel to the fire of anger when we do that. We should not disregard the person we owe and feed their anger. We should take care of our obligations right away. Don't force individuals to seek legal action when you know you are in the wrong. Being stubborn can also lead to violence. On the other side of the equation, it would be better to be taken advantage of than to retaliate in court against the brother who has wronged you. Overall the message of the New Testament is that we should try to solve matters out of court as Christians. One brother should never take another to court and also shouldn't have to (1 Cor 6:5-7). Such matters can be judged within the church using Matthew 18:15-17.

So now Jesus has fully equipped us with every tool necessary for dealing with anger. Deal with it right away. Paul probably was thinking about Jesus's teaching when he said, "Don't let the sun go down on your wrath" (Ephesians 4:26). Use your escalating language as a gauge. Just like we have a gauge on the dashboard of our cars to indicate when the engine is getting too hot, we should know when our anger is heating up. Don't just go through your religious routine when there is unresolved conflict. Do everything you can to stay out of court or it could lead to uncontrolled resentment and violence or even murder. Anger is dangerous.

Discussion Questions:

- How is the "hedge" of Jesus and that of the Pharisees similar?
- How does Jesus's superior hedge prevent murder by addressing what leads up to it rather than just the act itself?
- Is Jesus saying anger is the same as murder or that it can lead to murder?
- How can you use your own escalating language as a barometer?

- What four steps are we commanded to take if we find ourselves in the middle of a religious observance and remember our brother has something against us?
- What is Jesus's advice to those who face legal action due to leaving a matter unresolved?
- What conflicts have you yet to resolve?

Suggested Exercises:

- Pinpoint any unresolved conflict in your life and settle it before Sunday. If not, solve it on Sunday instead of going to church! If in church, leave; solve it; then come back!
- If you have a matter that is under the threat of legal action make all efforts to settle out of court while there is still time.
- Share with the group next week an example of how you were angered at home, school, work, or even church and how you were able to rectify the situation before it escalated.

10

Control Your Desires

Matthew 5:27-30

You have heard that it was said, "You shall not commit adultery";
but I say to you that everyone who looks at a woman with lust for
her has already committed adultery with her in his heart. If your
right eye makes you stumble, tear it out and throw it from you;
for it is better for you to lose one of the parts of your body, that for
your whole body to be thrown into hell. If your right hand makes
you stumble, cut it off and throw it from you; for it is better for
you to lose one of the parts of your body, than for your whole body
to go into hell.

Commands of Christ: . . . *tear* it out and *throw it* from you . . . *cut* it off
and *throw it* from you.

Again, as in the previous case of focusing on anger to prevent murder,
Jesus is now focusing on lust to prevent adultery. Jesus begins by saying
that they had heard since ancient times not to commit adultery. Then
He states, "But I say . . ." It's easy to get the misconception here from the
language proposed that Jesus is saying something different. It appears as
if He said, "The law says one thing but I say another." Not so again. He
is saying all that they have been taught in the past was to avoid certain
actions. Don't steal, don't kill, and don't bear false witness. But nobody
has shown them how. He is once again demonstrating the superiority of
his hedge of *prevention* to the Pharisees hedge of *tradition*, for they have
no answer about *how* to avoid adultery. The only deterrent for them is the

death penalty. Hopefully that will dissuade individuals from becoming involved.

Jesus's method is not just heavy consequences after the fact. Instead, it is how to avoid ever arriving at the point of breaking the law in the first place. One must focus on what leads up to the crime, not just on its execution and aftermath. Jesus might very well agree with the old adage, "An ounce of prevention is worth a pound of cure." This is the prism by which Jesus's statements about the law should be evaluated. He is teaching us better ways to refrain from breaking the laws of God, not that the laws of God are to be changed. The result of surmounting gigantic mountains of tradition is not being able to see the forest for the trees. He said the Pharisees tend to "strain at the gnat and swallow the camel" (Matthew 23:24). They miss the big idea by getting lost in the details.

He states, "But I say that whosoever looks at a woman to lust after her has committed adultery with her already in his heart" (Matthew 5:28). Some people then want to jump to the conclusion that lust *is* adultery. But the statement above does not say this. It concludes that adultery has happened "in his heart." It has yet to actually occur in reality. Once again, as in the issue with murder, thinking bad thoughts about someone and taking his or her life is not equally harmful. It simply pinpoints the cause. Jesus is more likely discussing "cause and effect." The cause is not the effect and the effect is not the cause. For example, eating poorly, smoking, and not exercising is not equal to death, but it can certainly cause it over time. Yet I will not be arrested and placed behind bars on the charge of attempted homicide if I decide to visit the donut shop. It is that type of ridiculous thinking that perverts the teaching of the Master. There are actual scholars who conclude from this passage that lust is adultery, just as is the act itself. Such thinking is dangerous, especially since many men struggle with such thoughts on a regular basis. It could easily lead to the conclusion that, "Oh well, since I'm already guilty, I might as well enjoy myself." What a horrible miscarriage of justice this would be against our glorious Lord. And no doubt this is the direction the enemy would love to divert this holy teaching. He wants to turn the holy into the profane. But our Lord here, the spotless lamb, is not advocating sin but righteousness as always. He is espousing the godly philosophy of keeping individuals from their secret sins, so that they may not be guilty of the "great transgression" (Psalms 19:13).

Jesus so desperately wants to drive this message home that I believe He again resorts to the use of hyperbole. The orders issued here seem quite outrageous, and I believe it was intended to be so. He is basically saying that if you simply cannot control your eyes it would be better to get rid of them altogether. The point is not about the functions of the human body. He wants to cut off sin at its source. That is the heart of his message, and He is using this overstated speech to make that point ever so clear. The only way to cut off lust is to catch it at the beginning. It is in the area of our thoughts that sin must be addressed. Once it develops to the point of action it is too late.

It is very much like the energy you find in a black hole. As long as you keep your distance you are safe. The slightest movement toward the funnel immediately puts you on a collision course. Once you begin to feel the gravitational pull there is only a brief timespan in which reversal is possible. Within a matter of seconds you will have already reached the point of no return if you don't take action. This is the nature of sin, that once a thought is entertained the collision course is set and the individual is rapidly approaching the point of no return (James 1:14-15). This is why external efforts at sin control are useless, and this is exactly what the Pharisees were engaged in.

I believe Jesus, on the other hand, insisted the battle is within, in the heart and mind (Mark 7: 21). Plucking out the eye and cutting off the hand is another way of saying to address lust at the root level. There is no record of any Christian who took this passage literally and then followed through with blinding himself. And this is with good reason, for even if you take this literally you will undoubtedly find it easier just to deal with your heart. If you control your lustful thoughts you will never have to worry about committing the offense of adultery. This is where we must focus our energy and resources, not after the fact.

Discussion Questions:

- Does Jesus teach that breaking the law inwardly is the same as breaking the law outwardly?
- If you don't work on not breaking the law inwardly you will end up breaking the law outwardly—do you agree or disagree?
- Should the death penalty be applied for bad thoughts or bad actions?

- What one word could we use to describe Jesus's hedge of protection for the law?
- Is Jesus more interested in the addressing cause of adultery or the effect of adultery?
- What is the difference between heart adultery and actual adultery?
- What are some ways to avoid intentional lusting as men?
- What are some great ways to avoid contributing to the problem as women?

Suggested Exercises:

- Guys: Keep a log of all the times throughout the day that you had to turn your head or redirect your attention. After exercising self-control for twenty-one days share with the group the methods that seem to work and what good habits you have developed.
- Guys: Read and consider a men's study group for the book *Every Man's Battle: Winning the War on Sexual Temptation One Victory at a Time* by Stephen Arterburn.
- Ladies: Please watch *What Guys Think about Modesty* on www.godtube.com.
- Ladies: In the spirit of trying to avoid contributing to the problem, please consider the following. Keep a log for twenty-one days of how many times you had to change once you checked with your father, husband or mature male leadership about what you were wearing before stepping out the door. Share with the group what you learned overall about what type of clothing is appropriate and what is not (1 Peter 3:2-5).
- Avoid watching any TV program or buying any clothing, magazines, or books where the word "sexy" or its derivatives are repeatedly used. Make a policy to avoid all R-rated movies. Filter and monitor your PC.

11

Mean What You Say

Matthew 5:33-37

*Again you have heard that the ancients were told, You shall not
make false vows, but shall fulfill your vows to the Lord." But I say
to you, make no oath at all, either by heaven, for it is the throne
of God, or by the earth, for it is the footstool of His feet, or by
Jerusalem, for it is the city of the great King. Nor shall you make an
oath by your head, for you cannot make one hair white or black.
But let your statement be, "Yes, yes" or "No, no"; anything beyond
these is of evil.*

Commands of Christ: I say to you *not to swear* at all . . . But your word *is
to be* yes-yes; no-no.

The breaking of promises (oaths) to God was another common problem
Jesus wanted to address. Apparently an elaborate system of swearing had
developed so as to guarantee an individual was telling the truth. The
text mentions people swearing by heaven, earth, Jerusalem, and their
own heads. In Matthew 23:16 Jesus heaps contempt on the Pharisees for
assuming that swearing by the gold of the temple holds more weight than
swearing by the temple itself.

It reminds us of our own pitiful methods of proving our intentions
are good. We will say things like, "Cross my heart and hope to die." On
the other hand we believe that as long as our fingers are crossed behind
our back, we are not obligated to abide by any agreement. I've heard of
others "swearing on their mother's grave" in order to prove the validity

of their speech. Then there's the old "scout's honor" routine. All of these pathetic examples illustrate the absurdity of swearing when it would be much better to just keep your word in the first place.

No doubt this is the same level of frustration the Master experienced as He heard all kinds of outrageous statements appealed to in order to validate any claim. Since they were a religious culture and a supposed example to the rest of the world; this nonsense ended up making most of these oaths a direct insult and embarrassment to God. Just like when we place our hands on the Bible in court to demonstrate our commitment to telling the truth, they were doing similar damage toward God's temple, throne, and reputation. We won't get away with using God's name to further our own twisted agendas.

So again we are offered the protective hedge of prevention in order to cure this disease of constant swearing by this, that, or the other. Jesus once again wants to find the source of the problem and eliminate that rather than trying to manage the sin once it has broken free and is on the loose, like a wild bull escaping its fencing. The religious leaders of the day told people to honor their pledges to not offend God. But nobody was aware of the fact that making pledges was already offending God! Jesus's prevention commands are as follows: 1. Do not swear at all! 2. Let your yeses be yes and your noes be no. The Pharisees' solution was for people to keep their promises. That wasn't working. Jesus's solution was not to make any. That, on the other hand, has a 100 percent success rate. Just say yes or no and hold firmly to either commitment.

If you think about it, this really is brilliant. After all, if our word meant something, would we ever need to back it up with further evidence? This I believe is the precise area in which Jesus wants to challenge us. Again Jesus will always penetrate to the heart of the matter. We must be people who keep our word. Being that sort of person is not easy. In order to be a person of your word, you have to hold on to your side of the bargain with a pit bull-like tenacity. Whether painful or not doesn't matter; we must follow through to the end on our decisions. It's like the postal service agent who says, "Through rain, sleet, or snow." Nothing will be able to shake us loose from our commitment to our word. We must say with the Roman procurator, "What I have written, I have written."

Don't say yes until you are 100 percent sure you can abide by that. Don't say no unless you are certain it will never change into a yes. Take notice of yourself in saying yes and no. If you see that you can't abide by that, don't make the agreement to begin with. It might be better to say maybe than to say yes or no and then change your mind. For example, if a father says, "Yes, we will go fishing next weekend," he is now bound by that yes regardless of the circumstances. Therefore it may be better to say, "There is a good chance." When you RSVP for an event, you are now bound to attend. You cannot make an excuse for yourself and remain a godly disciple. A disciple of Jesus Christ is bound to his word. We are to be known as people of our word. Our yes really means yes and our no really means no. And because that is the case, we never have to swear by anything. Swearing is no longer necessary or beneficial since the truth is already evident in our spoken word. Jesus is the truth, and as His disciples we are to be people of truth whose word means something. We say what we mean and we mean what we say.

Our society is built on the fact that mankind lies. This is why so much legal documentation is required any time you make a purchase or conduct any type of business transaction. You have to give your signature over and over again, promising to fulfill the terms and conditions of whatever the agreement is. In every court of law you must take an oath. Even the president of the United States has to swear to uphold the Constitution. Nobody can basically be trusted; hence, you have prenuptial agreements among the wealthy. But the fact remains that if a person's yes meant something, none of this would be necessary! Conversely, no amount of oath taking or contract signing can guarantee the person will be true to his or her word. If there is no inner resolve to abide by one's statements, no manner of regulation will suffice.

As disciples of Jesus Christ we must rise above the ways of the world. Shining our light means we have something different to offer. We are not liars like the people of the world. We shine because we are trustworthy. If not, then we need to urgently busy ourselves with the remedy. Many Christians have fallen into a lockstep with the culture on this issue and massive repentance is desperately needed.

Discussion Questions:

- The Pharisees' solution to oath-breaking was to keep your promises in the first place. What two preventive measures did Jesus offer that would keep you from breaking promises?

- True or false: keeping your word prevents you from both making and breaking oaths.
- What questionable methods have you resorted to to prove the validity of your word?
- How will you avoid those methods in the future?

Suggested Exercises:

- In the week to follow, keep track of how many times you agree to or decline something. In other words, keep track of your yeses and nos. Report back to the group whether you were able to stick to your decisions.
- As you held firmly to your no (for example, in response to a child's request for something he or she didn't need); share how hard it was to maintain your composure and refuse to give in. If you continue to stick to your word, how do you foresee this will improve the relationship between you and your children (in terms of the way they have tried to wear you down until you give in, in the past)?
- As you held firmly to your yes (keeping a promise to go fishing even though something comes up at work, or attending the wedding even though a home emergency arises), share how hard it was to maintain the original agreement without making excuses.
- Since swearing by the Bible is still practiced in many courtrooms, think about how hard it would be for you to refuse based on your convictions of what Jesus taught. Share with the group whether you would be up to this challenge if you share that conviction. If not, provide the scriptural rationale for abiding by this courtroom policy. Are there other options for conscientious objectors?
- How about wedding ceremonies? Discuss whether an oath is appropriate there or if there should just be a legally binding agreement. What's the difference between "vow" and "oath"? Should we be more careful about the wording used in our ceremonies?

12

Respond Gracefully

Matthew 5:38-42

You have heard that it was said, "An eye for an eye, and a tooth for a tooth." But I say to you, do not resist an evil person; but whoever slaps you on your right cheek, turn the other to him also. If anyone wants to sue you and take your shirt, let him have your coat also. Whoever forces you to go one mile, go with him two. Give to him who asks of you, and do not turn away from him who wants to borrow from you.

Commands of Christ: . . . *not to resist* the evil person . . . *turn* to him also the other . . . *release* to him also the coat . . . *go* with him two. To whoever asks you—*give*.

The next law Jesus wants to build a hedge of protection around deals with retaliation. It is believed that the "eye for an eye" statute was initiated in order to prevent a person from overdoing it when taking revenge against an adversary. Again it appears that Jesus's approach is somewhat like our saying, "Better safe than sorry." The only way to make sure you never go beyond the appropriate boundaries in retaliation is to avoid retaliation altogether. It's just like the teaching on oaths. Rather than trying to keep them, it would be better to avoid them altogether. Cut off even the very possibility of violating the law by total withdrawal from any hint of impropriety.

There is something new here in this teaching. Before, the command was preventing personal negative behavior by addressing it at the root

154

level, in the heart and mind. It's about stopping it in your head before it has a chance to express itself in your life. Now, however, the stakes have expanded to include another individual. This time it is not just about dealing with your sin but the sin of another person against you. Not only do you have to deal with your own reaction but their reaction to yours. You have to try and get inside the head of the other person as well as your own. It's not enough to restrain yourself and thereby be found innocent of all charges. It's about reaching out to the offender. It's about making an impact on the sinner to the point that you increase the possibility that he or she will open up to the gospel. Isn't that what Jesus did for all of humanity? He said, "If I be lifted up, I will draw all men unto me." By doing that He was in essence abiding by this very teaching. Instead of giving us what we deserve, He gave us grace. Instead of making us pay, He paid our way. And it was that dying act of love that has won over the world.

Jesus is saying that even though the law allows for reasonable retribution, you should instead return positive treatment for negative treatment. *Through Gates of Splendor* is a 1957 bestselling book that fully illustrates this concept like none other. Elisabeth Elliot wrote this book about her missionary adventure to reach the dangerous Huaorani tribe of eastern Ecuador in South America. In the process of doing so she and her missionary friends all lost their husbands. Five men, including Elisabeth's husband, Jim, were attacked by the fierce tribe and were murdered. All they were trying to do was befriend the natives so they could share the gospel with them, but just about the time it looked like they were becoming more receptive, everything backfired on the missionaries. What is amazing about the story is the response of the widows. Instead of packing up their bags and going home (not retaliating), they decided to face their offenders to offer them grace. This act of unbelievable bravery and forgiveness (positive for negative) melted the hearts of the Huaorani tribe and won them over for the gospel. There, dramatically illustrated, is the power of this profound teaching.

So in Matthew 5:38-42, where can we pinpoint the exact orders of the Master in terms of retaliation? The imperatives are as follows: don't resist; turn to him also the other (cheek); release to him also the coat (in addition to the cloak); go with him two (miles); and give to whoever asks you. All of these commands (other than the first) refer to returning positive treatment for negative treatment.

These are just examples from the life of first-century Judaism. For example, the Roman law required assistance from any bystander to a Roman soldier for the distance of at least one mile if called upon. Jesus was saying to do even more than what is required. The Jews despised the Roman Empire for taking over their nation and making them subjects to the emperor. They longed for the day when God would deliver them from their adversaries. Yet here is Jesus asking them to treat their worst enemies with kindness. How about you? Are you ready to show grace when you are mistreated? Pray for a readiness not only to avoid retaliation but to show grace under fire. Respond gracefully. "Kill" their resistance to the gospel with kindness.

Discussion Questions:

- What does the teaching against retaliation have to do with the law stating "an eye for an eye and a tooth for a tooth"?
- How does Jesus apply his hedge of prevention to this law about getting even?
- It's one thing to refrain from vengeance but quite another altogether to return good for the evil that is perpetrated against you. How hard is that for you?
- How did going to the cross prove that Jesus was practicing what He preached about not retaliating against all of mankind but instead returning to them good for their evil?
- How did missionaries return good for evil in the book *Through Gates of Splendor*?
- How will you show grace to your adversaries and increase the possibility of winning them over to Christ?

Suggested Exercises:

- Prepare a prayer of blessing for the next person who cuts you off in traffic and use it!
- Take on the attitude of a servant toward the person who was promoted over you on the job when it should have been you who got the promotion because you were better qualified.

- Extend the time period you are required by law to pay child support even though the divorce was not your fault in the first place.
- If you are drafted into the military, extend your term of service once the opportunity to be discharged presents itself.
- Prepare a wrapped Christmas/birthday/special occasion present for your rude bus driver or coworker. Or take him out to lunch.
- Volunteer at a drug rehab center (example: a branch of the Salvation Army).
- Join a letter-writing prison ministry (for example Prison Fellowship) or an outreach.

13

Favor Foes

Matthew 5:43-48; Luke 6:27-36
You have heard that it was said, "You shall love your neighbor and hate your enemy." But I say to you, love your enemies and pray for those who persecute you, so that you may be the sons of your Father who is in heaven; for He causes His sun to rise on the evil and the good, and sends rain on the righteous and the unrighteous . . . Therefore you are to be perfect, as your heavenly Father is perfect (Matthew 5:43-48).

Commands of Christ: *Love* your enemies and *pray* for your persecutors . . . You will therefore *be perfect* as your Father . . .

The theme of responding gracefully is further illustrated here in terms of one's interaction with enemies. The law about one's neighbors is clear, which is to love them. But what about your enemies? Naturally one would assume the opposite for them. So the tradition of men that was added to the law by Pharisees and the like was to follow that statement to its logical conclusion: to hate one's enemies. Jesus, as is often the case with tradition, declares His opposition to that conclusion. It is this hatred for anyone but their own people that made the nation so exclusive and ultimately useless in terms of providing a worldwide witness.

This was not God's plan. He wanted them to be inviting and accepting. He wanted a model citizenry that would attract the rest of the world. This isolation is the very thing that ended their role as servants of God and caused Him to go with "plan B," so to speak. He ended up rejecting them and turning to the church (Mark 12:1-12). This idea that we are the elect of God and nobody else is worthy is dangerous. This is the danger of hyper-Calvinism. We too, in the church, must stay on guard against such conclusions about our own superiority over the ungodly. We must remember that God is not willing that "any" should perish, but that "all" should come to repentance (2 Peter 3:9).

The bottom line for Jesus is redemption. What approach to life is most likely to attract people into the kingdom of God? Jesus believes if we live with God's perspective, we will stay more open and receptive. God the Father displays a mature perspective in the way He handles the sinful. He is not just decent to the righteous but provides for everyone. By doing so He gives everyone the freedom to choose. If life could only be sustained by faith in God, then everyone would be forced to believe. God doesn't want to force anyone even though He could. He wants genuine converts who weigh the options and finally come to their senses about Him.

A love relationship can never be forced. True love is always a matter of choice. The option of becoming someone's husband or wife is presented and then a decision is made in the affirmative only if the feeling is mutual. That, I believe, is what the Father is looking for and He wants to position His children to perpetuate it.

There is a scripture that comes to mind that will sum this up entirely. "This is a faithful saying, and worthy of all acceptation, that Christ Jesus came into the world to save sinners" (I Timothy 1:15). It's really not about the righteous. It's about the unrighteous. And the sooner we come to realize that the better we be begin to benefit the kingdom of God. It's about expanding the kingdom. The only way that happens is by getting sinners saved.

Here is the prime method by which they are attracted. When someone reacts to them gracefully, they are astonished. When their sworn enemy, whom they have persecuted, responds with an act of love, they are frozen in their tracks and forced to examine themselves anew. In this examination they will find themselves wanting. That is the nature of repentance. Repentance is simply a change of heart and mind. Every person who becomes a child of God must go through that process of repentance (change of mind) and belief (faith). That is the only way to enter the kingdom of God (Mark 1:15).

Therefore, how is Christ specifically directing us here? His marching orders are as follows: 1. Love your enemies. 2. Pray for your persecutors. 3. Be perfect like your Father is. Keep in mind that the perfection we are called to in this passage is not necessarily referring to sinlessness. Even though that is important, the word for "perfect" in the New Testament has more to do with completion or maturity. It is *teleos* in the Greek. *Teleos* means finished, or complete. It is something that has arrived at the full stage of maturity; it is fully refined. This perspective toward sinners is not the view of the novice or the beginner. This is only the territory of the seasoned veteran of the Christian faith. It is a concept that we must mature and develop into over an extended period of time.

If you think this way it means you are fully grown in the kingdom. Only the fully developed and refined soul is now positioned and prepared to do battle for Christ. For example, you can't take a raw piece of steel to a swordfight. First it has to be given over to the flames and shaped by the hammer under red-hot temperatures. Then it is sharpened and sanded and decorated and polished. Now it is ready to adorn the Master in His battle over the enemy.

So there you have it. Christ is calling us to complete maturity. He wants a finished (perfect) product. As such we can now respond in a redemptive fashion to a sinful and hurting world. Instead of becoming part of the problem, we will now be equipped to become an integral part of His solution.

Discussion Questions:

- How did Israel's hatred for their enemies end up disqualifying them as evangelists?
- How can our desire for righteousness turn into something ugly and exclusive?
- How does the concept of perfection enter in to the equation?
- What are some particular ways you can think of to show love to your enemies?
- What prayer would you pray for your persecutors?

Suggested Exercise:

- Write out a prayer for your worst enemy and share it with the group next meeting. Have them evaluate you according to its maturity level.

14

Father the Faithless

Luke 6:27-36

Do good to those who hate you, bless those who curse you, pray for those who mistreat you . . . whoever takes away what is yours, do not demand it back . . . if you love those who love you what credit is that to you? For even the sinners love those who love them. If you do good to those who do good to you what credit is that to you? For even sinners do the same. If you lend to those from whom you expect to receive, what credit is that to you? Even sinners lend to sinners in order to receive back the same amount. But love your enemies and do good, and lend expecting nothing in return; and your reward will be great and you will be sons of the Most High; for He Himself is kind to the ungrateful and evil men. Be merciful, just as your Father is merciful.

Commands of Christ: *Do well* to those who hate you, *bless* those who curse you, *pray* for those who mistreat you . . . whatever is taken from you, *don't ask* for it back . . . *lend*, expecting nothing in return . . . *Be merciful* as your Father is merciful.

This is a continuation of the previous teaching from the perspective of Luke rather than Matthew. The scripture cited above skips around somewhat to not repeat the commands already covered in Matthew. Yet here in Luke we have a fresh list of examples that in some instances are even more demanding than what we encountered before. It lists additional ways to return positive treatment for the negative. You are ordered by Christ to

161

do the following: Do good to those that hate you; bless those who curse you; pray for those who mistreat you; don't ask back what is stolen; lend without any expectation of recompense; be merciful as is your Father in heaven. He is not asking us to do these things, He is demanding it. Why? The emphasis at the end of the message sums it up. We do all these things in an effort to take on the perspective of our Father.

He is the absolute measuring point or standard for our lives. When you really think about it you realize we actually do have a very merciful, kind, and loving heavenly Father. Jesus stated that He is kind to the ungrateful and the wicked. He is showing us by example how a seasoned person of great wisdom and maturity will react to the lost. He sees them all as His children whether good or bad and is not willing that any of them should perish.

God so loved the world (sinful man) that He gave His only begotten Son, that whosoever would believe in Him would not perish but have everlasting life. It's not about making the guilty pay because that would result in total annihilation. It's about redemption. God doesn't want to throw the baby out with the bathwater. He wants to find a way to salvage humanity and put it back on the right track. He believes we are worth saving regardless of the trouble we've gotten ourselves into.

When the "sons of thunder" were ready to wipe out the Samaritans, Jesus was quick to remind them that they were working for the wrong side (Luke 9:53-55). The Father had not sent him to destroy life but to save it. May we also catch the Father's vision and then take action.

Discussion Questions:

- In what ways is God merciful to everyone, whether good or bad?
- Why do you think that is the case?
- Are you mature enough to deal with someone's hatred toward you in a way that you can continue to function in a pleasant manner without taking it personally?

Suggested Exercises:

- Even though you know a particular coworker despises you, find something positive to say to him or her this week. Even with all his or her shortcomings, there has to be something good about this person that is undeniable.

- Prepare a positive response in writing for someone who just cursed you out! Share that short composition or one-liner with the group and if it proves to be a hit, use it the next time it happens!

- Compose a prayer for a person you know who has been treating you badly. Be sure and keep it positive, trying to see things from his or her side of the equation and from a heavenly perspective as well. Pray this prayer for him or her in your private devotion time.

- The next time you lend a friend some cash, don't allow yourself to expect that money to be returned. If it is returned, fine. If not, let that also be fine. Do not demand repayment but leave the matter in God's hands.

15

Don't Broadcast

Matthew 6:1-18

Beware of practicing your righteousness before men to be noticed by them; otherwise you have no reward with your Father who is in heaven (Matthew 6:1).

Commands of Christ: *Beware* of your righteousness . . . *don't* ever *sound* a trumpet before you . . . *don't let* the left hand know what the right hand is doing . . . When you pray *don't be* like the hypocrites . . . *enter* your innermost room and close the door . . . *pray* to your Father in secret . . . When you pray, *don't babble.*

Jesus has a lot to say about *secret devotion.* The temptation that comes with doing good deeds is to accept the admiration of others that sometimes results. Before you know it, this admiration becomes your motive for doing anything good in the first place. When you accept all the glory, you take credit for God's work in your life. We don't even do the work, God does it through us.

Plus, when you act like you are not doing it for recognition but you really are, it makes you a hypocrite. This was the thing about the Pharisees that Jesus detested. He said they do everything to be seen of men. They broadcast their piety in terms of the way they dress and pray and how they prefer to be addressed (Matthew 23). To say that rabbis were highly respected would be an understatement. Their every word and expression was memorized by their students. This was because their statements could not be written down. It was too expensive in that day to record things because they did not even have easy access to pen and paper. The hides of animals had to be dried and sewn into scrolls first before any writing material was even available. Therefore, their teaching was passed down orally. There was a huge reservoir of oral tradition that had accumulated over many generations.

Everyone likes to be well thought of, and, if a true believer, we want to be considered spiritual. So it is not just something that the Pharisees struggled with. It is just as easy for us to fall into as followers of Christ.

As such, specific steps are necessary to avoid getting caught up in this sin. Jesus gives particular examples that will eliminate the possibility of failure. He orders the following: don't sound a trumpet; don't let your left hand know what your right hand does; don't be [pray] like the hypocrites; enter your innermost room; pray secretly; and don't babble. These are all actual ways to "Beware of your righteousness, not to do it before men."

The first admonition is to not announce your giving. Jesus suggests that some would even sound a trumpet to gather as much attention as possible. It reminds me of the harvest festival I once experienced in Ghana, West Africa. On one occasion a large gathering of church folks met and each person announced how much he was going to give. Each time an offer was made the place would erupt in applause and celebration. The name of the giver and the amount pledged was broadcast over the loudspeaker. Later in a sermon I had to warn them that this custom was directly opposed to the teaching of Christ. I told them that when they celebrated, the individual who gave should really enjoy that because that would be all they would get. As Jesus said, there would be no reward for them in heaven. They have their reward now.

The next demand is that we not allow our left hand to know what our right hand is doing. This has to be a metaphor, due to the fact that "hands" do not possess the capacity for knowledge but simply respond to the impulses of the brain. I believe He is promoting more of a spontaneous approach rather than a lengthy and calculated scheme. We must not allow ourselves to premeditate on the matter and thereby be tempted to give in a way that will see to it we gain the biggest political advantage, whether that be in terms of recognition or influence.

The prayer should be likewise. One should not agonize on exactly the best thing to say beforehand and then stage a grand presentation. It should be as natural as a regular conversation, without regard to the private or public nature of it. Hypocrites (play actors in the Greek) use it as an opportunity to convince others of their spiritual superiority, which is actually proving the opposite. Prayer makes or breaks our relationship with God. It is not to be used to improve our relationship with man. So keep it between you and Him in a private fashion. Don't let anyone know about your prayer life so that your prayer life will draw you closer to God.

Keep it real and personal with God. Chants and formulas are not what we desire in our relationship with others. We want them to be themselves. God also wants that in our prayer life. Just talk with Him like you would anyone you want to have a good friendship with, keeping in mind that He is who He is: the immortal King of kings and Lord of lords.

Discussion Questions:

- How can our common desire to be thought of as spiritual interfere with our motive for doing well?
- How can you make sure your reward for giving is received in heaven?
- What does it mean to not let your left hand know what your right hand does?
- If prayer makes or breaks our relationship with God, why do we sometimes use it to improve our relationship with man?
- How do you give secretly or in a way that will not bring attention to yourself?
- How do you pray secretly or in a way that will not bring attention to yourself?

Suggested Exercises:

- Make a large donation to the church or local ministry, but do it anonymously this year.
- Consider making your regular church giving anonymous. In other words, give cash without an envelope to identify yourself so that it cannot be discovered who gave it and you won't be able to claim it on your tax returns.
- Schedule your daily prayer routine at a time that nobody will be aware of your absence. Conduct this matter in seclusion where your voice cannot be detected by others. Perhaps a local park, an

empty chapel, room or the back porch will do the trick. Discuss with the group what the challenges of this assignment might be.

- When asked to say the prayer for a special event, try not to premeditate or write out your prayer in advance. Instead, consider speaking to the Lord what comes to you at that moment when you begin to pray. Make that the guiding principle of your life.

16

Pray a Certain Way

Matthew 6:9-13; Luke 11:1-4
Therefore pray like this: Our heavenly Father, please consecrate your name. Advance your kingdom. Generate your will on earth like it is in heaven. Give us today's portion of bread. Forgive us our debts as we forgive our debtors. Never bring us into temptation, but protect us from the evil one (author's translation of Matthew 6: 9-13a).

Command of Christ: Therefore *pray like this.*

The first thing that grabs our attention is that we are expected to pray in a certain way. This again is not a suggestion; we find it here as an imperative, which makes it a command. So Christ is saying, "Pray thusly." In other words, "Pray like so." The first word in the original Greek text is *Outōs,* which means *so* or *thus.* The imperative is *pray you* or *you are to pray.* So it comes out as "Thusly you are to pray." The *you* is in second-person plural, so it goes for everybody. We find here an answer to the disciples' request about teaching them *how* to pray.

That makes this portion of scripture extremely important to our faith. Jesus doesn't leave that question unanswered; He tells us exactly what to do. He provides for us the proper mind-set for approaching God. The Lord's Prayer is possibly the richest of all spiritual goldmines. There are many hidden revelations and mysteries yet to be unraveled in this, perhaps the greatest of all the compacted treasures of wisdom in the entire Word of God. We are now on holy ground!

Having agonized over this passage for many years, I have concluded what I consider to be the best choice of words available in the English language to replace the original Greek message beneath. Too often translators don't seem to have the time to wrestle with a passage and opt out after their first impression. Sometimes the hasty solution seems to simplify matters but at the same time misses the point entirely, which is to supply one word that has the closest resemblance to the original word in each sentence. By hastily rushing through a translation, the eternal weight of glory in a passage can be diminished and even lost to an entire generation.

The key for me is to match the original word with its twin, not just something in the same family. I am not overly concerned with making it appeal to our culture. I am more concerned with maintaining the original intent or expression. I would rather struggle with the English result than lose the original intent. There, however, is the painstaking aspect of translation. How can I best replace one word with another, making it meaningful to us without losing the original meaning? Sometimes that means meditating and struggling with one word for many years until one finally comes to an epiphany. My translation above is an example of that.

Notice that each line after the first one is a call (albeit in request form) to action. Every sentence begins with an imperative. This is not a command to us but a command to the Father. However, since you cannot command a higher authority it becomes a certain kind of imperative that is more concerned with asking than telling. The terminology for that is imperative of "entreaty." That is why I added "please" to the end of the first sentence of the prayer. That softens it to the point that it makes more sense in the context presented namely: a son of man respectfully addressing his heavenly Father.

One of the first questions that might come up in learning how to pray to God is how to properly address Him. What is the best word that captures who He is without any loss of dignity? Jesus chooses a term of endearment in the word "father." So right away, we see Jesus's concern for mankind to see Himself as part of the family of God, and not just those under His legal jurisdiction. How we see Him determines how we view ourselves in this relationship. This is what Jesus seems to be emphasizing here: relationship. We are not just the distant subjects of His vast domain where He rules and reigns from afar. No, Jesus immediately dispenses with the formalities and offers us an opportunity to encounter this Majestic Patriarch in a way that is more informal and that warms the heart.

This invitation is universal. Notice the first word of the prayer and consider that it is no accident: *our*. He is not just *my* Father as I pray to Him. He is everyone's Father. Jesus is encouraging us to pray inclusively. Our prayers should not be selfish but should include our fellow man. Yet it is in the midst of His immanence that the harsh reality of His transcendence is equally before us. He is not just our Father but our heavenly Father.

Regardless of the fatherly nature of God, the fact still remains that we find ourselves down here on this Earth without Him in the tangible sense of the word. The day will come when the tabernacle of God will be with men, but so far it has not yet materialized. And this is much of the driving force of the first part of the prayer so as it seems to pulsate with the desire that this chasm between heaven and Earth be filled. In the verses to follow, specific steps are requested that would indeed lead to the accomplishment of this objective.

The next verse is typically rendered, "Hallowed be thy name." Actually, it is better translated "consecrate your name." "Hallowed be" seems to have an uncertainty about it, as if one is saying these things ought to be. That would make this statement subjunctive, but technically it is imperative, so the phrase "hallowed be" is actually better rendered "make holy." Again, it is a call to action and not a wish that certain actions would someday occur. The Greek word there for *hallowed* is the same one we get the word *saint* from. It is *hagios*. So in order to translate the sentence correctly the imperative term we choose must come first in the sentence. "Consecrate" is that one word that can best take the place of the original *hagios,* instead of the two words "make holy."

In the real world that is so infinitely removed from heaven, the fact remains that the name of God is not at all as well-known as it should be. The first request to the Father in bridging this divide between heaven and Earth is that His name would become renown throughout all the world. That we would no longer have to insist that others know Him, but that all would know Him from the least unto the greatest (Jeremiah 31:34). As it is now, only those who are the closest to Him have discovered His holy name (YHWH) and are making every effort to keep it pure. We who are the children of God have learned from the third of the Ten Commandments not to take His name in vain. Extraordinary measures have been taken to do so, even to the point of eliminating it from scripture by replacing it with the term Lord in a mistranslation that is inaccurately serving a higher purpose.

Our well-known King James translation of "Your kingdom come" is another example of trying to make an imperative sound like a subjunctive. But in doing so the bite of it is diminished, and it seems so much like a wish that something would come true. This is not the case but is instead a calling upon God to take certain actions that would bring us all together as one happy family. We are praying that the God of heaven will be reunited with His earthly children.

In order to translate the passage accurately the action must occur at the beginning of the sentence. Hence "Your will be done" is somewhat backward in word order. It would make more sense to say "Do your will" than "Your will be done." We don't normally talk like that and so it demonstrates the failed attempt of the translator to make the command into an appeal. If it was subjunctive, that approach would make more sense. For example, one could say, "Oh that your kingdom would come, oh that your will would be done." But it is not subjunctive, it is imperative. Subjunctive is a wish of what could or should or might be. Imperative is a demand for immediate action. To show that it is an imperative of entreaty it is easier just to place a "please" at the beginning of all of the imperatives: consecrate, advance, give, forgive, and bring.

So the challenge is to provide an imperative at the beginning of each sentence that best replaces the original term in the Greek. Instead of "Your kingdom come," therefore, we want the action at the front: "Come your kingdom." Therefore, *advance* is offered as a better solution. *Advance your kingdom.*

The next line is translated "Generate your will," from the previously known "Your will be done." "Do your will" is not the best word to replace the original term (*ginomai*), which means to "become," "begin," or "generate." It contains the idea of being born or coming into existence. There is a different word for *doing* (*poieō*) and that word is not presented here in the original Greek of this passage.

Asking the Lord to please advance His kingdom and generate His will is saying the same thing. When the kingdom finally comes and is fully established on Earth, then His will can come to full and complete realization. As for now He has decided to leave things up to us. He lets us decide how we will manage our own lives. Therefore, we can see the devastation of a world devoid of heavenly management. We long for the day when the Lord truly reigns, when every knee shall bow and every tongue confess that Jesus Christ is Lord. This current reality is passing away and it is not our home. Our home is with God as our Father and as the King of our hearts. We are eager for the external reality of life as we know it to catch up to the internal reality of our faith and devotion to God. So we pray with eager anticipation that the world would return to its rightful owner. In the Lord's Prayer, we pray that the distance between heaven and Earth would once and for all be completely eliminated.

We pray toward the interests of God, and if we possess those interests, for our own as well. He wants us to relocate, in a sense. He wants to bring the world back to its perfect beginning under His bountiful administration. It is a reign of ideal peace where every need is met inside and out: "Give us today's portion of bread; forgive us our debts as we forgive our debtors." It is ultimately a place where we are never brought into a tempting situation but that we are protected from the evil one.

Some people may have been mistaken when they suggested that the prayer talks about what God wants first and what we want second. After further reflection I am now convinced that this prayer is all about what God wants. It just so happens that what He wants for us includes what we need as well. Not only is He interested in advancing His kingdom but has a father's heart toward the advancement of His subjects. He does not want His subjects to be self-sufficient but to depend on Him ("give us today's portion of bread"). He wants his children to be free from the bondage of unforgiveness ("forgive us as we forgive"). He wants us free from the endless cycle and prison of our passions ("never bring us into temptation"). It is up to us to make what He wants what we want as well. It is a prayer that is asking Him to do what He is already intending to do. As such it is a statement of faith in and solidarity with the eternal plans and purposes of God.

Discussion Questions:

- Is the way we are to pray suggested or mandated by Christ?
- How does the prayer aid our theology in terms of the best way to relate to God?
- How does the fact that there is no "I," "me," or "my" in the Lord's Prayer affect us?

- What does the name of God mean and why does that make it holy?
- Why is God's kingdom and God's will the same thing?
- What does the Lord's Prayer indicate God's will for us is?
- How can we use this prayer as a moral compass?

Suggested Exercises:

- In your personal prayer time begin to use the Lord's Prayer as a meditation anchor, to keep you focused on God's will. Next week, report back to the group how this improves your prayer hour.
- Report back to the group how using this prayer as a meditation anchor (keeping focused) guides you in your relationship with others.
- Report how the prayer helps you stay on target rather than getting distracted by the negative thoughts that are initiated by the enemy.

SECTION TWO:
Spiritual Toddler

17

Fast Privately

Matthew 6:16-18

Whenever you fast, do not put on a gloomy face as the hypocrites do, for they neglect their appearance so that they will be noticed by men when they are fasting. Truly I say to you, they have their reward in full. But you when you fast, anoint your head and wash your face so that your fasting will not be noticed by men, but by your Father who is in secret; and your Father who sees what is done in secret will reward you.

Commands of Christ: *Don't be* like the sad-faced hypocrites . . . *anoint* your head . . . *wash* your face.

When the hypocrites (Pharisees) fast, everybody knows it. They walk around looking depressed (downcast, disfiguring their faces). It's like a Hollywood actor who goes to every extreme to accurately portray a certain character. It's no wonder since the word *hypocrite* means "play actor" in the Greek. They probably don't even bathe to make themselves even more convincing in the role of a pious devotee.

That's not the right motive for fasting. It is a private matter between you and God. Your reward from God comes only when others are not aware of your spirituality. Notifying them results in a bit of admiration on the behalf of the public, but true spirituality is private; nobody should be aware of it. True devotion is done in privacy.

Of course God wants us to be more spiritual, and fasting is certainly not usually pleasurable to the body. But just like prayer, fasting can bring you the attention of others, and before you know it you're doing it to be noticed. We have to continually examine our motives with Christ. It is not enough to complete the act. It must be completed in sincerity to be legitimate. Attitude is the key factor with the Lord. Just look at the eight Beatitudes if you doubt that; the first and perhaps foremost of them is to be poor in spirit. That is a person who is meek and lowly and would therefore never think of broadcasting his or her spiritual efforts.

So what are the directives here? What actions are we commanded to take? They are uncovered in the imperatives that are listed here: 1. *don't be* like the hypocrites (the original Greek of the passage is not "don't put on a gloomy face" but "don't be like the sad-faced hypocrites"); 2. *Anoint your head;* and 3. *Wash your face.* In other words, carry on as you normally would with no indication that you are denying yourself in any way. Be cheerful, clean, neat, and appealing when you fast. This will ensure your reward from the Lord, rather than the reward that comes from the admiration of your fellow man. Keep it under the radar in order to prevent your neighbor from furnishing your reward because one reward will eliminate the other. Sometimes that can be tricky. You have to really be creative to avoid detection in terms of missing meals. Think that over and plan it out in a way that will be almost foolproof for the next time you fast. Now is the time to work out the details. You can reduce the risk of exposure by planning beforehand as you make sure you do things (fasting) in a way that pleases the Lord as His disciple.

Discussion Questions:

- What is there to lose by openly moaning and groaning about your fasting experience?
- What is there to gain from doing so?
- What is there to gain by fasting secretly?
- How hard is it to be a genuine believer with pure motives?

Suggested Exercises:

- Complete a happy fast! Pick a day to refrain from eating due to a spiritual need that may arise. Make sure that during your fast you avoid the following: 1. no hanging your head or frowning; 2. avoid allowing your personal hygiene, dress, and appearance to lapse; and 3. don't let anyone know about it (keep it between you and the Lord).

18

Don't Hoard

Matthew 6:19-24; Luke 12:33-34

Do not store up for yourselves treasures on earth, where moth and rust destroy, and where thieves break in and steal. But store up for yourselves treasures in heaven, where neither moth nor rust destroys, and where thieves do not break in or steal; for where your treasure is, there your heart will be also (Matthew 6:19-21).

Commands of Christ: *Do not treasure* to yourselves *treasures* on Earth . . . But *treasure* to yourselves treasure in heaven . . .

What do you consider life's greatest treasure? Many focus on possessions in our affluent society. But the problem is always the duration of that value. They say that once you drive a new car off the lot the value depreciates significantly (about 20 percent per year). So when you place all your value on those things, it is only a matter of time before you are sorely disappointed. But just think about eternity and you can multiply that disappointment exponentially. Jesus wants our entire approach to life to be revolutionized. The inward focus of "me and mine" must give way to an outward focus toward the needs of others. "Every man for himself" must become every man for every man.

Withholding leads to poverty in God's economy. But generosity leads to permanent wealth. If everybody gives, then the windows of heaven will be open and the blessings will pour down upon the earth. But when we close our hearts to one another the windows of heaven are closed. Give and it will be given to you, pressed down, shaken together, and running over (Luke 6:38). Worldwide poverty is the evidence that we as a human race have failed in that overall heavenly objective that nobody will lack anything they need.

So Jesus is calling us not to be part of the problem but to be part of His solution. When you go with God, you are also increasing your "eternal bank account." Eternal capital never loses its value. It is the treasure above all earthly treasure providing eternal dividends. Earthly treasure is nontransferable. However much you produce is precisely the amount you will be separated from at death. What matters is what will last. Therefore, personal earthly embellishments don't really matter. It's about how you can use that surplus in alleviating the suffering of those who are less fortunate. When you do that you have just gained the heavenly currency that you can take with you.

For example, there is a ministry called Living Water. They supply clean water to third-world countries. They dig wells and maintain them for underdeveloped areas around the world. It is believed that this simple solution will prevent a multitude of disease issues that arise because there is no sanitized water supply available. Clean water is something we take for granted but something others see as a luxury. By supporting organizations such as Living Water, one can be sure he will enter heaven with a warm welcome. But if a person decides to keep everything for himself, he will wind up as a fool having nothing to show for his brief, self-centered existence on Earth.

What you do with your resources shows where your heart is. Where your treasure is, there will also be your heart. Our heart does not belong to our possessions but to the Lord. Otherwise, why do we spend so much energy on chasing what has been called the "American Dream"? Other than our unbiblical fixation with feminism; why do we send mothers out of the home and into the workforce? Is it not for one reason and one reason only, that we may raise our "standard of living"? That should not be the number-one objective of the believer, and it shows that most believers in this country are fooling themselves. You can't serve God and mammon (material greed) at the same time, and that is exactly what the majority of us are trying to do.

I remember one time in a church service it was suggested that we "lower" our standard of living so as to have more resources available to provide for the needs of the poor. That was so rare a message that I'm sure the congregation was horrified by it and I've never heard anything like it since. Materialism is what we have bought into for the most part and it is our idol today. That is why the most important political topic around is always the economy. One of our former presidents tapped into that popular sentiment to get elected when he stated in opposition to family values that, "It's about the economy, stupid."

The urge to withhold resources and close oneself off from a needy world is illustrated in Jesus's parable about the eye. He said that if your eye is evil, then your whole body is full of darkness. An examination of the design of the eyeball shows this to be true. As we know, the aperture of the eye opens and closes to allow more or less light in, thereby illuminating our pathway. However, if the aperture were to tighten down, then no light whatsoever could come into our body and our sight would be lost. In this way the meaning of the parable becomes understandable. Tightening your grip on your possessions is analogous to a defective eye whose lens is no longer operational but is jammed shut. Likewise, you give someone the "evil eye" when you are envious of what they have. "Evil eye" in Jesus's day was just like saying in our day that someone was "green with envy." But when you keep an open heart toward others, you remain generous and giving in the spirit of Christ our Savior. The Pharisees were blind in this way. They were greedy, jealous, and selfish hoarders. On the other hand, we have Jesus, who gave, gave, and gave until there was literally nothing left to give.

Jesus never pursued wealth but totally entrusted his sustenance into the hands of God and attended to His will exclusively. He gave up his trade and the income it provided to live completely by faith. He was totally disinterested in the very thing we build our lives around: the economy. His cleansing of the temple showed his utter contempt for profitmaking ventures in the sanctuary. He focused on a higher ambition; that being the economy of the kingdom. He taught that it was the Father's duty and good pleasure to provide, not the individual's duty to solely provide for himself. He told the rich to give everything away to the poor and follow him.

Some in history have responded to that very wish, thereby ensuring an unspeakable eternal reward. Saint Anthony, for example, took Jesus's words to the rich young ruler literally: *If you want to be perfect, go, sell what you have and give to the poor, and you will have treasures in heaven; and come, follow Me (Matthew 19:21)."* He did just that; and became the father of monasticism in the process. Few have the courage to step out

181

in the same way Jesus did. Saint Francis is another one who forsook his wealth for the cause of Christ. It is said that he gave up even the clothes on his body, thereby leaving himself naked before the general public. Once a brown blanket was thrown over him as a covering it became his only cherished garment.

Throughout early Christian history the pursuit of wealth was frowned upon and instead it was the pooling of resources that was encouraged as occurred in the book of Acts. Today we are so far removed from that. It is more accurate to see the situation we are in now as "every man for himself!" We have so far removed ourselves from the tenets of our founder so as to barely be recognized as Christians anymore. Our lives show little to no difference from our unbelieving counterparts. Our dirty little secret is that what we do with our resources is what defines us.

So let's examine our lives and make the proper adjustment that would more firmly place us into that category that distinguishes us as one of Jesus's true disciples. If we are not handling our money correctly, then we are not operating as a disciple of Jesus. How should a disciple better manage his resources?

The question is, basically, what do we trust in? Do we trust in our career and paychecks, or in the Lord to provide? Are we giving everything away in faith or are we keeping it all out of fear? Do we hold on to everything too tightly or do we let it go? Do we constantly worry and fret over money or do we release it all into the hands of the Lord in an attitude of contentment? Do we celebrate the advancement of others or do we resent that we were not advanced?

Discussion Questions:

- How will earthly treasure prove to fail you in the end, both in this life and the next?
- How does one begin to treasure heavenly treasure?
- In God's economy, what are the results of withholding versus generosity both now and throughout eternity?
- How does Jesus's illustration of the malfunctioning eyeball demonstrate how a miserly, withholding, and condemning person will end up?
- Name some saintly individuals who surrendered everything they owned.

- How about Jesus? Didn't he essentially surrender everything?
- In what way can we reorder our lives to better reflect Jesus's philosophy?
- Knowing the most we can do, what is the least we can do to store up eternal treasure?

Suggested Exercises:

- At the fork in the road of your career choose the less profitable and more kingdom—centered path unless the other path ends up in philanthropy.
- Consider allowing your wife to stay home or at least work less in order to have more time with the children. Discuss the price that will be paid in choosing wealth over posterity. If there are no children discuss the value of having the wife stay home to manage the household well, rather than going out and jumping into the rat race with the husband just so you can have more things (Titus 2:4).
- Consider downsizing your lifestyle in order to have more resources to give to the less fortunate. Do you really need that many houses and cars? Discuss among the group members what it would take to scale down.
- Volunteer regularly for a disaster relief (Red Cross) or hunger relief organization (Feed the Children). Volunteer with Habitat for Humanity. Open up to the possibility of allowing the volunteering to develop into a career objective. These are all examples of storing up treasure in heaven.

19

Don't Worry

Matthew 6:25-34

For this reason I say to you, do not be worried about your life, as to what you will eat or what you will drink; nor for your body, as to what you will put on. Is not life more than food, and the body more than clothing? (Matthew 6:25)

Commands of Christ: *Stop stressing* about your life . . . *Look* at the birds . . . *Consider* the lilies . . . *Seek* first the kingdom.

Jesus commands his disciples to stop worrying about their lives (basic needs). Then He follows that with another list of imperatives that will aid in the process. How do you stop? Well, you look at the birds; consider the lilies; and seek the kingdom first. The command is not so much about ceasing anxiety in general as it is about missing the whole point of life. It is about asking yourself what your primary concern is and how it matches up with eternity. Is that all that life is about, food and clothing? It is certainly not. Jesus said, "For a man's life consists not in the abundance of things which he possesses" (Luke 12:15).

Instead of focusing all our efforts on our own needs, we need to be about the Father's business. We need to be asking ourselves, "What does the Father need?" This brings us to the heavenly guarantee. That's right, there is one! We are guaranteed that if we take care of His concerns He in turn will take care of our concerns. So we have two choices. Either we can worry about our own provision without any help from God, or we can turn our attention to providing what God wants with His help! He will let us take care of ourselves if that's what we want. But why not attend to the Father's business since our provision will then be automatically guaranteed? Why worry about something when you don't have to? This is the offer of our beloved heavenly Father.

Jesus is basically saying, "Look, it's what the Father does!" He takes care of creation and you just happen to be part of it. The birds, the flowers, the people—all part of God's establishment (that He naturally provides for). But should we be led astray into thinking we are on our own, we will find ourselves victims of our own errant philosophy. We are the part of the creation that has been afforded the extra gift of a rational mind, will, and emotions. We should not allow this to talk us out of our own security. God is not kicking us out of the house to make it on our own. We only leave His provision and shelter because we choose that path of independence. The message is to always come back home to the Father and stop living like a refugee.

We've got bigger fish to fry—as the expression goes. So stop fussing and fretting over the small stuff. Free yourself from the rat race so you can reenter the human race as an ambassador for the kingdom of God. Don't be overly occupied with the superficial so you can stay in touch with the supernatural. Souls are weighing in the balance and you could be the person to tip the scale in a heavenly direction. The kingdom of God must be expanded through the salvation of lost humanity. The Father wants His kids back on two levels. The first is turning them back around from serving themselves to serving Him. Secondly is in the adoption of those who have yet to experience His love. Seeking first the kingdom of God (Matthew 6:33) is seeking first the will of God. Turning over your will and surrendering to His is what it takes to experience salvation. Seeking first His righteousness means the same thing. It means that instead of relying on what you can do to earn your salvation; you accept what Jesus did to earn your salvation. It is not our righteousness but His that saves us.

Discussion Questions:

- Is this lesson about not being concerned or not being concerned about the wrong things?
- How does our independent spirit tend to lead to anxiety?
- Will God let us take care of ourselves if that's what we want?

- What needs to change so you can stop worrying about your basic necessities and start focusing on God's priorities?
- What's the difference between our kingdom and His? What do we want and what does He want? If we focus on His needs will He focus on our needs?
- What does it mean to seek the kingdom of God and His righteousness first?

Suggested Exercises:

- He said consider the birds and the lilies in terms of their effortless existence. We are to study how they are well provided for in the course of nature without earning it. Have two individuals pick one each of the two categories and do research on it. Report back to the group what you find by next week.
- Make a list of the usual things you tend to worry about during the week. Share that with the group at the next gathering. Allow each group member to do the same and then bring it to the Lord in prayer.
- Share testimonies as to how you are able to lay your burdens down on a regular basis. What methods seem to work for you? How can a person learn to let go?
- Make a list of what needs to change in your life to make God's will your number-one priority. God's will basically consists of your salvation and the salvation of others (plus discipleship). Share your findings with the group at the next meeting.

20

Don't Criticize

Matthew 7:1-5; Luke 6:37-42

Do not judge so that you will not be judged. For in the way you judge, you will be judged; and by your standard of measure, it will be measured to you. Why do you look at the speck that is in your brother's eye, but do not notice the log that is in your own eye? Or how can you say to your brother, "Let me take the speck out of your eye", and behold, the log is in your own eye? You hypocrite, first take the log out of your own eye, and then you will see clearly to take the speck out of your brother's eye (Matthew 7:1-5).

Commands of Christ: *Do not judge* in order not to be judged . . . first *remove* the beam from your own eye.

This statement by Matthew Henry sums it up: "Commonly none are more censured than those who are most censorious . . ." Here in this passage Jesus is unlocking one of the great mysteries of earthly existence. It is the law of nature I like to refer to as *reciprocity*. Basically it means in a wide variety of circumstances that you will reap what you sow; not in the same amount but exponentially. One seed planted will eventually lead to hundreds of seeds harvested. Jesus is telling us that you don't just refrain from judging just because it is harmful to the individual recipient. You refrain from judging because that same censorship will return back to you, and on a much grander scale than what you initially deposited.

I have worked with inner city homeless men for almost twelve years now. It may not be a well-known fact, but I speak from experience when

I say that men finding themselves in bondage, such as drug addiction or homelessness, seem to have one thing in common. You can't get them to stop complaining. They tend to have a very critical spirit, which leads them to the desire to escape what they see as the harsh realities of life through substance abuse. My contention is that it is not the substance that has them bound but their own attitude. By planting the seeds of bondage they themselves end up bound without measure. They receive back on themselves the contempt they heap all throughout the day on others. I often teach them that if they could ever just stop the judging they could effectively attack the root of their own imprisonment. But as it is, their addiction seems as if it were a mountain that can never be climbed due to that thick hairy root of fault finding that holds them fast to the ground like a tree trunk. Jesus is teaching mankind that by judging, we become our own worst enemy.

He provides a universal principle even more remarkable than Albert Einstein's $E=mc^2$. He is opening us up to the unlimited powers of the universe in this passage. He is showing us that we have the power to make or break our futures by making sure we have all the forces of nature behind us. The formula I have uncovered after carefully studying this passage seems to indicate the following pattern: Giving = Receiving the Same Exponentially or simply $G=RS^X$. It is all about filling in the blanks with positive seed (thoughts and actions). There is positive seed and negative seed and both are guaranteed to multiply and return. The key is to get things going in a positive direction where the good things, such as friendship and favor return to your life rather than contempt and harm. It is automatic. Whatever you give out whether it is in thought or in action will multiply and return to you.

Jesus is warning us about the power of our own choices to potentially destroy our lives. We tend to rush to judgment before getting the facts straight. But if we knew how that would unleash all the powers of hell against us we would do everything in our power to withhold our tendency to prejudge. We have to learn to pull in the reins on our passions, gaining control of our negative thoughts before they have a chance to gain momentum. Every effort is worth it to prevent us from digging our own graves. The future of our lives is in our own hands. I cannot overstate the importance of this groundbreaking insight by our Lord Jesus Christ.

He commands us to stop before it is too late. Once the thought is planted, it is over. It will reproduce and will fall upon us and keep us in bondage. He says "Don't judge in order not to be judged." In the Greek, the emphasis of how that same seed you plant develops and multiplies and returns upon you is unmistakably dramatized in the repeating of the same word all the way through. A literal word for word translation of what Jesus said goes like this: "With the judgment you judge you will be judged."

But some would think that is an impossible dream, asking, how can we stop judging? We must after all judge between right and wrong. The problem is we don't have all the information about them the way we do about ourselves. So we should turn it around on ourselves since we do know ourselves: "Take first out of your own eye the beam." Plus, if we judge ourselves, others will judge themselves. But if we judge them, they will judge us. It could make the difference between election and nonelection; promotion or demotion; favor or disfavor; winning or losing. Everything we give out does return with a vengeance! Woe to those who fail to watch themselves in this area.

Discussion Questions:

- How does finding fault with others hurt me more than them?
- How does finding fault with myself rather than others help me?
- How does Jesus's revolutionary formula $G=RS^X$ uncover the secrets of exponential success and exponential failure as well as the power to control those forces?
- To come to the proper conclusion about anyone's shortcomings you need all the facts. Who is the only person you always know everything about?

Suggested Exercises:

- Keep a mental log all next week about how many times you were critical of anyone, whether on TV or the radio or just in your daily interactions with coworkers.
- Share with the group in the next meeting how you were able to overcome those tendencies to judge prematurely. What methods did you use to withhold criticism?
- What did you tell yourself when you were about to conclude something negative?

21

Invest the Positive

Luke 6:37-42

Do not condemn and you will not be condemned; pardon and you will be pardoned. Give and it will be given to you. They will pour into your lap a good measure—pressed down, shaken together, and running over. For by your standard of measure it will be measured to you in return (Luke 37b-38).

Commands of Christ: *Do not condemn* and you will not be condemned; *forgive*, and you will be forgiven (released). *Give* and it will be given to you [exponentially].

Thankfully the principle works both ways. So it is not just mandatory to stop the negative but to start the positive. When you do that the good seed will also multiply and return. Now instead of failure and bondage, success and victory are on the way! It is all up to you what you choose to invest. If you invest poorly your dividends will be very poor. If you invest well your dividends will turn out very well. If you don't invest at all you will receive neither positive nor negative dividends.

So if you find that life really seems to be treating you unfairly, I would advise going back to the investment principle. Ask yourself, "What exactly am I entering into the system and is it positive or negative?" You will most likely find that you are reaping what you have sown. You are receiving back in a greater measure whatever it is you initially invested. We usually tend to blame someone else for our failures, but doing so only ensures those failures will continue. On the contrary, if you will retrace your own steps you might find the actual culprit is the one facing you in the mirror.

Above in Luke 6:37-42 Jesus contrasts this for us by commanding, "Don't condemn and you won't be condemned." On the other hand he states in the next verse, "Forgive and you will be forgiven; give and it will be given to you pressed down, shaken together and running over . . ." He is providing for us great ideas for investments that are guaranteed to multiply and return the positive rather than the negative. A lot of us are full of negativity, yet at the same time we wonder why our lives are so miserable. It is in large part because we are unaware of this universal principle and natural law that Jesus has disclosed to mankind. He wants to help us get our lives going in a positive direction so He explains what the problem is and how to solve it.

Notice the formula $G=RS^X$ (giving equals receiving the same exponentially) and the empty blanks _____ = _____^{X}. Now it is up to you to start the system working for you. Ask yourself what you really need in your life and then begin to invest that very thing into the lives of others. The blanks are empty now, but everything changes once you begin to fill those with positive investments. Stop the condemning, criticizing, and fault finding. Start encouraging, uplifting, and forgiving. Then you will find in time that others are more encouraging, uplifting, and forgiving toward you, and your life will begin to be set free from the former bondage of your poor decisions. You get a lot of whatever you give, so give well.

Discussion Questions:

- Since output is inexorably linked to input, how important is it to invest positive thoughts and actions into your life?
- Is it possible that when life is treating you badly you are actually the one to blame? Why is that often the case?
- Share some negative thoughts or actions you need to stop practicing so that those negative thoughts and actions won't come back to haunt you. Are you faithless, disrespectful, judgmental, unfriendly, uncaring, or stingy? Take an inventory.
- Share some needs you have in your life that you can expect to receive in abundant supply once you start investing those positive

things into the lives of others. Faithfulness? Respect? Friendship? Acceptance? Compassion? Financial aid? What is it you need?

Suggested Exercises:

- Decide what you need the most and then start investing that in others on a regular basis. For example, are you lonely? Need a friend? Start being friendly to those around you and keep track of the results. Make sure it becomes part of your daily routine and not just a onetime incident; that will only arouse suspicion. Over the weeks and months to follow share the results with the group.
- Do the same thing with your finances if you have a problem there.
- If nobody listens to you, practice listening to them better.
- If no one submits to your authority, check the way you are submitting to your authorities and make changes in your behavior on a daily basis. Keep track and share the results.
- Perhaps there is something you need that isn't mentioned above. Whatever it is (within reason), start investing to see results.

22

Be Persistent and Optimistic

Matthew 7:7-11; Luke 11:9-13

Ask, and it will be given to you; seek, and you will find; knock, and it will be opened to you. For everyone who asks receives, and he who seeks finds, and to him who knocks it will be opened. Or what man is there among you who, when his son asks for a loaf, will give him a stone? Or if he asks for a fish, he will not give him a snake, will he? If you then, being evil, know how to give good gifts to your children, how much more will your Father who is in heaven give what is good to those who ask Him! (Matthew 7:7-11)

Commands of Christ: *Ask,* and you shall receive; *seek,* and you will find; *knock* and it will be opened to you.

This command is fairly straightforward and therefore easy to comprehend. The context is prayer to God regarding something needed. Here it is the resolve in which the matter is approached that is considered. Do you just ask once and give up? Notice your kids. Don't they keep asking until they get an answer? So it is acceptable to remain God's child in our interaction with Him. Successful prayer requires a good amount of persistence and optimism according to Christ.

First is the idea of determination. You show that by continuing to ask even though nothing has transpired. Jesus emphasizes this by repetition and by the use of the present active imperative in the original Greek. The command is given in three different verb forms, which are basically identical in purpose. This is known as "parallelism." Rather than rhyming for emphasis, they repeat the same idea in a different way. Usually the emphasis is double but here it is triple. *Ask* and you shall receive; *seek,* and you will find; *knock* and it shall be opened to you. All three imperatives contain the idea of pursuing what you need from God. So why keep repeating the same idea unless you intend to suggest that persistence is necessary? The fact that they are found in the present active imperative further promotes the idea of continuing to visit the matter until it is resolved.

And why is there this thrust toward determination in our relationship with God? I believe it is the same thing our children sense in us. They will not address an individual who is not favorable toward them. But since they know we are in favor of them, they are optimistic about their chances of getting what they desire. Why is it that "everyone who asks receives"? This is a message not about how to get what you want but how gracious and loving is our heavenly Father. The saying is divided into three sections. First is the command of what to do (Matthew 7:7; Luke 11:9). Second is the assurance that you will receive (Matthew 7:8; Luke 11:10). Third is the reason you will receive: the goodness of God (Matthew 7:9-11; Luke 11:11-13). Taken together the majority of the teaching is about the goodness of God.

We must believe in His goodness for any of this to work out. So the first area to look at in successful prayer is our faith. Do we really believe in our Father's loving disposition toward us and willingness to help or do we think like orphans? That will determine everything, hence the emphasis on that crucial predisposition by Jesus.

My stepson is six years old and doesn't understand about money and how hard it is to earn. When he sees something he likes he says to us, "I want to buy that." It is as if he truly believes that "everyone who asks receives, and he who seeks finds and to him who knocks it will be opened." After all, as far as his experience tells him up to now, life is easy. When I need something, I go to my parents and get it.

I believe that is exactly the type of childlike faith the Father is looking for in us. The child does not think, *Yes, I really would like that so I will have to work, save, and maybe, if nothing else interferes I will purchase that one day.* Our needs are not earned independently from God, they are lovingly provided by God's grace.

God is willing to maintain the world He has created, and we are part of that mechanism. When we get too independent from God we suffer the consequences. He will allow us to live according to the way we believe. Do you believe everything is solely within your own power to obtain or not? Or do you believe you can rely on God? Before you can ask, seek, and knock, you have to answer that question.

Discussion Questions:

- Would you consider your faith more childlike or adult-like? Why?
- When you ask the Lord for something do you persist or only ask once? How many times do you ask, seek, and knock before finally giving up?
- Do you believe it is all up to you to provide for yourself or do you believe God wants to be involved in every need that arises?
- Do you see God more as a benevolent, heavenly Father or a demanding, distant deity?

Suggested Exercises:

- Write a list of things you really need help with right now in terms of provision.
  Include those items in your daily prayers until an answer of some sort presents itself.
- Share this experience with your group in terms of how challenging and rewarding it was. How was your faith tested and stretched? How did God communicate His answer back to you? How long did it take? Weeks? Months? Years?

23

Treat Others as You Want to Be Treated

Matthew 7:12; Luke 6:31

In everything, therefore, treat people the same way you want them to treat you, for this is the Law and the Prophets (Matthew 7:12).

Command of Christ: All things therefore that you want man to do for you, so also *do for them.*

If you want things simplified and streamlined Jesus is your man. He is known for his pithy statements that are brief yet infinitely profound and thought-provoking. This command is one of those jewels. It says so little yet says so much, just like a wise sage would prefer.

At another time we see that Jesus had whittled everything down to two commands: love of neighbor as yourself and unreserved love of God (Matthew 22:40). But here it is condensed even further into only one duty. This one action will do for you what all of the other 614 regulations and obligations of the Old Testament law purport to do.

It is fascinating that this maxim doesn't seem to include one's treatment of the heavenly Father. Perhaps it is the case that by treating others well, it so pleases the Father as to be seen as also treating Him well. It has been said that this teaching sums up what it is indeed to be a disciple, and I don't doubt the validity of that conclusion.

Everyone knows how they expect to be treated, and I daresay this treatment is beyond the minimum requirement. Yet this is indeed what is necessary to correctly carry out the objective. If we are to treat others as we want to be treated, we must first determine exactly what that is. What treatment do we expect from others? After we nail that down, we can proceed to the second step: treating them the same way.

Do you want to be criticized behind your back? No? Then that's the first place to begin. Refrain from doing it to someone else because you wouldn't like it. Have you ever heard someone say, "How would you like it if I did that to you?" It is as if it never crosses our mind to be considerate. But this is what discipleship is all about: consideration.

We cannot afford to operate in a kneejerk-reaction mode. We have to consider beforehand not only how we should respond but how we should initiate kindness to begin with. Rather than being positively passive we should be positively proactive. This way we can create our own constructive environment. If we treat others the way we want to be treated (positive seed), they will in turn treat us the way they want to be treated (positive harvest), generally speaking.

In order to become a true disciple, one's faith must be followed up by works. Faith without works is dead, and so is discipleship. Therefore, determine in your heart how you will carry through on your commitment to Christ's command here. Perhaps the way to start is to remember a time you were mistreated. Then find someone in that same circumstance and treat him or her positively. For example, one of my pet peeves is when I'm talking and the person turns and walks away or his eyes glaze over. In other words, he is not really listening. Or when he interrupts before I finish my sentence. Therefore, I will make it my duty to listen carefully to anyone who is addressing me, giving him my undivided attention and not responding until he is finished with his thought or point. These virtues have to be practiced in order for them to make any difference in our lives. Let's get to work.

Discussion Questions:

- How is it possible to keep every commandment in the whole Bible by just keeping one?
- How does moving from more than six hundred obligations to just having one simple objective encourage you and keep you from giving up?
- Do you feel energized and motivated enough now to give it a shot? Was this Jesus's intention?

- Why does being considerate in a proactive manner tend to create a positive environment for you?

Suggested Exercises:

- Determine one way in particular that you want to be treated on a specific issue. For example, I want people to be more friendly and inviting.
- This week make it a point of treating someone else in the exact manner you specified above that you want him to treat you. Report back to the group your experience.
- Imagine that you were in the role of supervisor instead of the person who is over you. Consider how you would want to be treated if you held that position. Begin to act on that new revelation this week and report back to the group your findings. Or if you are the supervisor, imagine what it would be like to be the person under you on the corporate ladder. How would you want to be treated as such?
- Before you cut in at the front of the long line of traffic, imagine how the people at the back feel who have waited patiently all this time as they should.
- Remember how you felt when you were in a foreign country and didn't know the language. Didn't you feel helpless? Consider the fact that there are many in this country suffering from this same condition. They need patience and a helping hand. Be ready to lend a hand, and even offer help without being asked.
- What types of tragedies have you been through? Floods? Fires? Tornados? Wouldn't it have been great to receive disaster relief? Plan your next vacation as an outreach to whatever part of the country is experiencing a natural disaster.

24

Choose the Path of Greatest Resistance

Matthew 7:13-14; Luke 13:24-30

Enter through the narrow gate; for the gate is wide and the way is broad that leads to destruction, and there are many who enter through it. For the gate is small and the way is narrow that leads to life, and there are few who find it (Matthew 7:13-14).

Command of Christ: *Enter* through the narrow gate.

Here we have another concise statement from Jesus that sums up the whole of Christian experience and lifestyle. It is basically a matter of swimming upstream. The tendency for us all is to take the path of least resistance, but Jesus is ordering us into the path of the greatest resistance. He Himself went down that road and it was arduous. He is not painting a pretty picture for us. He is telling us up front that association with Him could be hazardous.

The gospel is countercultural. It demands sacrifice, self-restraint, and perseverance. These are not popular concepts. The easy way is living for pleasure and being self-absorbed. Eternal life is the reward for a life of sacrifice according to Jesus. On the other hand, eternal damnation will go to the rest. He said there will be very few who will make it through. It is a fact that there are very few who are willing to sacrifice their kingdom for the Lord's.

When you stand up for the truth you often find yourself opposed to everything around you. Your home, church, city, and nation may be headed in one direction while you are going in another. It's hard to stay focused when you are called a lunatic and a fanatic for simply standing up for what is right rather than the traditional method.

It is a true story that the doctor who insisted on washing his hands before and after surgery was ridiculed and ostracized to the point of being accused of losing his mind. Yet this is now standard procedure for surgeons. We, like the prophets, are called to stand up under persecution and continue to proclaim the truth regardless. Blessed are those who are persecuted for righteousness's sake, for theirs is the kingdom of heaven.

When you call a friend or loved one out of the world you are calling him or her into a stricter observance of scripture and a reining in of passions. Only then can we become a vessel of honor worthy of the Master's use. Instead of being the master of your own destiny, you have now placed your life in the hands of God and are living by faith. You are turning from self-preservation to self-abandonment. The command is to "enter through the narrow gate." This can lead to a very poor, lonely, and treacherous existence, but that is the cost of living an authentic life. It is the cost of discipleship.

Discussion Questions:

- Name all the difficulties you can think of that Jesus endured, other than the cross itself.
- Are you willing to face those same challenges on the narrow road?
- List some current cultural trends that are diametrically opposed to the gospel.
- How have you recently been made fun of because of taking a stand for righteousness?
- Name some examples of sacrifices you've made on the narrow way leading to life.

Suggested Exercises:

- When the topic of religion comes up at the water cooler, school, or even a family gathering, see what happens when you take a stand for Jesus as the only way to God. Quote John 14:6 and report what happens.

- Address cultural trends and moral decline in Sunday school or small gathering where open discussion is encouraged. Discuss issues such as fornication, unwed pregnancy, homosexuality, feminism, and materialism and how those things have infiltrated the church and made it almost indistinguishable from the world. Report back to the group what you have found to be the majority: those in the church who want to downplay the behavior of those on the broad road (the "nobody is perfect" and "we're all sinners" crowd); or those in the church who reject the behavior of those on the broad road (holiness crowd).
- For one week be totally honest in your responses to all inquiries. Say what you really believe and not what you know the person wants to hear. Report what effect this had on you socially. Now imagine what your life would be like if this was your standard operating procedure!
- Share the gospel. Just sharing the gospel can cause so much disruption that it is amazing! It is not the path of least resistance.
- Long-term goal: try to truly live a nondenominational approach to Christianity and notice how suddenly every avenue for advancement within the established denominations is closed off to you. Research the hardships of those in Christian history who have attempted this sort of lifestyle.

25

Expect False Prophets

Matthew 7:15-23

Beware of false prophets, who come to you in sheep's clothing, but inwardly are ravenous wolves. You will know them by their fruits. Grapes are not gathered from thorn bushes nor figs from thistles, are they? (Matthew 7:15-16)

"Many will say to me on that day, Lord, Lord, did we not prophesy in your name, and in your name cast out demons, and in your name perform many miracles? And I will declare to them, 'I never knew you; depart from me you who practice lawlessness.'" (Matthew 7:22-23)

Command of Christ: *Beware* of false prophets . . .

It's interesting to find that the warning about false prophets follows Jesus's command to take the narrow path. The implication is that the false prophets will likely choose otherwise. They perhaps do not subscribe to the sacrificial lifestyle Jesus modeled. They are in it for the money and the adulation. It reminds me of some of the TV ministers today that preach a message of health and wealth. They say that "gain is godliness." They suggest that a lack of anything is due to a lack of faith. The scripture warns us to stay away from these imposters (I Timothy 6:5).

Jesus says the false prophets are wolves in sheep's clothing. He says the way you judge a tree is by the fruit. A good tree will have good fruit and a bad tree bad fruit. The false prophets of the Old Testament told the people that all was well, that they were not sinning, and that their safety was guaranteed. The true prophets on the other hand warned them that their idolatry would not go unpunished. The true prophets stood up for righteousness and holiness while the false prophets allowed the people to indulge and intermingle with worldly pleasures and other gods. The false doctrine perpetrated in Jeremiah's day was that because they had the temple of God they were protected (Jeremiah 7:4). Their safety was guaranteed no matter what they did. That theory was totally annihilated when the Babylonians ransacked the city and temple in 587 BC, burning it to the ground. Those who believed in that false sense of security were destroyed.

These false prophets are a lot like Judas. He outwardly followed Jesus as a submissive lamb. But inwardly his objective was most likely power and control. He was eager for Jesus to take the throne of Jerusalem so he could rise to his throne along with Christ. He wanted to get his foot in the door, to position himself for personal gain. Once Jesus stopped talking kingdom talk and started sharing how He was going to suffer and die, Judas was out of there. Even though he was blessed by Jesus at one point to do miracles, his heart wasn't in that. He was focused on his will and not God's. He never really gave his heart to Christ but was more likely trying to use Him for his own political purposes.

One of the key distinguishing factors about the false prophets' teaching is that it allows for iniquity. Look and you will find them on judgment day claiming to have been working for Christ, but there is one small problem: lawlessness. On judgment day, Jesus will say, "Depart from me, you that work iniquity" (Matthew 7:23). The word in the original Greek for "iniquity" is *anomian*. *A* means *no* and *nomian* means *law*. They lived their lives with no regard to God's law yet at the same time claimed to represent God. Like the Pharisees, they say one thing and do another.

Any doctrine that allows for sin is false doctrine. Nowhere in the Bible is sin just accepted point blank. It is to be fully resisted and overcome by the power of Christ. Holiness is always the battle cry in the New Testament. By contrast, the idea suggested by Martin Luther in the Protestant movement of the sixteenth century is dangerous. At one point he urged one of his colleagues to "sin boldly." Luther taught that we are both sinners and righteous at the same time. But the Bible declares, "Shall we continue in sin that grace may abound? God forbid!" (Romans 6:15) It also declares, "If the righteous scarcely be saved, where shall the ungodly and the sinner appear?" (1 Peter 4:18) In the Word of God, sinners and the righteous are contrasted with one another, not merged together.

There are many Christians who go around saying, "We are all sinners, and nobody is perfect." It is that attitude that is foreign to the Word of God. Jesus said on the contrary, "Be ye therefore perfect as your Father in heaven is perfect" (Matthew 5:48). Paul states, "Let everyone who names the name of Christ depart from iniquity" (2 Timothy 2:19) Striving for holiness and maturity is the message of the New Testament, not settling for mediocrity. It is the narrow road that leads to life and few will there be that find it.

Sometimes we try the narrow road and find that it is far from comfortable. Jesus said "the Son of man has nowhere to lay his head" (Luke 9:58) He lived in a state of poverty, but we find that system unacceptable and opt for affluence instead with society in general. We eventually blend in so much with society that we no longer have a testimony. To keep us from feeling guilty we contrive a false doctrine that tells us that riches are the way to spirituality. We end up drifting away from God and serving money; then we lose our desire for holiness. We become self-reliant and, as a result, the self-sufficient enemy of God.

We, like the people of Israel, think we are guaranteed safety and security because we are chosen. But there is no guarantee, and if we do not repent we will suffer the same fate. Jesus said the one who saves his life will lose it and the one who loses it for His sake will find it. Two of the major gods of our time are moral compromise and materialism. These gods must be renounced. It is time to renew our commitment to Christ and follow Him down that arduous yet rewarding path to holiness.

Discussion Questions:

- What are the implications of the fact that Jesus warned of false prophets right after urging us to choose the narrow road?
- What did Jesus mean when he said false prophets are like wolves in sheep's clothing? In what ways do you expect such people to behave? What is their ulterior motive?
- What was the main difference between the false prophets and the true prophets in the Old Testament? For example, what was Jeremiah prophesying compared to his counterparts?

- On judgment day, what will be the missing ingredient for those who prophesied and did miracles in Jesus's name yet are rejected by Jesus?
- What false doctrines are out there today teaching us to compromise with the world?
- What reformation doctrine can be dangerous if taken to an extreme?
- How can a hunger and thirst for righteousness inoculate you from any such falsehood?

Suggested Exercises:

- Memorize the Beatitudes this week to prepare your mind to recognize the counterfeit. Recite those by memory at the next meeting.
- Research the Beatitudes to fully understand the proper disposition for a Christian minister of the gospel. Report your findings to the group.
- Prepare a study on false versus true prophets of the Bible. Name their distinguishing characteristics and share them with the group. Or have each member of the group pick a particular prophet who stands out for them and share the opposition they faced in standing up for righteousness during a dark period in history.
- Share how one of those same prophets might react to the situation we find in our own country today!
- Do a study on organizations that use Jesus's name but are actually cults. Share with the group why they are not accepted in mainstream Christianity.
- Share with the group the recent findings that show how there is relatively no difference today between the lifestyle of the churched and the unchurched.[64] Use the reference in the footnote below as well as any new data you can discover though additional research. What worldly philosophy has permeated the church today to cause this to happen?

---

[64] McMullen, Shawn A., *Releasing the Power of the Smaller Church*, (Cincinnati, Ohio: Standard Publishing, 2007), 120.

26

Pray for More Harvesters

Matthew 9:37-38

Then he said to the disciples, "The harvest is plentiful, but the workers are few. Therefore beseech the Lord of the harvest to send out workers into His harvest."

Command of Christ: . . . *petition* the Lord of the harvest . . .

The orders here coming from our Commander focus not on the task itself but entreats the Father of the project. We are ordered to *petition* the Lord of the Harvest. There is a glaring deficiency that Christ is now facing. There is an enormous amount of harvesting to be done and only one man in the field. It is overwhelming and the temptation arises to seek aid from friends and coworkers. Nonetheless, this is not at all the Lord's standard operating procedure—that is, to take matters into His own hands. He is not taking the initiative here because contrary to popular opinion, this is not pleasing to God.

God the Father requires total submission to His plans and objectives, no questions asked. All decisions are made by Him alone. To second-guess God is to undermine His authority. So when one is faced with a dilemma, there is only one righteous solution, and that is prayer. We must find out what the will of God is in that particular situation before proceeding. It may seem that the resolution beckoning before us is only a practical matter, but we don't see the whole picture from beginning to end as He does.

Here on display before us is Jesus's philosophy of ministry. In John 5:19 He states, "The Son can do nothing of himself, but what he sees the Father do: for what things He does, these also do the Son likewise." In John 8:29 he says, "I always do the things which please the Father". Jesus knew to wait on God and find out His will before proceeding. He was teaching His disciples to do the same and not launch out on their own. They must seek the Lord before proceeding on any course of action to make sure it is His will.

The lesson is this: it is the Father who does the work. He doesn't necessarily send us to do anything but positions us so He can accomplish His plans through us. In the book *Experiencing God: Knowing and Doing the Will of God*, Henry Blackaby makes this point very well. He says God is not saying, "Don't just stand there, do something!" Instead, He says the opposite: "Don't just do something, stand there!" We don't do any work independently of God. He does the work and we are allowed to tag along. When He needs us He will call us.

This is a shocking revelation to some who have blown past God in their own ministries, and the way they focus on themselves proves it. It's easy to get ahead of God and very hard to wait. Our culture is not at all groomed for ministry in Jesus's style. But Jesus's style is the most productive. Remember, He said, "Every plant, which my heavenly Father has not planted, shall be rooted up" (Matthew 15:13). It is best as Jesus taught us to check with the Father before we head into the field and cause more damage than good. So let's retrain ourselves to restrain ourselves and pray before acting. It's better to do nothing at all than to get involved in a project outside God's will. See a problem? Talk it over with God and see how He wants to handle it. Initiative is wonderful in the workplace environment of our modern, fast-paced society but counterproductive and disastrous when it comes to being about the Father's business.

Discussion Questions:

- Is awareness of a shortage of evangelists in a region and an abundance of lost souls a sign that you are being called to evangelize that particular group?
- If not, what is this "awareness" calling you to do instead?
- How about Jesus? Did he function in His ministry on impulse or did He simply do as instructed by the Father?

- What scriptures support or prove Jesus's philosophy of ministry?
- How does the following statement by Jesus remind us of who is actually performing the work and who is merely an instrument of the work of God in the world? "Every plant, which my heavenly Father hath not planted, shall be rooted up" (Matthew 15:13).
- How does it feel to know God has everything under control?

Suggested Exercises:

- Name a glaring deficiency you see in your church or community. Is God calling you to get involved? What needs to happen for you to find out?
- Make your church's or community's deficiency a matter of prayer this week and return with your conclusions, sharing that with the group and getting feedback.
- Determine what level of involvement God is calling you to based on that prayer and feedback. It may be an extended time of prayer or direct, immediate action.
- Share with the group the process of determining God's will on a matter. How difficult was it for you? How much certainty can you expect, and what were the signs that confirmed to you this certainty? How much does this depend on a daily listening prayer routine as opposed to a crisis management mode of prayer?

27

Know My Strategy

Matthew 10:5-6

These twelve Jesus sent out after instructing them: "Do not go in the way of the Gentiles, and do not enter any city of the Samaritans; but rather go to the lost sheep of the house of Israel."

Commands of Christ: Into the way of the nations *you will not go* . . . but *go instead* to the lost (destroyed) sheep of the house of Israel.

Here we become privy to God's game plan regarding how to spread the gospel. The disciples have been watching Jesus's methods in terms of how He goes about spreading the word. Jesus had just mentioned the enormity of the task and asked them to pray for laborers. As they did, it became clear to the Master that these twelve were to be the ones called to render support. I also see this as a strategic part of discipleship training. This is on-the-job training. That is where you give your apprentice an opportunity to take over for a while under your supervision, so that when the time comes the responsibility of the enterprise will not find him ill-prepared.

First He anoints them with the same powers He uses to cast out evil spirits and heal sickness (Matthew 10:1). Then he lays out the boundaries as to where they are to minister (Matthew 10:5-6). It is interesting that God's plan is to approach his children first and give them a chance to repent before branching out to the rest of the world.

They are commanded not to go into the way of the nations but to go to the lost sheep of the house of Israel. We see the same perspective later after the resurrection of Christ as He lays down the strategic plan of

209

first starting in Jerusalem, Judea, and Samaria, ending in the uttermost parts of the world (Acts 1:8). The gospel is to extend itself outward from Jerusalem in concentric circles embracing the entire nation of Israel before encompassing the globe.

In Matthew 21:33-40 we see the entire historic plan from a bird's eye view. Jesus does this in the form of a parable about a vineyard owner who built it from scratch and then hired managers to watch over it. When the time came to gather the produce from his vineyard he found that the managers (husbandmen) he had left in charge were not willing to fulfill their end of the bargain. They beat or killed the representatives sent from the owner. When the owner sends many more agents they suffer the same fate. He finally sends his own son, thinking they surely will respect him. However, they destroy him as well because he is the heir to the property. This is the same story that we find in the history of Israel. God sent many prophets to the nation, expecting results. They rejected them and killed many along the way. Finally He sent Jesus, His only Son, and still it had no effect on them. They killed him as well. That was the last straw for the Father. Because of this, He destroyed Jerusalem in 70 A.D. and turned to the Gentiles to spread the good news.

Yet the overall plan of God is correct. It was the nation of Israel He had called to be His minister to the world. They, however, for the most part kept it to themselves. Not pleased with that He had to turn elsewhere. But first he gave them one last chance to repent. That is why Jesus said to start at home. Start with the lost sheep of Israel. Notice that He refers to even His own children and the sheep of his own pasture as "lost." The Greek word translated *lost* actually means *destroyed*. The nation has become ruined from within and is no longer useful to the Lord. It is not just the ungodly Gentiles who need the gospel.

So what can we learn from this and how do we apply this command? It seems like a specific plan for a particular generation, yet it was passed to us for a reason. I think one of those reasons is to learn to know what God wants before you proceed. His plan is meticulous and purposeful; it is not haphazard. It is imperative that we keep in touch with the heart of God and be one with His timing and direction. He has an *opportune timing* for everything (*kairos* in the Greek), and when you adhere to that strategic initiative the results are phenomenal. Jesus was able to know God's will for every situation because He was one with Him (John 10:30). To a great extent, it is no different for us. We have to maintain a certain amount of intimacy with God to be aware of God's specific plan and timing for us as well.

A second possible reason this strategy session was passed on to us was for us to see that we must totally rely on God. The picture that is set before us shows Jesus passing on the Father's plan to the disciples and the disciples carrying out that plan. There were no deliberations, just the issuing out of certain orders and the orders being carried out. Total allegiance is the only way to keep connected to the King. The King renders an edict and the subjects yield to it. We must never question His authority by downplaying the significance of scripture or by shelving the word of the Lord in favor of our own predispositions.

We tend to be very independent in this country and think for ourselves. But we are in a kingdom now and there is nothing independent about it. It is similar to entering the armed forces. When they say, "You're in the army now," that means you'd better make some adjustments and quick! You have to follow orders now. When you enter the kingdom of God you must do the same. You must trade in your operating and thinking systems for His. He will rule and reign forever and He will never take a vote on it. So get used to it! The gospel is often countercultural, so we must avoid contaminating God's kingdom with our worldly philosophy and personal preferences.

Father knows best. Anything we could come up with could never compare with one who has all knowledge and an eternity of experience. Trust Him; He knows what He is doing. "Man shall not live by bread alone but by every word (*rhema:* God's personal word to you) that proceeds out of the mouth of God" (Matthew 4:4).

Discussion Questions:

- How does the parable in Matthew 21:33-40 provide a panoramic historical view of God's plan of worldwide kingdom expansion?
- What does the parable show to be the mistake of Israel in the expansion of the kingdom that we could also be guilty of if not careful?
- Does scripture show that God was eager to replace Israel with the Church as his worldwide ambassadors or that it was only the last resort after multiple attempts at reconciliation?

- What are two lessons we learn today from the specific instructions Jesus gave his disciples during this particular outreach into the towns and villages of first-century Israel?

Suggested Exercises:

- Discuss with your discipleship group what ideas God has placed on your heart but has not yet revealed the "opportune time" for commencing.
- Discuss how hard it is to wait on God when you are so ready to take action.
- Discuss how you know when you are getting a "green light" from God. What methods does He typically use to signal you to move ahead?
- Begin a "listening log" that once you master, you will be able to use to more readily determine God's will on any particular matter. Make three columns and spaces for each day of the month. Write what you think God is saying to you during your daily prayers, Bible reading, and church attendance. Share your log with a trusted spiritual advisor so you can be mentored in the process.
- Share with the group how this listening log has helped you to be better aware of God's particular strategy and timing on ministry matters.

28

Fish For Men

Matthew 10:7-8

As you go, preach, saying, "The kingdom of heaven is at hand."
Heal the sick, raise the dead, cleanse the lepers, cast out demons.
Freely you have received, freely give.

Commands of Christ: *Preach*, saying, 'The kingdom of heaven is near.'
Heal the sick, *raise* the dead, *cleanse* the lepers, *cast out* demons.

Here we see a repeat of the type of ministry our Lord was involved in.
Along with a healing ministry, he consistently preached "the kingdom of
heaven is at hand; repent and believe the gospel" (Mark 1:15). We need to
keep in mind that He was speaking to a crowd that was desperate to rid
themselves of the Roman Empire. Jesus had to be well aware of the desires
of the masses as He in effect threw out that sort of bait that was sure to
captivate them. He did, after all, offer them a great deal of freedom. As a
matter of fact, the sort of freedom He offered was vastly superior to the
type they were eagerly awaiting.

Therefore I have concluded that what we see before us in this passage
of scripture is the following formula for successful evangelism: tie in what
they want with what they need. In the end, they will be thankful for
giving them much more than they ever bargained for. In today's society,
the opposite applies. You often get less than you expected from the offer
advertised. With Christ it is always much more than you ever could have
imagined. The statement about the impending arrival of God and His
kingdom must have gripped them to the core of their being, for they were

so desperate to be relieved of their bondage. Maybe the approach that would grip people the most in our culture would be to offer them a way to live forever! Again, if that's what everyone wants, you can tie into that what they need.

The second wave of commands is as follows: heal the sick, raise the dead, cleanse the lepers, cast out demons. You have to admit that if we all could do these things at will, quite a stir would be raised all over the world. Surely the attention of all mankind would be upon us. But alas, there are so few who believe in miracles anymore. Many scholars even dare suggest that there is no such thing, and that the record of those things in the gospels is fabricated.

My contention is that the gospels were not written to make us feel comfortable but uncomfortable with the uneventful way we are going about the Father's business. We have to rediscover His methods and follow through with His perfect plan. The question is: Does He still want us to carry forth with this command? Does Jesus want to anoint us as He did the twelve so we can do miracles? I notice that most believers are reluctant to agree with that conclusion, but they are at least agreeable with proclaiming the gospel message.

My suggestion is to stay open. One thing is sure, if you remain closed-minded to the supernatural, you will never find it. "All things are possible to them that believe" (Mark 9:23). If God wants to continue to move in that direction, it is up to Him, we are simply His humble servants. We are to simply pray, "Thy will be done." But the fact remains that when there is deliverance of any kind (from sickness, death, or demons), the kingdom has indeed arrived (Luke 11:20). We also (as did the disciples) need the power to become Jesus's witnesses (Acts 1:8).

Discussion Questions:

- In the process of fishing for men, how did Jesus tie in what the people of His day wanted with what the people of His day really needed?
- What do people want today? How can you use that to attract them to Christ?
- Does supernatural healing still exist? Should we remain open to the possibility that the Lord still may want to attract crowds by the performing of miracles in His name?

- Can miracles open people up to the gospel who were formerly closed off to it?

Suggested Exercises:

- Brainstorm among the group what it is that society is clamoring for these days and how we can use that as a bridge to the gospel.
- Design a campaign or tract that utilizes the conclusions of your brainstorming event.
- This week take the time to pray in Jesus's name for healing for anyone at home, school, or work who discloses a specific need.
- Seek God in your personal prayer times for guidance as to whether or not a healing ministry is still expected along with sharing the gospel as we fish for men. Share your conclusions with the group.
- Do a research project on the subject pinpointing the difference between faith-healing ministry at home and abroad in the Christian faith. Share your results with the group.

29

Step Out in Faith

Matthew 10:8b-10; Mark 6:8-10; Luke 9:3-4

Freely you have received, freely give. Do not acquire gold, or silver,
or copper for your money belts, or a bag for your journey, or even
two coats, or sandals, or a staff; for the worker is worthy of his
support (Matthew 10:8b-10).

Commands of Christ: Freely you have received, freely *give. Do not get* gold
or silver or copper (for your purses) . . . Later in Luke 22:36: But now if
you have a purse, *take* it. If you don't have a sword, *sell* your garment and
buy one.

The first way to show that you have stepped out in faith in your ministry
is to not charge for your services. Jesus pointed out to them that they
received from Him freely and they are to likewise give freely. A second
way to demonstrate your intention to walk by faith is to not over prepare
for the journey. Just go as you are and trust God to provide along the
way. Don't get gold or silver or copper for your trip. Don't bring extra
money. No bag, no extra coat, no shoes or staff. This approach is highly
questionable when compared to the way most missionaries prepare these
days. Usually the first thing you do is sit down and prepare a budget for
four years. Then you itinerate from church to church until that monthly
support goal is met. You stay on the field for four years and then return
for a second round of support raising. Usually the budget includes extra
for anything unexpected that might arise.

This is a far cry from what Jesus is suggesting here. However, it was a local mission at this time and not a worldwide attempt as of yet. Nevertheless, it is fascinating that Jesus required faith once it had been established that they were the ones who had been chosen for this particular ministry. He knows God is really the one doing the work and He is asking for those who are willing to enter with Him in the project. God will always provide for His own, especially those going to the trouble to enter into the harvest. The key is to make sure He called for you. The disciples did not ask to help in this project, they were asked. In answer to the prayer for laborers, they were chosen.

Can the same be said of us or do we just gravitate to things we are interested in and then say we are called to do it? That's an important question that must be answered before you put your life on the line. Never jump ahead of God because He will not support us going out on our own when He did not authorize it. Even if He did authorize it you must always exercise caution.

Notice that in Luke 22:36 the initial teaching seems to be reversed. In other words, now you must take the purse along with you. Even your security is not guaranteed. Because of that He orders you to sell your garment and buy a sword. So what are we to make of this turnaround? Was there a special provision and protection initially that is no longer available to God's ministers? This apparent revision of the previous policy was made right before Jesus's execution. Therefore it may not be a change in policy as much as a change in the atmosphere toward Christianity. In other words, it is becoming more dangerous to spread the gospel than originally. So the admonition to take a purse and to buy a sword is not because of a difference in God's willingness to provide supernaturally for the needs of the enterprise but because of a change in the level of hostility toward believers. We are not now taking our purse (or wallet) due to the fact that we can no longer have faith for expenses, but just in case we face adversaries and our monies will be needed for avoiding that persecution. I don't believe Jesus really intends for us to purchase a sword because He quieted the disciples when they brandished theirs (Luke 22:37ff.). He is just warning us of the change of public opinion toward Christianity in general.

So the bottom line on how to proceed is thus: 1. Determine if you are called. 2. Determine if God wants you to step out in faith rather than garnish support and wages in advance. 3. Step out in faith but be sensible.

Make sure you are proceeding according to His plan and with caution. No matter how much you prepare, faith will also be required. Just make sure faith is established in the reality of the call. That's the most you can do; the rest is up to Him.

Don't take any risks unless God is directing it. Smuggling Bibles into Russia, for example, is heroic, but it's suicide if the Lord isn't with you. None of us place death on our calendars like Jesus did. However, if we must, we should be willing to follow Him all the way to the cross.

Discussion Questions:

- What are two ways to step out in faith in terms of how to operate a ministry?
- What is the first item on the agenda to settle before launching out to the mission field or starting a new ministry?
- In what ways did Jesus and the disciples live totally by faith and not wait until everything was provided for them?
- In the beginning, He said to not overprepare, but toward the end of His ministry He said to be prepared and take extra money, protection, etc. Why did Jesus seemingly reverse His teaching?
- What does it mean to "have faith but be sensible"?

Suggested Exercises:

- Interview a long-term missionary and/or some full-time ministers. Ask key questions:
  - How did they know they were called?
  - In what way were they required to step out in faith to accept the calling?
  - How did they maintain a balance between faith and funding?

- Read *Experiencing God* by Henry Blackaby and Claude King. Share with the group what you learned about following God's lead.
- Share prominent biblical examples that we can follow in terms of how to step out in faith once the call has been firmly established.

30

Obtain Lodging by Faith

Matthew 10:11-14; Mark 6:11; Luke 9:5

*And whatever city or village you enter, inquire who is worthy in
it, and stay at his house until you leave that city. As you enter the
house, give it your greeting. If the house is worthy, give it your
blessing of peace. But if it is not worthy, take back your blessing
of peace. Whoever does not receive you, nor heed your words, as
you go out of that house or that city, shake the dust off your feet*
(Matthew 10:11-14).

Commands of Christ: *Inquire* as to who is worthy. There *remain*, until
you depart. As you enter the house, *greet* it . . . *Let* your peace come upon
it . . . *Let* your peace return to you . . . *Shake* the dust off your feet.

Here again it seems Jesus is requiring a walk of faith in spreading the
message from village to village. They were not to prepare everything
beforehand the way we do today. They were not to make reservations in
the nicest hotels. They were to enquire who is worthy and then remain in
that lodging until they depart.

This statement presupposes two things. One is that the participants
are not to expect that they will be among the wealthy of society, otherwise
they would go to great expense to make their stay as comfortable as
possible. The Father's business is a nonprofit organization in the true sense
of the word. A disciple does not charge for his services; nor was the disciple
charged for what he has received. They are to rely on God's resources and
not their own means of provision. Secondly is the fact that a lack of funds

is no excuse to halt the proclamation of the good news and the expansion of God's kingdom.

Again we tend to forget sometimes the nature of these things, that they are not suggestions. All these directions are given in the imperative mood and are to be understood as orders. How are we to respond to that? I know hardly anyone who carries on evangelistic methods according to this model. But perhaps that is why we are not blessed. On the other side of the coin, it could be a cultural difference that causes us to hesitate on this command.

Hospitality was a way of life in the Middle East but certainly not so in the twenty-first-century Western civilization we know and love. Nevertheless it should be. I'm sure there are worthy believers in any town who can be accessed, and for that matter even unbelievers who are simply open to hear the good news (especially overseas). But one must say it would take a lot of guts to really carry through with this challenge from our Lord.

We live a totally different way of life in modern society. There is insurance for everything. Nobody has to take any risks. But that also leads to a weak and dormant faith. I think we should listen to Jesus here and not just assume these orders are only for a specific group of people in a specific period of time and culture of the past. I believe this is a challenge for all ages, times, and places. That is why the disciples included this story and why we need to reconsider our perspective toward missions.

Finally, whoever you do end up staying with is to be blessed. Greet the house, and then let your peace come upon it. However, if they turn out not to be accepting and hospitable, they are not to be blessed. Let your peace return to you. If the town as a whole is unreceptive you are to shake the dust off your feet as a witness against them. So you are to enter and leave with your head held high. You are the best thing that ever happened to them whether they realize that or not. "How beautiful are the feet of them that preach the gospel of peace, and bring glad tidings of good things!" (Romans 10:15)

Discussion Questions:

- Why do you think the Father's business is to be nonprofit?
- Why does this fact make working in full-time ministry a real challenge?

- If you are not well-funded, is that a good reason to assume you are not being called to spread the gospel?
- Is this command just for the first disciples in their hospitable time or does it apply to every age?
- What might make it easier for some cultures versus others?
- Do we try to do mission work with as little risk and discomfort as possible? Why is that?
- What are the four options Jesus gave once you do establish a home base for your operations?

Suggested Exercises:

- On your next mission adventure, plan to stay in the local homes of the city or village you are ministering to rather than splurging on hotel accommodations. Report the wealth of rewards you received from that experience upon your return.
- Consider supporting mission organizations that support local ministers rather than wealthy ministers from the West. In many instances, outrageous amounts of money are spent to maintain a high standard of living and in the process little else is achieved in terms of conversions and discipleship. Gospel for Asia is one such group that supports indigenous ministry.
- Read *Revolution in World Missions* by K. P. Yohannan and report your findings.
- Determine to let nothing hinder you once the call is confirmed. Be ready at a moment's notice to pick up and go!

31

Be Cautious

Matthew 10:16-23

Behold, I send you out as sheep in the midst of wolves; so be shrewd as serpents and innocent as doves. But beware of men, for they will hand you over to the courts and scourge you in their synagogues; and you will even be brought before governors and kings for my sake, as a testimony to them and to the Gentiles. But when they hand you over, do not worry about how or what you are to say. For it is not you who speak, but it is the spirit of your Father . . .

Commands of Christ: *Behold,* I send you as sheep in the midst of wolves; so be wise as a serpent and harmless as a dove. *Beware* of men . . . *do not worry* about what you will say . . . *flee.*

Overall we see that the message in Matthew 10:16-23 is to proceed with caution. Jesus starts the warning out with revealing to the disciples the setting or context within which they will be called to operate. It will be a hostile environment. Jesus told them to pay careful attention to that fact. He said, "Behold, I send you as sheep in the midst of wolves." Based on that harsh reality the next statement makes a lot of sense. "Be wise as a serpent and harmless as a dove." In dangerous circumstances, care must be taken not to bring too much attention to oneself.

I know missionaries in China who have to use code words in their e-mails so as to not be noticed that they are advocating or spreading Christianity. Every time they share the gospel there is a risk because it is against the law. They cannot broadcast it on the media outlets in the city.

Instead, they offer business seminars and in the process discreetly offer the gospel. This is a good example of being as wise as a serpent and harmless as a dove.

Usually serpents can be both crafty and harmful. We are not to be so. In the history of Christianity there are many examples of brutal savagery in the name of Christ that actually has nothing to do with him. There were so many godly men burned at the stake, drowned or murdered because of small theological differences of opinion. Many Native Americans were killed for not becoming a Christians. No, we are not to resort to violence but be as harmless as doves. The Bible says, "And the servant of the Lord must not strive; but be gentle unto all men, apt to teach, patient, In meekness instructing those that oppose themselves; if God peradventure will give them repentance to the acknowledging of the truth" (2 Timothy 2:23-24). The command is to pay attention to your surroundings. Be wise and do no harm.

"Beware of men," says Jesus. The men he is referring to are the religious leaders who will flog you in their synagogues and take you before the judges and governors. When on trial, "Don't worry about what you will say." If you get into trouble in one area, flee to another. You have to stay on your toes and avoid trouble if at all possible. If it is unavoidable, have faith and don't be afraid. It may be God's will for you to spread the word among the officials.

It reminds me of the book *The Heavenly Man: The Remarkable True Story of Chinese Christian Brother Yun* by Brother Yun and Paul Hattaway. A Chinese man acquired a Bible and started spreading the good news while Chinese officials chased him from city to city. At one point he had to baptize new converts in the middle of the night in a frozen lake to avoid detection.

This is what Christ was talking about when He says to beware of men and be ready to be on the move when trouble arises. As we branch out into dangerous areas, we need to take all of Jesus's directions and warnings to heart.

Discussion Questions:

- Do you ever feel like a lamb in the midst of wolves when you try to live your faith in an unbelieving and immoral world? Is your church experience any better?

- Name examples of instances where you had to be as clever as a snake yet harmless as a dove in spreading the gospel to places or in situations that were hostile toward it.
- Name instances where you had to be wise as a serpent and harmless as a dove trying to change policy in the church from worldly to holy.
- Has Christianity always abided by this "harmless as a dove" policy?
- What are some practical ways to avoid using the sword or falling victim to it?
- Name some methods Jesus used to avoid detection or slip free from an accusation. How about his followers?

Suggested Exercises:

- Research the methods Jesus and Paul used to avoid detection or postpone their demise at the hands of the religious elite. Share your findings with the group next week.
- When sharing the gospel on the job it might be wiser to use a special occasion, such as Christmas or Easter, to mask the significance of what you are proposing. Once as a corporate chaplain I used the story of the candy cane during Christmas as a bridge to share the gospel with every single employee. Yet there was no backlash.
- Sharing a greeting card with someone who has lost a loved one is another way to show concern while providing an open door for discreetly sharing the gospel.
- Sometimes just sharing your testimony will naturally include the gospel without offence.
- When traveling to a foreign country, have a long talk with the local missionaries about what precautions to take that will avoid bringing too much attention to yourself and endangering your team without totally eliminating the spread of the gospel and the building up and training of disciples.
- This week try to steer the conversation toward eternal truths without it being detected or perceived as a threat. However, don't water it down so much that it is unrecognizable as gospel. Keep John 14:6 in the back of your mind. Report your experience to the group.

32

Fear God Alone

Matthew 10:26-31; Luke 12:32

*Do not fear those who kill the body but are unable to kill the soul;
but rather fear Him who is able to destroy both soul and body in
hell* (Matthew 10:28).

Commands of Christ: *Do not fear* them therefore . . . What you hear in
the darkness, *speak* in the light; and what's in the ear, *proclaim* upon the
housetop . . . *Do not fear . . . fear . . . Do not fear . . .*

All the imperatives revolve around the central subject of fear. The context
is persecution for Christ's sake. Jesus said that if they called him evil, then
all the more they would call his followers evil. It takes us back to the
Beatitudes again where Jesus states that we are blessed when "they revile
and persecute you, and say all kinds of evil against you falsely for my sake.
Rejoice and be exceedingly glad, for great is your reward in heaven, for so
they persecuted the prophets who were before you."

One must expect to be persecuted if they choose to follow Jesus. More
importantly, they are not to fear that persecution, which in many instances
can include violence or even death. It is easier not to fear false accusation
than to not fear a violent death. But Jesus tells us not to fear either one.
That is the imperative. He says, "Don't fear them . . ."

He goes on to say "what you hear in the dark speak in the light, and
what you hear in the ear proclaim upon the housetop" (Matthew 10:27). I
think the reasoning here is not to hold back on your message to the world
just because there is a threat to your image, and, furthermore, your safety.

225

We are to go ahead and speak out with boldness regardless. We are not to allow the threats of our enemies to stop us from speaking and proclaiming the good news. When the time came for the spread of the gospel, the apostles did not cease to preach in Jesus's name even though they were warned by the authorities. They did not cower before the authorities but spoke boldly and rejoiced when they were punished by flogging. However, we must remember that this was after they were baptized with the Holy Spirit. Before that they were in hiding and fearing for their lives. I think this tells us how we can become bolder and less fearful. We too need the infilling of the Holy Spirit to have the unmatched courage of Christ.

Jesus goes on to say that the one we should really fear is God. He's the only eternal threat. There is no place in time or eternity that is free from His influence or justice. The most a man can do to us is to destroy our body; and it is a body that is scheduled to expire anyway. He cannot cross the boundary into our souls. So the teaching is to get our fear moving in the right direction. Fear does have its place, but not toward one another.

Jesus doesn't place a lot of value on this brief lifespan that we so desperately hold on to. He only seems to value it in regard to its impact or lack thereof on things eternal. The things that last are naturally the greater treasure. This life does not last very long at all. Only what we do for Christ will last.

Toward the end of the speech Jesus provides the rationale for a life free of fear. We can rest in the fact that God values all of His creations, from the greatest to the smallest. The sparrow is one of the least of all creation yet they too receive God's complete attention and concern. If even they who are not much more valuable than a few cents are important to God, how much more important to God are we? He goes on to make a statement of great wonder and one that offers abundant comfort to mankind. He says that even the very hairs of our head are numbered. He loves us that much. He goes to that extreme in caring and in wanting to know every minor detail about us. How reassuring that is.

Knowing this it is almost impossible to fear that we will ever be without full consideration in every endeavor we face. What a great calming influence Jesus provides for us for eliminating our fears. We can trust that no matter what we go through, we are not abandoned by God, and He will work all things together for our good in the end.

Discussion Questions:

- No matter how careful we are we do tend to stick out like a sore thumb in an ungodly society. Once that society turns hostile, what's to keep us from clamming up?
- Why are we not to fear what people can do to us?
- How is a wasted life a greater threat than a righteous death?
- How does the fact that God cares to know the number of hairs on our head comfort us in times of distress?

Suggested Exercises:

- Research biblically the difference in the disciples before and after Pentecost and share that with the group. What did their judges deduce from their new display of confidence?
- Read a good Christian biography of a "brave heart" who took great risks for the kingdom of God and prevailed. Share your findings with the group.
- Go around the room and have each member of the group pray for strength and wisdom from God in terms of being free from the fears that freeze us in our tracks. Pray for that same boldness exemplified by the disciples after the day of Pentecost.
- Make this a daily part of your prayer routine until the fear lifts and share your victory with your fellow disciples.

SECTION THREE:
Spiritual Preschooler

33

Expect Conflict

Matthew 10:34-42; 11:15-18

Do not think that I came to bring peace on the earth; I did not come to bring peace, but a sword. For I came to set a man against his father, and a daughter against her mother, and a daughter-in-law against her mother-in-law; and a man's enemies will be the members of his household (Matthew 10: 34-36).

Commands of Christ: *Do not think* that I came to cast peace . . . Whoever has ears, *listen*!

The overall lesson here in this passage is to expect conflict. We are commanded not to imagine that Jesus came to bring peace to the earth at this time. We are ordered not to get the wrong idea about Him. Our thinking has to be correct. This is the area where Satan will most likely attack. Just as he did with Adam and Eve, his best efforts come when he can twist our minds around in the wrong direction. If we expect peace, we will function differently than if we expect war. Jesus is warning us to expect war. And this war will not only involve outsiders. Unfortunately, even those in your own home could turn on you.

This passage is talking about the possible cost of discipleship. Christianity maintains such a strong belief system that it will totally transform your way of looking at the world. You will no longer be in the mainstream of society pursuing what they pursue. They are only interested in the temporal, but you are focused on the eternal. You seem detached, uninterested, and socially unacceptable to the world. You are not driven to indulge your appetites in the same fashion. Those in your immediate family who have chosen the ways of the world (lust of the flesh, of the eyes, and the pride of life) will also disown you and your Master's eternal kingdom in exchange for the here and now. It reminds me of Paul's sad commentary in 2 Timothy 4:10 regarding a dear friend that he had lost: "Demas has forsaken me, having loved this present world." Paul, like many of us, experienced betrayal by someone really close to him.

Ultimately all must admit that nothing ought to come between them and the Lord. He must be our closest relationship, and should we have to choose between Him and family, we cannot do otherwise but serve the Lord. We just hope and pray we never have to cross that road. Even our very lives cannot claim our ultimate allegiance. Nothing is more important than our relationship with God.

It is like the martyrs of the Roman Empire who had to face the lions in the coliseums. All they had to do to save their lives was deny Christ. In many instances all they had to do was say, "Caesar is Lord." As true believers they simply could not do so, and because of that they provided the greatest witness to the reality of the Christian faith the world has ever known. Although we don't invite such conditions, we know that should we find ourselves in similar circumstances, His grace will be sufficient. We remain as wise as serpents and as harmless as doves as a general rule. Nevertheless, no matter how careful we are, we know it could happen. We know we could find ourselves in a position where there is no way out other than death. In that position, we will not fear those who can only destroy the body, we will stand firm in our testimony to the end. Whoever accepts us accepts the Lord, and whoever causes us to suffer is furthering the suffering of Christ. Eternity will reward and punish each favorable and unfavorable response.

We are basically called to identify with Christ and what He endured on Earth. At one point we recall how he was approached by his own people as mad and they were ready to take him away by force (Mark 3:21). We see that the religious leaders insulted Him and persecuted Him and said all manner of evil falsely against Him. We see how some called the miracles of the Holy Spirit the miracles of the Devil. We see how they mocked and scourged and crucified Him as he continued to love them.

This is the potential cost of discipleship, and we must pray for God's grace to endure it. If we undergo slander for His sake, we should be all the more thankful that this is all that is being done against us and that we don't also find ourselves as a lamb appointed for the slaughter. Thankfully we are called not to be sacrifices only but "living" sacrifices, holy and acceptable unto Him. But don't think that Jesus ushered in a day of peace, for that day is yet at the end of time when He returns as the world conqueror. Don't be led astray by false TV preachers who offer peace and safety or health and wealth, for that day is yet to come when the kingdom of God finally becomes an external and permanent reality. It will be judgment day when he separates the wheat from the tares and the good fish from the bad. Matthew 13:43 says, "Then the righteous will shine forth as the sun in the kingdom of their Father."

The following command comes in the form of that familiar formula: "Whoever has ears, listen." This command follows a long speech about John the Baptist who at that very moment found himself in prison awaiting execution. John the Baptist presents a tangible example of what it means to suffer for righteousness's sake. This is the very thing Jesus had been talking about. He had been explaining to the people that following Him could be dangerous. He did not criticize John the Baptist for his circumstances but hailed him as the greatest of all prophets. And soon he was to suffer the fate (murder) of many of the prophets of old.

He goes on to explain that the kingdom of God is more than the setting up of an earthly governorship. It is an assault on the kingdom of darkness. It is not a struggle against flesh and blood but against principalities and powers and wickedness in high places (Ephesians 6:12). When you enter the kingdom you enter a life and death struggle between good and evil. That is what occurs when you are saved and begin your journey into discipleship.

Welcome to the good fight of faith (1 Timothy 6:12). Fight well and endure hardness now as a good soldier of Jesus Christ (2 Timothy 2:3). The Marines have the slogan: "The Few. The Proud. The Brave." But perhaps that motto is even more appropriate for Christian discipleship. For it is the narrow road that leads to life and there will be very few who will find it (Matthew 7:13-14). Do you have what it takes to be a disciple? Can you deny yourself, take up your cross, and follow Him?

Discussion Questions:

- Once you accept Christ, doesn't that mean all your problems are over? Why not?

- We expect some conflict with nonbelievers in the world, but how scary is it to realize rejection can just as easily come from within the confines of your own household? Have you experienced this? Explain.
- Have you suffered a loss of a job or promotion due to your beliefs? Have you ever felt your life was in danger just because your personal convictions?
- What prevents you from accepting a threat due to your convictions as a legitimate possibility? What changes in society might raise the level of hostility to our cause?
- Are you one of the "few, proud and brave?" or do you still need some maturity?
- What reminders did Christ provide that keep us going?

Suggested Exercises:

- This command has to do with *acknowledgment*, in terms of the potential risk that genuine faith entails. Therefore, today, if you have supposed incorrectly that Christianity is heaven on earth, reconsider. Although we are instructed to pray for the kingdom to come, it has not yet fully arrived. In the real world we must reorient our thinking toward facing resistance. Be prepared to face conflict and know that your life as a true believer is a life consisting of an attempt to swim against the tide. The reward is very real but not necessarily experienced in this life. Prepare yourself mentally to fight the good fight. You will never regret any sacrifice for Christ.
- If you can make this statement with all confidence, consider signing off on the following:
  Having full knowledge of all the dangers and risks involved with true devotion to Christ, I pledge my allegiance, life and limb to the cause of Christ with no reservations.

Name: _____Date: _____

34

Submit to the Gentleman

Matthew 11:28-30; 12:18-21

Come unto me, all who are weary and heavy-laden, and I will give you rest. Take my yoke upon you and learn from me, for I am gentle and humble in heart, and you will find rest for your souls. For my yoke is easy and my burden is light (Matthew 11:28-30).

Commands of Christ: *Come to me,* all those who labor . . . *Take* my yoke upon you and *learn* . . .

Here we encounter the irresistible appeal of the Master as he presents Himself as the only viable candidate for our affections. Just before this statement in Matthew 11:28, we find Him setting the stage in verse 27: "All things have been committed to me by my Father. No one knows the Son except the Father, and no one knows the Father except the Son and those to whom the Son chooses to reveal Him." So He basically sets Himself up as the only possibility for knowing God. There is no other option because no one can know the Father as well as the Son. The religious leaders of the day claimed to know God's will, but they could never know God the way that God the Son knows Him.

It seems the religious leaders are way off the mark. They are proud, demanding, and hypocritical. They are the cruel taskmasters for the traditions of men. They would force you into the futility of trying to earn your own salvation. By doing this they have even unwittingly become the children of the Devil (John 8:44). Is that the type of leadership you are looking for?

Now compare that with the holy Son of God. If anyone should have a reason to be proud, He should. Yet He is not. He is not eager to increase your burden but to lighten your load. If you join up with Him you will find a gentle and humble soul. You will then find rest for your soul.

Isaiah declares that he will not be overbearing. He will not shout out in the streets to bulldoze His way over you because His voice is louder than yours. He won't give up on you no matter how bad of a sinner you have become (bruised reed or smoking flax). Isaiah 42:1-4 says, "Behold, my servant, whom I uphold; my chosen one in whom my soul delights. I have put my spirit upon him; he will bring forth justice to the nations. He will not cry out or raise his voice, nor make his voice heard in the street. A bruised reed he will not break and a dimly burning wick he will not extinguish; he will faithfully bring forth justice. He will not be disheartened or crushed until he has established justice in the earth; and the coastlands will wait expectantly for his law."

So there we have presented before us two options: submitting to the cruel, demonic enforcers of legalism or to the beloved gentleman of heaven. It's no wonder the world has flocked to Him in unprecedented numbers, making Christianity the largest religion on Earth. What a wonderful picture He has painted of Himself and that the Father has revealed to us about Him. And isn't it true that His yoke is easy and His burden light? After all we aren't asked to toil for our salvation any more. He has taken the brunt of the load all the way to the cross. What a wonderful Savior and Lord! Who would not be willing to serve Him with all their heart, soul, and mind?

So what exactly is He asking of us? 1. Come to me. 2. Take my yoke upon you. 3. Learn of me. Have you done that? Have you given up on your own efforts to win God's approval? He already approves of you. Can't you hear Him calling you to come to Him? That is the message of the gospel. "I love you just the way you are but too much to let you stay that way." He knows we can't save ourselves, so it's up to Him to resolve the broken relationship between us and God. It is an offer that is just there for the taking, as if He is saying, "Come to me, I am the answer. Your religious leaders can't provide what I can. I have direct access to God. I have the ability to take away your sins. Will you come? Will you let me handle this for you? I will give you rest. You will no longer be at odds with God. I will open up the way to reconciliation, allowing you to rest from your efforts."

Once you become a child of God, then we will work on your spiritual growth. This is the "I love you too much to let you stay that way" part mentioned above. At that point you will "take my yoke upon you." The taking up of the yoke was a Jewish idiom meaning submission to the training of a master. But His yoke is easy and His burden is light because He is there to encourage, guide, and provide the grace necessary to face any challenge. He says to us, once you are saved, now you will enter into discipleship training based on my commands. At that point you will "learn of me." "Learn" and "disciple" are practically the same word. Discipleship is a calling to apprenticeship. So by asking you to learn of him, He is asking you to become His disciple or apprentice. You will learn from the only teacher who is coming to you directly from heaven. You will learn from God Himself (John 6:45). If this is the offer, who in his right mind could possibly settle for anything less?

Discussion Questions:

- What type of person was Jesus according to Isaiah 42:1-4?
- Compare that with the Pharisees. How were the religious leaders so different and off target in contrast to Jesus?
- What were the people weary and heavily laden with?
- When Jesus offered them rest from their burdens, what was He saying about salvation by grace through faith and not works?
- What did Jesus mean by following that "rest" up with coming under His yoke and learning of Him?
- How do we learn from Him today? Where do we find His teachings?
- Is He really our Lord if we have no working knowledge of his philosophy and imperatives?

Suggested Exercises:

- If you have not done so, submit to the Gentleman today in the following ways:
  o Come to the Messiah and lay your burdens down. Or stop trying to earn you own way to heaven and receive the payment He made on the cross for your entrance into heaven. Accept him as your Savior and Master today.

o Accept the Messiah as your personal trainer. In other words, place yourself now under His yoke of discipline and benefit from His limitless wisdom. He is your master and you are His apprentice.

o Enter into a teacher/student relationship with the Messiah. Become one of His modern disciples by agreeing to apply to your life every one of the commands He gave his first disciples as recorded in the gospels.

• Share with the group which of the above (if not all) you most struggle with. Use your accountability partner to remind you to follow up on this in the days to come.

35

Stay Open-Minded

Matthew 12:22-37; Mark 3:20-30

Either make the tree good and its fruit good, or make the tree bad and its fruit bad; for the tree is known by its fruit . . . but I tell you that every careless word that people speak, they shall give an accounting for it in the day of judgment. For by your words you will be justified, and by your words you will be condemned (Matthew12:33, 36-37).

Commands of Christ: *Make* the tree good and its fruit good, or *make* the tree rotten . . .

Jesus was always bumping heads with the Pharisees because of their stubborn refusal to even consider the possibility they could be wrong. They never thought to question themselves about anything. They just assumed God was on their side because they'd earned it. No matter how reasonable you were with them, they could not accept you unless you were one of them. To be a Pharisee was to be perfect, and anyone who rejected that idea was of the Devil. But by being so obstinate and narrow-minded they wound up becoming the very thing they accused others of. They were the ones who were actually serving the Devil while imagining all along they were serving God. Their mental apparatus was totally shut down because they concluded they had already figured everything out. They were no longer open to discussion about anything, especially their own failures.

This closed-mindedness is a dangerous thing. Can a person be so blind to his or her own perspectives that God Himself couldn't talk any sense into him or her? In the gospels is the case in point presented to us of just how religious fanaticism can blind you to the very God you supposedly represent. It seems so odd that the most religious can also be the most rebellious, but it is indeed the case.

Being religious can lead to great evil if it is not from the heart. So often it can become a behemoth when it bypasses character on the way to a know-it-all perspective. Dr. Know-it-All is also too often Dr. Do-Little in disguise. We deceive ourselves into thinking knowledge of a matter is also taking action on a matter. We become a self-righteous hypocrite, and when that happens we find ourselves driving right into a brick wall named Jesus.

Paul the former Pharisee said that "knowledge puffs up" (1 Corinthians 8:1). The more information you acquire, the harder it seems to be to stay humble. So what we have to do is always keep that in mind as we further our education and take upon ourselves the various traditions of our perspective denominations. These lines that we draw in the sand against one another in the Christian faith are often based on those long-held and cherished traditions of old. But their age does not guarantee their accuracy and our presuppositions are all based on partial knowledge ("we know in part . . ." 1 Corinthians 13:9). Our greatest treasures of knowledge, tradition, and theology are all based on an unfinished understanding.

But Jesus has perfect understanding. So our thinking, no matter how refined, has to basically grow up to his. When He speaks we have to stop in our tracks and listen very carefully. We are obligated at that point to think it over. We have to be ready to discard everything we've ever known to be true about that particular subject. When Jesus reasons with us, we must open up to that discussion. If we bypass Him we settle for our own brand of comfortable ignorance, which leads to transgression.

The command to "make" the tree good or evil is a call to think things over. It is a call to reason together with the Lord. Although this is technically a command aimed at the Pharisees, it was also a warning to the disciples and the future Church not to make the same mistakes they did. The conclusion that the Pharisees came to about Jesus casting out devils by the power of Satan simply makes no sense at all. If you think about it logically, this is absolutely ridiculous. There are two opposing teams. One team is evil and one is good. They will always oppose one another. They will always expand their prospective territories at the expense of the other. But what is to be gained by the enemy casting out itself? Doing that is working for the opposition. Doing that is self-defeating and is thereby lending a hand to your adversary. Self-defeat is an oxymoron, yet this new low is the line of irrational thought the Pharisees had sunken to in their desperation to hold on to power and influence in the eyes of the people.

These kind of unreasonable conclusions come from those who rush to judgment. They assume the worst before really examining the facts. What they are saying doesn't make sense. They seem to be saying, "The opponent must be evil because he is not one of us. I don't need to discuss it, that one fact is enough to condemn them." It is the mentality that commonly defines exclusive cults. They close themselves off to the world and all reason and scrutiny. They imagine God is with them. They cease to examine themselves anymore. In refusing to do so, they close themselves off to God as well.

Jesus presents the evidence to them in a coherent manner. He is not using emotion or hype or supernatural powers. It is as if He is simply saying, "Let's examine this presupposition of yours and see if it holds water. A good tree has good fruit. A bad tree has bad fruit. Now, which tree am I? What kind of fruit am I producing here? Is it good or bad? If it is good, then be quiet. You have no justification for what you are saying here, it is simply a matter of prejudice and jealousy. Have you ever heard of an army fighting against itself? Does it not fight the enemy only? So how does your hypothesis of Satan driving out Satan make any sense? This miracle I performed is not an instance of bad prevailing over bad, but good overpowering the bad. I'm cleaning house because I'm the good guy. You are calling me bad because you are the bad guy. That is what is really going on here."

Maybe if they had actually examined Jesus's good fruit they would have also had the eyes to see the rotten fruit that they possessed. It was their closed-mindedness that doomed them to failure. Don't let the same thing happen to you.

Discussion Questions:

- How was Jesus's openness to sinners and message of salvation by grace such a threat to the religious leaders of his day?

- Share examples of policies and perspectives in church politics that are so wrong yet held to for so long that there is no room for discussion on the matter. (In other words, the "mental apparatus" has been shut down on this matter.)
- How does our partial knowledge divide us into separate denominations within the same Christian faith?
- How did Jesus prove that the Pharisees' conclusion about Him using the power of the Devil was likely more out of envy than logic? How did He use reason show the crowd that their accusations didn't make sense?
- How did the Pharisees' closed-mindedness lead to the point that God Himself couldn't even talk to them? Does this happen to us today?

Suggested Exercises:

- Name a long-cherished and firmly held belief of yours that was shattered by revelation. Share with the group.
- Open up the fact that there may still remain a great deal more in your life that needs to be rethought and reconsidered.
- Enter a college course on a subject you thought you were well advanced in, such as Christian history, theology, or even a subject covering the life of Christ. After completing the course make a note of how many factual errors you had to correct along the way and share them with the group.
- If you don't have time for the course, read the textbook offered and make a report on that.

36

Understand My Significance

Matthew 12:38-45; Luke 11:29-32

Then the men of Nineveh will stand up with this generation at the judgment and will condemn it because they repented at the preaching of Jonah; and behold, something greater than Jonah is here. The Queen of the South will rise up with this generation at the judgment and will condemn it, because she came from the ends of the earth to hear the wisdom of Solomon; and behold, something greater than Solomon is here (Matthew 12:41-42).

Commands of Christ: *Behold,* something greater than Jonah is here . . . *behold,* something greater than Solomon is here.

Here we have Jesus proclaiming his superiority in an indirect way. He has already stated many things about Himself that are extraordinary (light of the world, bread of life, etc.). Until we come to the realization of just who He is, we will continue to be lost. We will continue to fail. We will continue on with our religious exercise in futility. It comes down to this: "Who do men say that I am?" (Matthew 16:15) This is what the entire Church is built upon. This is what our relationship with God is predicated on. To understand His significance is to open ourselves up to eternity. To fail to understand that significance is to close ourselves off from it. If He is just a man, then his sacrifice has no redemptive significance. If He is God, He becomes the doorway to eternal life. This is the message He had to somehow convey to mankind without causing an uproar. However, when He did speak, even in veiled speech about his special relationship with the Father, it was considered blasphemy. People could not see beyond the natural.

Over time the disciples finally did come to the proper conclusion that Jesus is the Christ, the Son of the living God (Matthew 16:16). Once we realize that, suddenly His teachings and His actions—everything He says and does—takes on a monumental significance. The generation that experienced Him has to shoulder a greater responsibility for overlooking and underestimating Him. He asked them to think about the fact that the whole city of Nineveh repented at the preaching of Jonah. Yet why will they not repent at His preaching since He is so much greater than Jonah? The people of Nineveh will rise up against that generation on the day of judgment because that was the generation who rejected God's Son. All the Ninevites had before them was God's prophet and it was enough. History is replete with examples of individuals responding appropriately to the man of God. Look at the Queen of Sheba and how she responded to Solomon. Jesus is greater than Solomon or any of the patriarchs because none of them were deities. We have to realize that when we encounter the life and teaching of Jesus in the gospels, we are encountering God in human form. This fact should cause us to stop and give all the more earnest heed to what we are presented (Hebrews 2:1).

The command is to "behold": something greater than Jonah is here and "behold": something greater than Solomon is here. Stop! Look! Listen! Something amazing has just taken place. Something has transpired the likes of which we will never know again in all of human history! God has become a man and is now living here among us as a mere mortal. Do you understand the magnitude of this undertaking? If not, you must awaken to this one essential truth before anything else Jesus says holds any meaning for you. You must believe in who He is before you can receive His message of redemption. The evidence is all around you. Now put that together and bow before Him in humble worship. As the old hymn states, "Fall on your knees, oh hear the angel's voices, oh night divine, oh night when Christ was born!" It is the divinity of Christ on which everything rises or falls. Once you come to recognize this, you're hooked. You are willing to give Him your all. No sacrifice is too great for the King of kings and the Lord of lords.

When you see Him for who He really is, you begin to understand the following:

1. His exclusive role in the scheme of things. You begin to see the big picture as illustrated in the of the vineyard owner in Luke 20:9-15. He was the final attempt by the vineyard owner (God) to get the keepers (Israel) of the vineyard to come to their senses. When they did not respond to the son, they were destroyed and the vineyard (God's kingdom) was rented out to others (Gentiles).

2. As the divine Son of God, He speaks from a perspective that can never be duplicated. He has the sole vantage point of seeing from the inside out. We see through a glass darkly and look from the outside in into what we can make of the glory of God. His vision is that of a face-to-face eternal cohabitation (John 1:1). He is so confident in his superior understanding of God that He states in Matthew 11:27 that "no one knows the father except the Son and anyone to whom the Son desires to reveal Him." What he means there is obvious.

It is not that nobody knows God. Many people have a good relationship with God. But nobody has ever seen God or coexisted with Him as Jesus has. Only the Son can truly pass on the truth of the Father having stepped out of eternity to temporarily experience time and space. John 1:18 states: "No one has ever seen God, but God the only Son who is at the Father's side, has made him known." The Greek word for "made him known" is where we get the word *exegesis*. The Son as the sole divine resource is the only person qualified to exegete (explain) the Father. We must stop in our tracks when he speaks because He declares not only exclusive knowledge but His own special union with that deity in John 8:58: "before Abraham was, I am." *Egō eimi* is Greek for "I am." "I am" is another way of saying God's name, Yahweh.

We too must give Jesus His due. We must hold His teachings in a place of prominence over any other teaching of any other man. We must agree with the philosophy of those who decided to print the words of Jesus in red. We must grip ourselves by the shoulders and shake ourselves when we see His speech in the gospels and remind ourselves of just who it is that is speaking here. We must not allow them to become commonplace and lose their significance; we must guard them as the most holy of all speech we will ever encounter. We must remember the words of our Lord to keep them holy.

I conclude my remarks with Colossians 1:18: "And he is the head of the body, the church: who is the beginning, the firstborn from the dead; that in all things he might have the preeminence."

Discussion Questions:

- How does the value of the overall message, deeds, and sacrifice of Christ take on an epic proportion once His true identity is uncovered?
- How does the parable of the vineyard (Luke 20:9-15) reveal Jesus's role in the scheme of things?
- What are the implications of Matthew 11:27 and John 1:18 in terms of Jesus's special significance as the highest personal source for divine revelation?
- How was the confession of Peter in Matthew 16:16 a turning point in the disciple's relationship with Jesus?
- Do we keep Christ and His wisdom in the forefront of our churches and lives, or are we also guilty of downplaying His significance by treating Him like any other prophet or patriarch? Do we even give Him less respect than we do other Biblical characters?
- Why does He demand and deserve greater respect than any other man of God?
- How is that respect best achieved? How do we give Christ the preeminence in all things?

Suggested Exercises:

- Complete a study on Hebrews chapter 1 and Colossians 1:18 and relate to the group how this has helped you regain the proper perspective in terms of Jesus's significance.
- Brainstorm among the group practical ways to ensure Jesus's teachings remain in the forefront of the overall function of the church so as to ensure He remains the head of the church as it abides by His recorded agenda.
- Introduce the Christ-centered discipleship program in this book to your church whereby disciples are made to adhere to every one of Jesus's commands.

- Commit as many of Jesus's words to memory as possible. That way they will stay in the forefront of your thinking. The way you think will lead to the way you conduct your affairs and the affairs of the church.
- Formulate a Jesus club where all you do is memorize and discuss Jesus's perspective on life. Books from *The Jesus Library* (Michael Green, editor) series should add a great deal to the discussion.
- Put together a game show (such as *Jeopardy!*) that features all Jesus taught and commanded. Perform it before the church during a regular service on a monthly basis.
- Create a test having to do with the life and teachings of Christ for all elders and staff of the church. Make a high score a determining factor in accepting them into all key leadership positions.

37

Reunite with Your Heavenly Family

Matthew 12:46-50; Mark 3:31-35; Luke 8:19-21

Someone said to him, "Behold, your mother and your brothers are standing outside seeking to speak to you." But Jesus answered the one who was telling him and said, "Who is my mother and who are my brothers?" And stretching out his hand toward his disciples, He said, "Behold my mother and my brothers! For whoever does the will of my Father who is in heaven, he is my brother and sister and mother" (Matthew 12:47-50).

Command of Christ: *Behold* my mother and my brothers!

The command here is to notice something: look, here is my family. Jesus was seated, facing a crowd, and talking to them. His earthly mother and brothers couldn't get to him because of the crowd so they sent word. Jesus had his priorities straight. It was more important for the crowd to be united with their heavenly family than for Him to be reunited to his earthly family. For Jesus, as well as it should be for us, the spiritual reality always outweighs the biological reality. Eternity always holds the lasting significance whereas earthly things are only temporary at best. There is nothing in the world more important than bringing people into the family of God. If I am in the middle of sharing the gospel (as Jesus may have been), all other considerations will have to wait even, if it is my own family who need me. This was not the first time Jesus expressed His ultimate allegiance to the heavenly Father. When he vanished as a child and his family asked him why, He responded, "Didn't you know I must be about my Father's business?" (Luke 2:49) For Jesus it was the heavenly affairs, not the earthly affairs, which mattered most.

Our ultimate allegiance is also to the family of God even more than our own earthly family. Jesus was saying that those who were with Him and serving Him were the ones He considered his true family. We are to seek first the kingdom of God and His righteousness (Matthew 6:33). This is the priority. Seeking the kingdom and entering in to it by His work on the cross. Then you become one of the members of the family of God. You become a child of God by faith in the gospel. Then He is willing to call you one of His own if you further commit your life to Him in discipleship (Matthew 12:50). The Father loves those who do His will and wants to claim those individuals as His own children because they are precious to Him. This heavenly adoption transcends earthly attachment.

Does that mean that we must downplay the significance of our actual blood relatives and consider them of lesser value than fellow believers? Well, that depends. We know already that one of the Ten Commandments is to honor your father and mother, so Jesus is not advocating disrespect at all. As a matter of fact, many of the Ten Commandments (5, 7 and 10) are for the purpose of strengthening the family. Nevertheless as much as we love our families we can never allow them to come between us and God. Anything that is good can become an idol once it becomes the most important thing in life to us. One of the lessons here is that nothing can be more important to us than our relationship with God. Jesus goes on to say that "he who loves father and mother more than me is not worthy of me . . ." In Luke 14:26 He includes the children: "he who loves son or daughter more than me is not worthy of me." Nothing, not even our parents or kids, can come between us and Jesus.

We live in a day when the earthly mother of Jesus almost has equal significance to the Son of God in some circles. She is called the mother of God and is even worshiped and prayed to. This is an odd development, especially when we consider what Jesus did in this instance. While his mother waited outside and asked to see Him, He basically disregarded her wishes for a higher purpose. There is another popular ministry in our times called Focus on the Family. I have a high regard for this ministry and especially enjoy their conservative biblical approach. Yet sometimes I wonder, if Jesus was in charge, whether He would rename it Focus on the Family of God. It seems so from this incident reported by three out of four gospel writers. Jesus says to us in this event: Guess what? Some things are simply more important than others and you need to understand that.

There is a story of a man who was out sailing with his son and the son's friend. And when the two were driven overboard there came a moment where the father knew he didn't have time to save both. Amazingly he saved the friend of his son and not his own child. When the time came to find out why, it was simply explained that the father knew his son was going to heaven, but he also knew the friend would not. The son's friend was not a believer. But as a result of this event the friend gave his life to Christ and grew up to be a minister. Think about that. It may seem hard to accept but from God's perspective, the father actually made the correct choice. When you have a kingdom perspective, nothing is more important than eternity.

It is the same thing that Jesus did for us. God so loved the world that He gave His only Son that whosoever believes in Him shall not perish but shall have everlasting life (John 3:16). Look at Jesus on the cross for the ultimate example. Notice two things as He was hanging there suspended between heaven and Earth: One: Wasn't he concerned with the family He was leaving behind for their well-being in His absence? Oh yes, because even from the cross He was making arrangements for His mother to be taken care of by John once He died. Two: Did He not finally make the choice to leave them for a higher purpose? Indeed he did. So there you have it: even though our families are the most precious thing in the world to us, they cannot be allowed to compete for our affections toward God.

It is a lot like being called into a military conflict. At that point you are sacrificing time with your loved ones to provide for the greater good of mankind. It is entirely possible that you may end up permanently leaving them behind. In the kingdom of God, we are also called into battle to fight the good fight of faith. The consequences of this battle against good and evil are even more significant than any earthly contest will ever be.

How about you? As much as we love our families, when it comes down to it, will we make the right choice? Is anything more important to us than Jesus Christ? Do we love our families more than we love Him? Where are all our time, energy, and resources headed? Does He consider us one of His children? These are the important questions that must not go unanswered. Our ultimate loyalty must be to the Lord. We are to love the Lord with all our hearts, minds, and souls and have no other gods before Him. "Behold," says Jesus, "my mother and my brothers." Can you see the point? Are you included in that expression of love He gave to His disciples?

Discussion Questions:

- Did Jesus focus more on His earthly family or the family of God? Why do you believe that to be the case?
- Are you more tied to earthly pleasures, comforts, and associations or with the associations that lead to the pleasures of eternity?
- Are you bogged down in family affairs or final affairs? Where are most of your time, energy, and resources directed?
- How uncomfortable is it for you to consider these matters?
- How does the analogy of entering the military help you better understand how the urgency of the mission sometimes comes before all other considerations?
- Is Jesus calling us to be inconsiderate to family matters or considerate yet determined that nothing will prevent us from our ultimate spiritual purpose in life?
- How is Jesus on the cross the best example of this balance between home and purpose?

Suggested Exercises:

- Ask at least ten of your closest friends, family members, and church acquaintances to evaluate you on the following matter: Where would they say your ultimate loyalties lie based on their interaction with you over the past decade: home, work, school, or the kingdom of God?
- Take that information and begin to rearrange your priorities until the kingdom of God becomes the predominant answer when that same question is presented to them ten years from now.

38

Listen and Make Inquiries

Mark 4:3-9; 13-20; Matthew 13:3-9; 18-23; Luke 8:4-8; 11-18

So take care how you listen; for whoever has, to him more shall be given; and whoever does not have, even what he thinks he has shall be taken away from him (Luke 8:18).

Hear then the parable of the sower (Matthew 13:18).

He who has ears to hear, let him hear (Mark 4:9).

Commands of Christ: *Listen! Behold:* went forth a sower to sow . . . Whoever has an ear to hear, *listen.* Therefore *understand* the parable of the sower . . . *Take heed* therefore what you hear.

The command of our Lord here is to pay attention to this parable. He presents to us four kinds of "soil" with varying results. In the end only one out of four surfaces brings forth positive results. There are various levels of commitment when the gospel is offered to mankind. The hard path (that ends up leaving the seeds out for the birds to eat) is someone who didn't understand the gospel at all and made no commitment to it whatsoever. Other commitments of a slightly greater dimension are represented in the rocky and thorny soils respectively. It seems the individual represented by the rocky soil only made a superficial commitment and did not realize what it could cost him. When the heat was turned on in his life and he faced adversity, he flew the coop. The last of the bad soils is said to have a choking effect on the seed as the individual is exposed as an idolater who is more committed to the lesser gods of riches and the everyday cares of this life. The various negative responses show the truth about what was really going on in each person's heart. Their faith commitment was questionable.

I fear there are a great many of these types of people today, who simply don't know what they have gotten themselves into with Christ. They come to Him to get something without realizing they will also be required to give something up in return. They won't be required to give up much; they will be required to give up all. Nothing less than their entire life is required. The old saying, "He is Lord of all or not Lord at all," is certainly applicable here. When the Philippian jailor asked Paul, "What must I do to be saved?" the reply was to "believe on the Lord Jesus Christ" (Acts 16:31). Three fourths of the surfaces receiving seed could not produce precisely because of that one term that is so often misappropriated: Lord (Master). If you accept Christ for less than who He is, you have not accepted Him at all.

I tell those I lead to Christ that there are two sides to the coin of salvation. One side is accepting what He did for us. He laid down His life for us. The other side is when we lay down our lives (in terms of control) for Him. That's what it means to accept Jesus as Lord. If both sides of the coin are not minted, it cannot be spent. In other words, the salvation transaction is incomplete due to the response of the believer also being incomplete.

But good soil produces a good harvest. Yet even among the good soil there are various levels of produce represented in the thirty-, sixty-, and one hundred-fold returns respectively. That tells us that our commitment to the kingdom can always be improved for greater results. It tells us that although we are indeed the children of God and rejoice in our participation in the growth of the kingdom, there is always room for advancement. As He says in John, "The ones who are bearing fruit I prune, so that they can bear more fruit" (15:2). The original Greek word for *prune* (kathairei) is where we get the word *catharsis*. Pruning is a cleansing of our life in certain areas of sin that are preventing us from having an even greater impact. Our passions have to be reined in to an even greater extent in order for God to use us in more substantial ways.

It is like the wild stallion that is enjoyable to observe yet practically useless to mankind until its raw power is harnessed. The unwieldy beast has to be tamed. Then the newly acquired meekness of the animal will allow those powerful resources to be accessed for the greater good. Absolute freedom leads to total irresponsibility. But the more a person yields to the Holy Spirit the more impact he or she can have in the world.

We must come to the point that we trust the Master to make the best of the lives we have surrendered to His will. In this farming analogy, Jesus insists that the insight provided by Him into how the kingdom operates must be understood so our heightened awareness will lead to greater success. Failure to comprehend how the mechanism operates will guarantee a malfunction.

Another reality from the parable is that few will actually be saved, yet all are to be given a chance. The disciples were among that small minority who had the capacity to produce positive results from good seed. They had eyes that could see and ears that could hear, so they were truly blessed. However, woe to those who are blind and deaf to the gospel message. One of the major differences between a disciple and the general crowds is that when challenged by Jesus, the disciples wouldn't jump to wrong conclusions. They waited till the appropriate time and investigated further. They asked Jesus what He meant. They had a good heart toward Jesus and were not willing to give up on Him. They knew that whatever He said, there had to be a good reason for it. Just like the statement He made about eating his flesh and drinking his blood (John 6:53). They were not alarmed by that because they knew He was saying things to deliberately challenge the loyalty of the audience. In the end, it is as Jesus said, that the good get even more and the evil lose what little they had to begin with (Matthew 25:29).

To those disciples, He has one further command: "Take heed therefore what you hear." They may not have realized it then, but Jesus was passing on information that would be indispensable for the Church throughout all time! They must pay careful attention to what He is teaching them so they can in turn teach others when the time comes. Pay close attention! You will need to know this backward and forward. He's counting on you.

Believe it or not, we too as modern day followers of Christ have to struggle with the hard sayings of Jesus. Sometimes He says things that seem impossible. We have to do what the first disciples did and wrestle with those things in Christ and come up with the best solution. Dig, research, and persist until you come to a moment of clarity and enlightenment. For example: He said if we divorce and remarry without good reason we commit adultery. He said that if our eye offends us we should pluck it out. He said if a person strikes you on one cheek offer the other. He said to be perfect as is your Father in heaven. He said to give to everyone who asks. He said to love your enemies. This is just to name a few. We should not be like many in the Church today that seem to hide from Jesus. They don't address His commandments because they consider them too demanding or politically incorrect. Unfortunately, we don't have that luxury as a true disciple. We must stay committed to His commands and live those out as we pass those forward to the next generation to tackle. A genuine disciple never gives up on Jesus. He never throws in the towel. He does what the Master intended: he grapples with the hard issues until he comes to some sort of a peaceful resolution.

Discussion Questions:

- What are the three types of bad soil and what does it say about the shallowness of their faith commitment?
- What causes an incomplete salvation transaction? What is required on our side of the exchange? What are the two sides of the coin of salvation?
- What do you make of this statement: "If you accept Christ for less than who He is, you have not accepted Him at all."
- What is the purpose for planting? Is it just to make new life or is it so that this new life can produce something significant?
- What are some ways we can become more productive plants? How does character development play a role? How does a fuller yield lead to a greater yield in terms of produce?
- How will a fuller understanding of how the kingdom mechanism operates ensure our ministry will be less likely to malfunction?
- Sometimes Jesus tosses out some hard seeds/pills to swallow. What are some examples and what is the appropriate response?

Suggested Exercises:

- Write out the parable of the sower from memory; discuss its meaning and how that applies to the Church today.
- Compare Jesus's overview of how the kingdom of God functions to you or your Church's ministry approach. Share with the group

where you need to make adjustments so as to operate more effectively within the system. What needs to be loosened and what needs to be tightened? What is working smoothly and needs no adjustment?

- Discuss among the group how fuller understandings of the way the kingdom functions will improve your approach to evangelism. Examine your church's evangelism practices in light of the principles the parable uncovers.

39

Understand the Kingdom

Matthew 13:24-30; 36-43

So just as the tares are gathered up and burned with fire, so shall it be at the end of the age. The Son of Man will send forth His angels, and they will gather out of His kingdom all stumbling blocks, and those who commit lawlessness, and will throw them into the furnace of fire; in that place there will be weeping and gnashing of teeth. Then the righteous will shine forth as the sun in the kingdom of their Father. He who has ears, let him hear (Matthew 13:40-43).

Command of Christ: Whoever has ears: *listen*!

Jesus wants us to understand how the kingdom of God works. Therefore, He commands us to listen when He shares this parable that explains everything. He is giving us a panoramic view of the entire system throughout history from beginning to end and shows us His role in that venture. He utilizes a parable to introduce the method of how God's redemptive plan will unfold over time. He uses a farmer again to demonstrate the sowing and reaping aspects of the kingdom.

He states that a man planted good seed in his field, but that during the night an enemy came and planted weeds along with that initial wheat. Once the plants developed, the weeds were discovered and the attendants questioned the owner. He knew it must have been an enemy that had done this evil deed and that he would have to address it at harvest time. He could not uproot the weeds now because their removal would also endanger the produce. He could only resolve the matter at harvest by first pulling and discarding the weeds and afterward harvesting the grain. Without the key that identifies each character, the story is just another day in a farmer's life.

In verses 36-43 Jesus provides the clues necessary to interpret the saying because the disciples asked Him to. In the process, He unveils the supernatural battle that is unfolding between the forces of good and evil in the world. In the story, He identifies Himself as the planter of good seed and the Devil as the planter of the bad. The good seed represents the sons of the kingdom and the bad seed are the sons of the Devil. The harvesters are the angels who come in and do the separation at the end of time.

What one takes away from all this is the fact that evil will not be eliminated in the here and now. In this world, we will have tribulation, but we are not to fear because Jesus has overcome the world (John 16:33). Whether at home, in the church, or in the world, we will find ourselves side by side with the ungodly. Perhaps one of the lessons we gain from this is not to attempt to separate from wicked society and evil men, because apparently that is simply not possible. Even in the household of faith, evil is always present. After all, wasn't it the religious leaders of Jesus's day who were the main culprits, and who were condemned by Christ as children of the Devil (John 8:44)? What is even more horrible of a thought is the fact that even one's own home environment may not be safe. It is as Jesus stated: "a man's enemies shall be those of his own household" (Matthew 10:36). Yet you expect that you will face the enemy out in the world. What makes everyone susceptible is the fact that God has granted each individual the right to choose for himself and herself. This also demonstrates how easy it must be to make the wrong choice because no doubt the enemy will make his choice look, feel, and taste similar to the truth.

It also begs the question about why God allows evil in the world. It is not that He wants evil, but He does want us to have a free will and wants to see how we will exercise it before He brings the world to justice in the end. It is our abuse of a wonderful gift in being able to reason and conclude what we believe is the best course of action that has led to sin. But the gift itself is not a sin but a magnificent expression of love in offering us a precious thing called liberty. He did not create the evil world; we created it in our inappropriate response to the freedom He has given us. How should we respond to these harsh realities?

We are to live by faith (Habakkuk 2:4). The Bible declares that although the world around us seems to be falling apart and it seems that God is nowhere to be found, don't lose heart. God is still in control. We will prevail in the end if we continue to hold on to Him. The Old Testament prophet Habakkuk learned this lesson well almost six hundred years before Christ came to Earth. In that book he is first startled by the way his fellow believers, children of Israel, were treating each other. All he could see around him was violence (Hab. 1:2-3). The people of God in many instances had turned into cutthroats, and not toward the enemy but toward one another. He cried out to God, wondering in his heart why He would allow this injustice on the earth to continue unabated. God answered, but indeed it was an answer that alarmed him even more. He promised to send the Babylonians to wreak havoc and take revenge upon this evil generation in Israel. At that point Habakkuk was even more distressed by the fact that God would use the greater evil to punish the lesser evil. But not to worry, for the Babylonians would also have their day of judgment. In the end, Habakkuk learned just to leave things up to the Lord, knowing that no matter how bad it looks now, all will be rectified in the end (Hab. 3:17). We are simply to trust Him because He knows what He is doing. The just shall live by faith.

In a world where each person gets to decide for himself, it is inevitable that wrong choices will be made. Even though evil comes of it, this is still the best of all possible worlds, for the alternative is to not be made in God's image. It is not to have a free will at all but to have every decision predetermined to function for the good of all mankind. This would make all of us very much like robots. But the wonder of this life is that we are free! Free to make of our lives whatever we wish. God's wish is that we would include Him in that undertaking. But what a wonderful thing it is to have our choices respected when at any time He has the power to end all resistance and all life as well. When a relationship is based on love, that relationship must be presented with the opportunity to be accepted or rejected. Hence we have the very reason why the world operates as it does. It is to provide as an opportunity to decide for ourselves whether we want to serve the Lord. When we say yes, it can become a genuine experience where we say to Him that He is all I really want. I want You, Lord, more than I want anything else. It is what I have chosen because I love You. The only way you know if someone really loves you is if they don't have to say yes but do anyway. The world is the way it is because God wants to see what we will do if the choice is totally up to us.

There is one more item that suggests itself in this mechanism. Since it is allowed, what good does it do to suffer? As we know, it is by suffering that our faith is tested and has the opportunity to mature. Once it matures we can be used by God in a greater way. Patience, perseverance, self-control, knowledge, brotherly love, and godliness all come through testing. So suffering can be useful, albeit unpleasant at times.

Another benefit that we tend to overlook is the appreciation of heaven. If life were without trouble, it would be heaven already. We would have nothing to look forward to and we certainly would not appreciate that experience having already lived it. I believe this is another important way God uses suffering for our good. This life is preparing us for the next where there will be no pain, sorrow, sickness, or death—all of which we would take for granted had we not gone through these trials first. It is important to God that we appreciate what He does for us and that we do not take Him for granted, both in this life and the life to come.

Discussion Questions:

- What does the parable of the weeds give us a bird's-eye view of?
- What does the parable teach us about separating from the evil in the world? Is that really even possible, whether in the world or in the church?
- Is evil a result of a faulty creation or an abuse of the freedoms so graciously offered?
- How does God's giving everyone a choice prove His love for them?
- Why does God allow evil in the world? What good can come of it?
- How does the book of Habakkuk teach not to second-guess God?

Suggested Exercises:

- Explain in writing how the fact that the evil and the righteous are side by side in the church could change the way you preach your sermons or approach your ministry.

- Determine not to do the weeding out yourself since you really can't see anyone's heart. Resolve to allow that to be done at the end of time when Jesus separates the sheep from the goats. But at the same time determine not to allow that to be an excuse to accept sin in the Church with no follow-up according to Matthew 18:15-17.
- Eschew violent retribution of any kind in the home, church, or society at large. Respect the rights of individuals to choose as does the heavenly Father. Draw out an agreement for all to sign, abhorring and forbidding violence in Jesus's name.

40

Go through the Storm

Matthew 8:18-27; Mark 4:35-41; Luke 8:22-25

Now when Jesus saw a crowd around Him, He gave orders to depart to the other side of the sea . . . *and behold, there arose a great storm on the sea, so that the boat was being covered with the waves; but Jesus Himself was asleep* (Matthew 8:18 and 24).

Command of Christ: *He gave orders* for them to cross over.

When we take a second look, we observe in this passage that the *order* was given to cross over the lake. To say that Jesus didn't know what lay ahead would not be true to the many reports of His foreknowledge throughout the gospel records. Yet He did not cower from this premonition. As a matter of fact He was entirely content to sleep through the whole ordeal had He been given the chance. He totally trusted His safety into the Father's hands and knew that nothing would prevent Him from completing His ultimate mission. But obviously the disciples were not there yet. They still had much to learn, hence the reason for the command to move forward.

Yet it must also be admitted that it is easy for us to find fault with these men as we write our criticisms from our air conditioned offices 2000 years later. Facing a tempest on the open sea, however, would rattle the knees and nerves of the best of us. Nobody welcomes violent winds and waves. They simply overtake us when they are ready, whatever their variety. Whether it be the natural blasts of severe weather or the storms of life in general, they must come and the Lord will use these unsettling occurrences for our good. So the command from Jesus to them and to us is to stand up under the storm and struggle through it.

Andrae Crouch said it well in his song *Through It All*: "If I'd never had a problem, I wouldn't know that God could solve them." As we weather the storms we grow and mature in our walk with God. At first we are horrified and in fear of losing our lives. Over time, however, it is hoped by our heavenly Father that we will learn to trust in Him more. Deuteronomy 8:3 states, "So He humbled you, allowed you to hunger, and fed you with manna which you did not know nor did your fathers know, that He might make you know that man shall not live by bread alone; but by every word that proceeds from the mouth of the LORD."

God wants us to learn how to rely on Him in every situation. Jesus was one with the Father in helping bring the disciples to that place of absolute trust. The only way your faith can grow is for that faith to be tested. But none of us plan to test our own faith; it is just the ups and downs of life that test it for us. The key is to cease trying to avoid all risks, trials, and temptations. We are not to go around our problems but through them. Just as we increase our strength by testing and stretching our muscles, so our faith is made stronger by stretching it to the limit. The trying of your faith is "more precious than gold" because of the character it builds (1 Peter 1:7).

The old saying is true: "Sow an act and reap a habit. Sow a habit and reap a character. Sow a character and reap a destiny." It is through our trials that we are trained to be victorious in battle. God has a special assignment for us but we will never rise to the occasion without refinement.

If you have ever ministered to drug addicts you will notice one thing in particular that seems to identify many in general, which is a severe lack of maturity and responsibility. This is basically due to this one thing we have been talking about. They, in many instances, have spent twenty or more years of their lives doing everything they can to avoid conflict, pain, and storms of any kind through the abuse of mind-altering chemicals. Escaping the harsh realities of life is the very thing that ensures that you will always remain at the maturity level of a child regardless of what chronological age you are. Whether you use drugs or something else, the results are generally the same. Remaining defiant and immature will ensure you have no place of honor in the kingdom of God. You will become a branch that bears no fruit, and such a branch will be cut off from the vine (John 15:2). Even if you do produce, you can count on further pruning to enable you to produce even more. So we must find a way to change our perspective.

James says you should "count it all joy when you fall into diverse temptations—knowing this: that the trying of your faith works patience. But let patience have her perfect work, that you may be perfect and entire, wanting nothing" (1:3). Once we have been polished and refined (over a long period of time), we will find our purpose.

We need total trust, recall, courage, and optimism, just to name a few, to win our battles against the kingdom of darkness. So the next time a storm pops up, keep that in mind. Don't jump ship; just hold on with all your might in order to gain the insight, integrity, and fortitude you will need to overcome the enemy. It is, as they say, "What doesn't kill you will only make you stronger."

Discussion Questions:

- What does the fact that Jesus ordered them to cross the lake (all the while knowing a storm lay ahead) say to you about what He expects from his disciples?
- How do problems test our level of trust in God? Do you have any personal examples?
- How does the illustration of body building relate to the building of faith and other character traits in our spiritual man? Does the expression "no pain, no gain" apply?
- How does James 1:3 demonstrate the "no pain, no gain" principle of spiritual growth?
- How does the illustration of the marine's sword express the value of trials in the maturing process of the Christian?
- Does the fact that we are to expect storms and that they are ultimately good for us provide you encouragement for what you are facing lately? Explain.

Suggested Exercises:

- Have each person in the group pray a prayer of thanksgiving for the hardship that has fallen upon them lately, knowing that all things work together for the good of those who love the Lord and are called according to His purpose.

- Look back over your life to discover where you might have gotten off track with the Lord in avoiding a test or a trial or not responding appropriately to that storm. Ask yourself what specific character trait you forfeited in the process and determine to hang on when the next opportunity arises. Share your discoveries with a trusted fellow disciple who can hold you accountable.

- Share with the group specific character defects that were addressed and eliminated in the process of toughing out a storm.

- Inventory your life according to the fruit of the Spirit list in Galatians 5:22. Share with the group which fruit has fully developed in your life and that which has yet to fully develop. Determine to go through whatever it takes to fulfill God's purpose for your life.

41

Be Rejuvenated

Mark 6:31

Come away by yourselves to a solitary place and be refreshed for a while.

Command of Christ: *Come away* by yourselves to a solitary place and *be refreshed* for a while.

We discover something interesting in the life of Jesus that perhaps would not have been expected. There were regular attempts to get away from the pressures of ministry and to be refreshed by nature and solitude. Sometimes He would try the wilderness because that was a place where few people would dare to venture (Mark 1:45; 6:32; 6:46; Luke 4:42; 5:16). Other times He would go out of the country hoping not to be noticed so much there (Mark 6:31; 7:24). However, in many instances He would ascertain that his notoriety had preceded Him (Mark 6:33).

One can imagine the frenzy of excitement among the people once they realized physical healing was just a touch away. Day and night He was bombarded to the point that they could barely sit down to eat. So once the full disclosure of the situation is before us, it is not unreasonable at all to see why the Master saw it necessary to break away from the madness on occasion. The pace and volume of the needs were overwhelming and the need to keep Himself from wearing down was ever before Him.

The other side of the issue has to do with His and our relationship with God that is the very source of His and our ministry in the first place. So there are the physical and the spiritual limitations and the need to replenish what is lost in the course of a hard day's work. If not, there is a very real danger that neither your body nor your spirit will survive. The power to succeed in ministry comes from our relationship with God. That relationship requires quality time and undivided attention: hence you see Jesus striving not only to teach and heal but to get alone with God. The power to keep showing up for a good day's work comes from times of Sabbath rest and retreat.

Sometimes we are tempted to see retreats as an unnecessary expense and luxury. We too often see it as a benefit package for the corporate domain and not the house of God where we are called to sacrifice and to empty ourselves. Unfortunately, that will be the exact consequence if we continue to maintain a nonstop, overly demanding pace without reprisal. It will eventually end in the loss of our ministry altogether and the opting out for something more charitable toward the frailties of human existence.

So, one consequence of the failure to get away is the demise of one's ministry altogether. The other consequence of failing to get alone with God on a regular basis is ministry impotence. An unsuccessful venture for God can sometimes be much worse than bringing that entire venture to a close. And I believe these are two of the reasons we see our highest example (Jesus) behaving the way He does. He is constantly doing whatever He can to get away and get alone with God knowing that this is the source of His life's mission and success.

He also teaches his disciples to follow his example. In Mark 6:31 we have the consummation of the disciples' mission under Jesus's supervision, where He gave them power over unclean spirits and diseases and power to preach the gospel. After they went through all the villages, Jesus instructed them it was time to take a break and to assess the campaign. It was time to recharge for further exploits.

The order He gives them to obey without question is: "Come away by yourselves to a solitary place and be refreshed for a while." So it is not only essential that we cozy up to the idea of retreats, but we are actually commanded to do so. We are under mandate to take time out on occasion.

Now, according to Jesus, what must this retreat consist of? Well, the Greek words of the original passage clarify that for us. The first requirement is *kat'idian*, which means "according to yourself," or "alone." Seclusion or solitude is the first objective. Secondly is *eis eremon*, which means "into the wilderness," or nature. Third is *anapausasthe,* which means "be refreshed." This word means to allow one to cease from his or her labors in order to regain composure and vigor. So there you have, in the Master's own words, both the order to be restored and the specifics that are required to adhere to restoration in the best possible way.

There is no need to feel guilty about it unless you are not doing enough work to need a break in the first place. So my advice to myself and others, based on the Master's imperative, is: Don't neglect yourself and think you do not need any rest. The next time a retreat is offered, take it. The next time a vacation is available, take that too. In addition, take every opportunity on a daily basis to stay full of the Holy Spirit by spending quality time alone with God in prayer.

Discussion Questions:

- What is your first response to the fact that Jesus was known to break away from the crowds on a regular basis?
- Why do you think this is necessary both on a physical and spiritual level?
- What could become of our ministries if we fail to abide by Jesus's policy? Do you have any personal examples of burn-out that you would like to share?
- What are the three indispensable ingredients of a retreat according to Jesus in Mark 6:31?

Suggested Exercises:

- The next time your church offers a retreat, don't blow it off. Plan to participate.
- This week plan the type of vacation that includes daily opportunities to get alone with the Lord surrounded only by His creation.
- Suggest a wilderness retreat for your church this year, one where all electronic devices and cell phones are checked at the lobby.
- Establish a routine that includes daily, weekly, and yearly solitude, especially as it relates to your personal connection with the Lord in terms of prayer and meditation. Compare and contrast your methods and ideas with a trusted fellow disciple this week.

42

Seek My Kingdom and I'll Seek Yours

Matthew 14:15-21; Mark 6:35-44; Luke 9:12-17; John 6:5-13

The people saw them going, and many recognized them and ran there together on foot from all the cities, and got there ahead of them. When Jesus went ashore, he saw a large crowd, and he felt compassion for them because they were like sheep without a shepherd; and he began to teach them many things. When it was already quite late, his disciples came to him and said, "This place is desolate and it is already quite late; send them away so that they may go into the surrounding countryside and villages and buy themselves something to eat" (Mark 6:33-36).

Commands of Christ: *You give* them something to eat. *Go* and *see*. *Bring* them here to me. *Recline* them. *Gather* up the excess.

This story of the feeding of the five thousand is peppered with commands due to the nature of the undertaking. It started out with an attempt by Jesus and his disciples to get away from the pressures of ministry. They got into a boat and sailed over to a remote section of Bethsaida thinking they would be safe there. But somehow the crowd got wind of it and was there waiting for them when they arrived.

Jesus must have been impressed with both their persistence and desperation and therefore ministered to and taught them. He stayed there with them for some time and then it was getting late. The disciples realized the people were a good distance from the cities and were in peril. They needed to get going before dark. If they didn't make a move now to take care of their families and get them something to eat, they would wind up doing without and suffering from hunger and thirst on the way back home.

Jesus realized the people were so desperate to get to Him they had forgotten to make arrangements for sustenance. Eating was an afterthought while they stood at the Savior's feet totally enthralled with His teachings and the glory of God to heal. Yet had He not taught them to cease from being concerned with these things? Did He not say to "take no thought" about what you will eat and drink? And now, here was a massive amount of families who had done just that. Jesus had taught them that if they seek the kingdom first, all these other things would be added. I believe He intended to make good on that promise.

So why does He command his disciples first to give them something to eat? John 6:6 states that He actually asked them that question to "test" them because He already had a plan. When He presented them with the dilemma and insisted it was their responsibility, they began to do some calculating. It was concluded that eight months' wages would not really be enough to pay for the food for that colossal crowd. They began to see the enormity of the problem and the extent of the shortage. I believe this was the Master's point. Before we can truly appreciate the scope of the miracle we must understand the scale of the disaster. He didn't want the disciples to thoughtlessly follow him along and say, "Well, that was interesting, and there sure were a lot of people fed today. I wonder what's on the agenda for tomorrow." No, it's by entering the struggle and feeling the pressures and weight of it that our eyes are opened to the immensity of God's grace and provision.

I think this is oftentimes why we don't always get answers to our problems right away. He wants us to experience just how horrible and impossible the situation is and will continue to be outside His intervention. That way, when we finally are relieved of the burden, we will never forget just how amazing was the miracle that set us free and will ever be grateful that this bondage is no longer our unrelenting reality. "If the Lord had not been on our side, all our enemies would have swallowed us alive" (Psalm 124:3).

Once they realized the extent of the shortage, He began to issue a string of commands that would provide the "hands and feet" of the miracle He intended. All of these steps take faith to follow through with.

Had they not highly respected and trusted the Master, they would have only laughed at the instructions that followed.

He commanded them to go and see—but what is the use when no matter how much one person possessed, it is inadequate for the multitude. However, they did it anyway; they followed the command and reported back to him the number of items they had found. It seems that among all those people only one had perhaps been instructed by his mother to pack a lunch! Next he commanded they bring those items to Him. I wonder how difficult it must have been to convince the little lad to give up his lunch. Again, wouldn't we laugh at anyone who suggested such a thing? How can commandeering a little boy's lunch solve the hunger of the masses?

Again, a tremendous faith is required to follow through with every command. This does not appear to be a logical or reasonable course of action. However, we have learned as did the mother of Jesus that whatever He asks us, make sure you just do it (John 2:5)! After all, didn't he turn six huge water-filled pots into wine only when it was presented? The disciples too had learned one thing about the Lord. No matter how outrageous it sounded, just trust Him.

Next they were ordered to recline or gather the people into groups of fifty. To do this they were showing their confidence in Christ coming through with a miracle. After Jesus did, there were leftovers. Imagine how they must have felt as they went around and tasted, touched, and smelled the tangible resources that were once only in their imagination. He valued the surplus and so commanded them to gather up what remained. More than that there was the exchange that went on between disciples and the supernatural that must have caused a great and celebratory uproar in their spirits.

So here are the lessons learned:

1. We must fully appreciate the extent of the shortage.
2. More important than what you don't have is what you do have: bring that to the Lord.
3. Prepare then to receive exponentially!
4. Value the surplus. Behold what the Lord has done and be astonished! Taste it, touch it, feel it and never let yourself forget the glory of that moment.

We too can rely on God's provision. He promised us that if we put Him first there will be no need to be concerned with what we will eat or drink or how we will be clothed. Pray that God will increase your faith, that you too will focus on what is most important—leaving the basic necessities up to Him. May we seek earnestly for this kind of faith as his disciples. We need to search and discover ways to rely on Christ more.

Discussion Questions:

- Why were the five thousand plus people unprepared for the journey to find Jesus?
- Why did they all end up in the wilderness?
- How did this miracle of feeding the five thousand fulfill Matthew 6:33?
- Why did Jesus tell the disciples to feed all of those people?
- Why did He ask for the little boy's lunch?
- What were the four lessons learned by the disciples from this experience?

Suggested Exercises:

- Recall the last time you were so "hungry for Jesus" that you forgot to plan for lunch or you were so full of the Holy Spirit that you lost your appetite. Share that with the group or a trusted fellow disciple. Pray together for a personal revival.
- Examine your life as a whole. Is the will of God or your own your first concern? Repent if you discover it is your kingdom (personal ambitions, career, or lifestyle) that is your top priority.
- Meditate on the Lord's Prayer every morning before you start your day to keep your priorities straight. In time the external preoccupations will conform to the internal predisposition.
- Name an impossible situation you are facing right now that no matter how hard you try, you can't figure out a way to solve it. Share with your discipleship group how what you do have will not even make a dent in what you need.
- Determine whatever it is that you do have and give that to the Church (which is the body of Christ). Believe that Christ is yet willing to multiply what you have offered due to your devotion to

kingdom priorities. Pray the prayer of faith with your group and follow whatever further directions He may have for you. Cherish the surplus as God provides.

- Testify before the church how your needs where met by the Lord as you put His kingdom first and put everything else you needed in His hands.

Warning: These last three steps are not a "magic formula" with guaranteed results. It is simply a faith exercise based on what the Lord required of His disciples when they were in similar circumstances. Each person must first determine whether he or she has been called to participate.

43

Cheer Up, I'm Here

Matthew 14:24-33; Mark 6:47-52; John 6:16-21

When the disciples saw him walking on the sea, they were terrified, and said, "It is a ghost!" And they cried out in fear. But immediately Jesus spoke to them, saying, "Take courage, it is I; do not be afraid" (Mark 6:49-50).

Commands of Christ: *Cheer up*, I am; *do not be* afraid.

This command is one of assurance. He's telling them and us not to be afraid, that it will be all right because He is here. Our dark and dreadful pessimism can now be transformed into a sunny and cheerful optimism because of one thing: Christ is here. That's the way frightened sheep feel once they spot their shepherd. They know His presence is their joy, for in that moment there is no fear of harm in them. Having that feeling of security we can now let our guard down, relax, and enjoy life.

This is a story about God's presence. I believe it was the presence of God that enabled Jesus to walk on the water in the first place. Just prior to this incident Jesus was in the hills alone praying and connecting with God the Father. As He walked out onto the water He was walking in the Spirit having been energized by the powerful presence of God. The natural world is no match for the supernatural, and every threat it poses is rendered null and void being so vastly inferior.

Jesus was likely just enjoying his exhilarating connection with God and the byproduct of that relationship. The gospel story records that He "would have passed them by" had they not cried out to Him. He walked

274

on the same water in which the disciples struggled to even stay afloat. His connection with God was the difference. They had not spent hours in prayer alone with God like Jesus had. However, once He arrived, there was the presence of God again, to extinguish the harsh realities they had experienced. When He got into the boat with them the winds ceased.

So is it to be in our own lives. No matter what storm we go through on the outside there can be an abiding peace on the inside. The key to enjoying this type of lifestyle is found in Jesus's example of breaking away from the crowd to get recharged with the Holy Spirit. We need to keep our souls full so that it will be well with us both inwardly and outwardly in our ministries. In our efforts for the kingdom, we will be attacked from all sides in an attempt to move us off track from the goal of making disciples. It is our refreshment in the presence of the Lord that will keep us centered and unshakable.

This is what was discovered long ago by a man, Nicolas Herman, who was called Brother Lawrence. He lived and worked in a Discalced Carmelite monastery in Paris in the seventeenth century. One of the leaders of the monastery noticed that his countenance was always joyful and went to investigate. He found out that Brother Lawrence was doing something he called "practicing the presence of God." He had made it a habit of staying open to God throughout the day no matter how mundane his duty at the time (he worked in the kitchen). The result was a peace and a joy untold and unending. I believe our Christianity is what we make of it, and here is someone who invested in the kingdom and enjoyed a bountiful return.

Perfect love casts out all fear (1 John 4:18). God is perfect (Matthew 5:46) and God is love (1 John 4:8). So to stay full of courage, strength, and focus, we must find a way to walk in the Spirit, or continually practice God's presence. Jesus said we must abide in Him if we want to bear fruit (John 15:1-5). If we get disconnected we wither away and become useless. As soon as the lamp, TV, radio, or fan is unplugged it ceases to function within the capacity for which it was designed. So we must develop a plan similar to Brother Lawrence's that will find us keeping company with God on a regular basis.

The main artery to the heart of the matter is seeing how Jesus did it. He would regularly break away from the crowds and get alone with God (Luke 5:16). What is required for constant companionship is both uninterrupted and interrupted time with God. Uninterrupted is when you schedule a daily routine of going to your innermost room where your Father sees you in secret (Matthew 6:5-15). I recommend eventually working this time up to an hour a day since Jesus once told the disciples, "could you not watch with me one hour?" (Matthew 26:40) Secondly, there is the method Brother Lawrence used of "practicing the presence." He believed the presence of God was available in the most mundane of tasks just as it was at the holy altar. We just have to stay open to Him and heighten our awareness of Him throughout the day. After all, He is always present; it is just that we do not realize it or acknowledge it.

I believe this is what Paul was referring to when he said, "Walk in the Spirit and you will not fulfill the lusts of the flesh" (Galatians 5:16). Heighten your awareness of His presence and tap into it. Do not let any sin distract you from your goal of uninterrupted communion with God.

Discussion Questions:

- What was it that both enabled Jesus to walk on the water and calmed the storm for the disciples who were being tossed around in the boat?
- What effort did Jesus make to stay connected to God that we also must imitate?
- What was the method of Nicholas Herman that we could also emulate?
- How do the following scriptures—John 15:1-5; Galatians 5:16; and 1 John 4:18-confirm the need to practice the presence of God?

Suggested Exercises:

- Make an inventory of your daily routine and establish a time frame that is best for breaking away. Every day find time to get away by yourself and spend time with God.
  Try to accomplish this in a way that does not bring too much attention to yourself.
- Practice awareness of God's presence continually. Keep the lines of communication open regardless of what daily task you may be involved in. Share your experience.

44

Labor for My Love

John 6:26-40

Jesus answered then and said, "Truly, truly, I say to you, you seek me, not because you saw signs, but because you ate of the loaves and were filled. Do not work for the food which perishes, but for the food which endures to eternal life, which the Son of Man will give to you, for on him the Father, God, has set His seal" (John 6:26-27).

Command of Christ: *Do not labor* for food that perishes.

The context here is the aftermath of feeding the five thousand. The people were overwhelmed about what had happened and were eager to see what came next. They had lost track of Jesus because He had walked on the water to the other side of the lake overnight. Somehow they figured out that He was on the other side and were asking him how He got there. Instead of updating them with latest news of his supernatural exploits, He decided to point out that their desires had gotten out of control. This coveting had the potential to prevent them from arriving at the proper conclusion about the miracle. An opportunity to increase their faith in Him was slipping by unnoticed.

They were in jeopardy of missing the whole point: He had fed them to prove that when their motives are pure, God can be trusted to provide. But now because of the satiating bread, their motives had become clouded. They were focused on the gift and not on the giver. They were eager to be involved with the power of God to perform miracles, not realizing the greatest miracle is what God will do for us through His only begotten Son.

The gift should have turned them toward the giver with feelings of gratitude. It should have stirred within their hearts a desire to know him better. It should have caused them and us to fall in love with the Lord even more. For He not only teaches well (Matthew 6:33), He backs that up with wonderful compassion and heavenly provision. They should now be sitting at his feet to see how he will further lead them to God, how he will finally instruct us along the way to enter the kingdom of God and establish an eternal relationship with the King.

Jesus wanted them to know not how powerful His work was but how powerful His love was. Initially they had been drawn to God's kingdom and were now in dire straits because of it. He loved them for their sacrifice and was compelled to do something for them so they would not go hungry. The physical bread was only a stepping stone to the spiritual bread that was vastly superior. That spiritual bread was not baked dough but a person.

Jesus had an almost impossible task before Him because His job was to lead them to Himself. He did not point out the way; He was the way. He did not share the truth; He was the truth (John 14:6). Truth is not a concealed body of information that is strictly factual. Truth is a person. He didn't have access to the light; He was the light of the world. Oh that they would come to realize just who He was and just what He was willing to go through for them. The miracles were not an end in themselves. They were a means of developing a personal relationship with God through Christ that would last forever.

Don't labor for the food that perishes. Labor for what will last. Labor for His love. Jesus says to us, "I am it! I am what you are looking for. Find me and your search will be over. I am everything you need."

What do you want from Jesus? Are you merely just another satisfied customer with your insurance policy in hand? Is there a problem you need Him to solve? Are you hungry, sick, or lonely? Do you want to know what He can do for you, or do you want to know what you can do for Him? When He asks you, "What do you want from me?" I hope your answer will be, "I just want you, Lord."

Discussion Questions:

- What is the evidence that the people wanted more food and not more of Jesus?
- What faith lesson was their coveting interfering with?
- Why doesn't the gift turn us toward the giver?
- What was Jesus's impossible task?
- The miracles are the means to what end?
- Do you want to know what He can do for you or what you can do for Him?
- Which choice above shows you are not laboring for food but for love?

Suggested Exercises:

- Have you ever been distracted by a miracle and coveted the gift more than the giver? Share your experience with the group and the lessons you learned from it.
- Confess your fault to another trusted disciple. Provide him or her with recent examples of how you have focused more on the economy and earthly treasures over eternal treasures. Confess how you have spent more time and effort toward earthly over heavenly retirement. Confess how you have craved provision, power, and prestige more than a closer relationship with God. Pray together for forgiveness and inner healing.
- Write out a prayer stating your determination not to be sidetracked by the temporal over the eternal realities in life. Include repentance for leaving your first love.

45

Read between the Lines

John 6:40-60

*He who eats my flesh and drinks my blood has eternal life, and
I will raise him up on the last day; for my flesh is true food, and
my blood is true drink. He who eats my flesh and drinks my blood
abides in me, and I in him. As the living Father sent me, and I live
because of the Father, so he who eats me, he also will live because
of me* (John 6:54-57).

Command of Christ: *Do not grumble* with yourselves.

It is easy for a Christian to instantly condemn the Pharisees here for
grumbling about Jesus's claims. They say hindsight is 20/20. They are
encountering a man who is making incredible statements about Himself
that could very well border on blasphemy. They only saw Jesus as a poor
itinerate preacher, and they knew of his upbringing in Nazareth and were
familiar with his family unit. How can he say He is the bread that came
down from heaven? Yet for those of us who have truly come to know Him,
Jesus was simply explaining the facts.

The Christian symbol of the fish (*ixthus*) tells it all. Each letter of the
Greek word for fish tells us something about Jesus that ancient Christianity
had come to discover about him over time. *Iesous*=Jesus; *Xristos*=Christ;
Theos=God's; *Uios*=Son and *Swter*=Savior. Jesus, Christ, God's Son,
Savior: that is the core insight that defines our faith. It was this very truth
that would have set them free, had they the eyes to see it. Jesus told them

not to grumble because after all, only those who were informed by God could understand.

Only those who were close to God would have the ears to hear and the eyes to see. They would be mysteriously drawn to Him despite what He might say. Instead of being offended, these individuals would become all the more curious to find out just what exactly was going on behind all of these incredible statements and miracles. They would not be put off by what appeared to be outlandish claims, but it would stimulate their interest even further. And so it was with the disciples. Many were offended, especially by the flesh-eating statements. The disciples themselves were alarmed but refused to let go until they found out the full explanation.

This is the policy with regard to Jesus as his follower or disciple. Don't be taken aback by his bold rhetoric. You will always find after further review that He had a very good reason for making such a statement. There are many proclamations we cringe at as a disciple and we have to bite our tongues. For example, "If your eye offends you, pluck it out." "If a man slaps you on the right cheek, offer him the other also." "Sell all you have and give to the poor." "Bless those who curse you." "Unless you eat my flesh and drink my blood you have no life in you." "Be perfect as your father in heaven is perfect." "Let the dead bury their dead." How about the requirement to hate your father, mother, wife, children, brothers, sisters, and your own life in order to be a disciple (Luke 14:26)? When we encounter these hard sayings we are tempted to rush in and put out the fire that Jesus just started. Who are we to do so? We must respond to those powerful images as did the first disciples. Just study further to see what is the underlying principle.

Hyperbole is a tool that Jesus seemed to favor quite a bit. A hyperbole is: 1. Obvious and intentional exaggeration. 2. An extravagant statement or figure of speech not intended to be taken literally, as "to wait an eternity (dictionary.com)." But the way Jesus uses it, it almost seems literal, so it is not always easy to know right away what He really means. Oftentimes it just so happens that as the disciples pull Him aside for further explanation, we find that he was simply trying to make a point. He used rhetoric to shock the people to the point of triggering the type of response that ensured He would have their undivided attention. The biggest problem to overcome with the public is simply that: getting and maintaining their attention.

Jesus seemed to employ a variety of strategies to ensure that would never be a problem. Stories, parables, hyperbole, metaphors, miracles, etc., all ensured a captive audience. Yet more importantly I believe He would utilize that method to drive home a point. He wanted to shake the audience out of its complacency.

I believe Jesus also used metaphor due to being meek, lowly, and humble. He was faced with the unenviable position of having to proclaim to the world that He was it! How do you tell people that you are the answer without coming off as full of yourself? However, since it was the truth, He was beholden to oblige. He did very well with the "I am" passages: I am the way, the truth, the life. I am the light of the world. I am the door. I am the bread of life. I am the good shepherd. I am the resurrection and the life. He said everything but "I am God." But in every one of those metaphors, "I am God" is implied. Just think how much trouble the Christian faith has encountered over the metaphor used in the institution of the Lord's Supper? The statement "This is my body" has caused centuries of debate.

We have to learn to read between the lines with Jesus. From practice and a greater familiarity with his teachings we have to learn to distinguish between those instances when He is being literal and when He is making an intentional exaggeration to drive home a point. So don't complain, don't grumble, and most importantly don't give up on Jesus's statements. If you are willing to face them, hold on to them and wrestle with them; you will prevail in the end. In our encounter with the bold statements of Jesus, one thing is required: the tenacity of a bull dog. Whatever you do, don't let go!

Discussion Questions:

- What were the true followers of Jesus in the process of discovering about him that the Pharisees were blind to? How is that discovery preserved in the Greek word for "fish"?
- What is the dictionary definition of hyperbole; and how did Jesus utilize this to perfection in His ministry?
- How will a better understanding of Jesus's rhetorical methods tend to prevent a disciple from getting the wrong impression?
- What are some examples of Jesus's fondness for metaphor? How has His followers' misunderstanding of this led to confusion in the Christian faith?
- What is it that will help ensure we are able to distinguish between when Jesus is being literal and when He is using hyperbole?

- How does determination play a positive role in this undertaking?

Suggested Exercises:

- Do some research on the difficult sayings of Jesus and share your findings with the group. F. F. Bruce and David Bivin have done some good work in this area.
- Have each member of the group share their least favorite of all of the statements of Jesus. After discussing it, if there is still not closure on the issue, have everybody research the statement until the matter is laid to rest within their hearts. They can also interview individuals who have demonstrated a more seasoned and scholarly conservative understanding of scripture. Use a fellow disciple to be your accountability partner to make sure you follow through on the assignments.

46

Beware of Extremes

Matthew 16:5-12; Mark 8:13-21; Luke 12:1-3

Then they understood that He did not say to beware of the leaven
of bread, but of the teaching of the Pharisees and Sadducees
(Matthew 16:12).

Command of Christ: *Watch and beware* of the leaven of the Pharisees and
Sadducees.

Not long after Jesus fed the five thousand, he was intercepted by the
Pharisees and the Sadducees in another part of town, and they demanded
a sign from Him. Wasn't producing bread out of thin air enough? How
about the continual healings? All they really had to do was stick around
long enough to see Him in action. Jesus was outraged at this demand to
produce a sign and refused to accommodate them. He left them only with
a riddle about Jonah in the belly of the whale.

   As He left the company of those religious politicians He reminded
his disciples to watch out for them. Jesus referred to their false doctrine as
"leaven," or yeast. He told them to beware and be on the lookout for the
"leaven" of the Pharisees and the Sadducees. Here again we see Jesus using
a metaphor but not explaining it. Instead, He expected the disciples to
pick up on the spiritual and not the literal sense of the statement. But they
did not. They got the impression that Jesus was displeased with them for
forgetting to bring along bread. This amazed Jesus since He had on more
than one occasion produced bread out of nowhere. They should have
learned by now that seeking the kingdom meant that the necessities would

take care of themselves. It must have seemed as if they were hopelessly incompetent and so slow to pick up on the simplest lessons. So He took them to task for it. Then they finally understood that the leaven of the Pharisees and Sadducees was their doctrine.

To understand the platforms of these two parties one must investigate within the academic discipline of New Testament History. There you find their modus operandi in great detail. One basic way to understand these opposing viewpoints is through the conservative versus liberal perspectives. Although what we see in those two movements (liberal and conservative) in the twenty-first century is certainly a completely different animal, we can at least understand the fundamental principle behind it all. One group basically believes "anything goes" while the other condemns everything and would say, "Nothing goes."

The "anything goes" philosophy of the Sadducees is illustrated in their insistence that this life we live here on Earth is all there is. There is no reward/punishment stage in the afterlife because there is no afterlife. They saw no mention of a hereafter in the Torah (first five books of the Bible), which was among their narrowly defined canon of accepted books. They accepted no other Old Testament documents as God's Word. If that were the case, then one could see why they ended up living the lifestyle they chose, which was a great deal like the lifestyle of the rich and famous in our day. The Sadducees held most of the political power and were the wealthy elite of society. They were the highly educated upper class who kept their distance from the common people. When Rome wanted to do business with Israel, it would be the Sadducees and not the Pharisees who would be called upon to broker an agreement. They held the majority of the seats on the Sanhedrin and were responsible for the administration of the Temple. Their philosophy might on a smaller scale be summed up as, "Eat, drink, and be merry, for tomorrow we die."

The Pharisees, on the other hand, accepted a great deal more of the Old Testament. As a matter of fact the canon was not yet closed as far as they were concerned. They saw more evidence of an afterlife than is mentioned in the Torah alone. Yet Jesus did correct the Sadducees once in showing them that the afterlife, though not explicitly stated in the Torah, was implied (Luke 20:38). The Pharisees seemed to be more of a grassroots organization. They were considered part of the working class. They had no royal privileges, in contrast to their opponents. Rather than the Temple, their source of power centered around the synagogues. They ran the synagogues. The Pharisees were obsessed with ritual cleanliness. They wanted the purity of the priesthood in the Temple to be maintained among the general public. They actually believed that sin could be ingested by eating with unwashed hands for example. Jesus said they "strained at the gnat and swallowed the camel." They were so focused on the small rules, regulations, and traditions that they wound up missing the bigger issues of justice, mercy, and faith (Matthew 23:23-24). Their salvation was earned by keeping all of the traditions. In legalism, God's favor is not automatic; it is the result of obedience to the law. Yet much to their surprise, Jesus pointed out that it was that very law they ended up violating by leaning too heavily on the traditional interpretation and application of it. Jesus exposed the fact that their desire for recognition had caused their teachings to become self-serving (Mark 7:1-23) They actually ended up replacing the law of God instead of protecting it. They tried to change a person from the outside in, rather than the inside out, which tends to result in a work-based salvation.

So in the basic belief systems of these two well-known political parties we see the two extremes we want to avoid. One philosophy is too worldly and the other is too anti-world. You can be both too conservative and too liberal, and the centrist position is probably best. Paul spent most of his time keeping the spirit of the Pharisee out of the New Testament Church. It was a spirit that said, "No, you have to be a certified Jew first before you can be saved." That includes circumcision and the observance of all the feasts and diet regulations. This idea of earning God's approval for salvation is still alive and well today. We know salvation is by faith alone and not by works, lest any man should boast (Ephesians 2:8-9). But don't stop there, because now there is a danger of slipping out into the other extreme of saying works do not matter at all, and good conduct doesn't matter. That puts you now squarely in the camp of the Sadducees. That's why we should not stop at verse 9. For verse 10 of Ephesians 2 explains that "we are His creation—created in Christ Jesus for good works, which God prepared ahead of time so that we should walk in them."

So the balanced view is this: we are not saved *by* good works but *for* good works. Life doesn't end after salvation; on the contrary, it is just beginning. We are reborn, which means our whole life is yet ahead of us. It is now time to allow God to mature us and shape our character in such a way that we can accomplish a great work for Him.

Paul spent a good deal of his time correcting the extremes of "nothing goes" and "anything goes." This is still the duty of every church today. Look out for legalism and antinomianism. They are both dangerous and destructive to the Church. Nowadays the Church is hardly distinguishable from the world. It is lawlessness that abounds. Let us, the true disciples of Christ not be part of that. Nor are we to become so legalistic that we shun everyone in the Church and in the world. Beware of extremes.

Discussion Questions:

- What was the run-in with the Pharisees about that may have led Jesus to warn the disciples about those religious politicians?
- What metaphor did Jesus use to refer to the false doctrine of the Pharisees and the Sadducees, and why didn't the disciples catch on to it?
- What was the perspective of the Sadducees about life and the scriptures?
- What was the perspective of the Pharisees?
- What is the meaning of antinomianism and legalism, and how do these two extremes represent the two opposing parties?
- How do we reject good works when it comes to salvation yet embrace them when it comes to growing and finding our purpose in the faith? How can we stay balanced?

Suggested Exercises:

- Reread the New Testament armed with the facts of the opposing viewpoints and share the manner in which this insight provides both a clearer understanding of the text and a heads up on how not to lean toward one extreme or another.
- Over the next year keep track of your spiritual pendulum swings from an "anything goes" to a "nothing goes" extreme. Note the circumstances of these leanings and share what you have learned and how you have managed to pull yourself back to the center from time to time.
- Ask your most trusted fellow disciple and accountability partner to rate you on a scale of one to ten between the extremes of legalism and antinomianism. Get the opinion of a few more trusted

individuals and see if this is confirmed or denied (without sharing what others have said about you). Honestly evaluate yourself based on the information you gathered and go to the Lord in prayer about it, asking Him to forgive you for any extremes you have tended to gravitate toward and to help you stay balanced.

- Pray for your church and all the people of God in this country, that they will remain in the world without becoming part of it. If you have a discipleship study group, have each person say a prayer about this matter and encourage each one to make it a part of his or her daily prayer routine.

47

Resist the Devil

Matthew 16:21-23; Mark 8:31-33; Luke 9:22

Get behind me, Satan! You are a stumbling block to me; for you are not setting your mind on God's interests, but man's (Matthew 16:23).

Command of Christ: *Back off,* Satan!

The background leading up to this powerful rebuke was actually positive. Peter had just made his famous confession of faith in Jesus as the Christ and the Son of the living God. Once the disciples had all come to that conclusion, it was time then to share with them the rest of the story of redemption. Contrary to everyone's hopes and dreams, they would not ascend twelve thrones in their lifetimes. Instead, a sudden U-turn was made and Jesus was unexpectedly heading to the cross. God's plan was to sacrifice this Lamb of God for the sins of the world. Satan's plan was to convince the Master to do otherwise. After all, everyone could see that He alone deserved the throne of Israel. It was a very real temptation for Jesus because it was only fair that He should take His rightful place. He deserved honor, not the dishonor He had received thus far. However, it was not to be at this time in history. The Father had sent him not to be served but to serve and to give His life as a ransom for many (Mark 10:45).

So when Peter objected, it showed that he was not being led by the Father this time. Instead the motivation behind this seemed to be to protect his expected advancement to the status of royalty. Jesus told him he did not have in mind the things of God, but the things of men. Behind all of this Jesus saw Satan, who was trying to do the same thing he had attempted in the wilderness (Matthew 4:4) right before Jesus started his ministry. At that time he offered Jesus all the kingdoms of the world, if he would bow down and worship Satan. This passage illustrates what Paul said in Ephesians: we don't battle flesh and blood but the spiritual forces of evil. So after Jesus looked around at the disciples He soundly rebuked Peter for this false hope that was also in the hearts of all the others (Mark 8:33). By addressing Peter as Satan he drove home the point in the strongest possible way that Peter was now getting so off target that he was actually being used by the Devil. What a contrast between what Jesus had just said about him a few verses earlier, that he would build the church on his insight and give him the keys to the kingdom. Perhaps it was Peter's pride that got the better of him due to that seeming elevation of his status. Perhaps that is why he felt confident enough to try and correct the Master. By doing so he found that he had sailed right into a brick wall.

Peter got the point about Jesus being the Messiah and the Son of God, but he didn't understand how being crucified would draw all men to Christ. That concept was still over his head. We know it all from hindsight. I believe it was best explained by Jesus in John 12:24: "I assure you: unless a grain of wheat falls into the ground and dies, it remains by itself. But if it dies, it produces a large crop." Jesus knew the plan of God, but that didn't make it any easier to die on a cross. Jesus didn't want to suffer—nobody does. So when Peter came to his defense it must have made it even more difficult for Christ to accept his fate, although nothing on earth was up to Jesus's resolve on this matter. How hard it must have been for Jesus (who knew no sin) to become sin that we might become the righteousness of God (2 Corinthians 5:21).

So what is the lesson for us today as his disciples? One is to expect attacks and subtle tricks from the enemy. But when they come, we are to immediately go on the offensive. Jesus displayed for us this principle we see later in the New Testament of resisting the Devil so that he will flee from you (James 4:7). You need the eyes to see the enemy behind the person and not just the person himself. We battle not against flesh and blood. Don't talk to the Devil and entertain any of his ideas. Cut him off right away and refuse to have any association with his lies and deception. If not, you will end up like Eve, who kept talking to the enemy until she was finally convinced she deserved a better life than what God had provided. Don't even entertain such thoughts but bring every thought captive to the obedience of Christ (2 Corinthians 10:5). That is the only way to deal with the enemy. Don't even give him a chance to get his foot in the door. Tell him to get lost! Get thee behind me, Satan!

Discussion Questions:

- Who was Jesus facing when He said, "Get the behind me, Satan"?
- In what way had Peter fallen from the things of God to the things of man?
- In what sense did Peter and the rest of the disciples see Jesus as their ticket to royalty?
- How does Jesus's statement in John 12:24 explain the aspect of God's plan that the disciples were unaware of?
- How was this episode a repeat of the temptation Satan offered in Matthew 4:4?
- How does Christ's immediate and crushing response demonstrate the way to overcome?

Suggested Exercises:

- Imagine what you would rearrange inside your house if you knew Jesus was coming for a personal visit this weekend. Write those things down.
- Render an immediate and a crushing blow to all those things on the above list that are questionable in your life. Questionable employment, movies, entertainment, books and even churches should be rejected openly. All forms of compromise are on the table.
- Divide your group into two smaller groups of the same sex. Share with each other in the smaller group every thought that you have brought into captivity to the obedience of Christ this last week (2 Corinthians 10:5). Pray that this will become a daily practice.
- Discuss among the discipleship group "imaginations and every high thing that exalts itself against the knowledge of God" (2 Corinthians 10:5). What cultural norms in society militate against the Christian perspective? As a group, reject those things in a prayer of acknowledgement and repentance from each person.

48

Count the Cost

Matthew 16:24-27; Mark 8:34-38; Luke 9:23-26, 14:27-33

Then Jesus said to his disciples, "If anyone wishes to come after me, he must deny himself, and take up his cross and follow me. For whoever wishes to save his life will lose it; but whoever loses his life for my sake will find it. For what will it profit a man if he gains the whole world and forfeits his soul? Or what will a man give in exchange for his soul? For the Son of Man is going to come in the glory of his Father with his angels and will then repay every man according to his deeds" (Matthew 16:24-27).

Or what king, when he sets out to meet another king in battle, will not first sit down and consider whether he is strong enough with ten thousand men to encounter the one coming against him with twenty thousand? Or else, while the other is still far away, he sends a delegation and asks for terms of peace. So then, none of you can be my disciple who does not give up all his own possessions (Luke 15:31-33).

Commands of Christ: "he must *deny* himself, and *take up* his cross and *follow* me."

The news from the disciples' perspective went from bad to worse. Not only were their dreams of ascending to the throne with Jesus rapidly dissipating, their own lives were now at stake. They had chosen to live or die by Jesus and now it appeared the latter would prevail. First Jesus rebuked Peter for trying to correct him away from the path of suffering and death on a cross, and now He promised His followers that the destination of the Master is also the destination of the disciple. No doubt this had to be a rude awakening to his followers, and it elicited a variety of pathological responses. One may have been to stay in denial and just chalk it up to another one of those exaggerated statements the Master was prone to make. The other may have even been such a devastating disappointment as to lead to a great deal of anger and resentment, perhaps even to the point of betrayal in the end. So here's the basic message: "Not only am I going to suffer and die, but in all likelihood you will be called on to do the same!"

Being Jesus's disciple was about to become a lot more dangerous that it had been. His mission was not to take over but to provide a bridge between God and man through his own demise. He introduced them next to the three essential elements that will now make up a disciple of Christ. These are self-denial, suffering, and surrender. The command is to deny yourself, take up your cross, and follow Him. It requires what Jesus mentioned earlier to Peter. It calls for a shift of allegiance from the things of men to the things of God (Mark 8:33). The plans of God often demand self-sacrifice for a higher purpose, rather than self-indulgence at the expense of any finer objective. Rather than the public recognition and allegiance they had hoped for, they were now being asked to face the possibility of public humiliation and execution. They were being asked to follow Him in the sense of preparing themselves to experience the Master's experience.

So now, faced with this new twist of fate, they must come to terms with their own level of devotion. They had to think it over now. They must go back to the drawing board of their hearts and ask themselves if they have truly considered the cost. After doing so, were they ready to continue down this passageway of great risk and sacrifice? As if to help them in their decision, Jesus goes on to remind them that there is more to life than simply self-preservation. He states, "What good is it for a man to gain the whole world, yet forfeit his soul?" (Mark 8:36) The cold, hard truth about life that we all face is that none of us will make it out of this thing alive. So why not make your life count for something? Let your death be a seed planted rather than seed preserved. This is how Jesus changed the world. He said, "I assure you: unless a grain of wheat falls into the ground and dies, it remains by itself. But if it dies, it produces a large crop" (John 12:24). That is not to say that for the disciple, a martyred death is guaranteed. But we must be sure we understand in no uncertain terms that suffering is certainly to be expected on some level, and in many instances could include the ultimate sacrifice. If so, we know His grace is sufficient to meet that challenge as well as any other.

In the first three centuries of Christian history we see this grace poured out in dramatic proportions, as it was the most dangerous time ever to be a Christian. It was during that time that history records a remarkable desire on the part of Jesus's followers to be asked to make that commitment. They were ready—no, even eager—to give their lives as the ultimate testimony to the reality of their faith. They were the Christian martyrs and are called so because "martyr" is the Greek word for "testimony." And what greater testimony is there? It was so powerful and strong a witness as to eventually bring the Roman Empire to its knees. That same Christianity that was so despised and rejected became the official religion of the Roman Empire. Then it expanded from official religion to a rival to the throne itself.

In the meantime, we are to be as wise as serpents and harmless as doves (Matthew 10:16). In other words, our objective is not to be destroyed but to be as Paul stated, to be "living sacrifices, holy and acceptable unto Him" (Romans 12:1). We are to accomplish as much as we can in the limited time we are allotted to sojourn through this life. Either way you look at it, life is short. But should the day come when it is cut off even shorter, God's will be done. We say with Paul in Acts 21:13: "What are you doing, weeping and breaking my heart? For I am ready; not only to be bound, but also to die in Jerusalem for the name of the Lord Jesus." None of us plan for death, but all of us must be prepared for both that possibility and inevitability.

In Luke 14:27-33 Jesus tells us to make sure we think things over before joining Him. He gives a parable about a builder and a king. Each one had to estimate the price to be paid before entering the project or campaign, respectively. It would be embarrassing to find that we had to pull out halfway through because we did not estimate correctly. So think it over: are you prepared to give yourself 100 percent to this effort? Count the cost. Are you aware of what discipleship could cost you? Are you still willing to participate? If so why? What sufferings have you already experienced due to your commitment to Christ?

Discussion Questions:

- How did the news go from bad to worse for the disciples based on what Jesus stated in Matthew 16:24-27; Mark 8:34-38; and Luke 9:23-26, 14:27-33?
- What were two likely pathological responses to the challenge mentioned above?
- What are the three essential elements that will now identify a disciple of Jesus Christ?
- Now that they have discovered that their lives may be on the line for Christ, what statements does the Lord make to help them resolve to fully commit?
- Why is it better to be a seed planted than a seed preserved?
- What special grace was given to the first three centuries of Christianity to endure worldwide persecution? How did they overcome the Roman Empire?
- How does that encourage you for anything you might have to face as a disciple?

Suggested Exercises:

- Have you come to terms with the dangers inherent in following Christ as a disciple? Write out your own treaty as they did in the early days of the American Revolution pledging their lives, fortunes, and sacred honor to the cause of freedom. Pledge yours to the higher and eternal freedom that comes through the blood of Christ. Have everyone in your discipleship group who is willing sign your "declaration of independence" from the world and for the cause of Christ.
- Read the true story of the martyrdom of Perpetua and Felicity in 202 AD to the group. Discuss among yourselves what most impacted you about the story. Ask each person to examine himself and herself as to how every member believes he or she would fare in similar circumstances. Close with the hymn *I Have Decided to Follow Jesus* and a prayer for God's grace to handle any situation that should arise, knowing that there is a greater reward for those who pay the ultimate price (Hebrews 11:35b).

- Have each group member explain how each has accomplished or plans to accomplish the three requirements of a disciple:
  - Denying yourself. In what sense have you denied yourself as a disciple of Christ? What worldly desires, in terms of the lust of the flesh, lust of the eyes, and the pride of life have you given up?
  - Taking up your cross. In what manner have you taken up your cross as a disciple of Christ? What additional burden have you had to bear for the sake of the gospel? How have you had to suffer because of your devotion to Christ?
  - Following Christ. Are you following His lead or taking the lead in terms of the direction your life is headed?

SECTION FOUR:
Spiritual Schooler

49

Respond Appropriately to Revelation

Matthew 17:1-9; Mark 9:2-9; Luke 9:28-36

Six days later Jesus took with him Peter, James and John his brother, and led them up on a high mountain by themselves. And he was transfigured before them; and his face shone like the sun, and his garments became as white as light. And behold Moses and Elijah appeared to them, talking with him (Matthew 17:1-3).

Jesus came to them and touched them and said, "Get up, and do not be afraid." Lifting up their eyes, they saw no one except Jesus himself alone. As they were coming down from the mountain, Jesus commanded them, saying, "Tell the vision to no one until the Son of Man has risen from the dead" (Matthew 17:7-9).

Commands of Christ: *Arise* and *do not be* afraid. *Tell* no one of the vision . . .

This supernatural event follows the foreboding language of the previous command about taking up one's cross. And it is the cross that provides the greatest vantage point whereby the entire episode can be fully understood. The transfiguration was foretold toward the end of those statements by the phrase, "I tell you the truth, some who are standing here will not taste death before they see the Son of Man coming in his kingdom" (Matthew 16:28).

When we think of the Son coming into His kingdom, we normally think about eschatology (end times). We assume the previous verse provides the only clue for what is meant: "For the Son of Man is going to come in his Father's glory with his angels, and then he will reward each person according to what he has done" (Matthew 16:27). However, He was not referring to his second coming because this "last days" judgment is yet to occur. Rather, He was referring to an event that contained some of the glory of that final battle. Seeing Him enter His kingdom, or seeing the glory of the kingdom is something that can occur every time He performs a miracle. For instance, when He cast the demons from an individual, he said the kingdom of God had come upon them (Luke 11:20). So it is no stretch to suggest that His statement did not mean that the Second Advent would take place within that time period. It simply meant that they would get a taste of the kingdom of God as He was transfigured (*metamorphosis* in the Greek) before them.

So there is no need to suggest as theologian Albert Schweitzer did that Jesus was mistaken here by thinking the end would happen in his generation. Jesus did not know the time of His return, so it would not be a reasonable conclusion to suggest He made such a prediction in this passage. He stated that the time of the end was known only by the Father. He said to always be on the alert, for no one knows neither the "day nor the hour when the Son of Man comes" (Matthew 25:13).

So as Jesus predicted, there were some present who did see the kingdom of God come in great power not less than a week later. At that time He took Peter, James, and John up to a mountain to pray. As He was doing so His appearance began to transform in front of them. His face and clothes began to glow and two prophets from the Old Testament appeared with Him. And as if that wasn't enough, a cloud appeared and the voice of God commanded them to listen to Jesus. So what is the reason for all of this display of raw power and glory? Why was it meant to be kept secret? Well, it seems to all center around the revelation that Jesus had made earlier about His coming suffering and death. The fact that He was determined to see that through meant at least two things; one that the Father was so pleased with Jesus's willingness and determination to suffer for His sake and for the sake of humanity, He speaks for Jesus and expresses his love for his Son. He urges those present to get onboard with Christ and to support Him in His destiny. This is probably the second reason this event occurred. Jesus needed strength and encouragement to follow through on this monumental task. God spoke for Jesus and sent Jesus two famous prophets to encourage Him forward. For we know from the Gospel of Luke that it was His forthcoming crucifixion that dominated the conversation between the three of them (Luke 9:31).

So as the clouds lifted and everything returned to normal, we find the disciples face down and afraid to lift their heads. They were not aware that God's glory had faded away and now it was only the Master who stood before them. So the order comes from the Lord: "Arise and don't be afraid." Does He not treat them like the little children they are who cower before a frightening scene in a movie? He's telling them it's all right, get up and let's get going. You were privy to God's glory for a purpose, and that purpose was not to crawl into a shell. God's glory is for mobilization, not immobilization. Just like Moses before the burning bush, they were to be motivated to launch ahead with the plans that God had in store. They too no doubt found themselves unequal to the task.

The second command is "don't be afraid." Again it sounds like the same thing we tell our kids when they are frightened of the dark. The purpose of supernatural display is to motivate toward greater faith and zeal for the things of God. It is to ensure that everyone is clear about God's will and direction in any circumstance. Just like Gideon, we put our fleece before the Lord and the miracle confirms that we can rely on God to be with us in the challenges that lie ahead. Angels appear and announce God's plans so as to ensure that we have no doubts. What Peter had initially said is now being confirmed in this transfiguration. God is in essence saying to him, "You're right: He is the Christ, the Son of the Living God, so *listen* to him!"

The final command regarding the transfiguration is found in Matthew 17:9b: "Don't tell anyone what you have seen, until the Son of Man has been raised from the dead." At this point, telling everyone about Jesus's supernatural identity would be counterproductive, since they were all about to watch God's Son be mercilessly humiliated, rejected, and crucified. The two realities don't seem to coincide. Nobody would have ever guessed that the Messiah would allow Himself to be subjected to such cruelties. Instead, it was widely expected that the Messiah would be the one inflicting damage on others, that He would overpower the nation and the world with great ease and splendor. Yet here we see him as a lamb led to the slaughter. So the lesson is this: the public will not always understand God's personal revelation to you. Sometimes it is better to keep it to yourself. Maybe those things should only be shared with a small group of close friends (as did Jesus). We should exercise great discretion in the appropriate time and place to share personal revelations. Yet at the same time we should not go to the other extreme and discount all personal revelation as madness or as impossible. The Lord hasn't changed and He doesn't mind revealing things to individuals when He deems it appropriate. Modern technology and science has shielded us from the supernatural, and we are closed off to it for the most part. I think that is unfortunate. Look at the scripture and see that all things are possible with a God who knows no limitations. He is not obligated to function within the confines of our typical experience. "After this I will pour out my spirit on all humanity; then your sons and your daughters will prophesy, your old men will have dreams, and your young me will see visions" (Joel 2:28).

So should we become privy to a dream or vision, what are we to do with it? Follow Jesus's commands above: 1. Arise, and do not be afraid. Just ask yourself, what is God's purpose for allowing this and what exactly is He motivating me to do? To pray and reflect for greater clarity and then carry on with your life in a manner that incorporates those objectives that have been discovered? Maybe there is no action required. In that case, just allow yourself to be encouraged in the Lord. 2. Tell no one of the vision (until the appropriate time). God's personal message to you may not belong in the public domain. Just keep it to yourself as a treasure between Him and you unless there is a legitimate reason to do otherwise.

Finally we must ask ourselves an even greater question. Are we listening to Jesus? God spoke out of the clouds to insist that the disciples give heed to what Jesus was saying. Today disciples have no less of a mandate. We must carefully consider everything we have been taught and commanded by Christ in the gospels and incorporate those principles into our lives in every way possible. We will truly be His disciples only if we continue in his word (John 8:31).

Discussion Questions:

- What are the many different ways to see Jesus coming in His kingdom?
- What are likely the two reasons for the occurrence of the transfiguration?
- What command did Jesus give right after the event that let us know the purpose was not for immobilization but mobilization?
- Why did Jesus insist that this event be kept secret?

- Are dreams and visions a thing of the past or does the Bible say otherwise?
- Why does organized religion tend to discount and downplay such occurrences?
- How will you use discretion should you have a kingdom-coming experience?

Suggested Exercises:

- Recite from memory the appropriate response to revelation according to Jesus Christ.
- Apply this teaching to past experiences and share with the group how this would have helped. Explain how some things between you and the Lord should stay that way.

50

Learn from the Children

Matthew 18:1-14; Mark 9:33-50; Luke 9:46-50

He called a child to himself and set him before them, and said, "Truly I say to you, unless you are converted and become like children, you will not enter the kingdom of heaven. Whoever then humbles himself as this child, he is the greatest in the kingdom of heaven" (Matthew 18:2-4).

Commands of Christ: *See* that you do not disregard one of these little ones. If your hand or foot offends you *cut* it off and *cast* it from you. If your eye offends you *pluck* it out and *cast* it from you. *Don't hinder* him . . . *Have* salt in yourselves and *keep* the peace with one another.

The context for this teaching is an argument among the disciples as to who would be the greatest. Undoubtedly Peter must have assumed he was at the top of the ladder after everything Jesus said about him in Matthew 16:17-19. Nevertheless, pecking order seemed to be the subject that continually arose among Jesus's disciples (Luke 9:26; 22:24; Matthew 20:20). Even up to the night before His death He had to provide them with an object lesson to keep them humble toward one another by washing their feet (John 13:1-17). They could never get over the fact that they might be on the verge of becoming heads of state as they rose to power along with the Messiah to rule and reign over the earth (Daniel 7:14; Matthew 5:5; Luke 22:30).

When Jesus told them that there would be twelve thrones for them divided over the land of Israel, it must have excited them even more, beyond any hope of recovery (Matthew 19:28). It took the crucifixion itself to finally yank that spirit of ascendency out of their covetous souls. Yet it was such a powerful vision that it immediately resurfaced once they saw him return from the grave. The book of Acts records the disciples asking about this issue again as the resurrected Christ leaves them with their final instructions (Acts 1:6). They could not let it go, for it held all their hopes and dreams for advancement and prestige in this life. Yet his answer to their inquiry as to when they could take over was thus: "It is not for you to know times or periods that the Father has set by His own authority. But you will receive power when the Holy Spirit has come upon you, and you will be my witnesses in Jerusalem, in all Judea and Samaria, and to the ends of the earth." They had still yet to learn that the kingdom originates from within; and that which is without is yet to materialize.

Jesus continually steered them away from such visions of grandeur through various words, teachings, and lessons along the way. In this passage, we see a good number of commands using children as the item of supreme value to the lesson. Once Christ overheard their political squabble, He took a child into his arms and said that whoever is childlike is the greatest. He even warned them that unless they repent and become like that child, they won't even be able to enter the kingdom in the first place. So now the value of the child is taking on a new significance in the body of Christ. Much attention must now be given to this area of study in terms of just what a child possesses and how we can maintain that in our own lives. The command follows to not disregard one of these little ones. They embody a great deal more of a spiritual consequence than was once believed. They even have their own angels. They hold the key to what it takes to experience salvation. They are now to be seen as a great resource to be mined for untold spiritual treasure.

Additionally, if you ever think to harm them or even influence them in a negative direction, you will find yourself in extremely dangerous territory with God. It would be better to lose an eye or a foot than to cause one of these little ones to stumble. So if your hand or foot offends you cut it off and cast it from you. If your eye offends you pluck it out and cast it from you. In other words, do everything you can to avoid harming a child in any way. For the fires of an eternal hell surely await the perpetrator.

As they change the subject in Mark 9:38, it seems that Jesus is still using the perspective of a child to render the verdict. They bring up someone who is not on their guest list who is doing mighty works in

Jesus's name. They ask if they should do something about it. But isn't that the same argument all over again? Wait, they say, he isn't one of us. We are in charge, and here he is going about doing Christian service without our authorization. Who does he think he is? Again Jesus has to remind them that we are all serving the Lord, and we are all servants of one another. Authorization is not required, just allegiance. Jesus didn't necessarily call that man to "be with Him" in His ministry in a personal way, but He calls all to repentance and discipleship. A child would instinctively know and understand such things and would not try to make an issue political. Their innocence allows them the luxury of being open and accepting of others rather than closed and exclusive. We should learn from that as adults. So the command to the disciples is, "Don't hinder him . . ." He is for us not against us. The rationale is to leave well enough alone.

Jesus's final statement on the matter of authority structure and power grabs is this: "Have salt in yourselves and keep the peace with one another." This statement is akin to the one in John where He states that it is their love for one another that will distinguish them as His true disciples (13:35). If you keep bickering with each other about one-upmanship, you will lose your witness (saltiness). So just give up on this idea of climbing to the top of the corporate church ladder and love one another. Be a servant. Be like a little child who never plays politics. He just follows along and then goes out to play.

A child has innate qualities that are necessary for success as Christian adults. What are they exactly? Well, let me attempt to suggest a few ideas. One of the things an adult has that a child does not is self-reliance. A child does not mind you helping him put on his shoes or even his clothes. As a matter of fact, he or she may even prefer the attention. I have a six-year-old stepson who will at least offer a foot when the time comes to put his socks on. But he is actually capable of doing it himself. He is simply too young to understand that needing assistance is a sign of weakness and is frowned upon in the adult world.

It is this adult quest for independence and self-sufficiency that makes it virtually impossible to have a decent relationship with God the Father. We are told in the Lord's Prayer to routinely ask Him to provide today's portion of bread. Yet we live our lives as if it all depended upon us. So the first character trait that a child naturally possesses that we also need as adults is *dependence*. We all need to be more dependent on God and on one another. Second, we see that children naturally possess the quality of *trust* and are almost so to a fault. They will believe (trust, have faith) in just about anything you tell them. Some parents take advantage of that by suggesting to the children that there is a Santa Claus and a Tooth Fairy. I would counsel against this practice since they will find out later that adults make things up and will then wonder if what they heard about Jesus is just another fairy tale. Here again is an indispensable ingredient in a high-quality relationship with God. "Without faith it is impossible to please Him, for he who comes to God must first believe that He is, and that He is a rewarder of those who diligently seek Him" (Hebrews 11:6). A third quality is *contentment/humility*. They are content in the sense that they are not interested or even aware of the status of individuals to the point that they desire power or prestige. Jesus himself pointed out this quality in Matthew 18:4: "Therefore, whoever humbles himself like this child is the greatest in the kingdom of heaven."

They are content with their humble status in the scheme of things and they use that condition to their own advantage. While everyone else around them is fearful and in a state of panic over the latest news reports of impending doom, they are outside enjoying the fresh air and running around chasing the wind. They are content to let the adults make all the tough decisions about such matters. In feast and famine, peace and war, natural order and natural disaster, all children have one thing in common: playtime. You will find them in the most horrible and unimaginable circumstances inventing an opportunity for fun and games, maybe for the chance to escape their dismal reality. Due to their lack of adult status and privilege, they know it is useless to get involved with grown-up decisions about where they will live, what they will eat, and what they will wear. All of these things they gladly delegate into the hands of others and simply come along for the ride. What a wonderful attribute for the true follower of God to possess (Matthew 6:31ff).

Finally, we see that due to their disinterest and lack of awareness about the standing of any individual, they are equally comfortable with both the highest extremes of royal sophistication and the lowest and most despicable examples of human squalor. They don't seem to notice what everyone else observes in a person. The only thing they will judge an individual on is his or her capacity to be an effective playmate. They don't evaluate people. It seems that this habit is picked up over time from adults.

The last of the incredible qualities of a child that all adults should possess is *acceptance*. Children are naturally accepting of individuals. They will not judge people by their appearance or rank because those things are just not important to them. Oh if only we as adults could relearn what we have supposedly outgrown.

Discussion Questions:

- What was it that caused Jesus to bring up the matter of children—their special attributes and value to all of mankind?
- Why were the disciples so fixated on taking the highest throne possible in the kingdom of the Messiah? What had Jesus said that could have gotten them so excited as to continually debate one another?
- How had the disciples gotten the hereafter mixed up with the here and now? How had they misunderstood the nature of the kingdom as coming from the inside out and in that particular order over an extended period of time?
- The disciples were obsessing over their personal reign in the kingdom. But Jesus told them they couldn't enter the kingdom unless they do what two things?
- Name the particular attributes and natural inclinations of children that make them so special and such a great example for us all.

Suggested Exercises:

- Study your own children or a child you know personally in terms of dependence, trust, contentment, humility, and acceptance. Share the results of your study with your discipleship group. Then share how you plan to utilize the values you gathered in enhancing your personal walk with the Lord.
- Share how maintaining the humble attitude of a child will serve you well in your church ministry. How will it keep you from striving for power and influence rather than just remaining a meek and lowly servant like Jesus was? Give specific examples in terms of the current church politics you serve under.

51

Resolve Conflict Well

Matthew 18:15-17

If your brother sins go and show him his fault in private; if he listens to you, you have won your brother. But if he does not listen to you, take one or two more with you, so that by the mouth of two or three witnesses every fact may be confirmed. If he refuses to listen to them, tell it to the church; and if he refuses to listen even to the church, let him be to you as a Gentile and a tax collector.

Commands of Christ: *Go and correct* him privately. *Take* with you one or two others . . . *Tell* it to the church. *Let* them be to you as a pagan . . .

The context of this method is the rebuke of the disciples for wanting to be the greatest. He presents them with a long object lesson about humility using a child as a visual aid. So perhaps they begin to blame each other for causing the argument in the first place. This is also incorrect behavior. Now the disciples are acting like children all right, but in a negative and immature way. We are all too familiar with the phrase among siblings: "You started it!" It was possibly in this atmosphere of internal strife that Jesus first introduced the timeless principles of reconciliation.

He lays down the ground rules for resolving conflict in the Church. It is important to remember that these are not suggestions. He is not offering advice here. It is not one option among many; it is mandated that these specific procedures be firmly established in every organization of believers. His disciples are ordered to proceed accordingly.

If your brother sins against you, you are to take him aside privately and tell him his fault. The actual Greek words are best translated as "go and correct/reprove" him privately. This was not what was happening while the disciples were bickering with each other publicly. This only added fuel to the fire. The objective is to lay the matter to rest; come to a resolution. To proceed respectfully is to proceed discreetly. There is no question that sin needs to be addressed and eliminated in the body of Christ, not ignored, tolerated, or accepted. But if it is not handled in a spirit of meekness (Galatians 6:1), sin will be added to sin. You will end up with a net surplus instead of a deficit. So, careful attention must be taken when in the process of restoration. The whole purpose is to save and preserve the relationship not to damage it even further. The objective is not to eliminate the brother from fellowship, but to find a way to maintain the fellowship.

If the matter cannot be resolved between the two individuals in private, it is mandatory that it not end there. Jesus states, "If he listens to you, you have won your brother over. If he will not listen, take one or two others along, so that 'every matter will be established by the testimony of two or three witnesses.'" The "two-or-three-witnesses" requirement is not a new innovation but derives from Old Testament law for achieving justice in Deuteronomy 19:15. So here again we find evidence that Old Testament law is not to be disregarded in the New Testament Church. Nevertheless, the main thrust of energy in this second step is to give the person another chance to see his fault and repent. Oftentimes we find that some individuals just don't particularly like us, and we see that as their problem. It is easier to see our fault when it can be confirmed by several people that we really trust. Again it is the objective to free the individual from his or her sin, not to free the Church from the individual. So we go the extra mile (another command of Jesus) with this person by going to additional lengths to confirm his or her guilt. The increasing levels of addressing sin are very appealing. It is a gentle and thoughtful process that ministers to the person at fault with great care and concern. Every effort is made not to have to make this matter public because then his or her credibility is irretrievably lost.

The final and third step we are commanded to adhere to is that of telling it to the Church. No further explanation is given as to what this assembly consists of, but we do know the word "church" means "assembly" in the original Greek. It may be anachronistic to suggest that Jesus is pointing to the future here and is referring to the New Testament body of Christ. However, even if He is referring to synagogue discipline, this process will eventually fall into the hands of the New Testament Church. I believe he is giving them a way to solve the disputes they are currently facing as well as anything that will arise in the future. So in that sense it does belong to the New Testament Church.

Another matter of concern that arises is in this last stage of discipline is what is meant by assembly. Is it the assembly of elders or church leaders, or is it the entire congregation that must hear this matter? It would hardly make much sense to bring the matter before the entire congregation, yet we see this again in I Timothy 5:20: "Publically rebuke those who sin, so that the rest will also be afraid." Taken on face value, "tell it to the church" is just that; it includes everyone. Yet the next verse may open up a small window of understanding on the matter. It says, "If he also refuses even to listen to the church . . ." How can the whole Church be talking to one individual? Either it is an assembly of church leaders, or it is announced to the entire gathering and they proceed to deal with it in mob fashion. That doesn't seem plausible. The way the Greek word for church (*ecclesia*) was used during New Testament times has to do with a political assembly; something like a counsel to decide on a matter of state.

The entire assembly would not be equipped to handle matters of discipline for several reasons. One is that a vote would be required. There is no record of any democratic system in place in the New Testament. Everything was handled through a chain of command, so that option is historically out of place. Secondly, had they the opportunity to vote, it is more likely that sin would prevail and the reputation of the Church would be diminished instead of enhanced. The great majority of the assemblies are not typically walking in a seasoned and matured perspective. They would probably tend toward being overly tolerant. I think it is more likely that an inner court is held with the leadership presiding. Then the results would perhaps be announced publically.

Finally, if they will not listen to church leadership, Jesus commands his disciples to "let them be to you as a pagan or a tax collector." Pagans and tax collectors were basically outcasts. So the only logical conclusion from this statement is that they be dismissed from the assembly. Once again we must not assume that this is a permanent dismissal. All three steps are for the ultimate purpose of repentance and restoration. It just takes more drastic measures to get some people's attention. Nevertheless, a change of heart is required for fellowship to continue.

All of this strikes me as completely foreign to anything we know in the Western world. Is there really any assembly of believers that you know of who are actually abiding by these regulations? Whether they are or not is immaterial. Now that we know that this is the requirement of our Lord, it is imperative that we get to work on this project. An infrastructure has to be put in place in the Church where these three steps can operate seamlessly. The members have to be taught how it works and work it. Since it is a direct order from Jesus Christ, there is no way out but obedience.

So the question is how are we to make this happen in our churches? What type of educational programming or deprogramming is necessary? How can we have strong churches in an age of affluence, overindulgence, and consumerism? How can we keep gospel and culture separated to the point that the bad does not infiltrate and contaminate the good? These are the issues we face as we follow Christ on that narrow road leading to life. If not, we face the very real possibility of becoming totally indistinguishable from the world.

One solution is to just start practicing it as individual disciples to the point that the Church is forced to accommodate the volume of the present reality. So as a disciple, start working the system. Think of a situation you have right now in which Jesus's three-point process would provide the solution. They say the system works if you work it.

Discussion Questions:

- What is the contextual evidence that Jesus is both giving them a way to solve the disputes they are currently facing as well as anything that will arise in the future?
- How can public rebuke of a fellow believer potentially add sin to sin and lead to a further divide rather than reconciliation?
- Why is it necessary to recruit one or two more witnesses once the matter has been addressed privately but to no avail? Why can't we just leave well enough alone?
- If the two additional witnesses don't work, we are to tell the Church. What does that mean exactly? Why would telling the whole congregation for them to decide not seem like a reasonable approach? At what point would the matter be more likely to have been presented to the public?

- How might casting someone out of the Church actually be good for him or her in the end?

Suggested Exercise:

- Develop a "working" knowledge of Matthew 18:15-17. Next week start pulling openly sinful believers (breaking any of the Ten Commandments for example) to the side on all three levels if necessary. Report back your findings.

52

Know This: I Own My Disciples

Matthew 8:19-22; Luke 9:57-62

As they were going along the road, someone said to him, "I will follow you wherever you go." And Jesus said to him, "The foxes have holes and the birds of the air have nests, but the Son of Man has nowhere to lay his head." And he said to another, "Follow me." But he said, "Lord, permit me first to go and bury my father." But he said to him, "Allow the dead to bury their own dead; but as for you, go and proclaim everywhere the kingdom of God." Another also said, "I will follow you, Lord; but first permit me to say good-bye to those at home." But Jesus said to him, "No one, after putting his hand to the plow and looking back, is fit for the kingdom of God" (Luke 9:57-62).

Commands of Christ: *Follow* me. *Let* the dead bury their dead; but you are to go and *declare* the kingdom of God.

The context here seems to be a bit earlier in Jesus's ministry when His popularity was on the rise. At this point, a scribe (Greek: *grammateus*) offers his services to Jesus. He makes the statement that he will follow Jesus wherever he goes. But as is often the case, Jesus is able to see through the exaggerated speech to the heart of the man, knowing that when the going gets tough the tough (which this man was not) get going. His reply to the scribe implied that he could not expect a comfortable living situation in following Jesus. This would end up discouraging him and he would not be able to follow through on his initial investment. Perhaps this is why Jesus did not choose the person of education and sophistication to follow him; because their expectations for creature comforts would be sorely disappointed. The harsh realities of being the targeted sect for extermination within the confines of the Roman Empire would all too soon rear its ugly head. Only the strong would survive. "The foxes have holes and the birds of the air have nests, but the Son of Man has no place to lay his head" (Matthew 8:20). The master's lot in life would also be that of his followers in many instances.

The second person did not approach Christ, but Christ approached him to become a disciple (Luke 9:59). After being asked to follow Jesus, his excuse was to first allow him to bury his father. Perhaps he expected that it would be impossible to deny this justification for his delay. It is possible that he underestimated the Master. Number one, he likely did not realize who he was addressing. Secondly, he did not understand the magnitude of the undertaking Jesus was calling him to. When you are being addressed by God in the flesh, it will become apparent that He already knows your situation, and regardless of that fact, is still calling you to a work of unimaginable consequence. Jesus likely already knew about the man's father, yet He still thought of his mission as much more significant.

This is a shock to the system of all who encounter this story because we can't imagine this type of supposed heartlessness coming from the same man who was known for his compassion. Yet on the other hand, when you consider how Jesus views death in other instances, it may be quite the norm. He seems to hold contempt for all of the fanfare and mourning customs of the day when someone dies. He in one occurrence told the crowd to stop making a fuss because the deceased was just asleep (Luke 8:52). In another instance, He told them, "Our friend Lazarus has fallen asleep," when he actually meant he had died (John 11:11-12). He clearly seemed to think of death as a benefit rather than a loss in the sense that it was the end of all earthly troubles. Death is natural and is to be expected. The biggest thing to get out of it is the brevity of life and the short amount of time each person has to do something meaningful. This life is not the place to put down roots; it is an opportunity to invest in eternity. Eternity is the final resting place, not this world that will one day only be a faded memory at best.

This matter is also about the urgency of the situation at hand. When in the heat of the battle, you can't stop to deal with the dead, as much as they are loved. You must press on. The loss of a fellow soldier is not the end of the battle or the loss of the war. The war still rages on until the ultimate objective is obtained. This is the context of the reality Jesus faced. Lives in eternity were at stake. The bottom line is this: once a person dies, there is no further opportunity to repent. So you shouldn't squander your time on the physically dead because it is too late for them. Work with the spiritually dead, for there is still time for them to change. He was not calling him to minister to the dead but to the living. Let the others take care of that. With his gifts, he could be of far greater benefit elsewhere.

It is about the strategy of spiritual warfare and the overall perspective of the General. No excuse, however convincing, can ever reverse Jesus's sovereign pronouncement. We are to trust His unmatched leadership. He knows the best use of the available forces at hand. He knows what is necessary to achieve the finest result for everyone involved. The work of God in saving lives from an eternity in hell is so important that it dwarfs everything else we will ever know. "Follow me . . . let the dead bury their dead, but you are to go and declare the kingdom of God." Don't let anything, no matter how compelling distract you from that objective. Welcome to following Jesus, where you are ordered out of your comfort zone and sometimes away from everything you have ever known and held dear! Yet in the end you can only thank Him for the wisest and most prudent use of troops imaginable.

Finally, Luke adds a third individual who thought he was ready to follow Christ (9:61-62). He requests just to say good-bye to his family first. Yet here again Jesus concludes that he is not fit to be a follower. A soldier cannot become entangled with worldly affairs (2 Timothy 2:4). A true follower must immediately forsake everything and follow Jesus with no questions asked. Notice how it was so with the first disciples. Were they not in the middle of their livelihood and working beside their father when Jesus called them (Mark 1:17)? Did they delay? Did they protest? No, they immediately got out of the boat and followed him, even leaving their beloved father behind.

Like Lot's wife, the man was probably not actually as committed as he had originally supposed. So many individuals join the ministry with great enthusiasm and pomp and circumstance. They fully expect it to be a rewarding career only to regret later ever haven chosen that painfully narrow path of the cross and self-denial. One day they are thrilled to be in the ministry. The next day they want to quit. This type of double-minded personality cannot help but be a hindrance rather than a benefit to the kingdom of God.

This is a massive challenge to the Church today. Isn't such a total abandonment a completely foreign concept to most of us? Don't we even allow excuses that are far less compelling? Yet here Jesus refuses to accept any of it. As it was for the man who Jesus called to declare the kingdom of God (rather than bury the dead), it is a test as to where our ultimate loyalties lie. It seems there are only two options: abandon your excuses or abandon Christ. Likewise, who among us needs to reconsider his true level of commitment? Are you sure you can handle full-time ministry? It may not be as easy as it seems.

Discussion Questions:

- How did Jesus's reply to the scribe demonstrate both Jesus's full grasp of the situation and the scribe's less than complete grasp of the situation at hand?
- How did the second man Jesus called to follow Him possibly underestimate both the Master's level of awareness and the urgency of the situation?
- How does this situation serve as another illustration of Jesus's unique yet far more accurate view of death?
- In the throes of war it is not appropriate to stop and say good-bye to loved ones. A person must separate himself from worldly affairs to fully focus on military action and efforts. How does this apply to the final person Jesus pronounced unworthy to join his select company of disciples?
- What does the desire to turn back reveal about the person's true allegiance? Does it show that his heart isn't really in it, just like the heart of Lot's wife?

Suggested Exercises:

- Share situations in your past or even present where you either ran away from God's call or ran toward a call that was only imagined. Share with the group or a trusted fellow disciple what lessons you learned from the experience.

- Discuss among the group your tried and true methods for distinguishing God's voice from the cheap imitations (including your own). When do you know for sure that God is calling you to move on something? What sort of confirmations do you look for?
- Compare your view of this life with Jesus's view. Would you say you are entirely more focused on eternal or temporal realities? Confess this with a trusted disciple and pray together for a greater understanding of Jesus's perspective on life.
- Discuss among the group what situations have arisen that have caused you to miss a funeral, even of a family member. Were any of those related to a genuine calling?

53

Drink Deeply of the Holy Spirit

John 7:37-39

Now on the last day, the great day of the feast, Jesus stood and cried out, saying, "If anyone is thirsty, let him come to me and drink. He who believes in me, as the scripture said, 'From his innermost being will flow rivers of living water.'" By this he spoke of the Spirit, whom those who believed in him were to receive; for the Spirit was not yet given, since Jesus was not yet glorified.

Commands of Christ: If anyone is thirsty, *come* and *drink*.

They say, "You can lead a horse to water, but you cannot make him drink." The command in John 7:37 is to come and drink if you are thirsty. He is alerting the general public to a resource that will soon be made available to all. He states that this resource is for "whoever believes" in him. Verses 38-39 state: "Whoever believes in me, as the scripture has said, streams of living water will flow from within him." By this he meant the Spirit, whom those who believed in him were later to receive. Up to that time the Spirit had not been given, since Jesus had not yet been glorified. One can only wonder what it was about the last day of the feast that propelled Jesus to stand up and shout. Perhaps it was the weariness of dead religion that urged Him forward to scream out for change.

Notice first of all that this promise is for those who already believe. We know that "belief" or "faith" in Christ is the basis for salvation. The statement is that this experience was something that those who "believed in him were later to receive." This means those who were to experience

319

salvation had something to look forward to in the future. So Jesus is not referring to a born-again experience here. He is referring to an experience that is post-conversion. It is the experience that could not occur until Jesus was glorified.

Jesus told them that the Comforter (Holy Spirit) could not come until he had left (John 16:7). This matches the statement above that "the Spirit had not yet been given since Jesus had not yet been glorified." John the Baptist had promised something similar. He said, "I have baptized you with water, but He will baptize you with the Holy Spirit." Again this could not have been referring to salvation for it was experienced on the day of Pentecost well after the disciples had believed the gospel; for the gospel had already been provided them by the risen Lord in Luke 24:44-47. They had not understood why Jesus had to die on the cross until He explained it to them in that passage. This was the good news, or gospel, that is the power of salvation to everyone who believes (Romans 1:16). They were saved before Pentecost.

Just prior to Pentecost Jesus picks up on what John the Baptist had said from the beginning in Acts 1:5: "for John baptized with water, but you will be baptized with the Holy Spirit not many days from now." Jesus further explains the purpose for this outpouring from within a few verses later: "But you will receive power when the Holy Spirit has come upon you, and you will be my witnesses . . ." The purpose is not the conversion of the recipient but to help the recipient (who is already saved) get others converted. Even though they are already true believers, they need an extra zeal for boldness to proclaim the good news to the world. The Holy Spirit is called alongside us for support and encouragement. We need that grace to forge ahead against all odds, which was certainly the case in the beginning of the Christian faith.

Does this mean one does not have the Holy Spirit when he or she is born again? Of course not! You can only be born again by the Spirit (John 3:5). It is a spiritual rebirth, but it is that same Spirit that takes us further into the process of sanctification. Remember, the spirit baptism does not come from without but from within (John 7:38). So the source is already in place. It is just that this initial deposit starts to rise and overflows like a flood in the process. We are the temple of the Holy Spirit (1 Corinthians 6:19). The Holy Spirit is involved in everything we experience as believers, including what happens before, during, and after conversion.

So what is required for this coming and this drinking? Jesus said all that is required is "thirst," or desire, and the willingness to approach Jesus for a drink. The command is two-sided. There is the order to "come," which addresses our willingness to approach Christ. There is the order to "drink," which implies a willingness to quench our thirst. That's correct. This is not optional. You cannot opt out of this experience and still claim Jesus is your Lord because He has insisted that we all come and drink—if we are thirsty. If the Son of God Himself needed the Holy Spirit to descend upon Him and empower Him for ministry; how is it that we think we can do without this anointing? At his water baptism before He began his ministry there we find the heavens opened and the Holy Spirit descending upon Christ as a dove. Then in His inaugural address He is recorded as saying, "The Spirit of the Lord is upon me; for He has anointed me to preach the gospel to the poor . . ." (Luke 4:18)

Are you weary of your own lifeless religious rituals? Do you need an invigorating renewal from deep within? Then drink deeply my friend, drink deeply. He said He will not leave us to face the world all alone. He will send us another comforter (*Paraklēsis* in the original Greek). *Paraklēsis* means "called alongside." *Para* means *beside* and *klēsis* means *called*. Take advantage of this resource provided by Jesus Himself. He ordered us to drink because we need to. We need the insight, encouragement, and power to be successful in the mission of bringing more lost souls into the kingdom. Remember this, which Jesus also said: "If you then, though you are evil, know how to give good gifts to your children, how much more will your Father in heaven give the Holy Spirit to those who ask Him?" (Luke 11:13)

Discussion Questions:

- What was Jesus referring to when He said those who currently believed in Him would later receive an infilling of the Spirit that would rise up like a fountain within them?
- How does John 3:16; Romans 1:16; and Luke 24:44-47 prove the disciples were saved prior to Pentecost? What many other passages suggest the same conclusion?
- Which passages show us that the Holy Spirit is involved in both conversion and sanctification? What did Jesus say about the Holy

Spirit "baptism" in John 7:37 and Acts 1:5 that places it squarely in the category of sanctification?

- What is the only requirement for this thirst-quenching experience according to Jesus?
- What does Jesus command the thirsty to do? How does that make you feel to know that it is not optional?
- What religious baggage is closing you off from a willingness to drink deeply of the Holy Spirit today? How can you open up to Jesus more in this area?

Suggested Exercises:

- Discuss among the group what hindrances there were in your upbringing that closes you off to the Lord's encouragement to come and drink. Determine to allow nothing to come between you and obedience to your Master.
- Confess to a trusted fellow disciple the current dryness and deadness of your religious experience thus far and the deep thirst that is yet to be quenched. Then pray together for the experience Jesus spoke of in John 7:37-39.
- Share with the group how you have heard the Lord's command and have therefore incorporated this blessing and anointing into your Christian life.

54

We've Got Work to Do

John 9:4-5

We must work the works of Him who sent me as long as it is day; night is coming when no one can work. While I am in the world, I am the light of the world.

Command of Christ: We *must* work the works of Him who sent me.

In this instance there is no Greek grammar specification that would identify a particular term in this passage as an imperative. It is the force of the statement that propels us forward to take immediate action. In that sense it is an "implied" imperative. The use of the word "must" serves notice as to the urgency and necessity of the situation at hand.

The context is the conversation leading up to the healing of a man born blind. The disciples asked Jesus if the blind man or his parents sinned for him to have been born that way. He told them it was not the result of sin. It just presented an opportunity to show God's love. That window of opportunity was becoming smaller and smaller, and Jesus understood just how little time He had left to unveil God's glory to the world. We estimate that it was around three years that He had in all to accomplish God's will, and so we can surely understand why he made the statement: "While it is day, we must do the work of Him who sent me. Night is coming, when no one can work" (John 9:4). The psalmist asks the Lord to "teach us to number our days, that we may apply our hearts unto wisdom" (Psalm 90:12). This is likely the spirit in which Jesus addresses his disciples here.

It was true of His life and it is true of ours. Our lives are brief already, but even shorter than that is the time we have to do God's work. If you live 70 years, that comes to about 25,550 days. Not all of those days are used to share the gospel. A good deal of that time is spent just growing up. So that leaves us with very little time as adults to effectively make disciples in this world. We are the light of the world. Therefore, when our light goes out, darkness replaces it. This is why it is imperative that we take every opportunity to shine forth as he told us before (Matthew 5:14-16). When we hide, it is the same as not being there at all. We don't have time to waste in fear and timidity. The clock is ticking and soon our window of opportunity will pass into the night forever. As the song said, "Only one life, so soon it will pass. Only what is done for Christ will last."

Finally notice the change from "we" to "me." Jesus said, "*We* must work the works of Him that sent *me* . . ." I see a strong statement about chain of command and interconnectedness here. There is the Father at the top doing the sending in the first place. The one being sent is not doing His own works but those works that are being passed down from heaven. Jesus operates in total submission. He expects nothing less from his team. They are to be in such complete surrender to him as their head that He could make such a statement, that "we" are to accomplish "my" work. The only way that "we" can work for "me" is if "we" are one. This is similar to Paul's later illustration about us being the "body" of Christ. Only the head houses the mind. No other body part has a mind of its own but stays wired and connected in such a way to the brain that it instantly responds to its every impulse. All of the different parts function as a unit. So are we to be fully submitted to and united with Christ. We are to become so integrated with the Godhead that we are totally indistinguishable from one another. So it is not just about doing a job, but making sure that job is an expression of the Father. Otherwise it will be an exercise in futility. Jesus stated, "Every plant, which my heavenly Father has not planted, shall be rooted up" (Matthew 15:13). We have to grow to the point of maturity that Jesus demonstrated where we know that it is not our work for God, but God's work through us that makes the difference.

If we do stay interconnected we can rest assured that our lives on this earth will not have been wasted. God can do more with three years than we could do with three lifetimes. John 15:5 said, "I am the vine; you are the branches. The one who remains in Me and I in him produces much fruit, because you can do nothing without Me." Get plugged in so He can shine through you. In John 9:4-5 the Master is saying in essence, "Hurry up; we've got work to do!"

Discussion Questions:

- How does the word "must" (in John 9:4-5) demonstrate that this statement is also a command or a mandate rather than just a suggestion?
- How could the healing of a man born blind have more impact on society that healing a man who had gone blind recently due to old age?
- In Jesus's day all work had to be accomplished during the daylight hours. Once night came there was no more opportunity to work. How did Jesus see his three years of ministry in the same way?
- How will the numbering of our days awaken us to the limited time we also have to spread the good news? How will this fact result in a greater urgency toward the work of God?
- How does Jesus's statement about "we" and "me" underscore the necessity of oneness?
- How do we move from the "our work for God" mentality to a "God's work through us" perspective? What scripture helps us with this reorientation?

Suggested Exercises:

- Since it is the Father's work and not our own efforts that produces fruit, it is more important first to get on the same page with Him in terms of awareness of what He is up to in the world. Jesus said "The Father loves the Son and shows him all He is doing." So the first objective is a love relationship. Begin to shore up the following areas in your life to rebuild that appropriate intimacy level that is necessary for us to hear His voice once He is ready for us to get involved in any particular way:
  o Make sure He has your undivided attention in terms of prayer and meditation for at least an hour a day.
  o Keep Him in the forefront of your heart and mind throughout the day in the midst of your daily duties and responsibilities.

- Keep a "listening log" where you write down in one brief sentence what you think God is saying to you on a personal level during your prayer, Bible reading, and church attendance. Share this log with a trusted mentor for feedback.
- Keep yourself saturated in the Word of God to where it becomes second nature.
- Abide in Christ by seeking a personal connection with Him that is palpable. Worship the Christ of the gospels as your Lord and Master putting all His sayings to heart and to memory.
- Ask Christ for the power of the Holy Spirit to become His witness.
- Follow the lead of the Person who has now become close enough to you that you can truly sense His guidance.

*All of the above must be verified by your accountability partner on a monthly basis. Each item should be discussed and the disciple hitting on all cylinders before this level is considered complete.

55

Value Not Power But Life

Luke 10:17-20

The seventy returned with joy, saying, "Lord, even the demons are subject to us in your name." And he said to them, "I was watching Satan fall from heaven like the lightning. Behold I have given you authority to tread on serpents and scorpions, and over all the power of the enemy, and nothing will injure you. Nevertheless do not rejoice in this, that the spirits are subject to you, but rejoice that your names are recorded in heaven."

Commands of Christ: *Do not rejoice* that the spirits are subject to you, but *rejoice* that your names are written in heaven.

The context of this admonishment was a second sending out of disciples into Judea to spread the gospel. This time there were seventy involved, and they were very successful. They were understandably overjoyed with a powerful and successful ministry experience. The demons were subjected to them. They had the facility to cast them out, and it was that very ability they were rejoicing over. It was like discovering you have superpowers and then having to deal with the fallout from that discovery. For us the supernatural is breathtaking and inconceivable, but for God it is just natural and even uneventful. It is just a normal part of His everyday experience. It is not special or unusual to Him. Jesus had to teach them not to let it go to their heads; that this is to be expected when you are working side-by-side with God.

What are the dangers inherent in such a display of raw power? Well, we see Jesus immediately reference the fall of Satan. Self-esteem is good, but if it gets out of control, it can totally destroy you and eventually turn you into an enemy of God. Satan is the prime example. He had come to the point where he thought equality with God was something within his reach. Not only equality, but even superiority was entertained. Ever since then he has become the lead adversary in this unceasing battle between darkness and light. In the Garden of Eden we see the same temptation being offered to Eve that he had wanted for himself. It was the possibility of upgrading to a godlike status that led to both his and man's downfall. It is the potential to be lifted up with pride that is one of the greatest threats to the furtherance of God's kingdom. Because once you are convinced of your own greatness and superiority, it suddenly becomes all about the advancement of your kingdom. In God's kingdom there is only room for one king. Since that job is permanently taken, the rest of us are forever His servants.

This was not the first time Jesus had to quash an enthusiastic response that bordered on blasphemy. For we all remember that heated exchange between Jesus and Peter, where Peter was addressed as "Satan." Not long before that he had been given the keys to the kingdom, and now it seems on the basis of that affirmation, he had dared to overstep his authoritative boundary (Matthew 16:21-23).

So the lesson learned here is to proceed with caution. I don't believe that the enthusiasm expressed by these seventy disciples had yet progressed to the level of pride. But had not Jesus intervened at this very point, it may have. There is a fine line between exuberance and self-aggrandizement. First we rejoice to the heavens over our success. Then we begin to associate the success with ourselves. We look around us and compare our victories to others failures. We begin to realize that we are a rare item indeed, that we are being used in a special way. So we must be special to God! We are better than anyone else. We have a corner on God. So when you want to know what God wants, "Look me up because I'm your man," we insist. So it is imperative that we stay on our guard when we experience ministry success so that our initial joyful song of praise does not develop into a cacophony of spiritual pride.

We must always see ourselves as only the vessel that contains God's glory and not the glory itself. The most we can achieve in this life is to become a vessel of honor. 2 Timothy 2:19-21 says it perfectly:

"Nevertheless the solid foundation of God stands, having this seal: 'The Lord knows those who are His,' and, 'Let everyone who names the name of Christ depart from iniquity.' But in a great house there are not only vessels of gold and silver, but also of wood and clay, some for honor and some for dishonor. Therefore, if anyone cleanses himself from the latter, he will be a vessel for honor, sanctified and useful for the Master; prepared for every good work." Our job then is basically to remain His possession.

We remain his children by never allowing self-centeredness come between us. We should take Jesus very seriously but never take ourselves very seriously. We will never be the parent in this relationship with God. We will always be the child. We will never be the teacher of Christ but always the student (Matthew 23:8). We must constantly take an inventory of our lives and depart from any iniquity that could arise that will contaminate our vessel.

Blessed are the meek, for they shall inherit the earth (Matthew 5:5). We are valuable to God only inasmuch as we remain under his control. A wild stallion is great to watch but is of no use to mankind in a practical sense. Only when the savage beast within has been soothed and tamed can all that power be harnessed in a positive direction.

So it is with us and the Lord. Meekness is power under control. We are to let go of our rights, freedoms, privileges, and even our very lives to be of any value to the kingdom of God. Like the hammer in the tool pouch, we just remain intact until He calls for us. We don't jump out of the tool chest and do a dance because He just used us to drive home a few nails. We don't say to the other tools that we must be special, and the best tool of all. We remember that had He not designed us this certain way, we would have no value in the first place. The glory doesn't originate in us, it originates in the mind of the architect. He is using us to accomplish His work, not His work to accomplish us.

The display of power is not an end in itself. It is the means to the ultimate end of bringing someone to the Lord. So we can't get all caught up in the bait we are using to fish for men. We need to rejoice more in the catching of the fish. The greatest miracle of all is the acquisition of eternal life. All miracles, no matter how great on earth, are temporary. As Jesus said, everyone who ate the manna still died. It is the item that endures that contains the ultimate value. It is Jesus who is the bread of eternal life. The other bread only furthers our brief existence here on earth. In John

6:47-51 Jesus says, "Most assuredly, I say to you, he who believes in me has everlasting life. I am the bread of life. Your fathers ate the manna in the wilderness, and are dead. This is the bread which comes down from heaven that one may eat of it and not die. I am the living bread which came down from heaven. If anyone eats of this bread, he will live forever; and the bread that I shall give is my flesh, which I shall give for the life of the world."

Don't rejoice in having power over the Devil, rejoice in eternal life! What is eternal life? Eternal life is knowing Him (John 17:3). Nothing supersedes the relationship. That is what He died for. He died to initiate a relationship with us that will last throughout eternity.

Discussion Questions:

- What were the seventy disciples excited about when they returned to Jesus who had sent them out to share the gospel in Judea?
- Who did the disciples' power trip remind Jesus of?
- How can our initial song of praise end up a cacophony of self-importance?
- How can maintaining a humble view of ourselves for who we really are (just a vessel or a tool) keep us out of trouble? What scriptures support that viewpoint?
- How does a tame horse demonstrate meekness?
- Miracle working power is the means to what end? How did Jesus make that clear in John 6:47-51?
- What did Jesus die for?

Suggested Exercises:

- Discuss the value of mountain-moving faith verses faith in the gospel. Which one is the means and which is the end? Which one of those is temporary and which is eternal? Which one will change the geography and which will change the world? Pray a prayer of commitment and determination to keep everything in the proper perspective as you serve the Lord in whatever capacity you are called.

- Discuss methods to keep your pride in check. Research famous ministers who fell due to not having such a system in place and share your findings with the group.
- Research the differing approaches to church government and the checks and balances in place to maintain order. What are some of the strengths and weaknesses of the various approaches?

56

Stay Open and Generous

Luke 11:34-36; Matthew 6:22

The eye is the lamp of your body; when your eye is clear your whole body also is full of light; but when it is bad, your body also is full of darkness. Then watch out that the light in you is not darkness. If therefore your whole body is full of light, with no dark part in it, it will be wholly illumined, as when the lamp illumines you with its rays (Luke 11:34-36).

Command of Christ: *Inspect and be certain,* therefore, that the light in you is not darkness.

Here is another example of the same illustration being used for different reasons. In the Luke passage, the parable about the eye seems to be used as an appeal to the general public to open up and be more receptive to the gospel. They had seen so many miracles, yet their hearts were still closed to Jesus. He pronounced woes on His generation because they were more hardhearted than the Ninevites who repented at Jonah's preaching. Jesus did far more and greater works than Jonah, and yet they remained obstinate in their traditions. Jonah was a prophet and Jesus was the Son of God. God Himself couldn't even crack their stony hearts. In Matthew, the parable is used to emphasize opening up and being more generous. If you withhold your money and keep it all to yourself, you will never experience the sowing and reaping process that God has set into the very course of nature. Approval for your fellow man can also be withheld because he is not in your clique or a member of your "holy club." It can be withheld when you stare in envy at someone else's good fortune. We are not to build our life around wealth but to use our good fortune to help the less fortunate. Thereby we will have a rich welcome in heaven. Withholding our goods leads to making an idol out of them. So in summary, the Luke passage is about opening up to receive and the Matthew passage is about opening up to give.

Jesus uses the mechanism of human eyesight to drive home the point about being open and receptive rather than rigid and intolerant. He states that our eyes are the lamps of our body. In other words, they let the light in so we can see where we are going. Eyesight works by the amount of light that travels through the aperture in the center of the iris. The pupil expands to let more light in when it is dark and contracts to keep too much light out when in the direct sunlight. Jesus is saying that those who were unreceptive to His ministry were blind. Their pupils were bolted down tight and there was no possibility for any light to penetrate their darkness. This is a horrible place to come to and it is still an ailment that is prevalent today.

We get so stuck in our traditional way of doing things and our lifestyle that we become completely shut off to the light of God's Word. Instead of allowing it to enter into our hearts and change the way we have always believed, we end up changing God's Word to make it say what we have always believed. We might as well stop reading it because we no longer allow it to change us. Jesus was calling all generations to unwind and allow the light of the glorious gospel to filter in through the cracks of our concrete hearts.

A "darkened eye" or an "evil eye" was a Jewish idiom that meant a person was envious. Many in that day had become envious of Jesus. Because of that they shunned him. They were judging Him and excluding Him rather than opening up to him and welcoming him. They were giving him the evil eye of jealousy. But not only was this evil eye aimed at our Lord and Savior, it was aimed toward everyone who refused to join their "holier than thou" club. They were an association with an exclusive membership. Everything was for personal gain. There was no thought for the lost or needy soul. All monies were used to pad their own pockets and further their own cause.

As such they failed to achieve the purpose God had designed the nation of Israel for. They were not to keep all of the glory to themselves; they were to spread the good news throughout the earth. Instead of being a good example to the world, they had become an absolute disaster. They thought of the rest of the world as dogs and that only they were the privileged children of God. Instead of being thankful to be called to serve, they mistook the call as a preference for them over the rest of the world. That's why God had to judge them and pass on that same assignment to the New Testament Church. But as Paul said, we should be careful that the same thing doesn't happen to us. We were grafted in, but we could be easily replaced with the natural branch (Romans 11:18).

The overall lesson is not to harden your heart. Remain open, accepting, and generous. Thereby you will be identified as a true child of God. Jesus said, "Inspect and be certain therefore, that the light in you is not darkness." Examine yourself now and ask, am I open to new ideas, or do I think I have everything totally figured out in the Word of God? Do I see Christianity as only those in my denomination or in all denominations? Am I exclusive or inclusive of other cultures, opinions, and convictions? Will I ever find myself in the midst of sinners and even being called their friend? Do I read the Word of God to have control over it or to allow it to have control over me?

Discussion Questions:

- What two different points does Jesus make with the same illustration about the mechanism of the eye in Matthew and in Luke?
- What does an open pupil or aperture in the eye represent as opposed to one that is completely shut?
- How does our comfort with the traditional way of doing things lead to a closed mindedness that can shut us off from the convicting penetration of God's truth?
- The "evil eye" is a first-century Jewish idiom meaning what? How did this apply to the ways Jesus and those who follow Him have to suffer in their ministries?
- How did this policy of exclusivity prevent Israel from achieving the purpose for which God created them? How will it do the same to the New Testament Church if we don't learn from our predecessors?
- What is the overall lesson to be learned from Jesus's parable about the human eye?

Suggested Exercises:

- Honestly evaluate yourself on a scale of one to ten on the following questions. Then meet with a fellow disciple, compare notes, and pray for one another that you will remain open and receptive rather than rigid and intolerant. Allow an atmosphere of confession and repentance to prevail over that of rationalization or justification.
  - I accept all Christian denominations as equally valid.
  - I am equally accepting of people at every socioeconomic level in society.
  - I am interested in other cultures and their perspectives.
  - I carefully consider other opinions and convictions.
  - I rejoice when my plan is upstaged by something more sensible.
  - I am a friend of sinners.
  - People say I am very approachable.
  - I read the word of God with an open mind, allowing it to change me regardless of the way I have been brought up to believe.
  - I both question everything and like to be questioned about everything.

57

When on Trial, Trust the Holy Spirit

Luke 12:11-12

When they bring you before the synagogues and the rulers and the authorities, do not worry about how or what you are to speak in your defense, or what you are to say; for the Holy Spirit will teach you in that very hour what you ought to say.

Command of Christ: *Don't ever worry* about making your defense or what you should say.

We know from Christian history that the prospect of being put on trial was a very real possibility in first-century Palestine. In addition to the threat of the Sanhedrin was the fact that Christianity was simply not yet registered within the Roman Empire as a sanctioned religion. As such, it was vulnerable to attack as an illegal institution. At first they were hardly indistinguishable from the Jewish faith, which was sanctioned, but in time they became a separate and distinct organization with no official approval. Naturally they became a target for abuse; a scapegoat, if you will, when one was needed. For example, it is known that Nero blamed the Church for the fire in Rome in 64 AD. For hundreds of years they were mercilessly harassed and slaughtered by a string of Roman emperors until Constantine finally put an end to it in the fourth-century AD.

But what is fascinating about the Christian faith is the way they seemed to perceive their persecution as martyrdom. The word "martyr" is of Greek origin and is translated as "testimony" in the New Testament. Even though they were paying with their lives for their faith, they saw that as the single greatest testimony of all and not as a defeat. This was the Holy Spirit in them giving them the strength and determination that those times required.

This is what Jesus was promising here in His Word of preparation for the future. They were to expect resistance of all varieties. It would come from the synagogues, rulers, and authorities of all persuasions. The bottom line is that the Christian faith is an assault on Satan's territory and as such will be defended against. The enemy will use every sort of worldly leader and authority structure he can to thwart the kingdom of God. He will not even stop short of the Church itself. Satan's strategy is conquering through division. He aims to keep us in a constant state of tension with each other, whether it is one denomination or belief system against another or even squabbles within one's own preference.

It was the religious leaders of Jesus's day that were His greatest threat, and it is the religious leaders of our day that in many instances follow in their footsteps. Phariseeism is not just a blast from the past; it remains alive and well among the performance-based and legalistic leadership approach so often exercised by religious hierarchy today. Their objective is to rise to a place of power and prestige over other believers rather than to serve one another. That view is an ultraconservative view. You will find extremes on both sides of the divide. In the United States we see the Church as a whole divided into conservative and liberal camps. The liberal groups tend to downplay the divine origin of scripture while the conservative churches fight to uphold the inerrancy of scripture. This is why reports are constantly surfacing about the ordination of "gay" bishops and "lesbian" ministers. Those are the consequences of devaluing scripture. We find even within the same denomination churches who accept homosexuality and those who don't. Forty years ago, who would have even thought such things were possible? Syncretism is not just the verdict for ancient Israel, it is our current reality. A true believer could find himself victimized by extremes on either side of the equation.

So what is Jesus saying exactly? For one thing, He is teaching us to expect conflict. He is also saying not to be overly concerned about conflict, that it is to be anticipated. When you find yourself standing before one official or another, don't feel intimidated. Don't be afraid of man who can only destroy the body (Luke 12:4). Make sure to stand up for Jesus Christ in those situations because "whoever acknowledges me before men, the Son of Man will also acknowledge him before the angels of God. But he

who disowns me before men will be disowned before the angels of God"
(Luke 12:8-9). But don't worry and fret about what words you will use to
defend yourself. For Jesus promises that "the Holy Spirit will teach you at
that time what you should say" (Luke12:11). The command from Jesus
is this: "Don't ever worry about making your defense or what you should
say." As it was during the time of the Christian martyrs, so it will be for us.
When we are persecuted, Jesus is persecuted (Acts 9:4). We are the body of
Christ, and the words of defense will flow from the head. He will speak for
Himself on that day through us. We are just to remain one with Him.

Discussion Questions:

- Why was the prospect of a Christian being put on trial a very real
  possibility in first-century Palestine?
- Why did the early Christians not see martyrdom as a defeat?
- Where can the Christian expect resistance to come from and
  why?
- How is the true believer a threat to conservative as well as liberal
  extremes?
- Since it is just a matter of time before you face such a challenge,
  according to the Master, what is the best way to be prepared?

Suggested Exercises:

- Share testimonies of times you were called to give an account
  (put on trial, in a sense) because you stood up for what's right or
  spoke out against what was wrong. Decide within the group of
  disciples if this was a true persecution or just an imagined one.
  Get feedback from one another in the Lord. Determine the best
  way to handle such situations in the future with the aid of the
  Holy Spirit.

58

Prevail over Passion

Luke 12:13-34

Someone in the crowd said to him, "Teacher, tell my brother to divide the family inheritance with me." But he said to him, "Man, who appointed me a judge or arbitrator over you?" Then he said to them, "Beware, and be on your guard against every form of greed; for not even when one has an abundance does his life consist of his possessions" (Luke 12:13-15).

Commands of Christ: *Watch out! Guard* against all covetousness. *Sell* your possessions and *give* alms.

The context of this commandment is a monetary dispute between brothers, which Jesus was called on to resolve. One of the two appealed to Jesus to convince his brother to divide the inheritance with him. He apparently shouted out to Jesus from the crowd, putting Jesus on the spot, so to speak. Jesus's reply was, "Who appointed me a judge or an arbiter between you?" Then he said to them, "Watch out! Be on your guard against all covetousness; a man's life does not consist in the abundance of his possessions."

First of all, legal arbitration was not what God called Jesus to do. Jesus was not on His own schedule or planning His daily agenda. He strictly adhered to the parameters of activity as was so determined by the Father. So the answer to the question Jesus posed here was obvious. It was this man himself who was attempting to force Jesus into the role of arbiter. This public display of impertinence by the complainant proved that his passions were out of control. Is that the appropriate place to settle a private matter, and should the teacher be imposed upon to render a verdict with no information about the case?

The fact that rabbis were known to help resolve legal disputes does not erase the ugliness of this ill-mannered approach. What right did he have to corner the Master and place demands upon Him? The only one with that level of authority is God. So this illustrates how one's desires can be so out of control as to totally lose sight of all common decency, as if to say, "Only what I want right now matters." What else, other than inordinate desire, would drive a person to cry out in the midst of a crowd of people and expect a positive result?

So Jesus addresses the real problem instead of the one suggested by the malcontent sibling. The actual issue is coveting the inheritance and how that can bring two brothers who had just lost a cherished loved one to a dangerous place. No resolution would ever prove satisfactory as long as their desires were out of control. So why offer a solution for them when that solution is already obvious? Did they really need Jesus' advice on the simple matter of dividing something in half? No, but they did need his advice on the underlying issue that brought them to this point of contention in the first place. This is what they received. As is often the case with Jesus, he will not always give us what we want, but he will offer what we need. He is able to instantly penetrate through our façade to the heart of any matter.

Jesus's teaching on covetousness is a reaffirmation of the last of the Ten Commandments. Whenever necessary, He adds a great deal of emphasis to it; for it is in this final of the Ten Commandments that we find a back door. If left unchecked it will provide a pathway whereby all of the remaining nine can also be violated. Isn't it dissatisfaction and discontent that leads to other gods, making idols, disrespecting God's name, ignoring the Sabbath, disrespecting parents, committing murder, adultery, and theft, and bearing false witness? The obedience toward all commandments rises or falls on whether or not we can control our desires. We always seem to want more instead of being satisfied with what we already have.

This seems to be the basis of our political system here in the West, and it is not an exaggeration to suggest that it has become an idol to us. One illustration of this is the slogan that won a presidential election not too long ago in the United States: "It's the economy, stupid." What is sad about the statement is not so much the vulgarity of it as the fact that it outperformed the other camp who was promoting "family values" at the time. Now isn't that the truth for our generation? What do we really value the most? With both partners pursuing full-time careers in most cases one can hardly conclude it is the family. The lights are on but nobody's home. Are we not serving another master? Jesus said you can't serve God and riches. We have chosen money over Him. Why? It is the same reason why the two brothers were so much at each other's throats as to have one of them cry out in desperation in the middle of a crowd of followers. We simply are not satisfied with our standard of living. We believe we have to *have more* to be happy. This is the core of what the word "covetousness" means.

The original Greek word for coveting is *pleonexias*. It consists of the combination of two words: *pleon*, meaning "more," and *exias*, meaning "have." We don't believe we have enough money, possessions, positions, recognitions, power, or even sex partners. Just think about the entertainment industry for example. Is their fame and fortune not enough so that they have to continually run from one awards ceremony to another? There are the Academy Awards, the People's Choice Awards, the Tony Awards, and the Golden Globes to name a few. Once a year should be enough, but that's just the point. It is never enough. There can never be enough recognition to match what we think we deserve. Fill in the blank. There is never enough of anything we want. We always want more. But we already have more than anyone in history! Have we considered the fact that God may be blessing us in order to provide for those who have less and not so that we can have even more?

How far off the mark we have drifted in modern society where overindulgence is par for the course? Jesus is warning us to bring all of this hedonism to a halt, to get a grip on ourselves. He is commanding His disciples to have no part of this excess living we have come to expect where two-thirds of the world's resources are being consumed by one-third of the world's population. I believe He is calling us to radically simplify our lives and to use that excess to help the less fortunate. And the tenth commandment is the place to start.

We must first begin with our appetites. We must learn contentment. Paul said, "I have learned in whatsoever state I am, therewith to be content" (Philippians 4:19). Furthermore he states in I Timothy 6:8: "And having food and raiment, let us therewith be content." This is how a person can live by faith. They must mature to the point that whether we have everything or have nothing it is the same to us. We must remember that "I can do all things through Christ which strengthens me" is not referring to acquiring wealth but to acquiring contentment. This is the central issue of our time, which if we fail to remedy will plunge our culture into ruin. The handwriting is on the wall, and we must now do everything in our power to turn things around before it is too late. It is the nature of the beast that if you don't heed the warning signs you will suffer the consequences. When one encounters the sign "beware of dog," one proceeds with great fear and trepidation. How much more should we inch forward with caution when Jesus says, "Beware of covetousness"?

Discussion Questions:

- What was the context of Jesus's warning about covetousness?
- How was Jesus's question to the man about who appointed him arbitrator designed to return the discussion to the root of the problem?
- How did Jesus end up delivering the brothers the advice they needed rather than what they wanted?
- How can the last of the Ten Commandments provide a passageway to violation of the other nine?
- What is the evidence that our culture is way out of control in terms of overindulgence when it comes to the economy, recognition, and consumerism, for instance?
- What two words are compounded to form the original Greek word for covetousness? How does that put a finger on the root of the problem?
- What answers do Jesus and Paul suggest as far as the solution for coveting is concerned?

Suggested Exercises:

- Take a mission trip to a third-world country and see how they live from day to day. Live the way they live for a while if possible. This should heighten your awareness of the necessities of life and how much infinitely past that we live on a daily basis.
- Reorient your lifestyle toward a more simplified life. Cut the waste from your life: extra houses; cars; clubs; lands; etc. Lower

your standard of living significantly to have more money left to provide for the less fortunate. For example, you would have greater resources to provide for clean water, food, or to support indigenous missions in the poorer countries of the world. There are many organizations to support that focus on those very things. Discuss your spending cuts and redistribution plan with a fellow disciple and determine together the validity of the proposal.

- Discuss among the group the pros and cons of selling your church building and meeting in your homes instead. How would that free up a significant amount of resources that would be better spent elsewhere (evangelism, needy in your community, missions, etc.)?
- Discuss among the discipleship group what exactly the basic necessities of life are and whether or not you are content with that. Discuss methods for dealing with discontent.

59

Stay Engaged: Parousia Is Imminent

Luke 12:35-47; Matthew 24:42-51

But if that slave says in his heart, "My master will be a long time in coming," and begins to beat the slaves, both men and women, and to eat and drink and get drunk; the master of that slave will come on a day when he does not expect and at an hour he does not know, and will cut him in pieces, and assign him a place with the unbelievers (Luke 12:45-46).

Commands of Christ: *Keep* your loins covered and lamps burning. *Watch* therefore.

Jesus outlines the responsibility of a watchman in Luke and Matthew to illustrate what will occur on judgment day (Parousia) if we are caught off-guard. In the Western world we have no frame of reference to Jesus's story about the watchman. But in the underdeveloped countries of the East, it is a normal way of life to have someone constantly on the alert throughout the night watching over the property. This person sleeps during the day and stays up all night so that he will be ready to fend off any intruders. Thieves come at night, and in third-world countries their desperation only increases the likelihood of a strike. So it is a must to keep watchmen onsite. Advanced societies use security systems, and sometimes security guards. But Jesus is talking about the person who is not only responsible for the property overnight but also lives there.

He goes on to talk about the house manager, who is not only responsible for security but for the entire interworking of the household and every position in that organizational structure. Again, in underdeveloped countries it is common to have a whole crew of individuals working in and out of the household while the owners pursue more lucrative endeavors. Individuals are willing to be live-in housekeepers for practically nothing due to the fact that the alternative is starvation in many instances. This is probably closer to the situation we find in the New Testament where 90 percent of the people in first-century Israel were subsistence farmers. They were known by the Hebrew term *Amhaaretz,* meaning "people of the land," and they were just that, having only the cultivation of their individual farmlands to keep them going.

When you return home from an evening out, it is customary for the watchman to stand ready to provide reentry to the complex. He will meet you at the gate and open the doors for your safe passage. This is the context of the first section of Jesus's statements about staying ready for His return in Luke 12:35-41. He commands us, as His watchmen, to, "Be dressed, ready for service and keep your lamps burning, like men waiting for their master to return from a wedding banquet, so that when he comes and knocks they can immediately open the door for him. It will be good for those servants whose master finds them ready, even if he comes in the second or third watch of the night." He goes on to say, "But understand this: If the owner of the house had known at what hour the thief was coming, he would not have let his house be broken into. You also must be ready, because the Son of Man will come at an hour when you do not expect him."

So here we find the purpose of the parables. It is the return of Christ. At that time we will be judged on the basis of how we have performed during His absence. Some of us will go on to further God's kingdom while others will lose enthusiasm in His absence. It is all a test as to who will be the most faithful in the interim.

He goes on to provide a third parable as follows in Luke 12:42-46: "The Lord answered, 'Who then is the faithful and wise manager, whom the master puts in charge of his servants to give them their food allowance at the proper time? It will be good for that servant whom the master finds doing so when he returns. I tell you the truth; he will put him in charge of all his possessions. But suppose the servant says to himself, "My master is taking a long time in coming," and he then begins to beat the men servants and the women servants and to eat and drink and get drunk. The master of that servant will come on a day when he does not expect him and at an hour he is not aware of. He will cut him to pieces and assign him a place with the unbelievers."

So now we see a wide range of consequences meted out according to the level of faithfulness. On one extreme there is the expansion of his responsibilities and honor to place him over even more territory. On the other extreme is the loss of everything, making him equal to a nonbeliever, and thereby receiving the eternal damnation nonbelievers deserve (Matthew 24:51). There are also various levels of punishment between those two resulting in either "few" or "many" stripes according to the level of guilt (Luke 12:47).

So with all this said, it is imperative that all Christians take heed and watch every word they say and every deed they perform keeping in mind the day of judgment soon to come. One can have a rich welcome or a poor one depending on the investments one has made (2 Peter 1:11). Just think about it. These investments, whether good or bad, provide eternal dividends (Matthew 6:19; 25:14-30). It would be awful to end up saved but with no rewards. Throughout all eternity you will be known as the one who failed to do anything for Christ with your life. I don't believe that barely making it in heaven's door is as great as some make it out to be. Embarrassment is one thing, but eternal embarrassment is something entirely different.

In addition to the reward and punishment phase, we are to stay motivated by the fact that the day and hour of Christ's return is not known. This is the whole reason we must stay on the alert and keep occupied. Since we don't know the particular time, we have to be ready at all times. If we knew the exact day and hour, we could allow some downtime. But as it is, that option is not available. It could happen before this day is up for all we know. We don't want to be embarrassed and caught napping when He arrives. We want to be fully alert and fully engaged. We stay that way because we are expecting His return any moment and want to make the best impression possible.

So the command is to "watch," and "stay prepared." Are you expecting Him today? If not, you are not staying prepared; you are not keeping watch for His return. We must live like He could come at any moment. That way we will stay alert and occupied, meeting Him with joy and celebration rather than embarrassment and disappointment (1 John 2:28). Our relationship with God should not be hit and miss but a continuous stream of good works in the expansion of His kingdom here on Earth.

That way, when He returns He will be very proud and very pleased that He chose us to be His faithful servants.

Discussion Questions:

- How does the job description of a watchman in first-century Palestine (as well as is currently practiced in underdeveloped countries today) bring Jesus's parable to life as well as aid in your understanding of what Jesus is trying to communicate?
- How does the job description of a house manager in first-century Palestine (as well as is currently practiced in underdeveloped countries today) aid in a fuller understanding of what Jesus is trying to communicate?
- On what basis will the watchman and house manager be judged once the Master returns?
- On what basis will we be judged once Jesus returns?
- Name the four levels of reward/punishment that the servant of the Lord can expect.
- Is it possible to make it into heaven and yet still be reprimanded and embarrassed? How does that shatter the myth that there are no disappointments or regrets in eternity?
- How does not knowing the time of Christ's return keep us more motivated to stay engaged than if we knew the exact day and hour?

Suggested Exercises:

- Discuss among the group what regrets you would have if you knew your time to work for the Lord was over because today was the day of Jesus's return.
- Put together a skit or a short story with the theme of how a person would feel if the rapture occurred and now he or she only has regrets, but then suddenly he or she wakes up and there is a second chance! Have examples in the skit/story of the four levels of reward and punishment mentioned by Jesus in his parable about the house manager.
- Psalm 90:12 says to "Teach us to number our days; that we may apply our hearts unto wisdom." Have you done that? Calculate

just how many days you have left if you were to live to be seventy. Discuss your findings with a trusted fellow disciple and renew together your commitment to use the rest of your days more wisely.

- Pray together as a group for a heightened awareness and expectancy for the rapture; to know that today could be the day; to be aware that before you finish that sentence . . . !

- Discuss ways to spur one another toward a greater since of urgency and responsibility in light of our days drawing to a close and the world coming to an end. Example: every morning when you get up, say, "Today could be the day that Jesus returns," as a reminder and an affirmation toward faithfulness. Or every time you see a fellow disciple, greet him or her with the expression, "Maranatha!"

60

Settle out of Court

Luke 12:54-59 (context: 12:49-53 and 13:1-9)

And why do you not even on your own initiative judge what is right? For while you are going with your opponent to appear before the magistrate, on your way there make an effort to settle with him, so that he may not drag you before the judge, and the judge turn you over to the officer, and the officer throw you into the prison. I say to you, you will not get out of there until you have paid the very last cent.

Command of Christ: On the way, *give diligence* to be released from him.

Jesus knew that soon He would have to face the cross. That meant that the nation God had called Him to had rejected Him and His message from the Father. As such, the nation was in very real danger of facing God's heavy judgment for its insolence. Just like they had missed the warnings of the prophets in the past, they had now apparently missed the warnings from God's own Son (Matthew 21:33-40). But they were blind to the entire matter. They seemed to have no idea what trouble they were getting themselves into.

So Jesus makes a final appeal. He is doing everything He can to help them avert judgment. But alas, it is simply an impossible task due to their spiritual dullness. He says to them, "When you see a cloud rising in the west, immediately you say, 'It's going to rain,' and it does. And when the south wind blows, you say, 'It's going to be hot,' and it is. Hypocrites! You know how to interpret the appearance of the earth and the sky. How is it

349

that you don't know how to interpret this present time?" (Luke 12:54-56) Then He urges them to settle this matter before it is too late in a repeat of the parable about settling matters out of court. Before, He used this parable as a method of preventing anger. Now He uses it as a last-ditch effort toward reconciliation between the nation of Israel and God.

Unfortunately, it seems they had no idea what He was talking about. He was right again. They were clueless about what God was up to. They didn't see Him even though He was standing right in front of them. The consequence of this rejection of God's Son was the destruction of Jerusalem and the Temple in 70 AD. That is why Jesus, on the way to the cross, told the women, "Don't weep for me but for yourselves and your children" (Luke 23:28).

What about us? Haven't we received the same message? Haven't we rejected it for other gods? Did we not receive Jesus's message about the kingdom of God, and are we doing anything with it? It is easy to condemn another country and another culture in hindsight, but it is quite another thing to look at one's own country and be willing to see with clear vision how exactly it fails to measure up to Jesus's standards. The point of this passage is not to gain additional insight on Jewish history but to gain insight on the plight of all humanity and how we tend to drift from God as a whole. Instead of reading the text, we must allow the text to read us. We have to ask ourselves honest questions so that the blindness we saw in first-century Israel doesn't become our own. We too have the capability of ignoring God's Son, of overlooking his wisdom, wonders, and warnings. In the West we find ourselves trying to serve two masters: we want both Christ and riches. But Jesus said we can only choose one. Perhaps we have made our choice, but it has not been for Christ, though we say it has. In this country, we serve the almighty dollar, and that is our god. We are like the rich fool who spent all that time acquiring wealth to simply lose it all in the end. In heaven, what will we have to show for ourselves?

So just like He did with them, Jesus appeals to us to settle out of court before it is too late. We will also receive the judgment of God if we continue to place all our value in this life. He is calling us out of our kingdom and into His. Will we repent for our idolatry now or pay for it later? The command is just as pertinent to us as it was to ancient Israel. He is urging us to "give diligence" to be released from our debt before time is up; for if we end up before the court of heaven it will be too late. Jesus declares, "I tell you, you will not get out until you have paid the last penny." We are like the people God judged in Jesus's day. They thought of the Galileans as especially evil because their blood ended up mingled with Pilot's sacrifices. They figured that those who were killed by the tower that fell in Siloam were singled out for judgment due to being especially bad individuals. We think Israel was judged because it was so wicked. We assume they were worse than we are. But I believe Jesus is responding to us the same way He did to them: "I tell you no! But unless you repent, you too will all perish."

Discussion Questions:

- Just prior to Jesus's execution He advised the leaders of Israel to settle out of court. What was He trying to get them to see about themselves before it was too late?
- What was one of the immediate consequences of rejection of the Son of God for the nation of Israel? What further consequences are there?
- In what ways has our nation been guilty of the same thing?
- What actions should we take to avert similar catastrophes?

Suggested Exercises:

- Organize a multidenominational day of repentance among the churches in your city. Repent for materialism; legalism; feminism; homosexuality; fornication; and adultery. Repent for accumulation of wealth just for personal enrichment rather than the enrichment of others. Repent for overindulgence rather than sharing our excess with the hungry and needy around the world. Repent for violation of all of the Ten Commandments. Repent for failure to understand and instill the eight Beatitudes (and the principles of Lord's Prayer) at the very core of our being. Repent for overuse of the words "Christ-centered" when we have no idea either who the Messiah really was or what He taught. Repent of calling Jesus "Lord" when we are actually the masters of our own destinies. Repent for preference of our personal agendas over the kingdom of God.
- At the very least, repent of the above atrocities as individuals and as a group. Meet with an accountability partner if you can't meet as a group.

61

Exchange Humility for Honor

Luke 14:7-11

But when you are invited, go and recline at the last place, so that when the one who has invited you comes, he may say to you, "Friend, move up higher"; then you will have honor in the sight of all who are at the table with you. Everyone who exalts himself will be humbled, and he who humbles himself will be exalted" (Luke 14:10-11).

Commands of Christ: *Never take* the place of honor. *Sit down* at the lowest place.

Jesus (as was His custom) provides another lesson on humility. This is not surprising since He was the purest example of modesty and discretion. In comparison to the power hungry and status-seeking religious leaders of the day, He could only be described as "meek and lowly" (Matthew 11:28). Even though He was the eternal King of kings, he did not come to be served but to serve and to give his life a ransom for many (Mark 10:45). He could confidently say, "Blessed are the poor in spirit, for theirs is the kingdom of heaven" (Matthew 5:3).

The context for this lesson was an invitation to dine with a group of Pharisees, and He noticed their tendency to jockey for position and seats of honor. He proceeded to share a proverb with them to communicate this powerful teaching on how humility leads to honor, and, conversely, how striving for honor leads to humility. He told them at the dinner table, "When someone invites you to a wedding feast, do not take the place of honor, for a person more distinguished than you may have been invited. If so, the host who invited both of you will come and say to you, 'Give this man your seat.' Then, humiliated, you will have to take the least important place."

In the scenario presented above, the person perhaps sees clearly that he is the most notable of all the invited guests thus far. He is pleased therefore to take the seat of distinction and enjoy his good fortune. But he may not be aware that someone of even greater significance was also invited and has yet to arrive. Now he is obliged to relocate in disgrace before all, when all of this could have been avoided by showing a little humility. The reverse could have happened. He could have assumed a lesser position only to eventually be granted a greater distinction.

This illustrates the principle Jesus mentioned at the end. The one who humbles himself will be exalted and the one who honors himself will be humiliated. You will reap what you sow. In planting honor for yourself you are planting dishonor for others. Planting dishonor for others will result in receiving exponential dishonor.

As a disciple of the Lord, live by this principle: always give others the greater place of honor. We are ordered by our Master to "never take the place of honor." We are to always "sit down at the lowest place." It is not only a pattern of living suitable to dinner guests, it is a principle of life in every situation. The greatest among you is the servant (Matthew 23:11). Many of us play politics. We position ourselves to obtain the reins of power. This is often obvious when we watch the latest campaign for political office and the professional analysis that goes along with it. We find out how everything is a numbers game and that the candidate must appeal to the voter base that is most likely to get them elected. They will do and say just about anything to make people think they are on their side. Then, after the election, we learn the truth. Unfortunately, this is not just the predicament of worldly politics. We see that same scenario of every variety unfolding in the church hierarchy. Too often we are guilty of first measuring the political landscape and then running our own campaigns to achieve a title of some sort, rather than just serving in whatever capacity is needed at the time.

Jesus's system is to let others bring you higher. It is never to bring yourself higher. Just as He noted in the parable to take the least seat of honor at the dinner table, He also expects us to take the least seat of honor in the ministry and in church. We are not to plan ambitious schemes to advance ourselves within any church or ministry organization. We are to serve with all our hearts until we are requested to come higher. That way we know that it was not our choice but His. We ultimately belong to Him, so we must allow Him to place us where He wants us whether it is high or low in our eyes. The decision in those matters must always belong to the one who has called us.

This is why Paul constantly reminds the Gentile church that he was not appointed by man, but he is only holding the office of apostle due to the will of God (1 Timothy 1:1; 2 Timothy 1:1; and Ephesians 1:1). Paul did not expect any special treatment and paid his own way even when he didn't have to (1 Thessalonians 2:7-10). What a far cry it is from his example to what we see on display in our culture. The more successful you are, the more money you demand for an appearance. That is the way of the world and doesn't belong in the church. May more ministers be like Jesus and Paul. May they live by faith and even work a job on the side rather than expect that practically all of the church's resources should be devoted to their salaries. If we humble ourselves we will be exalted, but if we exalt ourselves, we who are His disciples and church authorities will find in the end that we are greatly humiliated, especially in terms of the type of testimony we portray to the world around us. Just think of how many souls recoil from the Church for this very reason.

Discussion Questions:

- How is Jesus the greatest example of humility ever?
- How did the Pharisees' eagerness to grab the limelight backfire on them?
- What are the two commands of Jesus that ensure His principle of always giving others the place of honor will be adhered to?
- How does this illustrate another principle about sowing and reaping?
- How does this teaching apply to church politics?
- How is our hunger for power and financial gain in the church a turnoff to nonbelievers?

Suggested Exercises:

- Agree with your fellow disciples to abide by the following policy in ministry:
  o Never ask for a raise.
  o Never seek personal advancement.
  o Never take a higher position unless you are asked to do so.
  o Never ask to speak; only speak when you are asked.
  o Take no position that causes you to see yourself as more than a servant.

62

Pamper the Poor

Luke 14:12-14

And he went on to say to the one who had invited him, "When you give a luncheon or a dinner, do not invite your friends or your brothers or your relatives or rich neighbors, otherwise they may also invite you in return and that will be your repayment. But when you give a reception, invite the poor, the crippled, the lame, the blind, and you will be blessed, since they do not have the means to repay you; for you will be repaid at the resurrection of the righteous."

Commands of Christ: *Do not invite* your friends, brothers, family or rich neighbors. *Call in* the poor, maimed, lame, and blind.

The context here for this passage is the same as the previous command. We are dealing with a dinner gathering of Pharisees to which Jesus was invited. Jesus had already brought out something He saw in their character that needed correction. First they were all eager to have the best seats. Apparently there was a seating arrangement that gave honor to the greatest among them, which was probably a ridiculous custom in the first place. Jesus didn't address the custom but the participants' eagerness to gain the upper hand on one another. Feeding into their desire for recognition, He suggested a way for them to achieve that without fail. Taking the lowest seat would guarantee recognition in a positive direction, whereas taking the highest seat would most likely guarantee disgrace. He encouraged them to reflect on their lives and to choose the wisest course of action rather than to act by brute force and instinct. As is His custom, Jesus cut to the heart of the matter.

In the following verses, Jesus continues on to the next issue that needed to be addressed. It must have been blatantly obvious to Jesus that the Pharisees were extremely exclusive in their approach to life and that being in their clique was of utmost importance in terms of acceptance. When Jesus said before that the sick needed a doctor, He was not just referring to the out-and-out sinners but this self-righteous bunch He found himself surrounded by on this particular occasion. So, like the great physician He was, He felt obliged first of all to "stop the bleeding." It was immediately obvious that this was the second area in which they were "hemorrhaging" the most. When the Pharisees held a luncheon or a dinner, they always invited their closest companions, family, and those with whom they could score the greatest political advantage. They probably never thought in terms of investing in the kingdom of God, only in themselves (it sounds a lot like today).

Jesus's message to them and to us is to "store up treasure in heaven where moth and rust do not corrupt and where thieves do not break through and steal" (Matthew 6:19). In Jesus's kingdom there is no poverty, whether it is physical or spiritual, for there is no respect of persons. All men have all needs met regardless of their party affiliation or academic prowess. In Jesus's kingdom we are to expand our family base to include all mankind as our brothers and sisters. Those who accept Jesus as Savior and Lord are those who make up our family, and the intention is to make sure everyone else gets a chance to be included as well.

Those who participate in His kingdom, which includes the expansion of His generosity to all, can expect eternal dividends. It is only right that we invest in the things that will last. Why invest in the temporary when it is possible to invest in the eternal? It is in the heart of God that no person be excluded due to a misfortune they may have encountered in this life in terms of poverty, loss of a limb, mobility, or sight. They are not to be treated as second-class citizens but offered the best we have, just like our most treasured companions and loved ones.

However, the harsh reality of first-century Israel was a far cry from that. It seems that any person who was blind was sentenced to a life of begging on street corners. Just think how it would be to lose a limb in that environment. There was no Social Security system, just the "lame beggar system." This class of individual was above all men most miserable and destitute. We know nothing of their plight in modern society. Even the poorest among us live like kings in comparison.

The way to gain in the hereafter is to suffer loss in the here and now. The sacrifices we make now will pay handsomely in the future. At one point Jesus suggested that even the smallest sacrifice will be duly noted and repaid. He said, "Whoever gives one of these little ones only a cup of cold water in the name of a disciple, assuredly, I say to you, he shall by no means lose his reward" (Matthew 10:42). He also told the disciples to expect to rule on twelve thrones (one for each of the tribes of Israel) because they had sacrificed everything to follow him (Matthew 19:28). He also spoke about how foolish it was to invest everything in this life without any thought to the future life (Luke 12:20). Nevertheless, we should also be careful that what we do invest is gold and not wood, hay, or stubble because all of our good works will be judged as to their value (1 Corinthians 3:13). No doubt our motives will play a big part in that, as well as our level of surrender to God's will.

All in all we are left here with two commodities that will not fail to provide a return due to their solid-gold rating. Return on stocks, bonds, and treasuries all fade in comparison to the eternal weight of glory that awaits those who participate in Jesus's investment plan. What are these two precious metals? They are composed of the two actions that Jesus commands. 1. Do not invite your friends, brothers, family, or rich neighbors. 2. Invite the poor, maimed, lame, and blind. So plan a big banquet and then make sure to invite all those who can never pay you back. This way you may suffer a net loss now, but in heaven you will profit handsomely because you gave with no thought of return instead of playing politics. This is what it means to be a disciple of Jesus Christ and to invest in eternity.

Discussion Questions:

- Who did the Pharisees invite when they held a luncheon or a dinner and why?
- How was that storing up treasure on Earth rather than in heaven?
- How did the disabled survive in Jesus's day?

- What are some scriptural examples of the above stated principle that, "The way to gain in the hereafter is to suffer loss in the here and now"?
- What are the two commands of Christ that have a solid-gold rating and will not fail to provide a substantial return on your investment in eternity?

Suggested Exercise:

- Discuss who in your community is the neediest. Make a list that you can use to plan your "poverty dinner party." Treat your guests like royalty, with the finest china and waiters with white gloves and even employing a local chef, all depending on what you can afford as a group. Fashionable attire, hairstyling, and suitable transportation to and from should all be considered. Call it Project Cinderella or Project Cinderella Man if you like. The sky is the limit.
- If you can't afford all the expense and don't have connections with retailers to give you a hand, consider inviting at least one needy guest over who you know will never be able to return the favor.
- Donate to a gospel rescue mission (those ministering to the homeless).
- Donate to a poverty relief organization overseas, where the real suffering is.

63

Don't Waste Shrewdness on Earthly Things

Luke 16:1-9

And I say to you, make friends for yourselves by means of the wealth of unrighteousness, so that when it fails, they will receive you into the eternal dwellings (Luke 16:9).

Command of Christ: *"Make friends"* of the unrighteous mammon so that when it fails they will receive you into the eternal tabernacles.

This context is a parable about mismanagement and the recovery of favor. It begins with the firing of an employee, sort of like a business manager, who was supposed to be watching over the finances. It was discovered he was wasteful and not acting in the master's best interest. He was called to give an account of his management and knew there was little time left before he would be out on the streets. So in the remaining time he had left he set about to prepare the way for himself to be welcomed into another position. He did that by giving every person who owed his master a break on their repayment plans. Instead of paying back the eight hundred gallons of olive oil that was due his master, he told them they only had to pay back four hundred gallons, but right away. Instead of a thousand bushels of wheat, he accepted only eight hundred from another debtor. He used his master's wealth to pave the way for his arrival into the home of another master to whom he had rendered aid by not requiring the entire debt to be paid back. He used "unrighteous mammon" to fall into the good graces of the others that he could potentially work for. Or at least it would keep him off the streets.

Jesus, along with the original master in the story, commends the shrewdness of the steward. Although he waited until the last minute, his performance may have provided him entrance into another position. Many wealthy believers today are in the same predicament. They have acquired a vast array of assets but have really mismanaged those by using it only for themselves and the comforts of this life. They have thus far provided little to no investment in heavenly assets. On judgment day, when they give account for their stewardship, they will find themselves with no "eternal habitation." They have wasted their lives thus far, but there is still time. Their lives are coming to a close, so in the little space they have remaining they should do everything possible to invest what is left. Then they will have at least something other than eternal poverty to look forward to.

Jesus said to "make friends for yourselves by means of the wealth of unrighteousness, so that when it fails, they will receive you into the eternal dwellings." It will fail once you leave this world. F. F. Bruce restates the principle thusly in his book *The Hard Sayings of Jesus*: "They will use material wealth to prepare for their earthly future. Why can't the children of light use it to prepare for their eternal future?" The heavenly minded can learn from the parable of the worldly business manager. If you have neglected investing in the kingdom of God it is not too late. Learn from this story and begin to act wisely as he did. Shift gears and reallocate your funds before it's too late. Work while it is yet day, for the night comes when no man can work (John 9:4).

This is not to say you can buy your way into heaven; this passage is referring to those who are already saved. But it is to say that you have not been provided these abundant resources without a reason. God has blessed you so that you can be a blessing to others. If you fail to do this you are mismanaging the funds of your heavenly Master. After all, they do not really belong to you but to Him. The greater your wealth, the greater your responsibility. Consider Paul's restatement of Jesus's principle in 1 Timothy 6:17-19: "Charge them that are rich in this world, that they be not high minded, nor trust in uncertain riches, but in the living God, who gives us richly all things to enjoy; That they do good, that they be rich in good works, ready to distribute, willing to communicate; Laying up in store for themselves a good foundation against the time to come, that they may lay hold on eternal life."

The redistribution of wealth is not the responsibility of the government. It is the responsibility of the individual believer. It is not to be mandated and enforced by law. We are to do so by our own choice and because we as individuals believe it is the best and most godly response. Think it over and ask the Lord what He would have you to do with your good fortune. If every wealthy person had this perspective, would we still be facing world hunger? Don't waste your shrewdness on earthly things alone. Have something to show for yourself on judgment day.

Discussion Questions:

- Why did the shrewd business manager go around to all of his boss's debtors and offer them significant discounts on their remaining debts?
- Who are we a business manager for and when will we give an account of our stewardship?
- How can we act shrewdly in the short time we have left to ensure our heavenly reservation in the Father's house is fully secured and accommodated?

Suggested Exercises:

- Reallocate the time you spend on earthly things toward heavenly things. For example, consider pursuing a career that is serving the interests of God's kingdom in terms of spreading the gospel, discipling, and ministering to the poor and needy. Or at least volunteer more with the time you have outside of your work commitment.
- Reallocate your energy and talents toward the needs of the local church or parachurch ministry. Ask them how they could use your particular area of expertise.
- Reallocate your resources from personal enrichment to furthering the cause of Christ. Since "retirement" is not found in scripture, consider using that time period for full-time ministry. You have so much to offer in terms of wisdom, and this light needs to shine forth rather than be placed under a bushel.
- The wealthy should donate everything they don't really "need" (e.g., extra cars, houses, and land) to gospel-centered charities.

64

Resist, Reject, and Resolve Sin

Luke 17:1-4

He said to his disciples, "It is inevitable that stumbling blocks come, but woe to him through whom they come! It would be better for him if a millstone were hung around his neck and he were thrown into the sea than that he would cause one of these little ones to stumble. Be on your guard! If your brother sins, rebuke him; and if he repents, forgive him. And if he sins against you seven times a day, and returns to you seven times, saying, 'I repent;' forgive him."

Commands of Christ: *Watch* yourself. If your brother sins against you; *rebuke* him. And if he repents, *forgive* him.

Jesus instructs us that sin is a part of life. We get offended regularly and we offend regularly. We live in a sinful world and to err is human. Yet Jesus does not allow us to get comfortable in that experience. He demands that we deal with it appropriately instead of just allowing ourselves to be sinned against or to sin against others without restraint. What is to be our response to these things? How then are we to live?

First of all we are to *watch ourselves*. We are to resist the Devil and sinful behavior as individuals. The number of scripture references to support this is astronomical, yet we tend to warm up to other theologies that allow for plenty of sin in our lives. One passage that says it all is 2 Timothy 2:19: "let everyone that names the name of Christ depart from iniquity." This passage may have stemmed from a statement Jesus made about how

363

bad it would be on judgment day for the unrighteous in Matthew 7:23: "And then will I profess unto them, I never knew you: depart from me, ye that work iniquity." The original Greek word for *iniquity* is where we get the word *antinomian* or *lawless*. It is clear that there is no excuse for the believer to hold on to any sin whatsoever. Our objective is to strive for sinless perfection, not sinful imperfection (Matthew 5:48). If we sin it should be on a rare occasion, not a way of life. It should be followed by horror, shame, regret, and repentance, not justification or rationalization.

We are to mature to the point that we rarely sin. 1 John 2:1 states, "My little children, these things write I unto you, that ye sin not. And if any man sin, we have an advocate with the Father, Jesus Christ the righteous." 1 John 3:9 further states, "Whosoever is born of God does not commit sin; for his seed remains in him: and he cannot sin, because he is born of God."

We are not without Christ; therefore, we should not think that we are sentenced to a life of bondage. If we walk in the Spirit, we will not fulfill the lusts of the flesh (Galatians 5:16). Shall we continue in sin that grace might abound? "God forbid!" (Romans 6:15) It is not about being a perfectionist, it is about perfecting your skills to be a winner in the kingdom of God. We have a race to win. We are all in a competition to do the most we can for Jesus Christ during our lifetime. Sin will interfere with that. It will come between us and God and prevent Him from accomplishing what He wants through us. He is looking for vessels of honor that He can fill (2 Timothy 2:21). He is asking us to "lay aside every weight, and the sin which doth so easily beset us, and let us run with patience the race that is set before us" (Hebrews 12:1). The contest basically boils down to this: who can accomplish the most for Christ during his or her lifetime by being the best at reigning in passions and submitting to Him? So watch yourself, stay in shape, and don't let sin hinder you from advancing the kingdom.

Not only will your sin interfere with success in the ministry, it will call down the wrath of God upon your life and beyond this life. He provides the example of offending one of these "little ones." He said it would have been better if you would have tied a millstone around your neck and plunged yourself into the sea than to offend one of them. We know from previous scripture that "little ones" normally refers to children. But it only highlights the ramifications of taking advantage of anyone in a vulnerable state. Whether they be a foreigner, homeless person, sick person, dying person, or disabled, there are harsh consequences for those who prey on the innocent and vulnerable. Resist such sins; watch yourself and watch others. That is the only response to sin that Jesus sanctions.

How about when a brother sins against you? Are you to just accept it and go on? Are you to ignore it and sweep it under the rug? Should you respond to him as if he were a pagan and turn the other cheek? Not at all! Jesus demands that you *rebuke* such a person. Sin is not to be accepted in the Church. The more you accept it the less of a witness the Church will be. We are to aggressively stamp out all sin in the Church. Rebuke the offender. Do as Jesus commanded in Matthew 18:15-17: Go and tell him his fault between you and him alone. If he receives you, you have won over your brother. If not, take along one or two others until the matter is resolved. If it can't be resolved, tell it to the Church. If the person disrespects the leadership of the Church, he should be eliminated from the congregation (1 Corinthians 5:5). The Church in the Western world is in dire straits with this issue right now. People just come and go with no rebuke. Unmarried couples are living together one Sunday and being baptized the next. Recent Gallup Polls show that the behaviors of nonchurchgoers are not much different than churchgoers. Divorce rates are the same, unwed pregnancies, premarital sex, etc. all seem to show little difference. This is because we have bought into a false doctrine about accepting sin among one another. We are not opposed to sin; we are indifferent to sin. Instead we should "rebuke them before all" (1 Timothy 5:20) that the congregation would learn. However, we are too fearful to lose financial support and numbers in attendance. Are we serving God or mammon? We must start cracking down on sin in our churches; the sooner the better.

But does "cracking down" mean cruel and vicious attacks? No. Here is the guideline in Galatians 6:1: "Brethren, if a man is overtaken in any trespass, you who are spiritual restore such a one in a spirit of gentleness, considering yourself lest you also be tempted." We need to take care of business, but not by brute force or in an uncivilized manner. There should be a spirit of calm and the atmosphere of common occurrence in such proceedings. It shouldn't be like a witch hunt, where an angry mob drags the individual to a rope hanging over a tree limb. No, we are all in danger of being on the hot seat at one time or another. We should treat the offender as we would want to be treated in the same circumstance. This practice is for the spiritually mature, not for the novice who will tend to make matters worse. A bull does not belong in a China cabinet. Only the spiritually mature will understand that they are to proceed in a spirit of meekness, considering the fact that they could also fall to temptation. However, having said all this, it is imperative that ungodly behavior be addressed on a regular basis.

In Jesus's system of conflict resolution in Matthew 18:15-17, the purpose is to bring the individual to repentance. Once this is achieved, *forgiveness* is in order. That is the final stage and command of Jesus in this passage we are considering: Luke 17:1-6. We are not eager overall to get rid of anyone but to restore him or her to fellowship. All that takes is that the individual will own up to his or her fault and repent of it. The Church has to operate like a self-cleaning oven. A mechanism must be in place to keep the church maintained: Spotless and shiny on the inside as it was meant to be. Only then can the church function properly as the light of the world. A city that is set on a hill cannot be hidden. Matthew 5:16 says, "Let your light so shine before men, that they may see your good works, and glorify your Father which is in heaven."

After Jesus explains the process of how we are to deal with sin, it is interesting what we find to be the response of the disciples. They immediately ask Jesus to increase their faith, and that really is the heart of the matter here. When it comes to pursuing a godly life where no sin is too small to ignore, it all comes down to what you *believe* is possible. If you don't *believe* you can stop sinning in any particular area, you certainly can't. If you don't *believe* that he who hungers and thirsts after righteousness shall be filled, then you *believe* the opposite. You *believe* that he who hungers and thirsts after righteousness shall remain unfulfilled. If you don't *believe* that the pure in heart will see God, then you will never pursue that grand adventure.

I, for one, believe the Beatitudes are for this lifetime and that the principles there drawn out are for all to strive for and achieve by God's grace. I'm not comfortable with speculating that Matthew fabricated these standards to appease legalistic Jews or with relegating those teachings to another time in the future kingdom of God. I would rather feel uncomfortable with the embrace of Jesus's imperatives and wrestle with their implications than to reason them away while sitting in my easy chair. Discipleship is painstakingly difficult. It requires more faith to achieve the impossible. Pray to Him today for greater faith and He will respond and assure you that even the smallest effort will produce unimaginable results.

Do not settle for a sinful lifestyle any longer. I say with Jesus: resist; reject, and resolve sin.

Discussion Questions:

- Why is it inevitable that we will regularly offend and be offended?
- If sin is part of our daily experience, should we just accept it?
- What scriptures allow for heaping helpings of self-indulgence? Doesn't Jesus, as well as every other apostle teach us to overcome sin? List as many passages as you can that support this view.
- Winners hone their skills to a state of near perfection. How does this apply to the way we should approach sin in our lives?
- How can we "crack down" on sin in the church without turning it into a witch hunt?
- What is the ultimate aim: banishment or reconciliation?
- How will addressing sin properly and routinely lead to the type of Church that can make a difference in the world and the one that Jesus is coming back for: "a glorious church, not having spot, or wrinkle, or any such thing; but that it should be holy and without blemish" (Ephesians 5:27)?

Suggested Exercises:

- Make a list of everything in your life right now that you are allowing to go on even though you know it is against the teachings of Jesus. List everything that falls under the category of "the lust of the flesh, the lust of the eyes and the pride of life" (1 John 2:16). Confess and renounce all ungodliness to a trusted disciple. If any of these sins are powerfully gripping your life in a form of addiction or bondage, take further action, such as acquiring an accountability partner/sponsor.
- When you have small group meetings, break off into even smaller groups of males and females, respectively. Let these be times of confession where all sin is addressed as well as anything you may be suspecting is sinful. Also, you can further break off into one-on-one confessions that you may be healed (James 5:16).

- Do a Gallup poll study on the behavior of churchgoers versus nonchurchgoers and share the results with the group. Discuss how the regular implementation of Matthew 18:15-17 could reverse those results. Pray together for the courage to begin addressing sin privately and corporately.
- Is there a brother or sister who has offended you because he or she sinned? 1. Go to him or her privately first and share the fault. Explain that you are using Matthew 18:15-17 and Luke 17:1-4. If the person apologizes, then restore him or her to full fellowship. 2. If not, take one or two other mature believers with you and approach the individual again. 3. If he or she does not "hear" the two or three of you, tell it to the Church officials. Try to take the offender from violation to full restoration if at all possible. If not, the Church may be forced to part company with this individual (with a hope he or she will still repent at a later date having learned his or her lesson).

SECTION FIVE:
Spiritual Adolescent

65

Don't Brag about the Minimum

Luke 17:7-10

He does not thank the slave because he did the things which were commanded, does he? So you too, when you do all the things which are commanded you, say, "We are unworthy slaves; we have done only that which we ought to have done" (Luke 17:9-10).

Command of Christ: *Say* that we are unprofitable servants who have done what we ought to do.

Perhaps if we were to actually go to all of the trouble to institute Jesus's orders about church discipline as previously mentioned, we might think ourselves very special indeed. After all, how many churches today actually follow through with the watching, rebuking, and forgiving template when it comes to sin? I would venture to say that it is a very rare jewel indeed in the Master's crown. But should this be the case? Absolutely not! Rather, it should be the norm, and the Church should be the light of the world rather than the shadowy darkness, blending in that it now does. So in this compromising atmosphere, one can easily imagine how simple it would be to fall into the temptation to think of oneself more highly than one ought (Romans 12:3). Yet in actuality we are, as Jesus's disciples, simply doing what we have been told. We are not yet even considering going above and beyond the call of duty. We find it amazingly difficult to even accomplish the two hundred-plus imperatives He has already left us with.

The fascination of this passage comes with the background introduction and illustration that provides us a glimpse into the daily routine of first-century Middle Eastern custom. As basically a third-world setting, it would have been common for the average household to be staffed with an assortment of servants (actually "slaves" in the Greek). In my travels and time living abroad I have experienced the lifestyle of the underdeveloped regions of the East. I saw firsthand when I lived in West Africa and the Philippines how the majority of households possess live-in servants. It is as true today as it was in Jesus's day that these individuals wait on you hand and foot. Far from an upgrade, it was, for my Filipino wife, sort of a letdown to come to this country where she no longer enjoyed the assistance of live-in household helpers.

Nevertheless, in Jesus's day as in ours in the East it is expected that the servant will prepare the meals, keep the house, and perform whatever other helpful activities are necessary. This was their job; it was part of their basic duties. Even though they do so much, neither you nor they expect anything less. Many of these precious individuals will, over time, begin to consider their masters as part of the family and vice versa. This is what Paul was referring to when he called himself a "doulos" or "slave" of Christ. The bonded slave of ancient Israel was one who once offered his freedom but chose to stay duty bound instead. His seven-year obligation was met, but because the master was so kind to him and he or she enjoyed the work, the slave chose to permanently attach himself or herself to that home. Perhaps this is what Jesus meant by "going beyond the bare minimum." But that is not a certainty.

The questions for us are these: Where do we stand in our service to Christ? Are we doing the bare minimum or are we going above and beyond the call of duty? Few people today even know Jesus's commands or that He gave us a long list of orders to carry out. Fewer still will practice them. Nevertheless, even if you are in that rare category of those who practice Jesus's commands, you are to *say* to yourself, "We are unprofitable servants who have done what we ought to do." If those of us who are engaged in the process are unprofitable, what does that make those who are not engaged? A great many individuals who read this material should say as well, "We have a lot of catching up to do in order to just break even!" As far as the faithful few are concerned, we must always be on guard to stay away from pride and self-righteousness. This will only lead to our eventually becoming like the most deadly of all of Jesus opponents: a Pharisee. We can do nothing on our own. Anything we accomplish is due to our connection with Christ (John 15:1-5). Never take the credit for anything. To God alone goes all the glory. Because of Jesus, our yoke is easy and our burden is light.

How will you keep your pride in check once you follow through on Christ's long list of demands? How will you maximize your efforts for the cause of Christ and thereby be seen not as unworthy but profitable?

Discussion Questions:

- We might consider our church pretty special if we abide by the Matthew 18 principle of resolving conflict and keeping the church pure. But how does it make you feel when you realize that is just one of Jesus's commands and there are 253 to go just to get to the bare minimum?
- How does the life of a first-century Middle Eastern house servant explain our relationship with Christ on this matter of what is expected of us as His disciples?
- What could be one way of going beyond the bare minimum with Christ?
- Which category do you find yourself in?
  o Ignorant of the requirements
  o Proud of myself by keeping some of the requirements
  o Overwhelmed by the sheer number of the basic requirements
  o Driven by love to go above and beyond the call of duty by extending my initial seven-year servitude to a lifetime of self-imposed slavery

Suggested Exercises:

- When you finish this course and have completed all 254 commands, say together as a group, "We are unprofitable servants who have done only what was required. Therefore we devote the rest of our lives to the service of Christ."
- Compose a pledge to Jesus Christ of Nazareth that is similar to the pledge to the American flag that can be used at discipleship graduation ceremonies. Include the concept of profitable versus unprofitable service.

- Confess to one another any pride that has surfaced since you began this journey of Christ-centered discipleship. It should be expected since it will be a rare item to even be involved at such a high level of performance. Pray together to maintain an attitude of humility throughout the disciple-making process.

66

Do As I Tell You, Regardless

John 11:38-43, 2:5

*Jesus said, "Remove the stone." Martha, the sister of the deceased,
said to him, "Lord, by this time there will be a stench, for he has
been dead four days." Jesus said to her, "Did I not say to you that if
you believe, you will see the glory of God?"* (John 11: 39-40)

Commands of Christ: *Remove* the stone. *Loose* him and *let* him go.

Here we are met with the story of the resurrection of Lazarus. It is known
that prior to Jesus's arrival, He received word of Lazarus's dire condition.
Instead of making haste to save him from dying, it seems Jesus purposely
delayed so that an even greater miracle could be experienced by all. The
whole drive behind the miraculous event was to turn doubters into believers
(John 11:42). They had to come to the point that they believed that Jesus
was indeed sent by God. But if you simply look at this situation from the
perspective of the participants, you can understand why a great deal of
questioning and anguish prevailed. Martha spoke for all when she said,
"If you had been here, my brother would not have died" (John 11:21).
Martha wanted to confront Jesus, but her sister Mary stayed home until
she was summoned. Perhaps she was too deeply hurt to face him, but he
called for her and she could not refuse him. When she arrived she said the
same thing: "If you had been here my brother would not have died." It's
almost as if everyone was saying, "Where were you?" All with one accord
knew one thing for sure: it was too late now because Lazarus was dead.

That is why, when they heard Jesus's orders to *remove* the stone, they were startled. It was actually the stone of their heart they first had to remove. For there, standing before them, was the resurrection and the life (John 11:25)! Martha was ready to acknowledge that at some later point in time life could enter, but behold, life was standing right in front of her! With Him, it is never too late. There are no circumstances that are able to render him powerless. He is the life. We all live and breathe because of Him. It is Jesus who decides if and when that breath is discontinued. Through him all things were made; without him nothing was made that has been made. In him was life, and that life was the light of men (John 1:3-4).

What His disciples had yet to learn was that it is not over until He says it is. Knowing just exactly who He is, we are compelled to obey even when all seems lost. Even when the situation seems hopeless and we feel helpless, we must remember that He is the hope and He is the help. We have to learn what His mother concluded early on. When she found herself in a jam about the wine running low, what did she tell them? Just "do whatever he tells you" (John 2:5). It may sound crazy, it may seem ridiculous, but listen: just do it! Believe me; He knows exactly what He's doing.

That's why the disciples followed through with his orders, albeit reluctantly. You see, He had already developed quite a reputation among them. They knew never to think twice about one of His orders. You don't have to understand it now, but you do have to trust Him always. Once you let Him in the door, He can gain access to your problem. But first there is the knock, and we must choose at that crucial juncture whether to answer it. Against their better judgment they did remove the stone, and because of that small act of obedience there came the next command that could also not be refused: "Lazarus, come forth!" It was similar to the miracle of the water becoming wine. The first command, which seemed ridiculous, was to fill the huge pots with water. Then there was the directive to draw it out for the governor of the feast. That is the precise moment when the water transformed into wine. When Jesus said, "Come out," that was the precise moment Lazarus came back to life. Nothing is impossible with God.

The final command was to "loose him and let him go." Again just as in the feeding of the masses, Jesus commanded them to enter into the miracle in a tangible way (pick up the fragments that remain). It was not just "doubting Thomas" who needed to touch and handle, but all of those who saw with their eyes but could not believe with their hearts needed to literally "grasp" the significance of what had just occurred. Jesus says to all of them as well as all of us today the same thing He once said to Thomas: "be not faithless but believing" (John 20:27). Their faith was dead and needed the work of loosing him and letting him go to be reignited (James 2:17). Before that exchange it seemed that although the dead had come to life, the living were still dead.

Are we not today so much like those in the story who gave up all hope and never expected anything beyond the natural course of events? Do we not instead rely solely on doctors and insurance policies and hospitals until all hope is lost? Do we not secretly value science the most and when science fails, our faith fails with it? We too in modern society need a healthy dose of "belief." We too need to interact with the fresh, new resurrection power of a living and reigning Lord. We who are not dead without are yet dead within. Dear Lord, breathe back into our impoverished souls your breath of life. Let us shout again with you in full assurance of faith: "All things are possible to them that believe" (Mark 9:23)!

Is there an impossible situation in your life right now that has caused you to totally give up? As long as you have the Lord, you don't have to give up. Keep seeking Him for His solution. When He gives you the order, make sure you follow through with it to the letter. What has He asked you to do that you are hesitating on? Have you yet to learn this one important fact about Jesus? That single undeniable piece of information is this: do as He tells you, regardless!

Discussion Questions:

- Why did Jesus postpone his arrival even though he knew Lazarus was dying?
- In what way did the people need their hearts of stone removed even more than the stone that was covering the tomb?
- What had his mother, Mary, learned about Jesus that the disciples had yet to learn?
- In what way was the raising of Lazarus from the dead similar to the turning of the water into wine?
- How did the next command to "loose him and let him go" resurrect their faith as well? How did it help them "grasp" the significance of what had just occurred?
- How could we in modern society use a healthy dose of belief?

Suggested Exercises:

- Discuss among the group how the Lord speaks to each of you on a personal basis and how you know for sure when He is telling you to take action. Discuss the difference between a general command to all disciples and a personal word to an individual disciple. Share examples of how you followed through with something personal the Lord told you that seemed questionable but turned out for the better.

- Share with your discipleship group or another trusted disciple things that you believe the Lord might be calling you to do. Discuss whether this could be scriptural or may just be a figment of your imagination. Pray together for continued guidance and if it is confirmed, proceed with the personal directive from the Lord.

- Developing a method by which you are relatively certain when God is calling you is the key to this command. It was a lot easier when Jesus was here in person. Today we walk by faith alone. Therefore it is essential that you develop a greater sensitivity to the voice of the Lord if you have not already done so. One way I train people to do this is through what I call a listening log. You keep a log of what you believe God is saying to you through the three channels of prayer, scripture, and church. It is a trial-and-error exercise that you do every day until it becomes second-nature to you. Every month turn your log in to a trusted advisor who can help you refine your listening skills. I would recommend this personal training process to those who are yet to fully develop in this area.

67

Don't Expect a Pleasant Return

Luke 17:20-37

For just like lightning, when it flashes out of one part of the sky, shines to the other part of the sky, so will the Son of Man be in His day . . . until the day that Noah entered the ark, and the flood came and destroyed them all . . . but on the day that Lot went out from Sodom it rained fire and brimstone from heaven and destroyed them all. It will be just the same on the day that the Son of Man is revealed" (Luke 17: 24; 27; 29-30).

Commands of Christ: *Don't ever go* after (them). *Remember* Lot's wife.

This teaching to the disciples begins with a question from the Pharisees, of all things. They asked Him when the kingdom of God would arrive. This is to be expected since Jesus was continually teaching about the kingdom and saying that it was coming soon. But He said, "The kingdom of God does not come visibly, nor will people say, 'Here it is,' or 'There it is,' because the kingdom of God is within you." Jesus knew something the Pharisees and the disciples didn't know. The kingdom of God starts from the inside. Indeed there will be a final battle when Jesus takes over the world by sheer force. But first it is offered peacefully. It basically comes down to surrender or submission to the King. You can do that willingly now or unwillingly later. But eventually it will be accomplished one way or another. When you willingly become a servant of God you are born again. You can now begin a relationship with God based on Jesus's sacrifice of His life for you. This is what Jesus meant when he said, "The kingdom of God is at hand:

repent and believe the good news" (Mark 1:15). God is already King; it's just that not everyone has recognized it yet. When you finally recognize this, it opens up the possibility of a relationship with Him.

Perhaps it is Jesus's thoughts on this topic that open Him up to a further discussion of these matters with His disciples. That is where we find the next directive. The long-term plan of the kingdom of God involves an initial deposit, a departure, and then a collection of the returns on that initial investment. Jesus plants that seed of His life for the initial deposit, then He leaves, and finally He returns to collect (Matthew 13:36-43). While He is gone the disciples will long for those days when He was there beside them in perceptible form. They will be tempted to run here or there, wherever it is said that He has returned. But He warns them not to do so. He tells them in Luke 17:22-24: "The time is coming when you will long to see one of the days of the Son of Man, but you will not see it. Men will tell you, 'There he is!' or 'Here he is!' Do not go running off after them; for the Son of Man in his day will be like the lightning, which flashes and lights up the sky from one end to the other."

When He does return it will not be as the meek and mild lamb we have grown accustomed to. It will be an apocalypse of epic proportions. He will explode onto the horizon and will obliterate all resistance once and for all at the end of the world. It will be judgment day: the final and all-decisive battle of world history, followed by an everlasting peace as Jesus finally sets up His literal throne. It is at that point that the kingdom of God will begin to take a visible form, for it will stretch out from one end of the earth to the other. The next time He shows up on Earth, this is the manner in which he will appear. We are to look for Him coming in the clouds with power and great glory (Matthew 24:30). We are not looking for a prophet or an earthly leader who claims messiah-ship. That has already occurred. That part of the plan of God has already been set into motion. There is no need to go backward or be fooled by an imposter. We are no longer looking for an earthly messiah but the heavenly Messiah arrayed in glory, majesty, and unapproachable light (1 Timothy 6:16).

He compares His return to two former catastrophic events that have befallen mankind. One is the fire and brimstone that wiped out Sodom and Gomorrah, and the second is the flooding of the earth during the days of Noah. These are not pleasant thoughts and they clearly communicate to us the fearsome and dreadful nature of Christ's return. We are only to pray that we are counted worthy to escape those things that are to come over the earth (Luke 21:36). He said his return will be like a bolt of lightning! "The Son of Man in his day will be like the lightning, which flashes and lights up the sky from one end to the other" (Luke 17:24).

So, knowing this, we should never be found guilty of following anyone else who claims to be Christ. If they are standing before us as a man, they no longer fit the description. When He comes back to Earth, He will come in all His glory. This glimpse into the future is what He has provided us in order to keep us faithful to him. Equipped and armed with this knowledge, we will never be tempted to follow a fake Christ. So don't go after one; you know better.

Discussion Questions:

- How is it that a kingdom that starts from the inside out means you can either accept Him willingly now or unwillingly later?
- Which category does Jesus's second coming fall into? Willing or unwilling? Internal or external? Mortal or immortal?
- Which phase of the kingdom of God are we in now? The initial investment, the departure, or the return on the investment? What parable illustrates these three steps?
- How does His return in a flash to wipe out all resistance in a cataclysmic power surge protect us from ever being fooled by a false earthly messiah who, in spite of being a mere mortal, claims to be Jesus?
- What is the primary agenda for the return of Christ—redeeming the world or conquering it? How does remembering Lot's wife keep you ready?

Suggested Exercises:

- Sign and date below if you agree with the following statement: "I cannot be led astray by a false Christ because I don't expect a pleasant return. He is returning to triumph over all of mankind as the King of kings and Lord of lords. This final battle will destroy every adversary the way the floods of Noah and the fire and brimstone of Sodom did."

Name: _____ Date: _____

68

Pray Persistently

Luke 18:1-8

'Yet because this widow bothers me, I will do her justice, otherwise by continually coming she will wear me out.' "Hear what the unrighteous judge said; now, will not God bring about justice for His elect who cry to Him day and night, and will He delay long over them? I tell you that He will bring about justice for them quickly. However, when the Son of Man comes, will He find faith on the earth?" (Luke 18:5-8)

Command of Christ: *Listen* to what the unjust judge says.

The command is to "*Listen* to what the unjust judge says" (Luke 18:6). To do that you have to know the parable (which provides the context for it) in Luke 18:2-5: "There was in a certain city a judge who did not fear God nor regard man. Now there was a widow in that city; and she came to him, saying, 'Get justice for me from my adversary.' And he would not for a while; but afterward he said within himself, 'Though I do not fear God nor regard man, yet because this widow troubles me I will avenge her, lest by her continual coming she weary me.'"

The purpose for this parable was to teach them "that they should always pray and not give up" (Luke 18:1). It is an argument from reason and logic. He provides evidence to make his case that even the worst among mankind will respond to persistence. If that is so, then it stands to reason that even more readily will the godly respond. At the top of the scale for godliness is God Himself. He as the most holy of all should be the easiest to get a positive response from. It all boils down to what you believe about Him.

As it was from the beginning it is still so today. Satan is at his best when he convinces us that God is the bad guy. What worked with Adam and Eve continues to work on all mankind. This is why one of Jesus's constant refrains was about the "goodness of God." That was central to His teaching and has to be central to our way of life. We have to remind ourselves in all of our trials and tribulations that when God seems so far away, indeed He is not. We have to constantly reaffirm the principle of "casting all your care upon Him, for He cares for you" (1 Peter 5:7).

Often we ministers will call out to the church from the pulpit, "God is good." And the expected response from the crowd is, "All the time." Then we will repeat, "All the time," and the crowd will affirm, "God is good." This type of mind exercise is necessary to battle the constant barrage of negativity from the enemy. This is one way to participate in "casting down arguments and every high thing that exalts itself against the knowledge of God, bringing every thought into captivity to the obedience of Christ" (2 Corinthians 10:5). We are to exercise ourselves "rather unto godliness" (1 Timothy 4:7). If the enemy can slip through with only one thought of negativity toward God, he will be successful in driving a wedge between us.

Jesus closes his teaching with a gripping statement: "When the Son of Man comes, will He really find faith on the earth?" (Luke 18:8) In other words, by the time Jesus returns to the earth to judge the world, what will He find? Will the walk of faith that He lived on Earth continue to all generations to come, or will it go the way of the dinosaur? Will we continue to trust God with our problems or look solely to technology? Will we allow our circumstances to defeat us or will we fight through to the victory with our faith? When we are persecuted for righteousness's sake, will we give up or will we fight the good fight of faith? Will He find mountain-moving faith that alters world geography or that which can barely be seen in a microscope? Maybe He will find no faith at all! That is the question He poses, isn't it? Will he find faith on Earth?

It was said that the Thomas Jefferson's Bible literally had holes in it; that he had gone through the New Testament and cut out every reference to the supernatural.[65] In the age of Enlightenment it was no longer acceptable to believe in miracles. They were relegated to the level of hopeful imagination, and an effort to embellish the actual truth of history that lie underneath these incredible fabrications. Many of the Founding Fathers of the United States had succumbed to deism, the belief that God started the world going and left it to play out on its own with no interference whatsoever. It was now up to individuals to make of it what they would.

Rudolf Bultmann, a German Lutheran theologian and New Testament scholar who was one of the major figures of twentieth-century biblical studies and a prominent voice in liberal Christianity, followed in this vein of thought by his attempt to "demythologize" the gospels. That basically means that everything you see that can be regarded as supernatural is no longer valid. I happen to believe the supernatural elements in the gospel story are legitimate and provide hope when one of us enters similar circumstances. For instance, you can't tell my daughter that divine intervention is just fanciful tales. When she was diagnosed with diabetes I prayed by faith that it would end. The night before her next appointment (to see what type of diabetic she was), I sat beside her in her bed and prayed that nothing would be found. That is exactly what happened. There are many more experiences like this one that I could share, but the point is well made. The days of faith are only over when you cease to believe.

The ball is in our court. Will we let faith die or will we strive to keep it alive? We must prevail; we must not allow war, famine, pestilence, natural disasters, or worldly philosophy to cause our salt to lose its flavor. Then we will be good for nothing except to be thrown out and trampled under the feet of men. Jesus said all things are possible to those who believe. Let's check our faith level. Let's keep it full and keep it alive and use it to prevail over anything the Devil throws our way. *Listen* to what the unjust judge says, and let that increase your faith.

Discussion Questions:

- What did the helpless widow employ to win over the powerful and influential judge?

---

[65] Findling, John and Frank Thackeray, *What Happened?: An Encyclopedia of Events that Changed America Forever: Volume 1* (Santa Barbara, California: ABC-CLIO, LLC, 2011), 26.

- What do you believe about God? Is He the hardest or easiest to persuade? Why?
- Satan is at his best when he convinces us of what? What's the best biblical evidence of this tactic and why does it keep working on us?
- When Jesus returns will He find faith on the earth? What historical evidence shows that the enemy is busy trying to strip us of every vestige of it, even to the point of removing it from the pages of our holy scriptures?

Suggested Exercise:

- Discuss the goodness of God as opposed to the wickedness of the unjust judge in Jesus's parable. How you see God determines everything. Discuss among the group how you think of God. Do you see Him more as a judge or a loving father figure? Pray together for greater insight into the innate goodness of God.
- Get together with a trusted disciple or a small group of disciples and ask the following question: "What current circumstance have you learned to live with that maybe you shouldn't?" Determine to continue addressing this issue in prayer as a group and individuals until some resolution is found.
- Read Hebrews 11 as an attempt to bolster your faith. Replace the names of those men of faith with your own. Use that information and apply those principles to your own current circumstances and expect the miraculous. Open up to the possibility of a supernatural solution.

69

Avoid Wrong Divorce

Matthew 19:3-9; Mark 10:1-12

He said to them, "Because of your hardness of heart Moses permitted you to divorce your wives; but from the beginning it has not been this way. And I say to you, whoever divorces his wife, except for fornication, and marries another woman commits adultery" (Matthew 19:8-9).

Command of Christ: Therefore, what God has joined together, man may not *separate*. (Therefore, let no man *separate* what God has joined together.)

The context of this debate is the Pharisees again trying to cause trouble with Jesus. They must have learned of Jesus's harsh stance against divorce and came to test him with scripture. Perhaps they intended to prove He was not abiding by the text but had separate views. The question posed to Jesus was whether or not a man could divorce his wife for any reason. Jesus's answer was only for one reason: fornication. In Jesus's day it had become the law to divorce for any reason the man chose. It had degraded to this point perhaps because of the uncertainty of the term "uncleanness." Moses had allowed the man to divorce his wife if he found some "uncleanness" there (Deuteronomy 24:1). It is translated as "nakedness" or "indecency." So from that, one might assume it is referring to adultery on one extreme or anything the husband deems inappropriate on the other extreme. In a male-dominated society it ended up meaning the latter: anything that displeased the husband. Jesus seemed to accept the fact that Moses may have left that matter open to abuse but that he was doing so in order to work within the hardened hearts of his time. In order to overcome this scriptural reference to Moses He had to appeal to a higher precedent. He went back to the creation account and illustrated very clearly how God designed the whole system in the first place.

He designed it for union and not for division. Division is a distortion of the original blueprint and an elimination of the purpose of that design. Again Jesus is using reason to argue against the Pharisees' desire to take advantage of scriptural loopholes. Union will strengthen society whereas division will tear it apart. It will eventually result in society coming to an end. By appealing to the "Supreme Court in heaven," Jesus pulls the prevailing assumptions more toward the direction of adultery for eliminating the marriage. Otherwise the bill of divorce is not accepted by God. If it is not accepted, the woman who was just divorced is still married to that man in God's eyes. The man who put her out is also in fact still married to her. That is why Jesus concluded that if they proceed with the wrong divorce, they will now have cause for it. For once the person remarries, this has also not been approved by God and therefore adds up to adultery. At that point there is legitimate cause for divorce. Once the union is violated, they are no longer one but two again. The union has reoccurred elsewhere.

In a society where women had no rights, Jesus had to speak out to those in power not to abuse it. Jesus did not speak in favor of a woman usurping the authority of the man to decide when divorce was warranted. He only said that the man should not misuse his authority. If a woman was divorced she was destitute as well. She could not go out on her own to make a living as women do today. Women in that day relied totally on their husbands to provide for them and they stayed home to take care of the house and children. A writ of divorce would only make it possible to pursue another means of support within the domain of another husband. A woman in Jesus's society did not have the ability to divorce her husband. Even so, in other countries women were beginning to acquire this ability on a limited basis. Therefore, you have the addition by Mark (written to a Roman audience) about the women not being allowed to divorce the husband either. The one who initiates it without proper cause is therefore the guilty party.

Today the pendulum has swung in the opposite direction. Women have just as much legal authority as men. Some might say they have the advantage. We are addressing an entirely different set of circumstances when we consider divorce in a modern-day setting. To approach this subject correctly one must first determine the parameters of Jesus's perspective in His day and then apply that to the current situation. In the context of a period of time where society was highly structured by a chain of command, Jesus would address the one with the most power not to abuse it, as well as the one under authority not to undermine it. Today he would most likely first demand that the traditional roles of males and females as designed by the Creator be reinstituted.

He does not advocate role reversal but for each sex to be held accountable for the role they were assigned by God. When a woman divorces a man against his will, it is more than dissolving a marriage. It is usurping the authority of both man and God. It undercuts the husband to the core of his being by stripping him of his God-ordained right as the final authority in the household. Once you overstep him you not only take away the marriage, you violate the social sanctity that was first established in the mind of God and forged into the spirit of the male species. Leadership for the husband is innate. It is just as essential an ingredient in the nature of a man as barking is for a dog or roaring is for a lion. Society's attempt to belittle these natural urges is equivalent to censuring birds for flying or fish for swimming. This is why we can see from observing Jesus's perspective on divorce in Matthew that the husband is not to be removed from headship for abusing his authority but admonished to behave honorably in his leadership role or face the judgment of God.

Overall we must conclude from this teaching that *fornication* should be the only grounds for divorce. The actual term in this passage is not adultery but *porneia* (Greek), which is translated as "fornication." But how does fornication apply to married couples? Isn't fornication pre-marital sex? It does include that idea but not exclusively. Fornication is actually any form of unlawful sexual intercourse. While adultery is covered in the term "fornication," fornication is not covered in the term "adultery." Adultery only covers what is done after the marriage and not what a partner may discover happened before the marriage. For example, if the man discovered after the wedding that his wife was not a virgin, this would also be acceptable grounds for divorce.

So the command from Jesus is this: *Don't separate* what God has joined together. Once adultery has been committed the marriage union has already been separated into a division and the unmarried division has merged into a union. The new union cancels out the old. That act was the final step in disobeying the Lord by not honoring God's sacred merger. The rest is just a formality. Consequently, if the marriage union has not been violated the marriage is still valid. Jesus's argument against divorce is based on His understanding of the two becoming one flesh.

Discussion Questions:

- With the determining factor being "uncleanness" according to the Law of Moses, how did this fact open the door to the husband abusing his authority?
- What portion of scripture did Jesus appeal to that seemed to trump the Pharisees' affinity for the teaching of Moses?
- How is wrong divorce a false divide and adultery a true divide as the result of a true union with another individual?
- What is the person who initiates divorce without a proper cause and remarries guilty of? Why is that the case?
- Should the final decision for divorce remain in the hands of the husband? Why?
- Why did Jesus choose the term *fornication* rather than *adultery* as the only acceptable reason for divorce?
- What is it that ends the marriage to the point that the divorce proceedings are just a formality for what has already been irreparably damaged?

Suggested Exercises:

- Discuss how the current legal system allows for divorce for just about any reason just as it did for men in Jesus's day and how you plan to live by a higher standard. Research and provide a list of all of the reasons that allow for divorce in our current system. Discuss how that no matter how awful those reasons are, only fornication is considered a legitimate reason for divorce. Decide the difference between Christ's view and the view of the world's view and agree to abide by Jesus's perspective.
- If you have been a victim of divorce, you are not guilty. If you have divorced a person for anything less than adultery, you are guilty. If you remarried you must ask for forgiveness for

committing adultery. If your former spouse remarried, you must seek forgiveness for causing him to commit adultery. You must also ask God to forgive you for separating what God had brought together as one.

- Discuss the fact that marriage is a covenant based on fidelity from both parties. Once that covenant is broken the offended party is no longer obligated. Remarriage to the same person following the divorce of that person is not a biblical concept (Deut. 24:4), nor is staying married to an adulterer to win him or her back over. Whoever committed adultery in the Old Testament was to receive the death penalty; therefore, remarriage to that person or staying married to that person would be out of the question. Agree to live within the biblical perimeters.

- Commit as a group to abide by Jesus's policy of divorce from this time forward, especially to avoid wrong divorce. There is absolutely no reason why the rate of divorce in the Church should be equal to that of the world. Make sure to include the phrase and philosophy of "for better or for worse; in sickness and in health; for richer or poorer" in your wedding vows and premarital counsel. Expect conflict in your marriage and don't expect everything to go your way.

70

Allow Children

Matthew 19:13-15; Mark 10:13-16; Luke 18:15-17

And they were bringing children to him so that he might touch
them; but the disciples rebuked them. But when Jesus saw this, He
was indignant and said to them, "Permit the children to come to
me; do not hinder them; for the kingdom of God belongs to such
as these. Truly I say to you, whoever does not receive the kingdom
of God like a child will not enter it at all." And he took them
in his arms and began blessing them, laying his hands on them
(Mark 10:13-16).

Commands of Christ: *Release* the children, and *do not forbid* them to come
to me.

Jesus had a soft spot for children, but that was not an idiosyncrasy, it
was wisdom. Children have a special place in the kingdom of God. It
was said by Jesus that unless you are converted and become like a little
child, you shall in no respect enter the kingdom of heaven (Matthew
18:3). In other words, they naturally possess the correct attitude and
disposition for a successful relationship with God. They are intrinsically
trusting, dependent, humble, and nonjudgmental. God placed them here
to show us the way! We need them to remind us how we ought to be in
our connection with God. They also still have a great deal of innocence,
and this makes them among the most vulnerable in society. Woe to those
who would take advantage of them (Mark 9:42). For Jesus, it seems the
ultimate crime is to abuse the powerless and the hurting. He came for

them. His ministry was focused on them. See Luke 4:18: "The Spirit of the Lord is upon me, because he hath anointed me to preach the gospel to the poor; he hath sent me to heal the brokenhearted, to preach deliverance to the captives, and recovering of sight to the blind, to set at liberty them that are bruised . . ."

Children were at the bottom of the chain of command in Jesus's day and in Middle Eastern culture. The father was on top, the wife was next, and the children were under her. They did not belong in adult issues and conversations. The men would discuss those matters among themselves and the children would learn at home and in school. They were not to be removed from their place. That is the extreme opposite of the Western society of the twenty-first century. Children are allowed untold freedom to play, to interrupt, and to disrupt any and every adult activity other than perhaps the workplace. The over veneration of children has almost taken on a religious fervor in our day. They are seen as untouchable angels who should never be scolded or reprimanded. And heaven forbid you should ever "hit" a child (a guilt-laden word designed to make spanking look wrong). Long gone are the days when the overall view toward children was that they were to be "seen but not heard." They are not only seen and heard, they are allowed to take over. The parents are now tagging along behind them in many instances. I have even known of an instance of a child being allowed to "divorce" his parents in a court of law!

Again the pendulum has swung in the opposite extreme of Jesus's words and context, and therefore we must be careful to restore the original setting before proceeding. Jesus would have never advocated allowing the children to be in control, just like He never advocated women being in control of their husbands. He is simply advocating greater love and acceptance toward them within that God-ordained structure. Again, they hold the key that unlocks the mysteries of the kingdom. Study them, enjoy them, celebrate them, and become a better person! Let them come to Christ; they are ready to do so. Let them participate in the Church; they are already present as fertile soil. They say 80 percent of people who come to the Lord (salvation) do so as a child. I myself came to Christ as a child and have never turned back.

This brings up an important issue about salvation, and that of children. Sometimes they are led to the Lord without understanding the nature of the commitment they are making. Care must be taken by parents to make sure they understand before they are baptized in water. In my work with drug addicts I have found in a high percentage of instances that many were led to Christ as a child but never realized what was expected of them. They had a religious experience but did not really give God control of their lives. They followed their supposed conversion experience with a twenty-year addiction to drugs. It usually turns out that they weren't really saved after all. Yes, they are ready for the gospel; just make sure the gospel is explained in such a way that includes repentance and faith (complete surrender). "Asking Jesus to come into your heart" for example, although a good beginning, may not express the seriousness and level of commitment that is truly necessary for a genuine conversion.

So the overall teaching is to make way for the children. Don't always exclude them in everything related to the Church. At the same time they should stay under authority and not "take over" the Church. Let the children have their place and the adults the more responsibility. Make them welcome, but also train them to respect authority and their elders. Disciplining children is also a way of loving them. Proverbs 13:24 says, "He that spares the rod hates his son: but he that loves him chastens him betimes." Children are to be kept under control but not overly controlled. Children are important to Jesus and should be important to us. They are not a nuisance to be brushed off and disregarded. Jesus says, "Release the children, and do not forbid them to come to me."

Discussion Questions:

- What are the characteristics of children that show us the way into the kingdom of God? How are they in a sense living examples for everyone to follow?
- How does the fact that children meant little to nothing in Jesus's society compared to the fact that they mean almost everything in our present society pose a problem in fully comprehending the significance of Jesus's teaching?
- Why do you think Jesus would most likely see both extremes as wrong and hold the middle ground between children being nothing and children being everything?
- In what way is this command saying that Christianity is not just for adults?
- How can we better release our children into the hands of Jesus and not hinder them?

Suggested Exercises:

- Come up with a new message and method to reach children with the gospel that is both on their level and serious enough to effect a change of heart in terms of a genuine conversion. Take the concept of "asking Jesus to come into your heart" and expand on that theme to the point that it includes the idea of total surrender. Include the ideas of Savior, Lord, and Messiah in your explanation of how to be saved. Have everyone in your group come up with a presentation and choose the one that is the most substantive as well as the most appealing.
- In terms of discipleship, discuss how the commands of Christ can be presented on a child's level so they can participate as well.
- Discuss among the group the value of the concept of children's church in connection with this command and how we can make that experience better.
- Discuss among the group or with a trusted disciple the importance of never lying to your child during his or her stage of innocence so his or her faith will not be damaged. What is the proper balance between fostering a vivid imagination and encouraging the acceptance of an alternative reality? For example, is it ever right to tell your child there really is a Santa Claus, only for the child to find out later it was untrue? Who's to say the child won't conclude the same thing about Jesus, who you say is real but can't be seen? Taking advantage of the innocence of a child could be an example of "harming one of these little ones" and must be avoided at all costs. The child's faith should be nurtured, not assaulted or even eliminated by careless jesting.

71

Rule by Serving

Matthew 20:17-28; Mark 10:32-45; Luke 18:31-34, 22:26; John 13:1-17

Calling them to himself, Jesus said to them, "You know that those who are recognized as rulers of the Gentiles lord it over them; and their great men exercise authority over them. But it is not this way among you, but whomever wishes to become great among you shall be your servant; and whoever wishes to be first among you shall be slave of all. For even the Son of Man did not come to be served, but to serve, and to give his life a ransom for many" (Mark 42-45).

Commands of Christ: The greatest among you: *let him be* as the younger. Whoever wants to be great among you *is to be* your servant, and whoever wishes to be first, *is to be* slave of all."

The context of Matthew 20:17-28, Mark 10:32, and Luke 18:31-34 is different from Luke 22:26 and John 13:1-17, but the lesson is the same and bore repeating. In the first instance they were on the way to Jerusalem, and as they walked, Jesus told them the ugly truth that awaited them: "Behold, we are going up to Jerusalem, and the Son of Man will be betrayed to the chief priests and to the scribes; and they will condemn him to death, and deliver him to the Gentiles to mock and to scourge and to crucify. And the third day he will rise again" (Matthew 20:18-19; Mark 10:33-34).

The second context is even more striking being the very night of his betrayal: "Now before the Feast of the Passover, when Jesus knew that his hour had come that he should depart from this world to the Father, having loved his own who were in the world, he loved them to the end" (John 13:1; Luke 22:14-15). The first setting was perhaps days before the passion and the second was the very night before. He was trying to prepare the disciples for His demise, but all they could think about was their anticipated ascendency to the throne.

It is impossible to imagine how they could shift away so effortlessly from the gruesome information that was just provided to them to subject matter on the opposite end of the spectrum. It is hardly what one would expect when reading along in the passage. He has just told them of His impending doom, which is immediately followed by their visions of grandeur. How can these two issues follow one another or be part of the same conversation? One's psyche is gripped by the irony of the entire situation, that they would dare bring up such things on the eve of His crucifixion. It just demonstrates either how totally clueless they were to the events unfolding before them or how painfully they were suffering from denial.

Luke sheds some light on the matter declaring that "they understood none of these things; this saying was hidden from them, and they did not know the things which were spoken" (18:34). One can't help but wonder if they were just writing off what Jesus said as just another one of His mysterious sayings that they might as well just leave alone for another time (or were at least hoping).

Perhaps it is this very shock factor that the authors of Matthew and Mark were intentionally trying to evoke by recalling that these two matters belonged side by side. You have the Lord on one side as a suffering servant and humble Lamb of God pitted against a conniving bunch of power-hungry savages on the other. How infinite indeed was the chasm between them? How Jesus was able to show such self-restraint here is another story in itself. Would not the great majority of us have flown into a vicious rage? But no, He calmly follows up with a lesson on humility. He sees this as an opportunity to correct them for still having no idea what His kingdom is really about. His lesson is about not conforming to worldly standards of behavior. In the world, it is expected that those who work and scheme and somehow arrive at the top are to receive the honor and be unquestionably obeyed. The rest of us can only dream of one day having such authority and influence. We are powerless pawns in the cruel chess game of life.

The prospect then of ruling and of sitting on a throne must have been so overwhelming as to have blinded them to every other fact of life that was repeatedly placed before them. The process of everyday life in this world is in direct opposition to the higher realities of God's eternal kingdom. It is not the powerful that rule in His world, but the docile. Blessed are the meek, for they shall inherit the earth (Matthew 5:5). Isn't it so hard not to allow the realities of this world to invade and overcome the policies and procedures of the world to come? It is like a fish which is in water but is actually not aware of it. The water is just the undetected reality of its life. That is the way things have always been and will, as far as I know, always be. Yet we are being told that there is better atmosphere, the type that will lead to eternal life for those willing to receive it. That is the kind of paradigm shift Jesus was making in this world with His disciples and it is indeed a shift of epic proportions to see service as the way to rule.

It is a lesson that has to be continually relearned and reapplied. So it was for the disciples right up to the end of their experience with the Messiah. The truth of the greatest individual being also the "slave" (Matthew 20:27) had yet to sink in as it is the case undoubtedly with most of us today. So, to further illustrate the point, he donned a towel and washed the disciples' feet. After, He reminded them that He was still their Lord and Master yet stoops to serve. If He was willing, so should they be all the more. These are the kinds of leaders he is looking for. Jesus wants those who will humble themselves, those who are poor in spirit, mournful, and meek and not proud, loud, and demanding. How devastating to one's pride this must have been. How alarming to the conscious of the disciples it must have been once they realized that our Lord was forced on the eve of His death to be occupied with this unthinkable object lesson. How it must have saddened them to the core to know they were not there for Him in his hour of distress but were instead preoccupied about their own vain ambitions.

And honestly, are we any different? Are we so consumed with serving Christ that we often refer to ourselves as His "slave," as did the apostle Paul? No indeed! I would venture to say that most of us are just like they were. As much as we want to point out the unremarkable nature of this motley crew of disciples to strive for fortune and glory, how are we really any different? Don't we want to be at the top, making all the decisions but not wanting to be held responsible for the outcome? What a wonderful world that would be. In every church of every kind throughout history it is the same story repeated over and over. Even an elementary student of Christian history can see this constant and unquenchable thirst for power among Jesus's supposed followers. May the Church say in unison one day, "We repent of our insatiable appetite for power." The command of our Lord on this matter is clear: "The greatest among you: let him be as the younger, and the one who rules like the one who serves" (Luke 22:26). And, "Whoever wants to become great among you must be your servant, and whoever wants to be first must be your slave" (Matthew 20:26-27).

Notice the Hebrew parallelism there (a poetic device). "Great" is paralleled with "first." And "servant" is paralleled with "slave." With that in mind there is no way to avoid what Jesus is saying any longer. Paul had it right. We are to be the slave of Christ and the slave of one another to please God. Maybe we could have finagled our way out of the situation by saying, "yes, I'm a servant." For example politicians claim to be "public servants." Nor do we mind being a part of the "service industry." We understand that concept—but "slavery?" Perish the thought! Now we have no more wiggle room. Jesus allows us no more creative avenues to think our way around it. We are faced with our hunger for power over our hunger for righteousness and must now bring it before him for confession. Let us do as Jesus said and follow Him down the road of service. For He came not to be served, but to serve and to give His life a ransom for many (Mark 10:45). The one who rules is to be like the one who serves.

Discussion Questions:

- What blinded the disciples from fully comprehending what Jesus had foretold about His earthly life soon coming to an end?
- How hard must it have been for the disciples to move from ruling by force to ruling by serving?
- Is not servant leadership still yet a rare jewel in the Church today?
- How does Jesus's parallelism of the term "servant" with "slave" eliminate any attempt to water down his lesson on humility?
- If even the King of kings approached us as a humble servant, why do we approach one another as kings and lords?

Suggested Exercises:

- Write out the title you currently hold and the ways in which you can reshape and recast that job description within the confines of servanthood. Discuss your conclusions with a trusted disciple or with the group of disciples you are working with.
- Hold committee meeting with the sole purpose of providing strategies that foster Christ centeredness in terms of maintaining an atmosphere that insists on Jesus Christ as the *only* head of the church. How can we keep the historical Jesus and His teachings at the forefront? How can we promote the philosophy of *one Leader and many servants* regardless of the place we find ourselves in the present-day Church political structure?

72

Let Go

John 12:1-8; 23-26

Let her alone, so that she may keep it for the day of my burial. For you always have the poor with you, but you do not always have me (John 12:7-8).

Truly, truly, I say to you, unless a grain of wheat falls into the earth and dies, it remains alone; but if it dies, it bears much fruit (John 12:24).

Commands of Christ: *Leave* her alone, for the day of my burial she keeps it. If anyone serves me, *it is imperative* that he follow me.

Jesus is one step closer to his final hour. It is recorded that at the time of this event, orders were already given to arrest Jesus once He was discovered in Jerusalem. He was now on the precipice of that triumphal entry with no exit. He stopped by Bethany on His way in, to no doubt say his last good-byes to his best friends and most devoted followers. He had been telling them all along that He was about to suffer and die on the cross, but none of them had understood it. Could it be that Mary was one of the few who did? One can only wonder if it was due to Jesus's speech about His final departure that sparked Mary to such an extravagant display. Yet we are not provided with the nature of Jesus's speech at this time, so there is no way of being certain of this. Rather, it seems more plausible that she just wanted to take every opportunity to show love, not knowing when she would see Him again. It is unlikely that she knew what this expression of worship would become; that indeed Jesus would see this as an anointing for His burial.

Now Jesus was at the point in His life where everything pointed in one sorrowful direction. He was so overwhelmed with His departure that it colored all of His thoughts and interpretation of every event. Imagine being in that place where all you can see is your impending doom. You know your days are coming to an end and now you see everything in a different light. Imagine the loneliness of this hour when surrounded by loved ones who have no idea what is approaching. Wanting to confide in someone, anyone, yet it is simply not possible.

John records Mary as pouring very expensive perfume on Jesus's feet. The other two (Matthew and Mark) report the pouring over the head. The context there is Simon the Leper's home and the woman is unidentified. Here in John, Mary is identified as the person responsible for this huge apparent waste of a year's wages. It makes you wonder if this event occurred with a different person other than Mary, since something similar had occurred once before with a woman who was repenting of her sins (Luke 7:36). Nevertheless, it seems most likely that the event is the one that was described in John, and that this alabaster box was enough to cover both his head and his feet. Mary was worshipping Jesus and giving Him a lavish offering of her heart, soul, and costly possessions. All the disciples could think about was the expense. They too should have gathered around and bowed to His feet along with her. But her being in the Spirit and they being in the flesh made for a conflict that Jesus readily corrected. He gave a command. The order was to "leave her alone." So often we as parents have to issue commands to our children in order to render a verdict that will end the conflict and render the guilty party defenseless. So it was with Jesus's disciples who were still little children in their faith.

What can we learn from this episode? Well, one thing for certain is to stay in tune with the Holy Spirit. Galatians 5:16 comes from a mature perspective when it declares "Walk in the spirit and you will not fulfill the lusts of the flesh." The disciples were too busy mentally transitioning into their thrones to be aware of the fact that their Savior and Lord was headed to the cross. They were not seeking first the kingdom of God. They were seeking first the kingdom of man.

And so it is with us as we build our empires here on Earth while never giving a thought to eternity and the things that really matter. And what about Jesus? How about the way He must have felt? What about the horrors that awaited Him in Jerusalem? What about the fact that the walls were closing in on His days on this earth? Who was there to support Him, to feel for Him, to weep for Him? Was He left alone to deal with everything Himself in his final hour sweating as if great drops of blood? Yes indeed. He was certainly left all alone.

And more importantly for us, is He still alone? Do we still have no feeling for His passion? Do we yet go through the motions every Sunday without a care? Do we say within ourselves that this is old news, or do we really remember Him in the bread and in the wine?

We have to let go. We can't control Mary, we can't control Jesus, and we can't control our own lives. They all belong to the Father. As we let go of Mary we worship with her. We admit that indeed it is so that we have lost our earthly kingdom, but we possess still a greater love for the King. We let go of Jesus and tell Him we are there for Him as He heads for the cross and all our political dreams and ambitions die with Him. We obey Jesus and we leave her alone as she goes about ministering to Him the way we should have been doing all along as He shared his broken heart with us along the way. We come to realize as the Master taught that "unless a grain of wheat falls into the ground and dies, it remains alone; but if it dies, it produces much grain. He who loves his life will lose it, and he who hates his life in this world will keep it for eternal life. If anyone serves me, let him follow me; and where I am, there my servant will be also. If anyone serves me, him my Father will honor" (John 12:23-26).

In other words, not only do you have to accept His demise, but it is in the accepting of His passing that you realize you may have just accepted your own. It is not the time for harvesting; it is the time for planting. It is the time for investing and not the time for cashing in on that investment. We so easily get ahead of God. We want to fast forward to the good part without any sacrifice.

But Jesus is saying now is the time for sacrifice of everything including your very life so that you may gain in the future. In that future is where all the glory lies. Yes, you have to let me go to the cross, and in the cross is where you will also find your own destiny. This world is not your home. There is a new world coming and that is the one where you will ascend your throne. Now your life must be a seed just as my life was. We are in this together and I know that you will not forsake me when the going gets tough. You want to serve me? You want to be a part of my kingdom; very well then. Know this: "If anyone serves me, it is imperative that he follow me." Now you are called to the same path: that of self-denial, taking up the cross, and following me. So, success for now is in the letting go of all things: her, me, and even your own life as you totally surrender it into my keeping.

Discussion Questions:

- How lonely must it have been for Jesus to be surrounded by his most loyal followers yet to be singularly aware of his impending doom?
- How must it have colored His every thought including the costly expression of love from the woman of God with the alabaster box of ointment?
- In what ways was Mary likely walking in the spirit and the disciples walking in the flesh?
- How do modern-day disciples continue to walk in the flesh with the way we approach Holy Communion and the way we plan out our lives in a strictly earthly dimension?
- What were the disciples holding onto so tightly that would not allow them to let go of Mary and Jesus and even themselves?
- Why is letting Christ go to the cross letting go of our own determination to avoid it?
- Jesus saw this life as an investment in the future but the disciples wanted a return on the investment in the here and now. How do we need to fundamentally change our perspective on the planting and harvesting aspects of the kingdom of God?

Suggested Exercises:

- The disciples had to let go of their hopes, dreams, and ambitions toward having power, prestige, and prosperity in this world and instead invest this life in the prospect of enjoying all of those things in the world to come.
  - Inventory your life privately and make a list of the hopes, dreams, ambitions, recognitions, and monetary advancements you have put aside for the sake of the kingdom of God. List the items you have yet to give up for the Lord. Ask yourself,

"What current investments do I make that I can take with me and what investments will I lose when I leave this world?"

o Share this with a trusted disciple and recommit your time, energy, and resources to the furtherance of the gospel and discipleship (the cause of Christ). Pray a prayer together of confession and repentance for the ways you have held on to your life and determine to let go and to completely turn everything over to the Lord. Determine to lose your life so that you can find it.

73

Have Faith in God

Mark 11:22-25; Matthew 21:20-22

And Jesus answered, saying to them, "Have faith in God. Truly I say to you, whoever says to this mountain, 'Be taken up and cast into the sea,' and does not doubt in his heart, but believes that what he says is going to happen, it will be granted him. Therefore I say to you, all things which you pray and ask, believe that you have received them, and they will be granted you. Whenever you stand praying, forgive . . ." (Mark 11:22-25a).

Commands of Christ: *Have faith* in God . . . *believe* that you have received it . . . *forgive* if you have anything against anyone.

On the morning following his triumphal entry into Jerusalem, He was hungry. He saw a fig tree on the way to the Temple (to cleanse it of the moneychangers). He expected to be refreshed and break his overnight fast by having breakfast. Instead, all He found was foliage. There was no fruit on the fig tree. He then proceeded to pronounce judgment on it saying, "May you never bear fruit again!" (Matthew 21:19) The next day they saw the fig tree withered up all the way down to the roots! They were amazed at this result of Jesus's word and faith. Jesus responded by encouraging them to exercise their faith. He said, "Have faith in God. For assuredly, I say to you, whoever says to this mountain, 'Be removed and be cast into the sea,' and does not doubt in his heart, but believes that those things he says will be done, he will have whatever he says" (Mark 11:22-23).

The tendency with this passage is to reason it away and to suggest that all of this was symbolic. It is too uncomfortable to realize instead that our faith leaves much to be desired in contrast to the Master's faith. So many commentators want to avoid this subject by turning a literal mountain into a figurative one or by suggesting that the fig tree represents Israel. Unfortunately, this is not reasonable since nothing about Israel or the mountain of life's problems is mentioned. All we have presented is an actual fig tree and an actual mountain range. It is easy to downplay through fear the reality that is set before us of a literal tree dried up from the roots and the logical conclusion following about a literal mountain being moved. The reason we want to water this lesson down is the very reason for the lesson: we too are of little faith. If God can create the whole world through Jesus in seven days (again, our faith can't perceive of a literal seven), why can't a simple mountain be moved? Our faith in the supernatural is practically nonexistent. But if we have any faith in the supernatural at all, then we are obligated to extend that to the unlimited nature of the One we believe in. That, after all, is really what this all boils down to: How big is your God? If He has limitations, then believe only thus far. If he has no limitations, then we are obliged to believe further. Anything less is a sin (Psalm 78:41).

Limiting the Holy One of Israel is a serious matter, for it will affect everything that follows for the worse. We will live at whatever level we believe is possible. If we believe we are slaves, we will always be so. If we, on the other hand, believe that we are the children of God in this world and that He is on our side that makes us practically invincible. We will proceed with great confidence over all our enemies and overcome the entire world. If God is for us, who can be against us? Jesus therefore commands us so: "Have faith in God!"

He then provides us with an additional secret to prevailing faith. He says that whatever it is you are asking for in prayer, you are to believe that you have already received it. You are to consider it done. This is what it means to have faith. When you have faith you do not expect the worst, you expect the best. When you are a child of God, expecting a miracle is normal, for God is, after all, a supernatural being. He does not operate within the laws of nature as do mere mortals. He controls those boundaries and they are less (much less) than the sum of Him. The creation can never equal the creator, it will always be less than. Creator > creation is the formula. So why do we act as if miracles are not possible? Why did

Thomas Jefferson cut out every reference to miracles in his Bible? Because his God was an absent God, a God who wound up the earth like a clock and then left it to run its course (see deism).

This is what happens when you use anthropomorphic imagery to describe one who is above and beyond all time and space. He transcends anything we understand, so how can we expect Him to operate within our temporal experience that He created in the first place for us? That is like us trying to fit into a bird cage. The cage was not created for us. Just because we placed that boundary on the bird doesn't mean we are now subjected to those same limitations. But somehow over time many theologians have bought into this fallacy about God and it soils all of their writings since the days of the supposed Enlightenment. So how do you have faith in God? One way is to consider it done! By the way, that is not a suggestion. Jesus commanded us to believe that we have received whatever we ask for in prayer!

Then last of all he adds a warning against unforgiveness. This is another tip about what could interfere with our prayers being answered. He said "when you stand praying, *forgive* if you have anything against anyone" (Mark 11:25). Again, I have identified the word above in italics as the "imperative" of that sentence. This means it is a direct order. Every time you have an imperative it is like adding the statement, "And that's an order!" to the equation. Notice that this additional command follows the previous command to believe you have received. So overall prevailing faith is the type of faith that expects positive results and doesn't allow unforgiveness to interfere. Not forgiving others will cause your prayers to be hindered (Matthew 6:14-15). If you don't forgive others of their sins, your Father in heaven will not forgive you of yours.

So the sky is the limit! The greater your God is, the greater you can expect the miracles will be! It all comes down to what you believe. One of my favorite lines of all time is from the movie *Indiana Jones and the Last Crusade*. Once Indiana's father is dying from a gunshot wound, he is forced to do something about it. The antagonist, who shot the elder Jones to force Indiana to find the cup of the Holy Grail, said, "Only the grail can save your father now. It's time to ask yourself *what you believe*." It is the same with our faith today. Is it all but extinct? Where is the power we once saw regularly throughout the New Testament? When the Son of Man comes, will he find faith on the earth (Luke 18:8)?

George Gray

Discussion Questions:

- Why do we tend to water down this story of Jesus cursing the fig tree and assume that the mountain He is referring to is not a literal mountain?
- How does the size of your God tend to determine what you will or will not be able to achieve in life?
- Discuss the power of "considering it done," no matter how impossible it may seem.
- How can unforgiveness stand between you and your miracle?

Suggested Exercises:

- Grade yourself on a scale of one to ten in terms of belief that you can have power over nature through Christ. On one end of the scale is that you can't effect even a grain of dust and on the other end of the scale is literally moving a mountain. Have everyone in the group share their score and explain their answer.
- Share with the group testimonies of times you avoided a natural disaster by faith: a tornado was turned around, a fire or a flood stopped short of your front door. Share a time you were healed of a terminal illness.
- Share times the scripture records that the natural course of events were interrupted or changed by the hand of God. Discuss whether you believe those things were literal or coincidental. Has God changed?
- Pray regularly for more faith to believe anything is possible. Open up to the supernatural reality of Christ. Encourage fellow disciples to seek to be the powerful witnesses Jesus intended us to be (Acts 1:8; Mark 16:17-18). Encourage them to face the challenge that will come to test their faith, for it is in the testing of it that it comes alive and becomes a force to be reckoned with.

74

Return to Your Rightful Owner

Matthew 22:15-22; Mark 12:13-17; Luke 20:20-26

Is it lawful to pay taxes to Caesar, or not? But he detected their trickery and said to them, "Show me a denarius. Whose likeness and inscription does it have?" They said, "Caesar's." And he said to them, "Then render to Caesar the things that are Caesar's, and to God the things that are God's" (Luke 20:22-25).

Command of Christ: *Give back* to Caesar what is Caesar's and to God what is God's.

Again we are unable to continue the sweet story of Jesus without this constant interference from the bitter religious leaders. This time it is the Herodians who join in with the Pharisees who were the personification of hypocrisy and scheming. They knew of Jesus's reputation of telling the truth no matter the consequences. This singularity and integrity stood out to those who knew only duplicity and deception in their daily dealings. So, knowing He would value honesty over personal safety, they hoped to propose a question by which the most truthful response would most certainly result in his demise. The question was crafted in such a way that either a yes or no answer would be equally condemning. If you say, "Yes, it is lawful to pay taxes to Caesar," you are condemned by Israel. If you say no, you are condemned by Rome (hence the need of the Herodians to witness the reply). Even so, they would end up being exposed and taken to school by this one person that they just couldn't seem to outmaneuver.

The question was, "Is it lawful to pay taxes to Caesar or not?" (Matthew 22:17; Mark 12:15; and Luke 20:22) He does respond honestly, but unfortunately, the truth detector is turned squarely on them. He says in reply, "You hypocrites, why are you trying to trap me? Show me the coin used for paying the tax." They show him a denarius, which is a silver coin worth one day's wages. It is interesting He didn't have one to show them. But since they were all about money, He knew He would find one on them. He then goes on to use that coin as an object lesson. With denarius in hand, He now reverses the dynamic by doing to them what they had intended to do to Him. He puts them on trial, and now they are the defendants answering questions from the heavenly prosecuting attorney. He answers their question with a question as well (a common tactic of rabbis in Jesus's day): "Whose image is this and whose inscription?" "Caesar's," they reply. His reply amazes them for some time to come. He said, "Give to Caesar what is Caesar's and to God what is God's."

So in reality He answers yes and no. Yes, you should pay your taxes. No, you should not add to that and worship them as gods. Give the emperor what he deserves and God what He deserves. They each have their place. The coin was created by the emperor and therefore it displays the image of the owner. People were created by God and they also display the image of their owner. The coinage belongs to the emperor and we belong to God. Jesus used the denarius as an object lesson to show them what they should and shouldn't do. The inscription on the silver coin read, "Tiberius Caesar, son of the deified Augustus." It's okay to use the coin as payment for taxes, but that is the extent of it. Their claims to deity were over the top. That belongs to God. When the emperor demands our worship, he is going too far, and that is where we draw the line. We should not forget that we bear God's image (Genesis 1:26) and that we belong to Him, heart and soul. This is the part the Pharisees missed. He had their bodies but not their minds, will, and emotions that were made in God's image. God didn't have their hearts. The command to them and to us is to return to your rightful owner.

Discussion Questions:

- How did the Pharisees intend to use Jesus's own values of honesty over personal safety against Him?
- Explain how it was that either a yes and no answer would have gotten Jesus into trouble.

- How did Jesus let them know He was on to them?
- How was He able to move from the "hot seat" to the role of prosecuting attorney with such ease so as to make total fools of them all?
- How does the image of Caesar on the silver coin show who it belongs to just like the image of God on mankind show who humans belong to?
- How was Jesus answering both yes and no?
- How did their attempt to destroy Christ end up in Christ's attempt to save them?

Suggested Exercise:

- Examine yourself in terms of how much of your life belongs to the Lord. On a scale between 10 percent and 100 percent, how much of your life belongs to the Father God? Have you ever completely surrendered to His will? Is He totally in control of your life or are you? If He is, rejoice! If not, repent!
- Take for example those decisions that take up most of the currency of our lives whereby God is either allowed to spend freely or is hindered from direct access. Score yourself on the following issues from one to ten in terms of totally lining up with God's will:
  o Career path
  o Marriage partner
  o The church I attend
  o Ministry involvement
  o Entertainment choices.

  o Discuss your conclusions with a trusted disciple or group of disciples. Pray with each other for the courage to return to your rightful owner.
- Determine not to be owned by the government, the economy, your job, or even your lover: you belong to the Lord first of all and your lifestyle should reflect that. Repent for putting Him on the shelf while you spend all your time, energy, and resources on self-preservation. Repent for marginalizing Christ and His kingdom to a person and philosophy you only have time for once a week if that. Repent for spending all of your time making money instead of making disciples.

411

75

Don't Be a Pharisee

Matthew 23:1-7; Mark 12:38-40; Luke 20:45-47

Then Jesus spoke to the crowds and to his disciples, saying: "The scribes and the Pharisees have seated themselves in the chair of Moses; therefore all that they tell you, do and observe, but do not do according to their deeds; for they say and do not do. They tie up heavy burdens and lay them on men's shoulders, but they themselves are unwilling to move them with a finger" (Matthew 23:1-4).

Commands of Christ: *Beware* of the scribes. All things therefore they tell you, *do and keep*, but *do not do* according to their works."

The old adage "actions speak louder than words" applies here. Jesus told the disciples and the people to beware of the religious leaders who no longer practice what they preach. So often we, like them, confuse knowledge of a matter with the performance of it. They obviously knew what should be done. Otherwise Jesus would not have commanded them to obey His orders. It's just that they were not practicing these things themselves. They were more concerned with appearances. Jesus provided a substantial amount of incriminating evidence that would convict them in God's court of law.

He presents to the people exhibits A, B, and C. Exhibit A: recognition. They wear long flowing robes to draw attention to themselves so they will be noticed and greeted in public. Exhibit B: elitism. Only the best seating arrangement will do for them in the synagogues and at banquets. Exhibit C: extortion. They devoured widows' houses instead of caring for them.

412

They take advantage of their position to minister to widows and minister instead to themselves. They act pious and make long prayers to convince the person they are swindling that they are legitimate. Verdict: guilty as charged with hypocrisy.

No doubt these same individuals will teach others not to covet recognition, to not be elitist or greedy. So do as they say, not as they do. Beware of them. They are not what they seem. They offer the bait of Satan. They will lure you in just to ensnare you into a life of servitude and bondage to the law. But Jesus has come that you may have life more abundantly. Whom the Son has set free is free indeed! They work from the outside in. Jesus works from the inside out. They teach that you work your way into God's favor. Jesus teaches that He will work to gain favor between you and God. God wants lovers, not lawyers. It's all about relationships. In a love relationship it is not about earning acceptance but about celebrating the acceptance you already have. In that celebration is birthed the desire to please the one you love. That is how your behavior ends up not only righteous according to the law but above and beyond the law (minimum requirements).

So what are some ways we can avoid the trap of legalism? How can you guard against religious pride (superiority complex)? One way is to remember that the greatest among us is always the servant (Matthew 20:17-28). If we keep a humble attitude of a servant we will avoid the pitfall of a power trip. We will not seek to lord it over God's church as do so many. Even if we are called to leadership it will always be as a servant of Christ and his sheep. We will be humble shepherds rather that cruel dictators. Paul did this by seeing himself always as the slave of Christ. Another is to remember that you will also be judged for the way you lead (Ephesians 6:9). You are never on top with no one to answer to. Keep it about relationship rather than rigorous adherence to religious principles. Reinterpret everything you have ever known to be true through the eyes of love and friendship.

Do justly, love mercy, and walk humbly before your God (Micah 6:8). When it comes to your own behavior, judge harshly so you will live a righteous life. But when it comes to others, lean toward mercy. Blessed are the merciful, for they shall obtain mercy (Matthew 5:7). You will receive back what you invest exponentially (Luke 6:38). If you want others to straighten up, straighten up yourself (you reap what you sow). If you want others to show mercy to you, then show mercy to them. Finally, God resists the proud but gives grace to the humble (1 Peter 5:5). Blessed are the poor in spirit for theirs is the kingdom of God (Matthew 5:3). If you walk humbly before God you can expect a great deal of favor and blessing in this life.

Discussion Questions:

- Why did Jesus command them to "do what the Pharisees say but not what the Pharisees do"? How does knowing what you should do not necessarily mean you are doing what you should do?
- If you know but don't take action yet expect everyone else to know and take action, what does that make you?
- What three pieces of evidence does Jesus provide that proves the Pharisees' guilt?
- How does the philosophy of Jesus summarized in the statement, "God wants lovers not lawyers" differ from the scribes' and Pharisees' approach to relating to God?
- What are two ways to avoid the trap of legalism and the superiority complex of religious pride that goes along with it?
- How did the Pharisees violate Micah 6:8 to the point of getting it totally backward, or doing the exact opposite? How can we use that same passage to stay on track with God?

Suggested Exercise:

- Could Jesus use the same evidence on you that He used against the Pharisees? Examine yourself in terms of legalism, elitism, personal recognition, and extortion. Confess your faults to another disciple that you may be healed. Repent of any of those tendencies and ask fellow disciples to help you stay relationship-focused through accountability.

76

Accept No Other Master

Matthew 23:8-11

But do not be called Rabbi; for one is your Teacher, and you are all brothers. Do not call anyone on earth your father; for one is your Father, He who is in heaven. Do not be called leaders; for one is your Leader, that is, Christ. But the greatest among you shall be your servant.

Commands of Christ: But *do not ever be called* Rabbi . . . *Do not ever call* anyone on Earth your father . . . *Neither be called* master, for you have only one master, who is Christ.

This teaching ties in rather heavily with the last warning against being a Pharisee. In their system of discipleship, each student was to one day work his way up to the master teaching position, or what is known as the rabbi. They were extremely hungry for recognition as a great teacher, leader, or master.

Christianity is markedly different. All of these designations belong to one person: Christ. We as Christians are forbidden to carry on in the same manner as the Pharisees did in constantly jockeying for titles and positions of authority. The top position will always be filled. It will never be open to us. We will always be His students and He will always be our teacher. We will never rise to the rank of top instructor in His kingdom and thereby have our own following. We are all called to remain Christ's permanent apprentices.

We are all brothers and sisters and we are all servants, but none of us are masters. This is the most important principle in all of discipleship; for if it is lost the very foundation on which Christian discipleship is built comes crumbling down. He did not send us to make our own disciples but to make disciples of Jesus. Disciples of Christ require His commands, not ours. We are simply passing down His orders, not our own. Our job is to keep the Lord as our only Master, Teacher, and Rabbi and never allow ourselves to think we can achieve the glory and position He alone deserves. The most brilliant among us are at best poor substitutes for Him.

The first command is, "Don't ever be called rabbi." If someone wants to honor you with that title, correct him and say, "No, there is only one Rabbi, and that is Jesus." We are not allowed to be considered a great teacher because that takes the focus away from the true teacher. What they will get from us is always less than what they can get from Him. It is His wisdom that will change our lives, not the idiosyncrasies of any of His followers. No matter how popular and gifted a teacher we may be, we are obligated to turn people away from us toward the true guide. Otherwise we will divert them from the source of all wisdom by claiming something not accessible to us. While they are focused on us they will lose sight of the only one who can really guide them. Our teachings are only valuable in terms of how well they communicate something he already said. We are not the way, but we must show them the way and stay out of the way.

The books of Matthew, Mark, Luke, and John hold practically all of His teachings to the first disciples. That is the information that will change their lives. That is the only knowledge where, if one puts it into practice, one will become a true disciple of Christ. The source of life and wisdom and understanding is in the gospels. When people come to us for a drink of living water, this is where we must lead them. He is the spring of the living water of wisdom. We must say with Peter, "Lord, to whom shall we go? You have the words of eternal life." We don't disciple people in our image but His. Discipleship as He intended it will cease to exist if we fail to hold on to this principle with every fiber of our being, imprinting it indelibly on our subconscious and that of the next generation.

The second command is, "Don't ever call anyone on Earth your father." This is a command that is regularly dismissed by those in the Catholic Church. This has become the prized possession of the priests, and they must now humbly repent. Even though they do act as a spiritual father as did Paul, ultimately none of us can truly claim to be anyone's father. Only God can produce children for Himself planting the seed of His Son for mankind so that whosoever believes can be saved. We don't own the gospel; we just pass on what we have received. We serve with Christ in the process of sowing and reaping.

This is not to say that the Catholic Church is worse than all other Christian denominations; it merely serves as the best illustration of this particular point, just as Judaism serves as the best example of overusing the word rabbi. Perhaps it is the Protestant Church that most misuses the word teacher. We regularly refer to our ministers as "pastor-teacher." This may be a direct violation of what Jesus is commanding. That may be their gift, but that is not who they are to be called according to the Lord. Jesus said you have one teacher and the rest of you are servants of one another. So even though we may have a teaching gift, it is used only to serve others by helping them discover Jesus's truth. Outside of Christ, there is no truth to offer. We have many who can teach but only one Teacher.

Jesus goes on to say, "neither be called master, for you have only one master, who is Christ. The original Greek word there for "master" can go in several directions. "Kathegetai" can be translated as leader, master, or teacher. Maybe even *master-teacher* would be the best translation. We don't allow ourselves to be seen as in charge so the church will never forget who really is in charge. Jesus is the head of the church, but it is up to us to keep it that way. He can't be Lord when we keep stepping in front of Him. We have to constantly remind ourselves and others just who is in charge here. This is not automatic even though Christ is sovereign. He allows us in his sovereignty to choose. We, like Paul, have to choose to "die daily" to our wills so that His will can remain paramount (1 Corinthians 15:31). That's why He insists we do everything we can to "remain" in him (John 15:4). For we all possess the potential to disconnect from Him.

Keep pointing to the only Rabbi, the only Father, and the only Teacher and never allow yourself to be seen as anything more than His humble servant. Regular inventory should be taken to make sure the church remains under His leadership. A Lordship infrastructure has to be set in place to maintain a yielded Church. Constant examination should be instituted with what the Church is doing in contrast to what Christ has commanded. Adjustments should regularly be made to ensure that Christ really is the head of operations. This matter of His Lordship should be taken very seriously and we must not assume that we are always in compliance.

He left His word with us to be the rule of our lives. Have we forgotten that? Have we laid it to the side in our board meetings and let the world reshape our churches in its image? Think about it. Keep Jesus on the throne by instituting policies that will facilitate it.

Discussion Questions:

- What is the primary difference between the Pharisees' system of discipleship and Christianity's system of discipleship in terms of moving up the chain of command?
- The Pharisees' system made disciples of each other; Christians only make disciples of Jesus. Therefore, what is the highest position we can achieve as Christian disciples?
- Why can't we allow ourselves to be called "rabbi" or a great teacher?
- What books of the Bible contain the teachings of the only person who really deserves the title of Master/Teacher?
- What's wrong with being called "father" in a religious sense? Didn't Paul see himself as such in terms of using the gospel to produce baby Christians and then helping those babies grow to full maturity?
- How can our designation as a "leader" or "master/teacher" in the Church end up usurping the role of Christ as the only head of the Church?
- Is the Lordship of Christ something that must be preserved or is it automatic?

Suggested Exercises:

- Write out a procedure by which the current Church hierarchical structure can be redefined in terms of servanthood. For example, how can each title and job description be reformulated from the perspective of a humility rather than control? How can all current models of Church leadership be redirected toward the servant leadership model? Use Mark 10:42-45 as the foundational scripture passage for this enterprise. Discuss your written program with your discipleship group or accountability partner. Consider which policy contains the greatest potential and present that to the leadership of the church.

• On the other side of the coin, what initiatives would work best to ensure that Christ remains the sole authority? How do we keep the Messiah and His perspective as encountered in the gospels in the forefront of every decision we make as a body of believers? For example, the higher one goes up the chain of command the more familiar that person should be with the life and teachings of Christ. They should be the instructors of such courses of study, the leaders of those who put Christ's words to memory. They should be the ones who are eager to bring the insight of Christ to bear on any issue. Reconstruct a church hierarchical system that combines the rise of power and influence with the rise of awareness and even a complete emersion into the personal philosophy of Jesus Christ. Share that system with your fellow disciples and the church leadership.

77

Fear God's Son

Matthew 24:1-3, 15-26; Mark 13:1-4, 14-23; Luke 21:5-7, 20-24

As he was going out of the temple, one of his disciples said to him, "Teacher, behold what wonderful stones and what wonderful buildings!" And Jesus said to him, "Do you see these great buildings? Not one stone will be left upon another which will not be torn down" (Mark 13:1-2).

Commands of Christ: Let the reader *understand*. Those in Judea must *flee* to the mountains. *Don't go down* into your house to get your things. Whoever is in the field *do not return* for your coat. *Pray* that your flight will not be in the winter or on the Sabbath. *Don't believe* (false Christs). *Behold* I told you beforehand.

Jesus's passion was at hand, and all He could see was colored by that overwhelming sorrow. He couldn't rejoice with the disciples' comments about the magnificence of the Temple as they sat across from it in full view. As splendid as it was, it was all for naught, for soon it would be reduced to rubble. All this would happen because of His rejection by the nation of Israel. Amazingly it was not out of revenge that He speaks about what they deserved for disrespecting Him. Instead he felt sorry for what was about to take place among His people and began to warn them to prepare any way possible to avoid this inevitable turn of events.

It is unavoidable that He must suffer rejection and crucifixion, but woe to those by whom these unthinkable crimes are executed. It would be better that they had never been born, than to dare to lay a hand God's anointed one, the Messiah, the Son of the living God. But not only had they mocked Him, they opposed him at every turn. Now they proceeded to do Him bodily harm. Not just a slap across the face—that would have been enough in itself for heavenly consequence. But to put this holy man through the excruciating torture and death of a Roman crucifixion is impossible to comprehend.

Instead of a crown of thorns, He should have had a crown of gold and a purple robe and a mighty throne with every conceivable honor known to man. They should have loved him as mankind's greatest treasure as the spring and fountain of eternal life and wisdom. Riches, honor, power, and dominion are due Him. This is appropriate. This is what He deserves, it is all due Him. His life story should have been one long triumphal entry. Day after day He should have received praise. Day after day He should have experienced homage and worship. But alas, they simply did not recognize God's Son. "had they known, they would not have crucified the Lord of glory" (1 Corinthians 2:8).

Knowing that this was His destiny, He humbly proceeded as a lamb to the slaughter. As such He was on a countdown. It is one thing to die. It is quite another to know beforehand the precise manner in which it will occur and have to live out those final dreadful days without being able to stop it. With all this weighing heavily on His mind, it is a wonder how He could have continued to think only of others. Even on the cross He prayed for those who hated Him, who are gloating over His demise. He worried about them and what their fate would be because of what they were doing. He reached out to His mother, who now without him would have no means of support. All of this while hanging from huge nails that were driven between the aperture of his wrists and ankles, and having to pull up and push down on those spikes in order to breathe!

So amazing and selfless is His love that we can barely comprehend it, much less ever hope to achieve this level of Christlikeness. It is out of that selfless perspective that we encounter all of the commands that follow. He was preparing them for this judgment day that would come on their nation. He didn't want them to fall victim when the Father's vengeance arrived. Seeing into the future, He was horrified by the carnage and wanted to save as many as possible, regardless that it was just recompense for what was being done to him.

Here are His instructions for the day of doom:

1. Look for the abomination of desolation. That is a sign that you need to flee! "Abomination of desolation" was a term used by the prophet Daniel to predict what would take place in the Temple. The Temple would be defiled in one way or another before the final disaster. In the second century before Christ it was done by the Greeks (Antiochus Epiphanies), who sacrificed a pig on the altar. The disciples were to watch out for any similar incident as a sign to take action to avoid the heat of the battle. Luke 21:8 provides an additional sign: "When you see armies surrounding Jerusalem you will know that its desolation is near." So he is saying when you see these things, "understand" their significance to avoid disaster.

2. Judean residents are warned to *flee* into the mountains for safety. To congregate in one spot would simply make it easier for the Roman soldiers to eliminate them. History records, however, that most Jews fled instead to Jerusalem, and that was where they perished as the city was besieged and burned to the ground.

3. *Don't go down* into your house to get your things. If in the field, *do not return* for your coat. To escape death, it is imperative that you not linger: leave immediately!

4. *Pray* that your flight will not be in the winter or on the Sabbath. A Sabbath day attack could be especially devastating since Jews would refuse to move out of respect for God. Unfortunately, in many instances it would also cost them their lives as their enemies would take advantage of it. Imagine if it happened in the wintertime, and there is no time to go back and get your coat! What a treacherous and desperate journey would lie ahead. At the height of the horror of war would be the perfect opportunity to expect the return of Christ, or in the case of the Jews, his first appearance. Perhaps this is why Jesus warns them to beware of false messiahs on that day of judgment.

5. *Don't believe* it if someone reports that the messiah has arrived. It will surely happen, so remember, *notice* (behold), I have told you beforehand. Christ as the Good Shepherd leaves behind a

must-do list to ensure the least amount of casualties to the flock. He provides them with an exit strategy for when that fateful day arrives. At His hour of greatest need, He can only think of our safety.

But the fact is one million, one hundred thousand Jews perished on that day. This should send a wakeup call not only to that nation but to any nation that defies God. Psalm 2:12 comes to mind when considering these things: "Kiss the Son, lest He be angry, and you perish in the way, when His wrath is kindled but a little. Blessed are all those who put their trust in Him." The Christian Church today may not openly defy Him, but it should beware of the way it tends to ignore Him and His teachings. A nation that is Christian in word only and not in action will open itself up to a similar fate. For is this not how the religious leaders of Jesus's day lived? Did the Master not say to them, "Well did Isaiah prophesy of you hypocrites, as it is written: 'This people honors me with their lips, But their heart is far from me'" (Mark 7:6)? Is that not the same place that Christianity has come to in this country? Let us examine ourselves and repent lest something worse comes upon us.

Discussion Questions:

- Why couldn't Jesus rejoice with the disciples about the magnificence and architectural splendor found in the Temple complex of His day?
- Was Jesus vindictive or saddened by the consequences of His rejection?
- What are the five pieces of advice He left with his followers to ensure the least amount of casualties once the time comes for Jerusalem to be judged for rejecting God's Son?
- At His greatest hour of need He can only think of the safety and well-being of others—even from the cross itself. What does that tell you about Jesus?
- The religious leaders of Jesus's day were guilty of honoring God with their lips, yet their hearts were far from Him. Don't we do the same thing to Jesus in the Church today? Don't we also, generally speaking, call Him "Lord" yet rarely do anything He asks?

- Could a similar way of treating God's Son today result in a similar kind of judgment?

Suggested Exercises:

- Discuss among your fellow disciples what exactly needs to change in Christianity to avert the judgment of God on our nation. In what specific ways as a body of Christ can we begin to take Jesus and His teachings more seriously? Write those objectives down and display them in a prominent place as a daily reminder. Agree with one another to do everything you can to promote and instill these new objectives into the body of Christ. Have everyone who agrees with these initiatives sign the agreement.

78

Know the Signs of the Times

Matthew 24:4-14, 27-30, 32-44; Mark 13:5-13, 24-26, 28-37;
Luke 21:8-19, 25-28, 29-36

Now learn the parable from the fig tree: when its branch has already become tender and puts forth its leaves, you know that summer is near. Even so, you too, when you see these things happening, recognize that He is near, right at the door (Mark 13:28-29).

Commands of Christ: *Learn* the parable of the fig tree. *Know* that it is near, right at the door! *Watch* out that no one deceives you. *Do not follow* after them. *See to it* that you are not alarmed. *Be* on your guard. *Don't premeditate* on your reply. In your patience *possess* your souls. *Arise and lift up* your heads: your redemption draws near. *Watch and pray, keep watch, watch!*

We start off the whole enterprise with the unavoidable fact that nobody knows exactly when Christ will return. Jesus states in Mark 13:32, "But of that day and hour no one knows, not even the angels in heaven, nor the Son, but only the Father." But what do we know? Jesus says we will know when it is "near" due to all of the signs that will be occurring on Earth just prior to the event. He makes that clear by His parable about the fig tree in Matthew 24:32; Mark 13:28 and Luke 21:29. Mark 13:28-30 states it like this: "Now learn this parable from the fig tree: When its branch has already become tender, and puts forth leaves, you know that summer is near. So you also, when you see these things happening, know that it

425

is near—at the doors! Assuredly, I say to you, this generation will by no means pass away till all these things take place."

What "things" is He referring to? Well, there is a long list He enumerated in the passages that precede that statement. He wants us to "learn" the parable and to "know" those signs so we will not be caught off-guard.

1. The first sign mentioned is the appearance of false Christs (Matthew 24:4; Mark 13:6 and Luke 21:8). Jesus said, "Take heed that no one deceives you. For many will come in My name, saying, 'I am he,' and will deceive many" (Mark 13:5-6). The command for this sign is to "watch out" and "not to follow after" these imposters (Luke 21:8).

2. The second sign is all nations turning on one another. "But when you hear of wars and rumors of wars, do not be troubled; for such things must happen, but the end is not yet. For nation will rise against nation and kingdom against kingdom" (Mark 13:7-8). The command to go with this sign is to "see to it that you are not alarmed" (Matthew 24:6). In other words, it shouldn't be seen as unusual but should be expected by Christians that wars will be on the increase toward the end of time preceding His triumphant return. It's all part of God's plan. Don't be afraid. God is in control.

3. The third sign is widespread famine, disease, and earthquakes. Luke states it like this: "And there will be great earthquakes in various places, and famines and pestilences; and there will be fearful sights and great signs from heaven" (21:11). It gives you the impression that everything is beginning to fall apart! But this is only the third of seven signs! In order for it to be noticeable, it must be both on a grander scale, more frequent, and more widespread than the regular reporting of world events as we know them today.

4. It gets much worse. First there are worldwide wars, then worldwide famine and earthquakes, and now worldwide persecution of Christians! Matthew 24:9 states: "Then they will deliver you up to tribulation and kill you, and you will be hated by all nations for My name's sake." Mark adds to "be on your guard" during this time. Jesus further orders us not to premeditate on what our

reply will be when we are brought before the courts to answer for ourselves (Mark 13:11). Jesus additionally admonishes us in Luke to be patient and hold on to the end to be saved (11:19). Jesus offers a lot of pointers here to those who will suffer the most for His name's sake. For it will be a dark chapter in the history of mankind when all the world turns against believers. He tells us to expect to be betrayed by false prophets, friends, and even our closest family members (Matthew 24:10-12; Mark 13:12; and Luke 21:16-17). Many of us will be put to death at this time.

5. The fifth sign is another worldwide phenomenon, but this one is very positive. "And this gospel of the kingdom will be preached in all the world as a witness to all the nations, and then the end will come" (Matthew 24:14). Perhaps it is the worldwide persecution of Christians that will finally show them the reality of the faith and the superiority of it in comparison to other faiths. But somehow in the midst of this worldwide torment, natural disasters, and war, the gospel will finally reach the ends of the earth.

6. The sixth sign is astronomical chaos. Jesus states in Luke 21:25-26 that "there will be signs in the sun, in the moon, and in the stars; and on the earth distress of nations, with perplexity, the sea and the waves roaring; men's hearts failing them from fear and the expectation of those things which are coming on the earth, for the powers of the heavens will be shaken." It seems that the character of this heavenly display will venture far beyond mere curiosity. It will after all cause the "distress of nations." So care must be taken not to assume that every small change in the atmosphere amounts to Armageddon. The devastation described here is apocalyptic. No one will remain unaware or unconvinced. It will be a global panic of unimaginable proportions.

7. The final sign, thank God, is the best. Jesus describes it so in Mark 13:26-27: "Then they will see the Son of Man coming in the clouds with great power and glory. And then He will send His angels, and gather together His elect from the four winds, from the farthest part of earth to the farthest part of heaven." What sweet relief—not only for now but for all eternity. During the final days of suffering believers are admonished to cheer up! "Now when these things begin to happen, look up and lift up your heads, because your redemption draws near" (Luke 21:28).

Mark (or Jesus in Mark) on the other hand admonishes us over and over again to be ready ("Watch and pray," verse 33; "keep watch," verse 35; and "watch," verse 37).

We have to stay on constant alert because it is as He said in the beginning: we don't know the day or the hour. I grew up in a Christian denomination where someone was always trying to predict the time when Jesus would return. A date would be set and the people would prepare. The date would pass and the people would return to their mediocrity. The whole point of what Jesus is saying is this: since we can't know the time, live as if it could happen today. Always be prepared. Always stay ready. We don't know the day, but we do know the signs. Jesus wants us to know these signs to keep us focused, aware, and not mislead.

Learn the parable of the fig tree and be informed about the last days. Memorize the seven signs so that you will never misunderstand or misread current events. False teachers and false prophets won't lead you astray because your information comes from the Master Himself. You will know and be fully assured of your salvation. You will never be surprised or caught off-guard. You will know to hold on to the end and therefore be saved. The generation that experiences these seven signs will not pass away until all is fulfilled.

Discussion Questions:

- According to Jesus, we can't know the day or hour He will return; but what can we know?
- Name as many of the seven signs as you can. (These are the signs that the end is near in terms of the return of Christ to subdue Earth.)
- Since we can't know the exact day or hour Christ will return, what is the best policy in terms of preparation?

Suggested Exercise:

- Memorize the seven signs that indicate Christ's return. Have each member of the discipleship group quote them from memory or recite them to at least one other disciple.

79

Remember Me

Matthew 26:26-30; Mark 14:22-26; Luke 22:17-20

And when he had taken bread and given thanks, He broke it and gave it to them, saying, "This is my body which is given for you; do this in remembrance of me." And in the same way He took the cup after they had eaten, saying, "This cup which is poured out for you is the new covenant in my blood" (Luke 22:19-20).

Commands of Christ: *Do this* in remembrance of me. *Take, eat*: this is my body. *Drink in*; all of you.

Perhaps this command from Jesus is what the Church needs to be reminded of the least. Thankfully, every Christian church, regardless of its affiliation, has some method of addressing this issue. Although all of Jesus's imperatives should be considered "ordinances," Communion, or the Eucharist, is the central ordinance for most of Christianity. It is considered the chief sacrament around the world. The term *eucharistia* is actually just the Greek word for "thanksgiving." And what word is more appropriate? For this observance is more about expressing our gratitude than anything else.

We do as He told us and "remember" him. We remember the extreme measures He was willing to take for us and thereby never question His great love for us. We recall with tears of appreciation His ultimate sacrifice, not just of one of our own but of God's own. Even in human terms we understand what Jesus meant when He said, "Greater love has no one than this, than to lay down one's life for his friends" (John 15:13). But just think of the additional fact that this man is also God in the flesh and now our amazement is exponentially higher. This one who sacrificed Himself for us is the Word of creation, by whom we all continue to exist. He who is the creator of the world knew beforehand what it would cost Him, yet He loved us so much that He created us anyway. What an amazing story and an amazing love. Who is worthy to even speak on these holy matters?

So we reticently approach this subject shoeless and prostrate. Sensing we are on holy ground, we carry on with fear and trembling. We are compelled to press onward having realized that these matters are not optional. But we are indeed commanded to give heed and to enter into this holy fellowship where only one of the participants is praiseworthy. We sit around the dinner table with Him and watch as He institutes what has been referred to as the Lord's Supper. We try the best we can to relive the disciple's experience. But we, like they, so often fail to grasp the significance of the occasion.

He says to them and to us, "Do this in remembrance of me." What are we to do? We are to take the bread and eat it, for this is His body that was broken for us. We remember as the bread is consumed that His body was ripped and torn and mutilated to provide healing and nourishment for our empty souls. As our jaws come crashing down on the remains, tears well up in our eyes and our emotions well up even more. It helps us remember the horrors of His passion, the lengths He was willing to go to in order to prove His love. In like manner we take the cup. It is much like the parallelism of Hebrew poetry, for we have the same theme repeated twice for emphasis but in a different fashion the second time. His body was destroyed and his blood was shed. These are two ways of saying the same thing: that He suffered and died for us. We are to take and eat, for this is His body. And lest we forget that message, it is repeated again in the cup as we drink in His offering. The offering is His blood, and the blood is His life; for the life is in the blood (Lev. 17:14; John 6:53). He gave His life for us. We should never forget it.

It is no wonder so much attention has been drawn to this sacred moment over time. Many theories have surfaced and some faiths have made this matter the whole of their purpose. Three major attempts have been made to put this holy matter into the proper perspective, and I doubt any of them are worthy of Him. Transubstantiation suggests that the words of Jesus in this passage are to be taken literally. In other words, at some point during the observance the bread actually does become His body and the wine becomes His blood. Consubstantiation is a lesser version of the same concept. It is saying that rather that transforming into the actual person of Christ, the presence of Christ is there in a special way. He is in, with, and through the elements, but the elements themselves do not change. Finally, there is the symbolic approach, which backs up one step further to say the bread and wine merely represent the body and blood of Christ. Jesus was fond of using metaphors and hyperbole, so it is not unlikely that He could have done so here as well. Regardless of how the matter is approached, it shows how it has become so important to us to have defined the very way we choose to worship.

But as is always the case, we should go back to the Lord Himself to keep everything in the proper perspective. After all, it is the things He said that we will answer to on judgment day, not our tendency to blow those things out of proportion. He said simply to practice this as a memorial to him. "For as often as you eat this bread and drink this cup, you show the Lord's death until He returns" (Corinthians 11:26). It is to us just as the Passover celebration is to Judaism. Why do they follow through with this ritual every year? One reason is so they will never forget what God had done for them. He did something remarkable and personal with them and them only. They should never forget that. To do so will cause irreparable damage to their relationship with God. So it is with Christianity. How can we forget Jesus's sacrifice? It must always be before our eyes and in our hearts. It must define our very relationship with God. It proves without a shadow of a doubt just how much He really does love all of humanity. Not only should we remember, we should allow that memory to launch us into action. The best way to say thank you for sacrifices He made for us is through sacrifices we continue to make for Him. That means not only showing reverence for the Eucharist imperatives but showing equal devotion for each and every other of the hundreds of commands He left us with.

Discussion Questions:

- Of all of Jesus's commands, why are we most familiar with this one?
- What does the term "Eucharist" mean? Why is it so appropriate?
- Why would God put Himself through such a grueling and agonizing death for us?

- How is the message of the bread and the cup a repeat of the facts for emphasis?
- What are the three most prominent theories regarding the bread and wine either becoming the body and blood or representing it? What does this tell you about the significance of this event for all of Christendom?
- What is the best way we can say thank you to Jesus?

Suggested Exercise:

- In this particular instance there is practically no need to offer suggestions on methods to memorialize the Lord's death, for it is widely practiced in our Communion services worldwide. The only thing we can do is try to think of any particular enhancement we could offer that would make the occasion more suitable to Jesus's liking. Discuss this among your fellow disciples. How can we make our current practice more pleasing to Jesus in terms of adherence to His expressed wishes on the matter?

80

Love the Way I Loved

John 13:34-35; 15:12, 17

A new commandment I give to you, that you love one another, even as I have loved you, that you also love one another. By this all men will know that you are my disciples, if you have love for one another (John 13:34-35).

Command of Christ: *Love one another* as I loved you.

Up until the night of His betrayal, the disciples were fussing and fighting for the position of greatest political advantage. They still expected a literal kingdom with literal thrones right up to the day of His arrest. They interpreted kingdom to mean rule and dominion over others and did not understand the concept of being a public servant. They wanted the fear, respect, and homage of men and even of their fellow disciples rather than the devotion that comes from a constituency that is greatly loved, cherished, and cared for, like a shepherd who watches over the sheep and knows them all by name. Rather than seeing one another as a brotherhood and as fellow disciples of the most loving teacher ever, they could only see one another as political rivals. Jesus saw their confusion and how they began to turn on one another, and it seemed the old adage "absolute power corrupts absolutely" had taken hold. It is only through the eyes of love that one's perspective of others can improve. Rather that thinking of how they can best serve you, you begin to consider how you can best serve them.

He needed to prepare them for His departure and make sure everything was in working order before He left. The first item on the agenda was love. He was about to demonstrate for them what His ministry was all about. To be his followers, they must also display those same values to one another. He said to them, "A new commandment I give to you, that you love one another; as I have loved you, that you also love one another. By this all will know that you are My disciples, if you have love for one another" (John 13:34-35). Instead of lusting for power and advantage over one another, we are called to serve one another out of love.

Jesus was known for something and it was not for overpowering individuals. It was showing love and compassion toward individuals and expecting that in return. It was his kindness that led them to repentance not fear of deadly reprisal. The only slavery that he inspired was that of the bond slave who loved his master so much that he wouldn't leave him even when offered the chance. He was as one author has stated, "a man for others." He didn't come to be served, but to serve and give his life a ransom for many (Mark 10:45). This is the perspective that the disciples where missing and what they desperately needed to catch up to before it was too late. For he would not always be around to referee and help keep the peace between them. People would recognize his disciples not by their lordship over, but love for each other.

We see this concept repeated again in John 15:12-17: "This is my commandment, that you love one another as I have loved you. Greater love has no one than this, than to lay down one's life for his friends. You are my friends if you do whatever I command you. No longer do I call you servants, for a servant does not know what his master is doing; but I have called you friends, for all things that I heard from my Father I have made known to you. You did not choose me, but I chose you and appointed you that you should go and bear fruit, and that your fruit should remain, that whatever you ask the Father in my name He may give you. These things I command you, that you love one another."

He sandwiches the teaching above with the principle of loving one another as fellow disciples; not only loving but loving the same way that He loved. What is the same way He loved? He leaves no question as to his intentions when He states that he will lay down His life for his friends. It is the type of love that causes you to be willing to lay down your life for someone. There is no greater love than that, for it is our very lives that we hold most dear. It is a selfless love that is willing to forsake one's own right to exist in favor of another's right to exist. We are to love like Jesus. Jesus loved unselfishly.

In John 15, Jesus focuses on three things that need to be in place in his absence. One is intimacy with Him. Two is faithfulness to His commands. Three is loving one another. He goes on and on about how keeping His command is a vital part of their relationship, and the command of all the commands is their obligation to love one another even more than they love themselves.

How can we be more like Jesus and learn to value another person's life more that our own? That is the question that the first disciples had to grapple with, and it remains our greatest challenge as true believers and disciples today. Blessed are the poor in spirit, for theirs is the kingdom of heaven (Matthew 5:3). Blessed are the meek, for they shall inherit the earth (Matthew 5:5). These are the attitudes that are essential to becoming the type of disciple that will change the world. May the Lord grant us heavenly grace to bring a blessed reality into what seems like an impossible dream.

Discussion Questions:

- Rather than seeing one another as a brotherhood and as fellow disciples of the most loving teacher ever, how did the disciples view one another?
- How was this fact a threat to the church Jesus wanted to found on self-sacrificial love?
- What was to be the distinguishing mark of those who are known as Jesus's disciples?
- What are three things that must be in place once Jesus is physically absent according to John 15:12-17?
- Is such a selfless love even possible to the point that you value another's right to exist more than your own? Provide an example.

Suggested Exercise:

- Have you ever loved someone so much that you would trade places with him or her on his or her death bed? Discuss what would have to take place to see your fellow disciples in the same light. Pray for a closer relationship with your fellow soldiers in Christ.

SECTION SIX:
Spiritual Adult

81

Don't Give Up

John 13:36-14:3, 14:27

Peace I leave with you; my peace I give to you; not as the world gives do I give to you. Do not let your heart be troubled, nor let it be fearful (John 14:27).

Commands of Christ: *Do not let* your heart be troubled, nor *let it be* fearful. *Trust* in God and *trust* in me.

Jesus is speaking to the disciples in heavenly terms but they are still interpreting everything in earthly terms. He said to them, "Where I am going you cannot come" (John 13:33). Naturally they would want to know where, since they were always with Him. And it seemed odd to them that He was speaking about going away somewhere where they couldn't follow along. So Peter asked, "where are you going?" (John 13:36) Again Jesus answered in a nonspecific way that required spiritual insight as well as picking up on the implications. He said, "Where I am going, you cannot follow now, but you will follow later" (John 13:36). Perhaps now He resorted to riddles since they could not handle the direct approach he had used before. As much as Jesus tried to warn them, they could not or were not willing to accept His death. But the destination He spoke of was in heaven with God the Father. They could not yet follow because it was not yet their time to face death. It was His demise that would finally force them to come to terms with what He had been saying all along.

Jesus knew this would be the greatest test of faith they had ever known, so He urged them not to give up once everything they had expected

439

came crashing down. Through their own denial their plans of rising to power only grew day by day so that when the bubble finally burst it was catastrophic. All their hopes and dreams were crucified with Him. They had no idea about what they were later to proclaim as the gospel: That it was necessary for Him to suffer and die to prepare the way for mankind to reconnect with God on a personal level. In light of this apparent reversal of fortune He tried to encourage them to stand firm. He dictated the following advice—in other words, things are going to get ugly so, trust me. "Trust in God and trust in me" (John 14:1); "Do not let your heart be troubled neither be afraid" (John 14:27). When your world turns upside down, know that I am still in control. Everything, believe it or not, is proceeding according to plan.

He was suggesting, once I leave you will have to learn to live by faith. Instead of rising to power now, you will earn the right through your faith to ascend your thrones at a later date of God's choosing. Trust me until we meet again, for you must now prove yourselves worthy of the rewards of the faithful. You have performed well with me by your side. Now let's see how well you can do on your own. Until then, I'll be constructing your mansions. In the meantime, love one another and keep my commands. Just like I have overcome the world by my Father's command, you will overcome the world by my command. The sacrifices you make now will pay off in heaven. Don't focus on the here and now, focus on the hereafter. You will also prevail in the end through the humiliation and suffering you endure now in my name. Fight the good fight to the end and never look back. The one who saves his life shall lose it, but whoever loses his life for Christ's sake shall save it.

How has your faith been tested lately? Don't be surprised when all you believe in comes crashing down and you end up holding on to Jesus for dear life. These things are necessary to prove you and refine you. In the end you will become a very productive disciple, as did the original disciples. That is why the trying of your faith is more precious than gold (1 Peter 1:7). Comfortable Christianity doesn't produce much, but under duress we find out who the true believers are, and it is those true believers who change the world.

Discussion Questions:

- What did Jesus mean by saying, "Where I am going you cannot come"?
- Why was it so hard for the disciples to understand that?
- In what way would they soon come to realized that the total upheaval of all their hopes and dreams meant that everything was going according to plan?
- In what way does renouncing ascendency to the throne in the present to live by humility and faith alone make one worthy of the throne Christ will provide in the future?
- In what way did Christ find it necessary to crucify their plans along with Him in order that they become more willing to accept His plans of worldwide evangelism and discipleship?
- How can we decrease so that He can increase in our lives?

Suggested Exercises:

- Name the fleshly desires that you have yet to renounce for the kingdom of God. What are you striving for in terms of creature comforts, power, and recognition that you are willing to confess and crucify for the sake of a better plan? Can you say with Paul, "I am crucified with Christ; and it is no longer I who live, but Christ lives in me; and the life which I now live in the flesh I live by faith in the Son of God who loved me and gave himself up for me" (Galatians 2:20)? Find a trusted disciple and confess your faults one on one, accepting prayer for deliverance.
- Name a time in your life when everything fell apart. Looking back on it, was it coincidence or part of God's plan to shake your world in order to realign your perspective and priorities toward the world to come? Share this testimony with the group.
- Write out a prayer expressing your current struggle and the belief that God will turn it all around for your good.

82

Trust in the Trinity

John 14:6-18

How can you say, "Show us the Father"? Do you not believe that I am in the Father, and the Father is in me? The words that I say to you I do not speak on my own initiative, but the Father abiding in me does His works. Believe me that I am in the Father and the Father is in me; otherwise believe because of the works themselves. Truly, truly, I say to you, he who believes in me, the works that I do, he will do also; and greater works than these he will do; because I go to the Father (John 14:9b-12).

Commands of Christ: *Believe me* that I am in the Father and the Father is in me; but if not, *believe* because of the works themselves.

There is such interconnectedness between the Father, Son, and Holy Spirit that it can be said that to receive one is to receive all three. And this is the mystery of the Trinity as Jesus begins to express it in the passage listed above. In John 14:6-8 you can see one person mentioned as being the other due to their union. To see one is to see the other (John 14:9). Sending the Holy Spirit is seen as a visit from the Son (John 14:17-18). As we see with Jesus's conversation with the disciples about this matter, it is not something that is easy to explain, it is just a fact that one has to deal with by faith. Many attempts have been made throughout the history of Christianity to get a handle on this issue but with no really satisfactory conclusion. When you attempt to communicate the nature of God in human terms, you will always come up short, for it is beyond our comprehension and capacity. We cannot speak authoritatively on a matter that we cannot look into objectively or scientifically. The nature of God must by definition be something of the highest complexity and beyond the reach of mortal man. Creation can scarcely understand itself, much less its creator.

Jesus alone could say what He said about the Father because He completely yielded to Him at all times. This special union never known by any other man is principally what made Jesus's humanity so unique. Unlike us, there was absolutely no sin to interfere with their relationship. There was no hindrance or cloudiness or uncertainty or distance. It was an open heaven in his spirit all the time. Their relationship was a perfect union, where humanity and deity lived in complete harmony (John 10:30). As such he was no longer His own man. He was completely possessed, but not unwillingly. He so identified with the purposes and plans and thoughts of God that they were His own. He could no longer distinguish between His will and that of the Father, for their wills were one. Seeing Him was like seeing the Father, for He no longer had his own identity. He had merged His identity with the Father's by preferring God over Himself. That's why He could confidently say, "If you had known me, you would have known my Father also; and from now on you have known Him and have seen Him" (John 14:7). He's saying that they are so one now you can't tell the difference between them.

For Phillip to follow that statement with "show us the Father" is really an insult. He had just told them that by seeing Him, they might as well be seeing the Father. So to ask for the Father is to disregard what Jesus had just revealed to them. Jesus was not just in agreement with the Father, he and the Father were one. He had so submitted to God that He had really ceased to exist as an individual. He wanted the disciples to see that fact. He wanted them to learn how to let go of everything and belong to Him, just as He had done with the Father. He wanted them to believe that He was in the Father and that the Father was in Him.

They needed to grasp the significance of that fact so they could repeat it upon His departure. After all, the context of this whole dialogue was the fact that He was soon leaving them. When that happened they would have to learn to connect to Him by faith, just as He had done while in the flesh with the Father. He goes on to say that to help with this process He would send them the Holy Spirit. Then at the end He said He would not leave them as orphans, but He will come to them. Again, receiving Him is receiving the Father, and receiving the Holy Spirit is receiving Him. The mystery of the Trinity is momentarily unveiled. He is speaking of those heavenly things that only the mature believer can consider. As the curtain of the holy of holies is slightly lifted the truths of the nature of God are presented before us as only flashes of light. We are left to deal with the ramifications of all Jesus said. We don't have full knowledge, but based on what He left us with, we can at least conclude that there are three persons and one substance. All three are God but not all three are the Father. That is the mystery of the Trinity. We are left to struggle with the reality that there are three and that somehow these three are one. We are commanded to believe this!

Believe it and then do everything you can to duplicate it in your relationship with Christ. Be one with Christ. This is not just for selfish reasons; the advancement of the kingdom depends on that union. For it is in that total surrender that becomes a solid connection that we become channels of His grace, just as He was the channel of God's grace. The reason we don't see as many miracles as before may be due to a weak connection with Christ. Right after expressing his divine union and mighty works, He insists that this supernatural ministry is continue on in His disciples as they unite with their risen Lord. Notice the connection in John 14:11-12: "Believe Me that I am in the Father and the Father in Me, or else believe Me for the sake of the works themselves. Most assuredly, I say to you, he who believes in Me, the works that I do he will do also; and greater works than these he will do, because I go to My Father." His connection leads to mighty works and so should ours. Soon after He says in John 15:4, "Abide in me and I in you." That is the union and intimacy level required for results. "If a man remains in me and I in him, he will bear much fruit" (John 15:5). He is the vine and we are the branches. We are interconnected to the point that His grace can be channeled through us into a hurting world. It can be said that the ministry of Christ continues on Earth through us. His love, generosity, compassion, power, and wisdom live on through us. When they see us, they continue to see Jesus to the extent we participate in His divine master plan.

So believe first of all that the Christ of humanity is interconnected to the God of eternity so that you can repeat that connection in your relationship with the heavenly Christ. The mighty works of Christ bear witness to His oneness with the Father, and so should our works bear witness to our connection with Christ. Improve your union and improve your ministry.

Discussion Questions:

- Jesus said that to see Him was to see the Father. What does that say about their complete union to the point of no longer being able to distinguish between the two? Nevertheless, did He ever claim to actually be the Father or just one with Him?
- As the only man to totally surrender to God to the point of no longer possessing a will of His own, it is understandable then how He could say He and the Father were one. That being the case, discuss how a request to see the Father would have been considered an insult to Christ.
- Jesus modeled oneness with the Father by faith because the disciples would be asked to reduplicate that experience with Christ once He left the earth. Explain how the disciples were to be sent by the Son in the same way that the Son was sent by the Father. Discuss how our oneness with Christ is just as important as Christ's oneness with the Father.
- If seeing Jesus was the same seeing the Father, is seeing you the same as seeing Jesus? If not, what changes need to be made in your life to achieve oneness with Christ?

Suggested Exercises:

- Address specific areas of self-will, pride, coveting, and ignorance that must change in order to lose your identity in Christ to the point that experiencing you is experiencing Him or seeing you is seeing Him.
  1. Ask yourself, who is actually making all the decisions in my life? Do I wait for the Lord's direction or assume it is solely up to me?
  2. Do I believe I have much to offer the kingdom of God or know that without Him I can do nothing?
  3. Do I crave power and recognition or do I hunger to serve?

4. Have I saturated myself in every word Jesus said to the point that it defines me, or is my contact with this material superficial?

5. Is my love for God and others found in self-denial, cross-carrying, and Christ-following, or the opposite?

Write out a personal inventory that includes examples of how you are either successful or lacking in each area. Swap this soul-searching information with a trusted fellow disciple for discussion, confession, and prayer.

83

Stay Connected

John 15:1-11

Abide in me, and I in you. As the branch cannot bear fruit of itself
unless it abides in the vine, so neither can you unless you abide in
me. I am the vine, you are the branches; he who abides in me and I
in him, he bears much fruit, for apart from me you can do nothing
(John 15:4-5).

Commands of Christ: *Stay* in me, and I in you. *Ask* for whatever you wish, and it will happen to you. *Remain* in my love.

We are like a neon light powerfully piercing the darkness and arresting the attention of all passersby as long as we stay plugged in to the electrical outlet. All of that raw energy inside us that is causing us to glow so vividly is immediately blackened once the switch is flipped and the source is quenched. In connection to the previous lesson it is that union with Christ that He exemplified with the Father that has to continue to be maintained between us and our Lord.

Jesus clarified that in no uncertain terms in John 15:1-11: "I am the true vine, and my Father is the vinedresser. Every branch in me that does not bear fruit He takes away; and every branch that bears fruit He prunes, that it may bear more fruit. You are already clean because of the word which I have spoken to you. Abide in me, and I in you. As the branch cannot bear fruit of itself, unless it abides in the vine, neither can you, unless you abide in me. I am the vine, you are the branches. He who abides in me, and I in him, bears much fruit; for without me you can do

447

nothing. If anyone does not abide in me, he is cast out as a branch and is withered; and they gather them and throw them into the fire, and they are burned. If you abide in me, and my words abide in you, you will ask what you desire, and it shall be done for you. By this my Father is glorified, that you bear much fruit; so you will be my disciples. As the Father loved me, I also have loved you; abide in my love. If you keep my commandments, you will abide in my love, just as I have kept my Father's commandments and abide in His love. These things I have spoken to you, that my joy may remain in you, and that your joy may be full."

Jesus uses the ordinary patterns of nature to illustrate for us what is expected and what is essential to our success in the kingdom of God. He names the major characters in the plot as the vine, branches, and farmer. God is the one who has planted the vineyard; He is the farmer who acts as the vinedresser in this particular aspect of his garden. The bottom line for the owner of the vineyard is produce. Without produce there can be no profit. More produce results in a larger profit. He is interested in getting the most out of His vineyard. There is an interconnection of purpose between the vinedresser the vine and the branches. Jesus identifies himself as the vine. It is just as He described while here on Earth. The vine has no mind of its own; it simply responds as a vine normally responds once stimulated to produce. The farmer plants a vine and expects that the vine will do what it was designed for as long as he takes good care of it.

We are the branches and we are branching out of the vine, or Christ. We are seen as a natural extension of him. As the nutrients flow from the vine and through the branches of the vine, fruit begins to appear. The vine relies on the vinedresser and the branches rely on the vine. But when seen as a whole, the entire process relies on the Father. It is expected that as long as the farmer does his part, the plant will always produce. That is the natural order of things and it always occurs this way. If there is no product, then the plant is perceived as an oddity and must be done away with. It is seen as a useless item that should be replaced so that more fruit can be harvested instead of wasting the valuable space.

So knowing the expectations of God, Jesus sets in motion a failsafe plan. This plan will ensure that we don't fail God and end up discarded in a trash heap. He knows who He is. He is the true vine. He is the type of vine that will produce bountifully every time. So since that is the case, the best way to guarantee success is to stay connected to him.

Unlike the usual system where a branch naturally stays connected, we do have a mind of our own. Even though it should be considered totally odd and a freak of nature, we have the ability to detach ourselves from Him. The moment we do, our light goes out; for it is not us who bear the vine, the vine bears us. Jesus commands us not to do that. We are not to fly off the handle and chase our own ideas and ambitions. We are to always remain in the mode of servant and follower and never take on an air of leadership or independence. This is not a democracy. It is and will always be a monarchy. Ideas such as thinking for ourselves and making our own way are foreign and end up causing the course of nature to end up mangled, deformed, and even detached from the life-giving source. As such we will shrivel up and die and will end up serving another purpose: mainly as dried-up twigs for the fire.

Instead, we are to go with the flow. In the natural order of things we are in Christ and Christ is in us and this allows God's grace to channel through. Then we get to enjoy all of the results of that as we see miracles all around us. It almost seems to us that we are the ones accomplishing something. But we know down deep inside that it is only due to our connection with Jesus. Unlike real branches we do have a mind of our own. But we are to keep that mind and will one with His mind and will. This is not difficult because we love Him with all our hearts and want to share in His work and become part of His solution for the world.

And that leads us to the next command, namely, "Remain in my love." It is not about producing for a harsh taskmaster who does not care for us or who only cares for His own well-being. To remain in Him we have to stay in love with Him. It is a relationship that drives everything in God's system, not an earning of His distant approval. He already proved His love for us by paying the ultimate sacrifice. Now it is our turn to prove our love for Him!

How do we do that? Just like He had a life to give, we also have one to give. We can choose whether or not we will keep it for ourselves or lay it down for Him and others. He lets us choose. But we know what He wants us to choose. He wants us to choose Him, the true vine. He is the best choice for this world. But we have to believe that first, before we will be willing to step out in faith. Then, based on our faith and love commitment to Jesus we eagerly search out any way possible to make the Lord happy. He doesn't leave us in the dark as to how to achieve that, for Christ states that it is in the keeping of His commandments that He will know that we love Him. And this show of love will lead also to further affection from the Lord. It is the method Christ used while on Earth to stay in his Father's love and it will likewise be our method of staying in Christ's love. Our love leads to our submission, and our submission leads to the Master's love. This is how we change the world through Christ. It all stems forth from a love relationship.

Have you ever withheld something from your children due to their disobedience? I'm sure this is the regular state of affairs for every parent. It is the same in our relationship with our Father in heaven. But the reverse is also true. It is the obedient child who receives the praise and positive reinforcement. So Jesus follows the command to stay obedient with the command to *ask whatever we wish*. After all, our Father is not like earthly fathers who are limited in their resources. He has no limitations. So Jesus can confidently say, "Ask for whatever you wish and it will happen to you!" Our obedience leads to His affection. His affection leads to our being well cared for and well provided for. Nothing can be out of the reach for those who are one with Christ. For union with Christ is interconnectedness with all of the powers of the universe. The only thing that limits us is the level of our independent thinking whereby we find ourselves disconnected.

Every church body and Christian organization takes it for granted that they are Christ-centered. It is a popular expression today. But have we ever really asked ourselves what that means? Have we then followed that up with a plan to ensure it stays that way? How can we be Christ-centered when we don't even know much less attend to Christ's commands? He says to us today as he did in his day, "Why do you call me 'Lord, Lord' and do not those things which I say?" (Luke 6:46) Do we think that union with Christ is automatic and permanent once we are saved? Evidence shows this to be the case. For while 80 percent of Americans claim Christianity, only 2 percent of churchgoers ever share their faith. Equally small percentages ever have a quiet time with the Lord in the word and prayer. Unwed pregnancies and divorce rates are just as prominent in the Church as anywhere else.

Ours is a passive and corrupt version of Christianity. Christ commands us to abide in Him and in His love not because it is easy to do but because it is difficult and requires undivided attention and effort. Remember, the Lord's work on the cross may be finished, but ours has just begun. It is totally up to us now what we will make of our Christian lives. It all starts with love and intimacy. Reconnecting with Christ on a personal level will guarantee results because He is the true vine.

Discussion Questions:

- Comparing your life to a storefront, would you say you are "well lit with the open sign glaring," or is it "dark, empty, and deserted with a small flickering light in the background"?
- What is the Vinedresser interested in, bottom line?
- How is this fact manifested in the elimination of unproductive branches?
- Are we saved to sit or saved to produce?
- How is this fruitfulness guaranteed?
- Is it safe to say that a growing relationship with Christ produces results?
- Is it safe to say that a poor relationship with Christ could end up in eternal judgment?
- Is that positive relationship automatic? Does the Church today act as if it was?
- What specific way does Jesus offer to maintain a positive loving relationship with Him?
- What is the biggest hindrance to union with Christ?
- What is the biggest hindrance to a loving relationship with Christ?

Suggested Exercises:

- Score yourself on a scale of one to ten, with one being the lowest and ten the highest, in the following categories. Share your results with a trusted fellow disciple and pray together for greater devotion to the Lord.
  o Since I was saved I have become active for the kingdom of God.
  o Since I was saved I have continued to focus on union with Christ through yielding my life over to His will. I die daily in an effort to lose my identity in Him.
  o To see me is to see the Lord, because I have lost myself in Him.

451

o   I don't accept sin as a fact of life; I aggressively attack sin in my life so that nothing will interfere with my connection to Christ and the flow of His Spirit through me to others.

o   One of the ways I am one with Christ is by the way I memorize His every word. There is no subject that comes up that I am not aware of His opinion of it.

o   I take Christ's commands seriously. I know how many there are, and I am constantly working on how best to obey each one. I have committed my life to adhering to them and helping other Christians know, love, and keep them.

o   My relationship with Christ is strong because I don't just call him Lord but do what He says as it is written in the gospel records.

o   My performance for Christ is based on my love and admiration for Him as my Savior and Lord and not as some slavish bondage to salvation by works.

84

Expect Danger

John 15:18, 16:1-4

These things I have spoken to you so that you may be kept from stumbling. They will make you outcasts from the synagogue, but an hour is coming for everyone who kills you to think that he is offering service to God. These things they will do because they have not known the Father or me. But these things I have spoken to you, so that when their hour comes, you may remember that I told you of them. These things I did not say to you at the beginning, because I was with you (John 16:1-4).

Command of Christ: *Remember* the word that I said to you.

The whole point of this passage is to prepare the disciples for the rough road ahead. Most of the time when persecution comes we get discouraged and wonder what is happening. Knowing that it is only because of our faithfulness to Christ strengthens us in the time of trial. Then we know that it is not due to our failures but our successes that we are being targeted. Jesus knows that suffering is ahead for His disciples for they must carry on His ministry. It is His ministry that kept being attacked in His day and it is His ministry that continues to be attacked today. He speaks of Himself as one with the Father. He states that when He is attacked it is the Father being attacked. When He is hated it is the Father being hated. And when we, his disciples, are hated, it is really Christ who is being hated.

Jesus states that we would not be hated if we were one with the world. But because we are one with Him, we must continue to suffer

His fate. The world continues to reject the righteousness of Christ for their own preference of the lust of the flesh, eyes, and the pride of life (1 John 2:16). We who are poor, mournful, meek, righteous, merciful, pure, and peaceful cause people to feel guilty about their own lack of these qualities. This results in our persecution. We pose a threat to their self-indulgent philosophy of life. We are to *remember* that He said to us, "No servant is greater than his master." This will bring us comfort in our hour of resistance. If we expect it and know the reason for it, we won't be as disheartened. It might even have the opposite effect on us. Like the early Church, we could find ourselves instead wearing persecution as a badge of honor (Acts 5:41).

So what exactly are we in for? First is the hatred from the world, which was mentioned earlier. We don't join in with them, we don't engage in their barroom, dance-club mentality. We therefore easily end up as the odd man out. I recall one evening when I was in restaurant management when the supervisor took all of us managers out to eat. Within a few minutes I found myself standing out like a sore thumb because every one of them made their way to the bar for a drink. These types of situations continually arise and expose us as being very different indeed from the average bear. Another oddity is the way we don't strive for wealth so much. Everyone around us is killing themselves to get ahead. They are all in competition to see who can have the highest standard of living. We live in the one-third of the world's population that is consuming two-thirds of the world's recourses. The bumper sticker for this generation is: "He who dies with the most toys, wins." The philosophy of the world is, "Get all you can, can all you get, and sit on your can." But true believers don't believe that. Instead, they are content with what they have and are storing up treasure in heaven. Our Master told us that you cannot serve both God and riches. We are simply not captivated by the rat race.

What else can we expect in terms of danger? Well, it unfortunately appears as if the Church can be even more dangerous than the world. It was the religious system and leadership of Jesus's day that was most hostile and posed the greatest threat to his safety. Jesus said that they will toss His disciples out of the synagogue. This was the Church of Jesus's day. And it is the Church of our day that can also be the most resistant to change. We have become so much a part of the culture now that one can scarcely tell the difference between us. As such, the Church has now, for all intents and purposes become the world and therefore the same hatred applies.

But the thing about religion that is so heinous is the fact that one can justify one's brutality in the name of God. Once you spiritualize your malice, it seems to you as an act of bravery and religious devotion. Just look at the disaster of 9/11. These were not acts of crime for selfish gain, they were perceived by the perpetrators as holy sacrifices in the work of God. Jesus predicts that this will happen to us as well. He says, "A time is coming when anyone who kills you will think he is offering a service to God" (John 16:2). Even the worst sinner can see his wrongs, but the religious sinner will never see his wrongs for they are disguised as a sacred offering. This is why Jesus told the Pharisees that even though the harlots and the tax collectors were coming to him, they never would, but would die in their sins. There is no blindness so heavy and impenetrable than religious pride.

So expect danger and even death; Jesus said, "but you also must testify, for you have been with me from the beginning." The Greek word for *testify* is where we get the word "martyr." And it is the following verse after mentioning the word "testify" (John 15:27) that Jesus mentions the possibility of our being killed. But we are not to fear those who can destroy the body, for God can destroy body and soul. In the end it is the loss of life that provides the most convincing of all testimonies as to the reality of the cause of Christ. It was the martyrs among the Christians during the early days of the Roman Empire that caused Christianity to soar to the highest level of impact on society ever. In the end it was not the Roman Empire that prevailed but Christianity. It is the mechanism by which the Roman Empire would eventually give way to the Holy Roman Empire in the unfolding of world history. Death is not defeat for Christians, just as it was not defeat for Christ himself. Rather it is a seed that will keep multiplying until it has overrun the entire earth.

There is a perilous side to following Jesus. But thankfully the other side of Jesus's ministry will be ours as well. Just as they kept His word they will keep ours. The joy of making disciples in the midst of all the chaos will bring us untold satisfaction. The delight of ministry is invigorating. However, the bottom line is this: we are not on a picnic with Christ. No, the truth is we have entered into a life-and-death struggle between good and evil. We are now on the front lines of the battle. This is not a time of peace but of war. The lives we live must reflect the danger we are in. We are to endure hardness as a good soldier of Jesus Christ (2 Timothy

2:3). But we know that we will win in the end and that every sacrifice, no matter how small, will be greatly rewarded in this all-out war effort.

We will be the heroes of our faith should we prevail. But should that be the case we will gladly cast our crowns at the Master's feet, for it is He alone who has caused us to triumph. So we must keep our heads up and fight valiantly, keeping in mind what the disciple who walked on the water said: "Beloved, think it not strange concerning the fiery trial which is to try you, as though some strange thing happened unto you: But rejoice, inasmuch as you are partakers of Christ's sufferings; that, when his glory shall be revealed, you may be glad also with exceeding joy" (1 Peter 4:12-13). Don't expect peaceful conditions in a time of war. Instead, fight courageously for a brighter tomorrow.

Discussion Questions:

- How do we know that faithfulness to Jesus's ideals, principles, and lifestyle means the road ahead will be hazardous?
- How is it possible to take persecution as a compliment?
- How does our eightfold character development process as enumerated in the Beatitudes (acquiring the mind of Christ) put us on a collision course with the self-indulgent lifestyle and philosophy of the world?
- Can you think of some examples where you stuck out like a sore thumb in the world because of your high standards?
- What makes religious persecution so heinous and practically impossible to turn around?
- What do the words "testimony" and "martyr" have in common?
- Explain this statement: "Death is not defeat for Christians, just as it was not defeat for Christ himself. But rather, it is a seed that will keep multiplying until it has overrun the entire earth."
- If becoming a disciple also means "we have entered into a life and death struggle between good and evil," why do we expect a life free of any conflict?
- What scriptural passages come to mind that demonstrate our Christian life is a lot like entering into a military conflict?

Suggested Exercises:

- Interview a military commander on this subject: The Best Way to Prepare for Battle.
  Meet with your accountability partner/ trusted disciple or a group of disciples and determine how best to apply those military strategies to your Christian life. How can the true disciple best prepare for the spiritual/physical warfare that inevitably lies ahead?

85

Prepare for a Life of Faith

John 16:23-28, 33

*In that day you will ask in my name, and I do not say to you that
I will request of the Father on your behalf; for the Father Himself
loves you, because you have loved me and have believed that I came
for the from the Father. I came forth from the Father and have
come into the world; I am leaving the world again and going to
the Father* (John 16:26-28).

Commands of Christ: *Ask* and you will receive that your joy may be full.
But *take heart*; I have overcome the world.

The spiritual walk that we live every day was about to become the common
experience of the disciples. They would soon have to learn how to live by
faith and not by sight. For three or so years they had lived by sight. They
had felt, heard, and seen all His miraculous words and deeds. But now
Jesus was addressing them in an odd way, saying, "In a little while you
will see me no more, and then after a little while you will see me." They
were dumbfounded by this statement because they still had no idea he
was about to die on the cross. In their theology, Messiah and crucifixion
did not mix. No matter how much Jesus tried to speak plainly to them,
they didn't have the ears to hear it. So again He spoke to them in vague
terminology. Yet even so, it is only with hindsight that we can understand
exactly what he meant. After all, it is the way we live as Christians today,
never having experienced the delight of walking with Him in the flesh.
When we need something we ask the Father in His name. And this is

what Jesus was encouraging them to do. He was preparing them for the time that he would no longer be visible to the naked eye. Now they would have to ask through prayer rather than in person to have their needs met. He puts it this way: "In that day you will no longer ask me anything. I tell you the truth, my Father will give you whatever you ask in my name. Until now you have not asked for anything in my name. Ask and you will receive, that your joy may be full" (John 16:23-24).

In essence, Jesus is saying something like this: "Look, I'm not going to be around anymore for you to ask for things. From now on you will ask in prayer when you have a need. Pray to God in my name and you will get what you need. Your joy will be full because you will realize that our relationship has not ended, it has just taken on a new dimension. I am still with you in spirit and it is my name that guarantees success. Instead of interacting with me in person, it will be prayer that you will rely on to keep our companionship alive. This is the only medium I will leave you with to keep connected to me other than the words and commands I have taught you." In another place he promises not to leave them all alone like orphans. I'm sure that after knowing him for so long, his departure would have felt a lot like being abandoned.

This is why he promises to replace Himself with a mighty force in the third Person of the Trinity. Once He is gone they will need a considerable amount of comfort and encouragement to fill that huge vacuum He leaves behind. That is why He says He will send them the *Paraclete* (in the original Greek). *Paraklēsis* has been translated as "Comforter" and "Encourager" in different versions because it means "one who is called alongside to support, encourage, and guide." He is basically saying the Holy Spirit will be sent to you to take over where He has left off.

There were three dimensions to His role on Earth:

1. He was in complete surrender to the heavenly directive. Jesus stated that the Holy Spirit, just like Him, "would not speak on His own; He will speak only what he hears" (John 16:13).
2. He would be the channel for direct communication with God, as stated in John 16:14-15: "He will bring glory to me by taking from what is mine and making it known to you. All that belongs to the Father is mine."
3. He would encourage and guide believers (John 14:15-18).

So He is not leaving them stranded. He is encouraging them to live a life of faith based on prayer and scripture. He is leaving them with a special Guest and Guide in the Holy Spirit, so there is no way they can get discouraged. Direct contact with God is still a possibility due to the arrangement He has prepared for us. But we must choose to tap into this resource and stay connected to it.

Finally, even with all this support, He knows living in this world is not easy. He wants to encourage them before He leaves. He says, in essence, "I have told you these things so that in me you may have peace. In this world you will have trouble. But take heart! I have overcome the world." We don't have to be down or depressed; instead, He orders us to take heart! Get up, go out, and face the world with hope and energy because it can be done! Be of good cheer! We can do it with Christ! Christ Himself is cheering us on!

Discussion Questions:

- What sort of life was Jesus preparing the first disciples to live by that our generation of believers has always lived by?
- What will cause the disciples to finally joyfully realize that just because Jesus has returned to the Father doesn't mean their relationship with Him has ended?
- Who will Jesus send to fill that void that will be left in His absence?
- What three general areas will the Holy Spirit specialize in according to John 16:13-15 and John 14:15-18?
- How does John 16:33 cheer us up as we deal with the harsh realities of life?

Suggested Exercises:

- Share with a trusted fellow disciple (or disciples) the following:
  o Name a time your joy was full because you turned to the Lord by faith and He answered your prayers.
  o Explain how answered prayer and knowledge of the overcoming power of Christ helps you "be of good cheer" regardless of the tribulations that come your way.
  o If you've never experienced the above scenarios, pray together for the courage to move forward.

86

Stay Prayed Up

Matthew 26:36-46; Mark 14:32-42; Luke 22:39-46; John 18:1

So, you could not keep watch with me for one hour? Keep watching and praying that you may not enter into temptation; the spirit is willing, but the flesh is weak (Matthew 26:40-41).

Commands of Christ: *Sit here* while I go over there and pray. *Remain here* and *watch* with me. *Keep watching and praying* lest you enter into temptation.

The context is the garden of Gethsemane and the very night of his betrayal. The disciples still seemed to have no clue as to what was on the horizon. But Jesus knew everything that was about to happen all too well, and it was tearing Him apart. He stated to them, "My soul is overwhelmed with sorrow to the point of death!" Having entered His greatest hour of need, this would be the time to turn to your most trusted friends. Yet it seemed to them a trivial matter and they were ready to call it a night. Perhaps they dismissed this false alarm as just another teaching device to make a point they were too tired to consider. Jesus anxiously prepared as best as He knew how for His impending doom. He turned to the Father in prayer. He was seen going back and forth, back and forth, nervously trying to organize the disciples for the maximum advantage.

First He sat the company down while He went off to pray alone. But he still would appreciate the comfort of his closest companions. Surely Peter, James, and John could provide the encouragement He needed in this troubled state. While the others sat a good distance away, these three

461

remained perhaps only a stone's throw from Him as he sat alone with God. He was hoping they could also support Him with prayers of their own to the Father. He commanded them to "watch" with Him, which really means to stay alert and prayerful. He returned some time later to find them dosing off—far from alert and prayerful. He groaned with mental anguish and dismay as He found that even in His greatest hour of distress His disciples are no more able to rise to the occasion than before. They couldn't even handle the easiest and lightest duty of one hour's prayer support. He just wanted to know someone was with Him, that He wasn't alone, that He didn't have to face this thing by Himself, that at least there were a few close friends He could turn to for support. That wasn't asking too much, was it? But for these oblivious few, it was indeed beyond them. Everything He had been saying all along seemed as meaningless chatter, and so it was still, they knew not the purpose for which they had been summoned to watch and pray.

So it was that upon His return He found them sleeping. He wondered aloud why they couldn't even provide one hour support for Him in his hour of need. All He wanted was a little prayer support and He couldn't even get that. He saw in them a dangerous precedent that would make them vulnerable to the enemy. They were neither aware nor prayerful. Their spirituality seemed shallow, and it was a wonder He didn't give up on them. But He concluded that their spirits were indeed willing but their flesh was weak.

As it turned out they wound up sleeping themselves right into a brick wall. Suddenly they were attacked and did as Jesus predicted and "entered into temptation." They fell victim to the enemy's assault. They all ended up fleeing the Master. They left Him stranded to save their own necks. But even then He never gave up on them. That is a great source of hope and encouragement for the rest of us.

What lessons can we learn from this episode? First is Jesus's example of turning to prayer in His hour of need. He was initially overwhelmed with distress, but it was in His prayer hour that He found the strength to carry on. But notice the command to "sit here." The reason for this command was so that He could get alone with God. Jesus made it a regular habit of finding time with God and doing it in solitude. We too must remove every distraction and allow the Lord our undivided attention. I hear many people excuse their poor prayer habits by insisting they pray to God constantly throughout the day. But the practice of praying without ceasing, though it is a good practice, is not undivided. It is divided prayer. Jesus taught us that in addition to that we need to give our undivided attention to prayer.

Secondly, He asks a few of them for prayer support. It is also a good practice to employ prayer warriors on your behalf. Prayer warriors are mature individuals who are used to spending a good amount of time alone with God. They can be relied on to at least be willing to spend hours at a time in prayer. One hour was the amount of time expected by Jesus for his disciples. How about you? Does that seem like an impossible achievement? If so, then begin in fifteen minute intervals until you work your way from thirty to forty-five and then arrive comfortably at one hour a day. It is the only way to stay alert (watch) with God's plan and timing for your life.

Thirdly, He mentions that it is this watching and praying that will keep you from succumbing to temptation. The reason the hedonistic culture of our times has crept in and taken over the Church is due to our lack of prayer. The church is no longer a "house of prayer." It is more like a house of sermons or lip service. The same is true for our individual lives. We too will fall victim to this wicked and adulterous generation if we don't purge and protect ourselves daily through long periods of solitude and prayer. Jesus said we are to daily pray, to "forgive us our debts as we forgive our debtors." Our relationships with others will only survive through forgiveness, and our righteousness will only survive through confession and repentance. Those who hunger and thirst after righteousness will be filled and the pure in heart will see God. Purity of heart is possible and must be maintained in order to sustain a healthy relationship with God. Don't believe the lie of the Devil that says "we will never be more than a sinner." There is no sin that Christ is unable to help us overcome (2 Peter 1:2-4; 2 Timothy 2:19). Instead of settling for mediocrity, we should strive toward perfection (Hebrews 6:1). We have a race to win (Hebrews 12:1). Through prayer we achieve a holy life and through prayer we overcome every challenge.

Discussion Questions:

- Did Jesus have the disciples hold hands in a circle and pray together or did He separate them into groups to pray while He prayed alone?

- Why did Jesus have eight disciples sit down in one place and take three others with Him a little farther only to leave them and go a little farther Himself?
- What does this incident teach us about corporate versus private prayer? Do we place perhaps too much value on public prayer and too little value on private prayer?
- Why do people try to excuse themselves from a daily private prayer hour by suggesting that they stay in an attitude of prayer throughout the day?
- What did Jesus expect from His three closest companions at this point of distress?
- When He found the disciples asleep, what was Jesus's merciful conclusion?
- How did Jesus's deep and abiding prayer life prepare Him to stand firm in the face of adversity?
- How did the disciples' superficial prayer life leave them vulnerable to an attack that would scatter them abroad?
- Do we have to repeat the disciples' mistakes to learn or can we not learn from their failures and avoid making the same mistakes?
- Has the Church become a house of hypocrisy rather than a house of prayer due to the fact that a lack of prayer has caused it to "fall into temptation," as Jesus warned?

Suggested Exercise:

- Schedule an hour-long private prayer time into your daily routine. Share that plan with a trusted disciple. Make sure that it is uninterrupted prayer and not a Bible reading or devotional plan, which should be done separately. Sometimes the enemy tricks us into thinking our devotional time is prayer time when it really consists more of reading and reflecting than actual talking and listening to God.
- Suggested principles to make the most of your prayer hour:
  - If you are not accustomed to praying for an hour at a time, begin with fifteen minutes and work your way up to an hour at fifteen minute intervals every three months over a year's time.

o Make sure it is a quiet place where there will be no interruptions or distractions.

o Pray and meditate slowly and carefully on the Lord's Prayer to help your prayers to begin heading in the right direction.

o Pray and meditate slowly and carefully on the Beatitudes (from memory) to keep your prayer focused on changing you rather than judging and changing others.

o Keep a listening log so your prayer can focus not only on what you want to say to the Lord but hearing what the Lord wants to say to you. In the log write down only what you feel He said to you during your prayer hour, not what you said.

o Share your log with a trusted mentor/disciple for further guidance and growth.

87

Do Not Resort to Violence

Matthew 26:47-56; Mark 14:43-52; Luke 22:47-53; John 18:2-12

Put your sword back into its place; for all those who take up the sword shall perish by the sword. Or do you think that I cannot appeal to my Father, and He will at once put at my disposal more than twelve legions of angels? How then will the scriptures be fulfilled, which say that it must happen this way? (Matthew 26:52-54)

Commands of Christ: *Put away* the sword in its sheath. *Let it be.*

Well, the moment for Jesus's betrayal and arrest had finally come. After Jesus had wrestled through His fears in prayer and was strengthened to face His accusers, here they came with clubs, swords, lanterns, and torches. Perhaps even more painful than the nails of the cross was the nail piercing his heart as one of His own disciples betrayed Him with a kiss into the hands of sinners. It is recorded that this band of soldiers was sent by the chief priests, elders, and Pharisees.

Perhaps it was Peter's lack of watching and praying that found him totally out of sync with God's will for the moment. It was not a time to fight and to wield a sword in Jesus's defense. It was Jesus's time to lay down His life. At one instant Peter is lunging at Christ's opponents and slicing off an ear (perhaps in an attempt to take off the man's head). In the next instant they are all running for cover. What is the difference in the two states of mind presented in the gospel records? Well, maybe it was due to the fact that it appeared at first like just another standoff between Jesus and his opponents that would end up in His favor again as He outwitted and outmaneuvered them.

But this time Jesus openly concedes that it is time for Him to suffer. Having never seen Him at a loss under any circumstance, it must have been frightening indeed. Suddenly their lives were also in danger. Again Jesus is forced to face His hardships alone, without a friend in sight.

Still yet Jesus is the teacher. But what command is issued forth even in the midst of this upheaval? Under the greatest duress as well as the most serene environs Christ is always the same. He finds the presence of mind to scold the lead disciple all the while being readied for the kill. He strongly reacts to Peter's overreaction of violence. He demands that he "put away the sword in the sheath."

Peter is perhaps once again thinking in political terms. He always wants to be the first to step out in faith for Christ. He doesn't want to live a quiet and cowardly life in relation to the Master. He wants to show Him that he believes. That he is not like the others, he has faith in the Master that Christ will prevail in every test. But he guessed wrong this time. There would be no miraculous escape; for it is as Jesus was trying to explain, that He must suffer and die.

Again Peter finds himself on the wrong side of the equation in his zeal. In fighting for the life of Christ he was fighting against his crucifixion. This is also what Satan was fighting against. Again Jesus has to say to him in a sense, "get behind me, Satan." Peter still does not have in mind the things of God but of man. He is still thinking politically (although it is in the guise of a loyal subject) and by what means no doubt he can keep the upper hand over the others. With this demonstration of valor, how can he not remain as the greatest among all the disciples?

Even now Jesus refused to waste a teachable moment. He was more concerned for their character than His own safety. He lectured Peter with the wisdom of the ages by saying that "all who draw the sword will die by the sword" (Matthew 26:52). By saying so He is instructing him to reconsider the path he has begun to take, for it will certainly have a deadly end. Peter had forgotten the previous teaching to never resist the evil person (Matthew 5:39). He had also failed to realize that his feeble attempt was nothing compared to the firepower Jesus already possessed. He had no decrease in His powers at this time; He simply refused to resort to them in His own defense. It was not time to defend Himself anymore. It was time to offer Himself as a sacrifice for the sins of the world.

So the third point of the lecture to Peter is about the necessity of His demise in order that the scriptures may be fulfilled. He had already explained before in public that once He is lifted up (hanging on the cross) He will draw all men unto Himself. This is all part of God's plan. It is the solution. He is not going to overpower the world as most believers thought about the Messiah, but He is going to allow the world to overpower Him. And this investment will be like a seed that keeps multiplying until it recovers the entire earth.

So as Luke records in 22:51: "Let it be!" Don't fight it. This was meant to be; for in this one act of self sacrifice the world will never forget just how much God loves it. "God so loved the world that He gave His only Son, that whosoever believes in him should not perish but shall have everlasting life" (John 3:16). This is the loving act that has captured the hearts and imaginations of all mankind. It was not His supernatural powers that drew us to Him but His willingness to give all of that up to identify with us in every way as human beings. To do what He didn't have to do. To pay a debt He didn't owe. "The way, as personalized in Jesus, was the way of suffering and triumph through humiliation" (New Bible Commentary).

How about you? Have you been tempted to resort to violence in fighting for the kingdom of God? Perhaps the Crusades (1095-1291) are an example in Christian history of a time when this was done. To save Israel from being overrun with Muslims, Christians entered into a bloody struggle to claim the Holy Land for Christ. Unfortunately, this has given Christianity a bad name because this sort of violence would have never been sanctioned by Christ. Is there such a thing as a "holy war"? Perhaps that was so in the Old Testament when the people of God were instructed to possess the land. But now our kingdom is within. There is no need to fight over religious lands. When Christ returns He will do all the fighting for us. Both Mahatma Gandhi and Martin Luther King Jr. provide historical examples of how one can use Jesus's methods to win the victory. Violence and true Christianity just don't mix.

The whole point of Christianity is that even though He had the power to do so, God never forced anyone to believe. He quietly allows each person to decide and respects that decision. For the ability to reason and to come to our own conclusion is the very part of us that best reflects the image of God. It is the way of peaceful protest and character development that best mirrors the image of Christ. "Who, when he was reviled, reviled not again; when he suffered, he threatened not; but committed himself to him that judges righteously" (1 Peter 2:23). Jesus used reasonable persuasion, and when He was rejected He gave it to God. "And a servant of the Lord must not quarrel but be gentle to all, able to teach, patient, in humility correcting those who are in opposition, if God perhaps will grant them repentance, so that they may know the truth" (2 Timothy 2:24-25).

Discussion Questions:

- What was one of the reasons Jesus was ready to face His death but Peter was not?
- What explains the sudden shift in Peter from crusader to coward?
- Explain how Jesus command to "put away the sword" meant that rather than fighting a heroic battle on Jesus's behalf Peter was actually fighting with Satan against God's plan.
- Did Peter once again (see Matthew 16:23) have the things of God or man in mind by making this move?
- In Peter's defense, he was at least willing to believe that Jesus could never be taken unwillingly. By fighting for Jesus, he was saying, "I believe as the Son of God, that Jesus, is invincible." Hadn't Jesus had mentioned earlier that the disciples would now need to add a sword to their list of basic necessities as disciples? Agree or disagree?
- How did this scene in the garden of Gethsemane help crystallize the fact that Christianity is not to be a religion of the sword?
- What other scriptures come to mind to support this concept?

Suggested Exercises:

- Determine together to never become part of any organization that tries to spread the gospel by force. Discuss the Great Commission with your fellow disciples and how those passages prove that we are to leave the results to God in terms of the judgment for those who don't believe. Discuss how Jesus is pointed to as our example of this in 1 Peter 2:23. Agree together to abide by that same policy.

Discuss how Christians should be wise as serpents yet harmless as doves. Agree together on this policy of Christ as well.

- Memorize the following statement from the Bible Commentary: "The way as personalized in Jesus is the way of suffering and triumph through humiliation."
- Tell of a situation where you were tempted to resort to violence but were able to restrain yourself for the cause of Christ. How have you had to put away your sword in obedience to Christ?

88

Come and Dine

John 21:1-4

Jesus said to them, "Come and have breakfast." None of the disciples ventured to question Him, "Who are you?" knowing that it was the Lord. Jesus came and took the bread and gave it to them, and the fish likewise. This is now the third time that Jesus was manifest to the disciples, after He was raised from the dead (John 21:12-14).

Commands of Christ: *Cast over* the right side of the boat for a catch. *Bring* some of the fish you have just now caught. *Come* and have breakfast.

The water gets a little muddied at this juncture in the historical sequence of events following the resurrection of Christ. But it appears to be the time right after Jesus's private appearance to them but before the final appearance and Commission. They were in Galilee where He told them to wait for Him, but perhaps the waiting proved to be unsettling. Impetuous Peter rose to his feet and declared he was going fishing, and the others went right along with him. Unfortunately, however, it is all for naught; for they catch absolutely nothing the entire night. Nevertheless, all of this seems to have been prearranged by Christ, for he met them there on the shore as they returned in the wee hours of the morning. Jesus calls to them as they are yet a hundred yards away, asking if they caught anything. They admit the truth. He instructs them then to put the net on the other side of the boat and they hit the jackpot. I'm sure it must have jogged their memory and reminded them of their initial calling by Christ.

They were not to return to their previous professions and forget about the higher calling. He wasn't kidding when He told them that from now on they would fish for men. They were to utilize all of their fishing skills on a spiritual level. He called them because they knew how to catch fish. They knew how to work hard and to be persistent and all of the tricks of the trade to make a living. All of this would be beneficial for the kingdom, yet without Christ it would still come up empty. As long as they stayed connected to the risen Lord they would have remarkable success. The key was to do just as they had done as fishermen and never give up.

One senses that Peter may have come to that point of giving up. He may have said to himself, "To heck with it, I'll just do what I know will work." Perhaps he was weary of uncertainty and fear and was just ready to go back to something safe, familiar, and secure. Maybe they were all tired of just sitting around doing nothing. That was the perfect time to remind them that God was still in control. They were not to worry or be discouraged. Jesus was going to work everything out for them in His time.

So Jesus seizes their attention and rekindles the fire of evangelism within their bones. He summons them just to sit down and talk it over. He wants to encourage them that everything will be all right. What better way to do that than sit down to a nice breakfast? This is just what the doctor ordered, so He commands them to come over and have some breakfast. "Just bring some of those fish I just caught for you and we'll have a nice meal together." Isn't it fascinating how the Lord understands our worries and fears and wants to bring peace to us? He wants us to rest in Him. We are not to take on these burdens as our own responsibility apart from Him. We just need to settle down first and get our bearings. When you go with God you go with peace in your heart. We are not to launch out in desperation. We are to wait for a peace about the situation before proceeding.

So what are the lessons we can learn from this exchange between the disciples and the risen Lord? First, don't stress out! God is still in control. The kingdom, power, and glory all still belong to Him. The scope and timing strategy are His. We are not to take that on as our own responsibility. To work with Him requires prayerful patience and trust. It is so easy to launch out and get ahead of God. But we are to resist that temptation and just wait contentedly. In the mean time we can just enjoy more of His presence. We are like tools in a tool box. We don't jump up and down and clamor for Him to choose us! No, we lie perfectly still. We remain in the position He last left us in. When he has the need he will call on us. But in the mean time we just enjoy the fact that we belong to Him and that He will use us when He is ready.

Secondly is the practical use of table fellowship (eating together and conversing) as demonstrated by the Lord. When everyone is relaxed and enjoying a meal, their defenses are down and their thoughts are allowed to rest. This is a good time to allow open and frank discussion. It is in small group gatherings in homes around dinner tables that you really get to know people. In a crowded foyer of a church is not the place where people will open up to one another. Let's use this principle we see in the early Church of breaking bread together in one another's homes so that we can have more than just a superficial acquaintance with one another. Small groups are not just a modern phenomenon; they are an ancient wisdom originating from Christ himself. *Koinonia* (the Greek word for "communion") is essential for a healthy Church. Friendship and intimate relationships should be the norm, not the exception. Jesus says to come and dine so that the winds and waves that roar within us will be still.

Discussion Questions:

- Why did Peter and the others resort to returning to the fishing trade?
- How did Jesus remind them about why they had left that profession in the first place?
- Is there a lesson here about lack of success in catching fish (winning souls) without the Lord as compared to the overwhelming success of catching fish with the Lord?
- Why does Jesus use table fellowship to set the stage for good discussion?
- What two lessons about patience and *Koinonia* can we garnish from the exchange between the disciples and the risen Lord in John 21?

Suggested Exercises:

- Invite fellow disciples over to your home for dinner on a regular basis. If you already practice table fellowship often, share that method with your fellow disciples.

473

89

Lead as a Good Shepherd

John 21:15-19

He said unto him the third time, "Simon, son of John, do you love me?" Peter was grieved because he said to him the third time, "Do you love me?" And he said to him, "Lord, you know all things; you know that I love you." Jesus said to him, "Tend my sheep" (John 21:17).

Commands of Christ: *Feed* my lambs. *Shepherd* my sheep. *Feed* my sheep. *Follow* me.

The immediate context for this passage is the resurrected Christ's appearance to the apostles on the shore of Galilee when they had breakfast together. But the context that Jesus has in mind is the night of his betrayal when Peter promised him in no uncertain terms that, "Even if all fall away on account of you, I never will" (Matthew 26:33; Mark 14:29). So after they ate breakfast the conversation turned to Peter, who though he had promised allegiance was unable to deliver. It was important to get to the bottom of this for two reasons. One was the guilt that would haunt Peter if he chose to suppress his sorrows, and second was to rebuild his leadership on a firmer foundation, namely one of humility and perseverance. The conversation that ensued consisted of asking Peter the same question again and again to test his resolve never to overestimate his allegiance again and at the same time to determine what was left of his allegiance.

You can break John 21:15-17 down into questions, answers, and resolutions. It is even more amazing when you are able to uncover the hidden richness of the original Greek text. First of all Jesus corners him about his previous declaration that he loved him more than all the others; for though they all forsake Jesus, Peter claimed he would go to the death with Him. He asked Peter, "Do you really love me more than these?" The term for love there is *agape*. This is love that is unconditional and remains firmly entrenched regardless of the circumstances. It is interesting that Peter's reply was a lesser form of love. By using *phileō*, he basically responds, "Yes, I like you."

Why does he respond with "like" when Jesus is asking about "love"? Has he learned his lesson not to make false promises? Has he learned not to imagine he is further along than he had supposed? It would seem so, for no matter how much Jesus pokes and prods he still pops up with the same reply: "I like you." After all, once Jesus gets the "like" response, He asks the same question again. Perhaps he was not satisfied with the first reply, for technically by responding with "like," Peter was not really answering Jesus's question. He did not answer whether or not he loved Jesus more than the others. He just said, "Yes, Lord, you know I like you."

The second time, Jesus leaves off the comparison with the others and focuses on the fact that Peter chose *phileō* over *agape*. He asks Peter again about his love, and once again Peter holds fast to the certainty that he does like Jesus, and that Jesus already knows this. Jesus's response to Peter's expression of fondness for Christ elicits a command perhaps to prove it. If you like me, then "*feed* my lambs." If you like me, then "*shepherd* my sheep."

After two attempts to elicit a love response from Peter, Jesus seems to accept at least the suggestion that Peter likes Him a lot. So his third question for Peter is in accord with his previous twisting of Jesus's question around from loving to liking. Jesus seems to be saying, "Okay, so, you like me, do you?" Forced to settle for less, perhaps Jesus has to make sure of that. He asks a third time, but really it is a different question. "Do you like me?" Peter is hurt that Jesus keeps pounding away at him, yet it is his fault for never really responding appropriately to the question. Perhaps if he had done so, he would have had a chance to confess his failures to Christ and repent afresh for his wrongdoings. Perhaps Jesus would have ceased asking the same question over and over if Peter had responded correctly in the first place.

The bottom line for the whole episode is, if you really do like Him, love Him, or anything of the sort, prove it in the following manner: "Feed my sheep!" This seems to be the primary purpose of the entire exchange. It is not to embarrass Peter. Rather, it is to motivate him to employ in a positive direction that burning zeal that surely must explode within him to make things right with Christ. Is not our Lord offering him a way to do just that? His desire to make up for denying Christ can be achieved by doing one thing: shepherding the sheep that Jesus will have to leave under His care after He departs. One of the ways Peter can uniquely do this is by using the lessons he learned from his past failure to strengthen other followers who will undoubtedly undergo the same testing in the near future.

Christianity was to begin under Peter with great suffering. It was born in the fires of martyrdom. It therefore needed a leader who had already been tried by those fires. It is not important to degrade Peter for his failures. But it is important that Peter, as the main leader of the Church upon Christ's departure, learn from those mistakes and use that to help others who would soon face that same dilemma. Peter was not initially able to keep his word. He did not fight to the death for Jesus at first. But history shows that in the end, he did go all the way to the cross with his Lord. This is why Jesus's final command to Peter from this exchange was, "Follow me." He meant to literally "follow me to death on a cross." Peter lost a battle, but he won the war. He had to learn to see the big picture. He didn't sit around and pine away over his personal issues. He didn't throw in the towel and go back to being a fisherman. No, he understood why these things were necessary and gained strength from the experience to carry on. This is what Jesus was trying to help him achieve as they sat around the shoreline finishing off breakfast.

What is the good news for us in this story? Well, the utmost hope is that no matter how badly we fail the Lord, He will never give up on us. If we learn from our failures, it is all worthwhile. We should never totally give up our ministry because we find out we are not really as grand as we thought. Perhaps that is exactly what the doctor ordered. If we think too highly of ourselves, we can never be a servant of Christ or his lambs. But it is imperative that when we fall, we learn from it and make adjustments that will ensure we don't get blindsided the same way again. We must also see the value in our failures for helping others who struggle with the same issues. We will never feel empathy for another's failures unless we have experienced them ourselves. Had this not happened to Peter he would have most likely rejected those who refused to suffer for Christ and made them outcasts in the Church instead of comforting them in their guilt and confusion. When we fail Christ we feel bad enough already; we don't need someone from the Church to come along and make it worse.

Herein most likely lays Jesus's strategy. He wants Peter to protect His sheep. He doesn't want Peter to scatter them. He wants His investment to multiply, not diminish. They need to be loved and nurtured and led through the horrors that lie ahead as the Church faces its greatest threats for survival. For things to go well upon Jesus's departure it is imperative that the union between Him and Peter be firmly reestablished on all levels. In spite of all that has occurred, Peter will be called upon to oversee the Church and take on the primary task of leadership. Jesus knows that Peter has what it takes, and in the end he will rise to the occasion.

He has the same thoughts about you. What responsibility has He challenged you with? How have you learned from your mistakes so that you can now better provide for the well-being of the sheep He has entrusted you with? Don't quit. Become a greater leader through trial and error. Practice makes perfect. Strive for refinement to ensure the enrichment of others.

Discussion Questions:

- Peter claimed that even if all the others denied Jesus, he never would. How does that context help make better sense of the question Jesus asked Peter in John 21:15?
- Did He keep asking Peter the same question for the three denials, or was Peter simply not answering the question properly?
- What were these questions testing Peter on?
- How would this ordeal actually prove to be beneficial to Peter's leadership in the end?
- What is the good news about failing in ministry? What two positives can come out of it?

Suggested Exercises:

- Talk about the responsibilities God has challenged you with in ministry or elsewhere and how learning from your mistakes made you a better leader. Share with your accountability partner (trusted disciple) the pressures you feel in ministry where failure does not appear to be an option—yet on the other hand, you are only human. Pray together for the comfort and encouragement of the Holy Spirit.

- Confess your thoughts of giving up on ministry altogether, if that is the case, and work through those issues through the prayer and support of fellow disciples.
- Discuss the trial-and-error aspects of leadership as fellow clergy members, not to excuse complacency but to encourage one another not to give up. Encourage confession and healing rather than concealment and unresolved guilt.

90

Spread the Gospel

Mark 16:15-20

Go into all the world and preach the gospel to every creature. He who believes and is baptized will be saved; but he who does not believe will be condemned. And these signs will follow those who believe: In My name they will cast out demons; they will speak with new tongues; [1]*they will take up serpents; and if they drink anything deadly, it will by no means hurt them; they will lay hands on the sick, and they will recover.*

Command of Christ: Having gone into the entire world, *preach* the gospel to every creature.

Mark 16:15-20 contains the core of the overall plan to save the world. The first sentence says it all, in a nutshell: "Go into all the world and preach the gospel to every creature." From this command we get the basic plan of God that covers all the essentials. First we see that it is a global enterprise. And the whole system rises or falls on one act of obedience, namely to *preach* the gospel. Once the gospel is believed, total world transformation has begun. The preaching of the gospel is the lighting of the fuse that leads to the explosion of the heart and life. For the declaration of scripture is: "But as many as received him, to them he gave power to become the sons of God, even to them that believe on his name" (John 1:12). At that point, a person is reborn. Old things have passed away and all things have become new.

To ensure there is no confusion as to who is eligible, Jesus tells us that it is for "every creature." God so loved the world (everyone) that He gave his only Son. He did not just die for the good ones but for everyone on the entire planet. It is astounding that this term would be chosen here because technically, *creature* covers just about everything. The trees and the animals can even be included in that term. But this is not the point of the passage. Jesus is using hyperbole (overstating the case) again to ensure the message is loud and clear that every single person on earth is to be told. Don't leave out any country, city, town, village, or individual. It is a comprehensive plan covering all of humanity. No one is to be excluded for any reason.

The following statements describe the responsibility of the respondents to the gospel. Our job is to proclaim; their job is to believe and be baptized. Whoever believes and is baptized shall be saved, and the one who does not believe shall be condemned. We are saved by faith and not works (Ephesians 2:8). So even though baptism is mentioned along with faith, we know that it is to follow faith. But it is so crucial to obey that it is placed alongside the requirement of faith. This places water baptism in a new light. It is more than just a symbolic ritual; it holds within it an interconnectedness with salvation itself. It does not accomplish the cleansing but it does help the recipient picture what is going on inside him. It gives him a way to act on and thereby prove his faith in Christ. For faith is not just knowing about someone, it is trusting in someone. The Greek word for faith is *pistō* and is perhaps best translated as "trust."

I often give the illustration of the boy at the edge of the pool and the father encouraging him to jump into his arms. The only way to show he has fully trusted his life into the hands of his father is by taking that next step. Saving faith is about giving up control of your life. That is why Paul told the Philippian jailor that you must believe in the Lord Jesus Christ to be saved. If you don't accept Jesus for who He truly is, you have actually not accepted Him at all. He is Lord and Master and requires your total surrender. That is the type of faith necessary for true conversion. You are not just to accept him as Savior but as Savior, Lord, and Messiah.

Jesus said that the kingdom of heaven was within our reach. Therefore we must "repent and believe the gospel" (Mark 1:15). So there you have the two stages everyone must pass through to truly be saved. First they must have a change of heart. Repentance in the Greek is *metanoiō*. It simply means to change your mind. Everyone must decide for themselves that they need to head in a new direction. Once they are convinced of this they will be open to believe something different. It is in the believing that salvation occurs. That true belief of the gospel can be confirmed in the act of water baptism.

Salvation is a powerful and explosive event. It is the greatest miracle on Earth. So it is no wonder that signs and wonders would follow that conversion of the soul into eternal life. Why do we suddenly shut down when the Bible goes on to describe the powers that will follow the new convert? Let us be careful not to downplay these results, which will also be a great testimony and be responsible for spreading the good news even further and faster than before. New believers are promised power over the attacks of the enemy whether by snakes, scorpions, or any other creature that may lie in wait. Even if someone tries to poison us he will not be successful. It is no wonder that they will speak new languages either, for notice what happened on the day of Pentecost. Salvation is also a great move by the Holy Spirit on a person and these signs should not be cause for alarm. Healing of disease is also a common occurrence in the ministry of Jesus, as well as it should be in our own. Since when has healing ended? New converts will lay their hands on the sick and they shall recover. Let's not shy away from the supernatural but rejoice and allow the Lord to do as He pleases. He knows best how to change the world.

So where do we start? In Luke 24:47 we notice that they start where they are currently located and then branch out into Judea, Samaria, and the outermost parts of the world. So what is holding us back? We can start today in our own neighborhoods and then branch out from there to every person on the face of the earth! This is an impossible task and it is only fitting that it remain the responsibility of the only One capable of pulling off the impossible. Let us proceed then hand-in-hand with Christ (Matthew 28:20).

Discussion Questions:

- What is the primary ingredient responsible for saving the world?
- Why does Jesus say "every creature" must hear the good news? Is He serious?
- What is the difference between mental assent faith and saving faith, and how does baptism play a role in confirming genuine belief or trust?

- Jesus said that to enter the kingdom (be saved) one must "repent and believe the gospel." What does that mean exactly, to repent and believe?
- Why should believers shy away from miracles since their salvation was the greatest miracle of all? Also, isn't salvation a relationship with the greatest miracle worker the world has ever known?
- Where do we begin if we want to carry out this command?

Suggested Exercises:

- Brainstorm with your group of disciples the best method of getting the word out in each of your neighborhoods, and then help each other "preach the gospel" in your respective areas. Whatever method you use must include the good news, which is best summed up in John 3:16. Whoever accepts should be baptized in water as soon as it is confirmed that he or she has fully surrendered to Christ. Following that, the person should be discipled by taking him or her through and helping him or her practice every command Jesus gave to His first disciples.
- Once your neighborhoods are covered, discuss how to expand in terms of your town, city, state, nation, and world. Utilize word of mouth, advertising, Internet, or whatever technology provides the best potential for success. This effort is monumental and must be developed over the long haul. In that sense it is never fully completed, but there should at least be a major infrastructure established that is adjusted and refined from time to time.

91

Finish What You Started

Matthew 28:18-20; John 20:21-22

And Jesus came up and spoke to them saying, "All authority has been given to me in heaven and on earth. Go therefore and make disciples of all the nations, baptizing them in the name of the Father and the Son and the Holy Spirit, teaching them to observe all that I commanded you; and lo, I am with you always even to the end of the age" (Matthew 28:18-20).

Commands of Christ: *make disciples* of all the nations. *Behold* I am with you.

As we expand on the theme of worldwide gospel proclamation, other important issues arise. Matthew points out that once people accept the gospel, our work has just begun. Now they are to be discipled. But just what all does that process entail? Are we merely being asked to encourage them along in their new life with Christ, or are there specific steps and procedures in place that must be strictly adhered to in a particular way? According to Jesus it is the latter. There is a required process that is spelled out in great detail as to the indisputable characteristics that constitute a genuine disciple of Jesus Christ. At first glance this procedure is not readily apparent, but upon further examination and reflection the essential ingredients begin to clearly and distinctly manifest.

Notice first the passage under consideration, Matthew 28:19-20: "Go therefore and make disciples of all the nations, baptizing them in the name of the Father and of the Son and of the Holy Spirit, teaching them to observe all things that I have commanded you; and lo, I am with you always, even to the end of the age." On the surface it seems as if there are many objectives and one might have difficulty knowing where to begin. It appears that Jesus is demanding that we do a number of different things with no orderly sequence or indication as to the priority. For example, there is the directive to go worldwide, to make disciples, to baptize, and to teach obedience of His commands. But how can we get clarity about the order in which to proceed and how to bring it all together?

Thankfully, by using an in-depth analysis of the underlying Greek structure of the passage, we can exegete the precise objective. A surface understanding of the text is a lot like a doctor who makes a diagnosis based on the symptoms alone. But when he wants to be certain, he will order a blood test, an X-ray, or an ultrasound to see in greater detail the exact nature of the problem. Let's see what we can discover from the underlying text. First I notice that the only real command in the Great Commission is to "make disciples." This is one word in the Greek, which is in the imperative, is *mathēteusate*. The other three words translated as commands are not imperatives. They are actually participles. But the fact that they are participles is what helps bring this entire passage together.

You see, there is a Greek grammar regulation that states that an imperative statement followed by a string of participles turns it into a main clause and subordinate clause respectively. In case everything just got blurrier instead of clear, let me illustrate it in outline form. Here is how the main clause and subordinate clauses are to be arranged according to the passage above:

Make disciples of all nations:

A. Going into all the world
B. Baptizing them in the name of the Father, Son, and Holy Spirit
C. Teaching them to keep all I have commanded you

Notice how the first word of A, B, and C all end in "ing." That tells you that they are participles. Therefore, they are to be subordinated to the main command of making disciples. In other words, Jesus is not telling us to do four different things. He is telling us to do one thing and then explains the three steps necessary to achieve that one thing. It is like when you are first learning how to drive and you are told to start the car. Then you are further advised to place the key in the ignition, turn it clockwise, and press slightly on the accelerator. The goal is to start the car, and the instructions that follow provide a step-by-step procedure for accomplishing that goal. This is exactly what is taking place in the Great Commission, and the way it was translated sometimes makes that difficult to surmise.

Perhaps a better translation would have been, "Make disciples of all nations *by* going into all the world, baptizing them [in the name of the Father, Son, and Holy Spirit] and teaching them to obey everything I commanded you" (emphasis mine). In simply adding the word by, the whole process is more clearly and accurately translated to show the primary objective as well as the steps required to complete that objective. Adding the brackets help you to not lose sight of the three-step process.

So the fundamental issue in the Great Commission is to *make disciples*. Yet there is actually one more imperative at the end and it is not to be overlooked. After Jesus lays out the strategy, He insists they not forget one final thing. He reminds them that this is not a mission, but a *co*-mission. He orders them to "Behold: I am with you always, even to the end of time." Earlier He stated that all authority/power in heaven and on Earth was given to Him. That was in verse 17, which is followed by the command for us to make disciples in 18 and 19. So why would it be important for Him to have all power and authority if it is only up to us to accomplish the task? The answer is because it is not solely up to us. Only as we unite with Christ is He allowed to accomplish the work through us. So in essence we have in verses 17 and 19 a sandwiching of the task at hand with the personal presence, power, and authority of the risen Lord. As we carry out His plan we are promised that He will be working alongside us in the task of world evangelization and discipleship. We are not acting alone or independently of Him. We are working as a unit; as the very body of Christ. Through us He lives on and continues to draw all men unto Himself.

This is a comforting thought when one considers the enormity of the assignment. For we find ourselves in the Great Commission embarking on a God-sized undertaking.

Discussion Questions:

- Matthew does a great job in pointing out that once a person accepts the gospel, our work has just begun. Are we merely being asked to encourage them along in their new life with Christ, or are there specific steps and procedures in place that must be strictly adhered to in a particular way?

- Does the way Matthew 28:19-20 was translated cause more confusion than is necessary about how to make disciples? In what way?
- Is it better understood as a "recipe," with a list of the essential "ingredients" necessary to make a disciple or to use a general statement about discipleship?
- How does the realignment of the participles (going, baptizing, and teaching) under the imperative (make disciples) clearly bring out the goal along with all of the particular ways to achieve it?
- What one word, if it were added to the current translation, could clear up a great deal the current confusion and misunderstanding associated with the Great Commission?
- In addition to the command to make disciples, is there any other command to be found in the Great Commission? If so, what is it and how does it change our role in this enterprise from one who has received an assignment to one who is called to a co-assignment?

Suggested Exercises:

- Research Matthew 28:19-20 (known as the Great Commission) and solidify in your heart and mind just exactly what Jesus is requiring of the Church. Refer back to the opening sections of this book where the matter is addressed in great detail. Confirm or deny those findings with further research. Share this with your fellow disciples so your discipleship program can proceed with great clarity and confidence.
- Establish a system in your church whereby any new convert can immediately be plugged into a discipleship program that teaches them to practice all of Jesus's commands to his first disciples. This book was written for that very purpose, so utilize it. The gospels were most likely written for that purpose; utilize that information as well.

92

Wait

Luke 24:49; John 20:22; Acts 1:8

And behold, I am sending forth the promise of my Father upon you; but you are to stay in the city until you are clothed with power from on high.

Commands of Christ: *Stay* [sit there] in the city until you are endued with power from on high. *Receive* the Holy Spirit.

Once again the emphasis is made about the utter necessity of proceeding with caution and only under the anointing of the Holy Spirit. Jesus himself progressed this way in His earthly ministry (Matthew 3:16; Luke 4:18.). In Matthew we just saw how the task of world evangelization and discipleship were to be sandwiched between the power and presence of the Lord Himself. Now we see in Luke 24:49, John 20:22, and Acts 1:8 that they are ordered to wait until empowered by the Holy Spirit as well. The command from the resurrected Lord in Luke 24:49 is to "Stay [or "sit there" in the Greek] in the city until you are endued with power from on high." This shows us how vital the presence of God is in the conducting of all our affairs on His behalf. It is so easy to get ahead of God and operate according to human wisdom. This is the work of God and we are neither capable nor expected to carry it out on our own. We will only succeed as we branch out of Him. He is the vine and we are the branches. We succeed by producing fruit that He has generated through us as we remain in Him. We are not just following orders and then reporting back to the general our individual actions on his behalf. No, in God's economy it is He alone who does the work. It is as Jesus said, no plant that was not planted by the Father would remain (Matthew 15:13). He does the actual work and we get to tag along. We tend to have this upside down by getting God's work mixed up with our own independent lifestyles and personal responsibilities.

In *Experiencing God: Knowing and Doing the Will of God*, the great work by Dr. Henry Blackaby and Claude King, the first three of seven steps are eye-opening. Using the example of the ministry of Moses, we are first reminded that God is at work. Secondly, God invites us into a relationship with Him that is real and personal. Only then is the person asked to join Him in His work. The work never becomes ours or our responsibility alone. It is the relationship that is really the primary responsibility. This is what this last command is all about. The relationship defines and drives the responsibility.

Another point made in this book is how we have been raised to work in the opposite direction of God. We are scolded time and again with the expression, "Well, don't just stand there, do something!" Instead, the authors wisely point out that to experience God, we must immediately reverse that process. We should instead say, "Don't just do something—stand there!" So Jesus arranges for the disciples to do that very thing in the upper room. He tells them to wait until they are endued with power from on high. And what are the results? Thousands come to Christ!

God has a plan for exponential growth, and the best we can do as mere individuals is work in the area of addition and subtraction. It is imperative that we get connected to Him and stay that way. Before we decide to make any ministry attempt, it should first be confirmed by the Holy Spirit. We get ideas all the time of things we think we would like to do for God—but are those coming from us or Him? Until you know, don't proceed any further. Jesus said, "The Spirit of the LORD is upon Me, because He has anointed Me to preach the gospel to the poor; He has sent Me to heal the brokenhearted, to proclaim liberty to the captives and recovery of sight to the blind, to set at liberty those who are oppressed; to proclaim the acceptable year of the Lord."

He knew exactly what His mission was because He'd waited more than thirty years first to find out. He didn't begin until the Holy Spirit descended upon Him. He was a man of prayer and solitude, which opened Him up to a unique intimacy with God. This is also the way we are to proceed. Only a divine connection can produce supernatural results. Stay patient and stay connected.

Discussion Questions:

- What scriptural evidence do we have that we are not to accomplish the worldwide mission of making disciples independently of the Lord?
- Can we safely say that it is so much the work of God through us that we are to view it as Him doing the actual work and us merely getting to tag along? What prevents us from going that far with it?
- Did Jesus view His ministry that way (that it was totally the Father's doing)?
- According to Dr. Henry and Richard Blackaby, what slogan have we been brought up to believe that is actually backward from what God expects of us in ministry?
- What are the three reasons Jesus was so confident about what God was calling Him to do? Could His disciples not benefit from those same principles?
- If Jesus and his disciples needed to be empowered by the Holy Spirit before beginning their ministries, why do we think we can do without it?

Suggested Exercises:

- Personally begin to pursue the three fundamental areas of preparation for ministry (making disciples of all nations) that Jesus was involved in and report the results to a fellow disciple. Have that disciple hold you accountable by checking back with you from time to time as to how you are progressing in those areas.
  - Never launch out with your own plans or ideas. Wait until the Lord confirms it in some manner. Learn to wait on God for confirmation. For example, you should experience a personal impression from God during your prayer time, Bible reading time, and your interaction with your church family. It might

take years for such signals to materialize, but that is always better than getting ahead of God.

o Consider your personal intimacy level with God. In many instances, it is your lack of closeness that is the cause for the delay in the first place. Every disciple should follow the Master's example of breaking away to solitary places for communion with God in prayer. Jesus once expected at least an hour of prayer from his disciples when He needed their help. I think that is a good rule of thumb in terms of the minimum amount of time necessary to connect with God. It so often takes a good amount of time just to get past all the racing thoughts about the current circumstances in your life before entering into your heart and mind the holy of holies.

o Finally we see the powerful surge of the Holy Spirit that came over both Christ and his disciples prior to their campaigns for the gospel. We also must, without question, be "endued with power from on high" (Luke 24:49). Seek the saturation of the Holy Spirit in terms of that initial "battery charging jolt" to get you moving and the daily walking in the Spirit to maintain it. Jesus has specifically designated the Holy Spirit as our permanent and indispensable companion (*paraklete*—called alongside) in ministry, referring to Him as our Comforter or Encourager (John 14:16-17).

Conclusion

If you have reached this portion of the book in earnest, you are now likely quite aware of this author's motivations for writing this material. The Church needs a tool to help them carry out the mandate Jesus left us with in Matthew 28:19-20 regarding just exactly how He wants disciples to be made. It is my sincere hope that this volume will provide just such an effective equipping mechanism that no believer would dare be without. If not, my hope is that at least many will be inspired to make Jesus a more central character in their attempts to lead others to grow in their Christian faith.

Christian discipleship as defined by Jesus is keeping all the commands He gave His first disciples. This is why I have gone to great extremes to uncover every imperative I could find that detailed his earthly ministry. I have carefully combed through each of the four Gospel records to uncover every mandate no matter how small, keeping in mind that some will be repeated. It is like a harmony of the gospel commands minus the repetition. I have also pointed out to the reader key passages that prove beyond any doubt what exactly Jesus expects of us as we attempt this grand objective of making more disciples for Him. I have written this manuscript with the conviction that the best way to arrive at Jesus's perspective is to allow Him to speak for Himself via the word of God.

For all who have taken Jesus's commands to heart and have arrived here having completed that arduous but rewarding journey, you have my most hearty congratulations! I consider this the highest of all honors known to man. Make sure you celebrate this monumental achievement in a manner that is worthy of it. As far as I am concerned, the Congressional Medal of Honor pales in comparison. Eyes have not seen and ears have not heard, I believe, the extent of the award that awaits those who have dared take up this challenge. Most importantly, you have proven your loving devotion to Christ, for He has most certainly said, "If you love me you will keep my commandments."

Maintain your love for Him by continuing to treasure and obey Jesus's commands as well as to call others to that honorable standard. Now that you have completed your discipleship training, you are fully qualified to take this material and lead someone else down that same road of success in the kingdom of God. As you do so, lean heavily toward application rather than just information. Don't forget what Jesus really wants: adherence to, not just acquaintance with His commands. Confide in the fact that making one disciple will lead to untold additional conversions; whereas making one convert ends there. It's the master plan that will make the difference. The only master plan for making disciples is the Master's plan for making disciples.

Bibliography

Bauer, Walter. *A Greek-English Lexicon of the New Testament and Other Early Christian Literature*, transl. and eds. William F. Arndt and F. Wilbur Gingrich. Chicago: The University of Chicago Press, 1957.

Bivin, David and Roy Blizzard Jr. *Understanding the Difficult Words of Jesus*. Austin, Texas: Center for Judaic-Christian Studies, 1983.

Black, David Alan. *Learn to Read New Testament Greek*. Nashville: B&H Publishing Group, 1994.

Blackaby, Henry Dr., Richard Blackaby and Claude King: *Experiencing God: Knowing and Doing the Will of God*. Nashville, Tenn.: Broadman &Holman Publishers, 1994.

Booth, Roger P. *Jesus and the Laws of Purity: Tradition History and Legal History in Mark 7*. Sheffield, England: JSOT Press, 1986.

Brooks, James A. and Carlton L. Winbery. *Syntax of New Testament Greek*. Lanham, MD: University of America Inc., 1979.

Brooks, James A. *The New American Commentary: Mark*. Nashville, Tennessee: Broadman Press, 1991.

Bruce, A. B. *The Training of the Twelve*. Grand Rapids, Michigan: Kregel Publications, 1971.

Charlesworth, James H. *Jesus Within Judaism*. New York: Doubleday, 1988.

Daube, David. *The New Testament and Rabbinic Judaism*. Peabody, Massachusetts: Hendrickson Publishers, 1998.

Donahue, John R. SJ and Daniel J. Harrington, SJ, eds., *Sacra Pagina Series. Vol. 2, The Gospel of Mark*. Collegeville, Minnesota: The Liturgical Press, 2002.

Erikson, Erik, H. *The Life Cycle Completed*. New York: W.W. Norton and Company, 1982.

Esterline, Dan, A., Sr. *A Weekly Discipleship Journal: 52 Commands of Christ.* Enumclaw, Washington: Winepress, 2003.

Findling, John and Frank Thackeray. *What Happened?: An Encyclopedia of Events that Changed America Forever: Volume 1.* Santa Barbara, California: ABC-CLIO, LLC, 2011.

Foster, Richard J. and James Bryan Smith, eds., *Devotional Classics.* HarperSanFrancisco: 1993.

Friedrich, Gerhard, ed. *Theological Dictionary of the New Testament,* Tr. and ed. Geoffrey W. Bromiley. Vol. VI. Grand Rapids, Michigan: Wm. B. Eerdmans Publishing Co., 1968.

Geddert, Timothy J. *Believers Church Bible Commentary: Mark.* Scottsdale, Pennsylvania: Herald Press, 2001.

Gerhardsson, Birger. *The Origins of the Gospel Traditions.* Philadelphia: Fortress Press, 1977.

Gingrich, Wilbur. *Shorter Lexicon of the Greek New Testament.* Chicago and London: The University of Chicago Press, 1965.

Hull, Bill *The Disciple Making Pastor.* Grand Rapids, Michigan: Baker Books, 2007.

Jeter, Hugh, P. *Commands of Christ.* Houston, Texas: 1stBooks, 2003.

Johnson, Timothy Luke. *The Real Jesus: The Misguided Quest for the Historical Jesus and the Truth of the Traditional Gospels.* HarperSanFrancisco: 1996.

Keck, Leander E. ed. *The New Interpreter's Bible.* Vol. VIII. Nashville: Abingdon Press, 1994.

McMullen, Shawn A. *Releasing the Power of the Smaller Church.* Cincinnati, Ohio: Standard Publishing, 2007.

Melton, Loyd, PhD. Lecture tapes for New Testament History. Cassette 8, Trinity College and Seminary: 1999.

Minear, Paul, S., *Commands of Christ: Authority and Implications.* Nashville-New York: Abingdon Press, 1972.

Nicoll, W. R. ed., *The Expositor's Greek Testament.* Grand Rapids, Michigan: Wm. B. Eerdmans Publishing Company, 1961.

Niederwimmer, Kurt. *The Didache: A Commentary,* trans. Linda M. Maloney, ed. Harold W. Attridge. Minneapolis: Fortress Press, 1998.

Pring, J. T. ed. *The Oxford Dictionary of Modern Greek.* Oxford, England: Clarendon Press, 1982.

Rienecker, Fritz and Cleon Rogers. *Linguistic Key to the Greek New Testament.* Grand Rapids, Michigan: Zondervan Publishing House, 1976.

Shlager, Neil, ed. *Science and Its Times.* Vol. 5. Detroit: Gale Group, 2000.

Stassen, Glen H. and David P. Gushee. *Kingdom Ethics,* Downers Grove, Illinois: InterVarsity Press, 2003.

Strong, James. *The Exhaustive Concordance of the Bible: Showing Every Word of the Text of the Common English Version of the Canonical Books, and Every Occurrence of Each Word in Regular Order.* Electronic ed. Ontario: Woodside Bible Fellowship, 1996.

Whiston, William, transl. *Josephus: Complete Works.* Grand Rapids, Michigan: Kregel Publications, 1963.